Jay Robert Nash's
CRIME CHRONOLOGY

BOOKS BY JAY ROBERT NASH

FICTION
ON ALL FRONTS
A CRIME STORY
THE DARK FOUNTAIN
THE MAFIA DIARIES

NONFICTION
DILLINGER: DEAD OR ALIVE?
CITIZEN HOOVER
BLOODLETTERS AND BADMEN
HUSTLERS AND CON MEN
DARKEST HOURS
AMONG THE MISSING
MURDER, AMERICA
ALMANAC OF WORLD CRIME
LOOK FOR THE WOMAN
PEOPLE TO SEE
THE TRUE CRIME QUIZ BOOK
THE INNOVATORS
ZANIES, THE WORLD'S GREATEST ECCENTRICS
THE CRIME MOVIE QUIZ BOOK
MURDER AMONG THE MIGHTY
OPEN FILES, THE WORLD'S GREATEST UNSOLVED CRIMES
THE TOUGHEST MOVIE QUIZ BOOK EVER
THE DILLINGER DOSSIER

POETRY
LOST NATIVES & EXPATRIATES

THEATER
THE WAY BACK
OUTSIDE THE GATES
1947 (LAST RITES FOR THE BOYS)

Jay Robert Nash's
CRIME CHRONOLOGY
A Worldwide Record, 1900–1983

Jay Robert Nash

Facts On File Publications
New York, New York ● Bicester, England

Jay Robert Nash's Crime Chronology

Library of Congress Cataloging in Publication Data

Nash, Jay Robert.
  Jay Robert Nash's Crime Chronology

  Includes index.
  1. Crime and criminals—Chronology. I. Title.
HV6030.N37 1985   364′.9   83-14046
ISBN-087196-663-8
ISBN-0-8160-1009-9 (PB)

Printed in the United States of America

10 9 8 7 6 5 4 3 2

Cover design: Eric Elias
Interior design: Teresa Delgado, A Good Thing Inc.

Jay Robert Nash's
CRIME CHRONOLOGY

MURDER

JAN. 9

Louise Masset is hanged at London's Newgate Prison for murdering her three-year-old illegitimate son, Manfred, (whom she had suffocated and left in a woman's lavatory at a train station), to be free to pursue her love affair with 19-year-old Euduore Lucas.

MARCH 23

Louis Rice, a black who had testified for another black accused of murdering a white man, is lynched outside Ripley, Tenn.

JULY 23

After raping 13-year-old Susan Priest, Elijah Clark, a black, is taken from the Huntsville, Ala., jail, dragged to the scene of the crime and lynched.

JULY 29

Italy's King Humbert I is assassinated by Gaetano Bresci at Monza, near Milan; Bresci, an anarchist weaver from Paterson, N.J., had saved up wages for his return to his native land and the murder.

AUG. 20

Franz Theodore Wallert butchers his wife and four stepchildren; he will be hanged at Gaylord, Minn., on March 29, 1901.

SEPT. 22

Mary Bennett is found strangled on a Yarmouth, England, beach; her husband, Herbert John Bennett, will be arrested for the murder on Nov. 6, 1900, convicted, and hanged for the crime at Norwich Prison on March 21, 1901.

SEPT. 23

Millionaire William Rice is chloroformed to death by his valet, Charles Jones, in Rice's palatial New York City apartment, at the direction of Rice's lawyer, Albert T. Patrick, in a wild scheme to obtain the tycoon's money; Jones will turn state's evidence, and Patrick will get the death sentence, later commuted to life; he will be pardoned by New York Governor John A. Dix on Nov. 28, 1912.

British wife-murderer Herbert John Bennett, shown in a magazine sketch during his trial. (Sept. 22, 1900)

American millionaire William Rice, after whom Rice University is named, was chloroformed to death by his valet. (Sept. 23, 1900)

DEC. 23

Widow Thirza Isabella Kelly is stabbed to death by 17-year-old John Edward Casey, who breaks into her Great Yarmouth, England, home in a clumsy attempt to seduce her; Casey will be given a life sentence the following year.

ROBBERY

JAN. 11

William Wall and Wild Bunch member Matt Warner, after serving several years for robbery and murder, are released from the Utah State Penitentiary. Both men have reformed.

FEB. 28

Lonnie Logan, Wild Bunch member and brother of Harvey Logan (Kid Curry), is surrounded in a farm-house outside Dodson, Mont., by a posse hunting him for bank robbery; Logan runs from the house through deep snow, blazing away at deputies, who shoot the 28-year-old bandit to death.

APRIL 5

While chasing Wild Bunch train robbers in eastern Ariz., George Scarborough, killer of gunman John Selman, Sr. (himself killer of gunman John Wesley Hardin), is shot by unknown parties from ambush; he will die the following day.

APRIL 17

George "Flat Nose" Currie, Wild Bunch member and much-wanted train robber, is caught rustling cattle by possemen outside Castle Gate, Utah, and is killed in a wild gunfight; town citizens rush to the slain outlaw and skin his body for gruesome souvenirs.

MAY 16

Kid Curry (Harvey Logan), of the Wild Bunch, kills

Last of the Old West's great outlaw bands, the Wild Bunch (left to right, seated): Harry Longbaugh ("the Sundance Kid"), Ben Kilpatrick ("the Tall Texan"), Butch Cassidy; (left to right, standing): Bill Carver and Harvey "Kid Curry" Logan. (Jan. 11, 1900)

Sheriff John Tyler and Deputy Sam Kenkins in Moab County, Utah, as the lawmen attempt to arrest him for robbery.

JULY 9

Tom Horn, ex-lawman turned hired gunman for a cattle consortium, shoots and kills suspected rustler Matt Rash near Brown's Hole, Wyo.

AUG. 29

Butch Cassidy, the Sundance Kid, Kid Curry, O. C. "Deaf Charley" Hanks and other Wild Bunch members rob Train No. 3 of the Union Pacific between Tipton and Table Rock, Wyo., of $5,014.

SEPT. 8

Scores of looters descend upon Galveston, Tex., after the city is devastated by a hurricane; many are shot by troopers.

SEPT. 19

Butch Cassidy and the Sundance Kid rob the First National Bank of Winnemuca, Nev., of several thousand dollars.

ORGANIZED CRIME

JAN. 7

Future California gambling boss and syndicate member Simone Scozzari is born in Sicily.

MARCH 15

Al "The Owl" Polizzi arrives in the U.S. from Siculiana, Sicily; with a police record dating from 1920, he will operate rackets under Moe Dalitz in Cleveland, Ohio, and will help to organize the national crime syndicate; he will be termed by U.S. Senate investigators as one of the "most influential members of the underworld in the United States" before his retirement to Coral Gables, Fla.

WHITE-COLLAR CRIME

MARCH 4

Albert J. Adams is exposed as the king of the numbers racket in New York City, running more than 800 policy shops that cater to more than 1 million customers a day.

MARCH 9

Policy king Zachariah Simmons is exposed by *The New York Times* as paying off thousands of dollars each year to New York City politicians and police to protect his fixed lottery and numbers operations.

MISCELLANEOUS

FEB. 1

The most lavish brothel in the U.S., the Everleigh Club, owned and operated by Ada and Minna Everleigh, opens at 2131–33 South Dearborn Street, Chicago; the sisters will earn millions before their retirement 11 years later.

AUG. 15

Race riots break out in New York City; mobs attempt to kill black entertainers Ernest Hogan, Williams & Walker and Coke & Johnson, who escape from theaters with rioters in pursuit.

DEC. 18

Edward A. Cudahy, Jr., 15-year-old son of a millionaire Omaha, Neb., meat-packer, is kidnapped by Pat Crowe, who will ransom the boy two days later for $25,000 in gold pieces. Crowe will escape to South Africa and, after many adventures, return to the U.S. in 1906, where he will return the ransom money; he will be tried and acquitted, mostly because he has, he claims, struck out at the powerful meat trust tycoon; for years thereafter Crowe will send his kidnap victim Christmas cards.

1·9·0·1

MURDER

FEB. 13

Bessie Taylor, second victim of mass poisoner George Chapman, dies in London; her death is mistakenly attributed to "exhaustion from vomiting and diarrhea."

MARCH 4

Immigrant Frank Latito is shot to death on a busy Denver street in broad daylight; police arrest Frank Sposato in the crowd and hurry him from the Italian colony through mobs threatening to riot; Sposato will go to trial on Nov. 19 and be proved innocent. The Latito murder remains a mystery.

MARCH 13

John Henderson, a black accused of murdering a Mrs. Younger, is dragged from the Corsicana, Tex., jail by a mob of 5,000, is tied to a stake and burned alive. A local jury will later commend the mob for its act of horror.

MAY 11

After black man James Brow is shot to death by a mob of whites for assaulting Della Garrett of Birmingham, Ala., the local coroner states that the wrong man has been killed.

JUNE 22

In a fit of jealousy, George Middleton of Pottersville, N. Y. kills his wife; he will be electrocuted at Clinton Prison on July 29; so crude is the electric chair that it will take four shocks over 12 minutes to kill him.

JULY 19

Fourteen-year-old Willie Nickell, son of Kels Nickell, is shot and killed near Mountain, Wyo. Western gunman and ex-lawman Tom Horn will be charged with the murder on Jan. 13, 1902. He will be convicted in Cheyenne on Oct. 26, 1902, and will be hanged on Nov. 30, 1903; his last words, to executioner Joseph Cakhill: "Ain't losing your nerve, are you, Joe?"

JULY 25

Wild Bunch member Kid Curry rides to the Winters-Gill ranch near Helena, Mont., and waits through the night to shoot and kill rancher Jim Winters as he brushes his teeth on the porch the next morning. It is a vengeance killing by Curry, who escapes on horseback; Winters had killed Curry's brother John five years earlier.

AUG. 7

More than 500 whites burn John Pennington, a black, at a stake outside Birmingham, Ala., for a brutal attack on Mrs. J. C. Davis.

SEPT. 6

Anarchist and unemployed worker Leon Czolgosz, inspired by Bresci's killing of King Humbert a year earlier, stands in a receiving line at the Pan-American Exposition in Buffalo, N.Y., ostensibly to shake hands with President William McKinley. Hiding a .32-caliber pistol beneath a handkerchief, Czolgosz slaps McKinley's outstretched hand away and fires a fatal bullet into the abdomen of the twenty-fifth President of the U.S.; McKinley will die eight days later; Czolgosz will be electrocuted at N.Y.'s Auburn Prison on Oct. 29; his last words are, "I am not sorry."

Anarchist Leon Czolgosz shoots President McKinley. (Sept. 6, 1901)

DEC. 25

Willis Burton Van Wormer and Fred Van Wormer, along with cousin Harvey Bruce, drive to the home of their uncle, Peter A. Hallenbeck, and shoot him to death for foreclosing a mortgage on the Van Wormer's stepmother's property in Greendale, N.Y.; Bruce will turn in the Van Wormer brothers and receive 18 years in prison, the Van Wormers will be sent to the electric chair on Oct. 10, 1903; Fred will survive two shocks and be placed again in the chair until dead.

ROBBERY

JAN. 17

George Henry Parker shoots to death wealthy farmer William Pearson on a London-bound train, for his purse; Parker leaps from the train at Vauxhall as a passenger, Mrs. Rhoda King, wounded in the robbery, points him out to pursuers; Parker is caught and will be hanged on March 19, 1901.

MARCH 27

Adam Worth, the greatest thief of the Victorian era, returns the priceless Gainsborough painting *Duchess of Devonshire*, which he stole 25 years earlier from Christie's Gallery in London; the return of the painting is made in Chicago, Ill., through detective William Pinkerton; for his act, Worth is allowed to return to live out his life in London with all charges against him dropped.

Kid Curry kills rancher Oliver Thornton at Painted Rock, Texas, when Thornton learns he is the notorious Wild Bunch member and train robber.

APRIL 25

Black Jack Ketchum is hanged for train robbery in Clayton, N.M.; to the crowd assembled before the scaffold Ketchum cheerfully shouts, "I'll be in hell before you start breakfast, boys!" To the hangman he yells, "Let her rip!" A mistied rope causes the western outlaw's head to be torn from his body as he falls through the trap.

APRIL 26

"Chicago May" Churchill, Eddie Guerin and others burglarize the American Express office in Paris, taking more than $100,000 in French francs and checks; on June 14, 1902, Guerin will be sentenced to life; and Churchill will receive five years' penal servitude; at the end of which she will be deported from France.

"Chicago May" Churchill, who helped rob the American Express office in Paris. (April 26, 1901)

Eddie Guerin, "Chicago May's" lover and the mastermind of the $100,000 American Express robbery in Paris. (April 26, 1901)

JUNE 17

California stagecoach robber "Old Bill" Miner is released from San Quentin after serving 20 years for holding up the Sonora stage.

JULY 3

Butch Cassidy, the Sundance Kid, Kid Curry, O. C. Hanks, Ben Kilpatrick and others rob the Great Northern train near Wagner, Mont., taking about $40,000 in cash.

NOV. 8

Wild Bunch member Ben Kilpatrick ("The Tall Texan") is arrested with his common-law wife, Laura Bullion (alias Della Rose), in St. Louis, Mo.; $7,000 in cash from the Great Northern train robbery is found in Kilpatrick's luggage; Ben Kilpatrick will plead guilty to train robbery in St. Louis on Dec. 12 and receive 15 years in Atlanta Federal Penitentiary; Laura Bullion will receive a five-year sentence in the Tennessee penitentiary.

DEC. 13

Kid Curry, toughest gun of the Wild Bunch, gets into a brawl in a Knoxville, Tenn., poolhall, wounding three policemen called to subdue him; he escapes and is hunted for three days by posses and bloodhounds before he is finally spotted on Dec. 15 by merchant A. B. Carey of Jefferson City, Tenn. Carey calls the police (the first time a phone is used to capture a felon in the U.S.); Curry is captured and taken to Knoxville, where he is sentenced to 20 years' hard labor for train robbery and is fined $5,000 on Nov. 30, 1902.

ORGANIZED CRIME

APRIL 18

John Bonventre, uncle of Joseph "Joe Bananas" Bonanno and member of the Apalachin syndicate meeting in 1957, is born in Sicily.

OCT. 1

Nineteen-year-old Johnny Torrio, who emigrated from Orsara, Italy, becomes a Brooklyn prizefight manager; he will later become the crime czar of Chicago and one of the chief architects of the U.S. crime syndicate.

NOV. 13

Mock Duck, leader of the Hip Sings tong in New York City's Chinatown, fights a pitched battle with hatchet men of the On Leong tong on Doyers Street, shooting four rival Chinese gangsters; Duck is re-leased for lack of evidence and testimony against him, the On Leong faction having carried away their wounded and refusing to make statements.

WHITE-COLLAR CRIME

FEB. 14

George Lehman, alias "Nigger Baker," is convicted of running a "green goods" (counterfeit money) scam in New York City, after his exposure by reformer Anthony Comstock. The con man is given a long prison term.

JULY 12

Ross Potter, passing himself off as Alfred Parsons, Lord Rosse of Burr Coth, Ireland, is convicted of passing worthless checks to Seth Low, president of Columbia University, and other New York City social lions.

DEC. 10

The New York Times on this day describes Albert Adams, king of New York City policy gaming, as "many times a millionaire."

MISCELLANEOUS

JULY 7

Professor Paul Uhlenhuth makes blood type discoveries that lead to forensic proof that German child-killer Ludwig Tessnow is guilty of slaughtering two young boys near Rugen; Tessnow will be executed at Griefswald Prison in 1904.

AUG. 20

White mobs howl through the streets of Pierce City, Mo., during race riots; several blacks are injured.

SEPT. 28

Antonio Maggio, infamous anarchist, is arrested for conspiracy to murder state officials in Sante Fe, N.M.

OCT. 14

Annie Rogers, consort of the notorious western outlaw Kid Curry, is arrested in Nashville, Tenn., and charged as an accomplice to Curry and the Wild Bunch. She will be sent to the Tennessee Penitentiary, to be released on June 19, 1902.

DEC. 15

A wild gun battle breaks out on the rue Popincourt in Paris between white-slavers Leca and Delbord and a half dozen other men over the possession of a prize whore; several people are wounded.

1·9·0·2

MURDER

JAN. 25

After an affair with Charlotte Cheeseman, George Wolfe batters in the girl's head with a chisel in London's East End and dumps the body in the Tottenham Marshes; Wolfe then enlists in the army but will be tracked down and convicted; he will be the last man to be hanged at Newgate Jail.

APRIL 1

A mob drags Walter Allen, charged with assaulting 15-year-old Blossom Adamson, from his Rome, Ga., jail cell and hangs him; his body is then riddled with bullets.

JUNE 1

Rose Harsent, of Peasenhall, Suffolk, England, is found dead on the kitchen floor of her employer's home, her throat slashed and body charred; William Gardiner is charged with the murder, but after two trials he will be released and disappear.

JUNE 25

New England mass poisoner nurse Jane Toppan is tried for several murders; though she insists she's sane, the murdering nurse is sent for life to the Taunton (Mass.) State Asylum for the Criminally Insane.

SEPT. 25

John Kensit, founder of the Protestant Truth Society, is attacked by large Catholic crowds as he leaves a Liverpool, England, auditorium; he is struck in the eye by a hurled file and will later die of his injury; John McKeever, a Liverpool youth vocal in his abuse of Kensit, will be tried for the murder of the religious leader but be acquitted. Kensit's murder remains unsolved.

OCT. 22

Maud Marsh is poisoned with antimony by mass murderer George Chapman in London; she is his third victim.

NOV. 10

Emma "Kitty" Byron stabs Arthur Reginald Baker, her lover, to death in London because he refuses to marry her; she serves only six years in prison, such is public sympathy for her.

DEC. 1

Edgar Edwards slaughters shopkeeper John William Darby; his wife, Beatrice; and their infant child while calling ostensibly to purchase their shop in Camberwell, England. Edwards then guts their store and steals more than £200, carting away goods and their dismembered bodies in sacks, which he buries in his backyard at night. A few weeks later he will attack another grocer advertising his shop for sale, prompting the police to discover the remains of the Darby family; Edwards, though insanity is rampant in his family, will be found guilty and hanged in 1903.

ROBBERY

JAN. 8

Sophisticated American-born thief Adam Worth, who committed countless robberies worldwide in the 19th century, dies in London.

MARCH 12

Bank and train robber Butch Cassidy, to escape posses searching for him nationwide, sails from New York City for Argentina aboard the *Soldier Prince* to take up robbery in South America; the Sundance Kid and the Kid's common-law wife, Etta Place, follow Cassidy to Buenos Aires, sailing from New York on July 10 aboard the *Honorius*.

APRIL 15

O. C. "Deaf Charley" Hanks, Wild Bunch member, after several cross-country escapes from detectives hunting him for a two-year-old train robbery, gets drunk and shoots up a saloon in San Antonio, Tex.; he is killed by two officers while resisting arrest.

MAY 8

Martinique is devastated by a gigantic eruption of the volcano Pelee, which destroys the city of St. Pierre, killing between 30,000 and 36,000 persons (an estimated 30 people survive, only four in St. Pierre); dozens of ghoulish looters will later land and rob the city banks; French sailors from the cruiser *Suchet* will land on the island and shoot several thieves before the looting is stopped.

JUNE 9

Train robber Harry Tracy, onetime member of the Wild Bunch, escapes from Oregon State Penitentiary with outlaw Dave Merrill after killing three guards; Merrill's body will be found near Chehalis, Ore.; and Tracy will later admit to murdering Merrill after reading in a newspaper that Merrill has secretly turned state's evidence against him in exchange for a lighter sentence; Tracy will be trapped by a posse near Davenport, Wash.; on Aug. 4 and, following a fierce gunfight, will commit suicide.

SEPT. 21

Lady's companion Madame Giriat strangles her wealthy employer, Eugenie Fourgère, to death at Aixles-Bains, France, to steal her jewelry; Giriat brings down suspicion on herself with a histrionic display for the police and will be found guilty and sent to prison for life.

DEC. 28

George Collins and Bill Rudolph ("The Missouri Kid") rob a bank in Union, Mo., blowing open the vault and taking $28,000 in cash and securities.

ORGANIZED CRIME

JAN. 2

Mafia chieftan Gerardo ("Vito") Gatena is born in Newark, N.J.; his criminal career will date from 1923, involving robbery, hijacking, bribing a federal juror and suspicion of murder; he will rise to family head of New Jersey and coruler of state syndicate with Abner "Longy" Zwillman.

JAN. 15

A pitched gun battle occurs between two warring factions of white-slavers near the Place de la Concorde in Paris, with several gang members on both sides wounded.

JULY 4

Meyer Lansky is born, at least officially, Maier Suchowljanksy in Grodna, Russia (this birthdate was later set by an immigration official because Lansky's parents couldn't remember his real birthdate); Lansky will rise to be a board member and treasurer of the U.S. crime syndicate, one of the most powerful men in America.

Bill Rudolph ("The Missouri Kid"). (Dec. 28, 1902)

George Collins, Rudolph's partner in crime. (Dec. 28, 1902)

AUG. 6

Future beer baron of the Prohibition era Arthur Fleggenheimer is born in the Bronx, N.Y.; he will be better known as Dutch Schultz.

AUG. 24

Carlo Gambino, who will rise to reigning *cappo di tutti capo* (boss of bosses) in the New York Mafia families, is born in Palermo, Sicily.

NOV. 22

Joe Adonis, later New York rackets kingpin and Mafia chief, is born Giuseppe Doto (or Dato—the family used both names) in Montemarano, Italy.

WHITE-COLLAR CRIME

FEB. 15

Chicagoan Jim Roofer opens the first wire store (a Big Store con game using a phony betting parlor and rigged racing results).

APRIL 10

Con artists launch another version of the Baker scam, convincing hundreds of suckers with the surname of Baker to invest in a legal battle to gain the so-called inheritance of Col. Jacob Baker, which includes all of downtown Philadelphia, valued at an estimated $3 billion.

JUNE 6

Retired western lawman Bat Masterson and friends are arrested in New York City and charged with running a crooked faro game; charges will be dropped, and Masterson will be cleared as a victim of police persecution (he claims jealousy as the motive).

DEC. 1

Richard Canfield's luxurious New York City gambling spa is raided by lawmen led by DA William Travers Jerome.

MISCELLANEOUS

APRIL 18

Denmark officially abandons the criminal identification of *bertillonage* (wherein various physical measurements are recorded) and adopts fingerprint identification.

SEPT. 2

A burglar named Jackson is convicted in London's Old Bailey through the prosecuting efforts of attorney Richard Muir, who persuades a jury to accept fingerprints (the science of dactyloscopy) as evidence; this is the first fingerprint conviction in legal history.

OCT. 17

Alphonse Bertillon photographs fingerprints left by the murderer of Joseph Reibel (a dental servant found dead in the dentist's Paris office) on a glass cupboard. Checking the photo against prints in his files, he matches them with those of ex-convict Henry Leon Scheffer, who will later confess to the killing; thus Bertillon, an archfoe of the fingerprint method, inadvertently undermines his own *bertillonage* system of identification.

DEC. 8

Crewmen Gustav Rau and William Smith lead a mutiny aboard the British ship *Veronica,* sailing from Ship Island, Mexico, to Montevideo with a load of timber. Captain Alexander Shaw and his mates are murdered and thrown overboard and the ship is burned. Five surviving mutineers will be picked up; Smith and Rau will be convicted of piracy and murder in Liverpool in 1903 and hanged.

MURDER

MARCH 16

"George Chapman" (Severin Klosowski) is tried at the Old Bailey in London and is found guilty of poisoning Maud Marsh, one of three known female victims. (Chapman had been a strong suspect during the Jack the Ripper murders of 1888, but since his method of murder was poison, as opposed to the Ripper's brutal slashings, most authorities have now eliminated Chapman as the real Jack.) He will be hanged in London on April 7.

MAY 4

Curtis Jett and Tom White, sheriff's deputies and members of the Hargis clan, which is at war with the Cockrill family in Jackson, Ky., shoot and kill lawyer James B. Marcum, a Cockrill ally, on the steps of the city courthouse in view of dozens of witnesses; Jett and White will be sent to prison for life.

JUNE 10

Violent anti-monarchist "Colonel Apis" (Dragutin Dimitrijevic) and several other army officers break into the royal chamber of the Belgrade palace of King Alexander (of Serbia), assassinating him and Queen Draga; Apis will organize the murder of Archduke Francis Ferdinand II years later to precipitate World War I.

JUNE 22

A mob in Wilmington, Del., drags George White, a black man, from jail and burns him at the stake as the suspected killer of 17-year-old Helen Bishop.

JUNE 23

Samuel Herbert Dougal is found guilty of murdering Camille Holland in Essex, England, after a two-day trial at the Old Bailey; he will be hanged on July 14 at Chelmsford Prison.

JULY 14

Ed Claus, a black convicted of rape, is hanged outside Eastman, Ga., by a large mob while his rape victim, Susie Johnson, witnesses the lynching.

JULY 20

F. Ward Gurley, DA of New Orleans, is shot and killed by Lewis W. Lyons, who believed Gurley was persecuting him. Lyons will be hanged on March 24, 1905, in New Orleans for the murder.

JULY 27

Jennie Steers, a black woman, is lynched near Shreveport, La., after she is accused of poisoning 16-year-old Elizabeth Dolan with doctored lemonade.

SEPT. 25

Milovar Kovovick and Milovar Patrovick, angered over being fired, murder steel-plant owner Samuel F. Ferguson and bookkeeper Charles L. Martin in Pittsburgh; Kovovick will be executed, while Patrovick will get 20 years.

DEC. 14

Wife-murderer William B. Ennis is electrocuted at Sing Sing (Ossining, N.Y.), becoming the first police officer sent to the chair.

DEC. 31

Prostitute Dora Piernicke of Toddenham Court Road, London, has her throat slashed by an unknown client; the murder becomes a sensation but is never solved.

ROBBERY

JAN. 16

Outlaw Henry Starr, doing 15 years in the Ohio State Penitentiary for murder and robbery, is pardoned by President Theodore Roosevelt, who has wired the badman: "Will you be good if I set you free?" Starr promises and is released. After his release, he will rob more than a dozen banks (and be the first to use an auto in a bank robbery) before being fatally shot in a bank robbery at Harrison, Ark., in 1921.

FEB. 2

Train robber and Wild Bunch member Henry Wilbur "Bub" Meeks is wounded as he attempts to dash through the front gateway of the Idaho State Correctional Institution.

JUNE 22

John Herbert Dillinger, who will become the most

notorious bank robber of the 1930s, is born in Indianapolis, Ind.

JUNE 27

Kid Curry makes a small noose from the wire on a broom and lassos a guard around the neck in the Knoxville, Tenn., jail where Curry is being held. Curry pulls the guard to his jail cell, takes his pistol, and frees himself with the guard's key; once outside the jail Curry leaps on Sheriff Fox's horse and makes good his escape.

JULY 8

Gustave Marx, Harvey Van Dine and Peter Neidermeyer, who call themselves "The Automatic Trio" (Chicago police label them the "Car Barn Bandits") begin their spree of eight robberies in which they kill eight men, including two detectives, and wound five others before being captured on Nov. 27.

SEPT. 23

Old Bill Miner single-handedly stops and robs a train near Corbett, Ore., taking a few hundred dollars.

DEC. 7

Chicago's State Board of Pardons releases Jimmy Dunlap, who has been one of America's most notorious burglars and bank robbers for forty years, after a three-year term in Joliet.

DEC. 23

After a devastating train wreck outside Laurel Run, Pa., scores of looters strip the dead bodies.

ORGANIZED CRIME

FEB. 14

John Anthony DeMarco, later to become an important Ohio labor racketeer and gambling kingpin, is born in Sicily.

SEPT. 22

Joseph Valachi, chief informant against the Cosa Nostra in the 1960s, is born in New York City.

OCT. 29

Russell A. Bufalino, whose criminal career will begin in 1927 and who will be called by the McClellan Committee "one of the most ruthless and powerful leaders of the Mafia in the United States," is born in Montedoro, Sicily.

DEC. 16

The Chicago Graft Commission closes forever the doors of the Lone Star Saloon and the Palm Gardens, meeting places for city gangsters; owner Mickey Finn (who invented the knockout drink) has his license revoked.

WHITE-COLLAR CRIME

JAN. 14

Edgar Zug, who advertises himself as a "White Witch Doctor," is convicted in Newark N.J., on a "gypsy blessing game," a scam wherein his victims pay him enormous amounts to drive away evil spirits.

APRIL 27

Policy king Albert Adams is sent to Sing Sing to serve 18 months for running the New York City numbers racket. The 62-year-old Adams gives the warden his occupation as "gentleman."

JUNE 1–JULY 8

Super con woman Sophie Beck swindles the Story Cotton Company of Philadelphia out of $2 million.

OCT. 3

Benjamin A. Chilson, known as "King of the Ringers," disguises western racehorse McNamara as a poor-odds horse called Fiddler and wins a fortune in the last race at Morris Park in New Orleans.

MISCELLANEOUS

APRIL 3

Parisian authorities pass stiff laws against vagrants and pimps in the capital, instantly enforcing the edicts and arresting hundreds of prostitutes and their pimps.

APRIL 26

Objecting to a black boarding with whites, 38 men break into a Bloomington, Ind., home and whip Rebecca and Ida Stephens and their black roomer, Joe Shively.

JUNE 7

Dozens are injured during the Motormen's Riot in Richmond, Va.

1·9·0·4

MURDER

FEB. 7

A black couple, Luther Holbert and his wife, convicted of murder, are burned alive at the stake by a mob in Doddsville, Miss., for killing white man James Eastland.

MARCH 14

Thomas Tobin, a particularly brutal killer, is executed at Sing Sing, in N.Y., despite his desperate attempt to prove himself insane by racing madly about his cell while yelling that rats are chasing him.

MARCH 26

Five blacks charged with various crimes are dragged from the St. Charles jail in Little Rock, Ark., by a raging mob and shot to death.

MAY 3

Allan Mooney, who has been convicted in a sensational trial of killing two women at Saranac Lake, N.Y., is electrocuted at Dannemora Prison.

JUNE 4

Caesar Young is shot to death by Floradora showgirl Nan Patterson as they ride in a New York City hansom cab; Patterson will plead not guilty, claiming that her erratic lover committed suicide, but the entry of the bullet points to murder. The beautiful showgirl, however, will later convince a jury of her innocence and will be released to pursue an accelerated theatrical career.

JUNE 11

For the first time in history, bloodstains are used to convict a murderer, as Theodore Berger is sentenced to death for killing T. Beclin in Berlin, Germany.

ROBBERY

JAN. 19

Bill Rudolph ("The Missouri Kid") attempts to rob the National Bank of Louisburg, Kan., but is sur-

rounded and captured by a posse of farmers armed with pitchforks. He will be sent to Leavenworth.

MARCH 26

Bank robber George Collins is executed in St. Louis for murdering a Pinkerton detective; he is given a shot of whiskey and a beer chaser before mounting the scaffold to be hanged; his neck does not break, and he slowly strangles to death.

JUNE 7

Three masked outlaws rob the Denver & Rio Grande Railroad at Parachute, Colo., for a small amount of cash; a posse runs down the trio the following day between Glenwood Springs and Rifle, Colo., two of the men escape, but one wounded man shoots himself; the body, first identified as cowboy and rustler Tap Duncan, is later positively identified by Pinkerton agent Lowell Spence as Kid Curry (Harvey Logan).

AUG. 3

Jean-Baptiste Detollenaere, a professional criminal, robs and kills a postman in Paris for 400 francs; Detollenaere will be guillotined in 1905.

SEPT. 3

Old Bill Miner robs a Canadian Pacific train at Mission Junction, B.C., taking $10,000.

ORGANIZED CRIME

JAN. 4

Joseph Rosato, who will later become a syndicate boss in New York narcotics and labor racketeering, is born in Naples, Italy.

FEB. 2

Notorious New York City gangsters Monk Eastman and Paul Kelly have a shoot-out with Pinkerton detectives; Eastman is arrested but later released.

JUNE 4

James V. Lasala, who will later become syndicate narcotics chief of northern California, is born in Brooklyn, N.Y.

NOV. 4

Chinese tong leader Mock Duck is wounded in a gun battle in front of his Pell Street, New York City, home; police catch one of the tong gangsters who attacked Duck, but he is released when the victim refuses to identify him.

WHITE-COLLAR CRIME

FEB. 10

Lou Blonger, head of the con clan in Denver, Colo., appoints Kid Duffy his full partner; both will launch expensive and successful scams against banks.

OCT. 11

New York City policy king Albert Adams is released from Sing Sing; the once-dapper millionaire is described by the press as "broken in health and bent with disgrace."

NOV.2

Mrs. Cassie Chadwick of Cleveland is sued for $190,000 on a personal note, which she refuses to pay to a Boston banker. On Nov. 26, the Cleveland *Press* will reveal that Mrs. Chadwick is a notorious swindler who has used the aliases of Elizabeth Bigley, Madame DeVere, Mrs. Springsteen, Mrs. Scott and Mrs. Hoover. On Nov. 28, the Citizens National Bank of Oberlin, Ohio, near Cleveland, will close its doors, its president, Charles T. Beckwith, admitting that he has loaned Mrs. Chadwick $240,000, four times the capitalization of the small bank, after Mrs. Chadwick had tricked him into believing that she was the illegitimate daughter of Andrew Carnegie. Beckwith had also made Mrs. Chadwick personal loans amounting to $102,000 after she showed him a forged promissory note from Carnegie for $2 million. On Dec. 8, Cassie Chadwick will be arrested, while ill in bed in the New Breslin Hotel in New York City, on charges of fraud and imprisoned in New York City's Tombs. She will be indicted and brought to Cleveland on Dec. 14, where a huge crowd will greet her at the train station with shouts of "Where's the money?" and "Where's Papa Andy?" She will be convicted of fraud and sentenced to prison, where she will die on Oct. 10, 1907.

MISCELLANEOUS

JAN. 10

Billy Roberts and Jack Stewart escape from Dannemora Prison, in New York.

MARCH 8

As a result of the murder of a white policeman and the subsequent lynching of a black man, Richard Dickerson, a race war breaks out in Springfield, Ohio.

MAY 18

England leads 13 nations, later joined by the U.S., in ratifying a global agreement to suppress white-slavers.

1·9·0·5

MURDER

MARCH 2

Jeanne Weber, an insane Parisian housewife, begins a mass-murder spree by strangling her sister-in-law's 18-month-old daughter Georgette. (See "Murder," March 26, 1905.)

MARCH 26

Jeanne Weber murders her brother's seven-month-old child Germaine in Paris by strangulation. (See "Murder," April 5, 1905.)

MARCH 27

Alfred and Albert Stratton are found guilty in a London court of murdering Thomas Farrow, a Deptford shopkeeper, in the first murder conviction through the fingerprint identification system. The brothers will be hanged.

Herman Billik of Chicago poisons Martin Vzral for $2,000 insurance money, which is turned over to Billik by an infatuated Mrs. Vzral; Billik will allow her $100 for her husband's funeral expenses, then permanently vanish.

MARCH 28

John Appleton confesses in Great Yarmouth, England, to murdering miner William Ledger, whom he killed with Joseph Earnshaw in 1882. Appleton will be sentenced to death for the 23-year-old murder but later reprieved and given a life sentence.

APRIL 5

Jeanne Weber tries to strangle her sister-in-law's 10-year-old son Maurice in Paris. (See "Murder," Jan. 29, 1906.)

APRIL 12

William A. Williams, in a berserk rage, slaughters Mrs. John Keller and her son in St. Paul, Minn.; Williams will be hanged on Feb. 13, 1906.

APRIL 13

Arthur Deveureux poisons his wife and twin sons in London and seals their bodies in an airtight tin trunk, which he deposits in a warehouse. His mother-in-law will track down the trunk, and Deveureux will be hanged at Pentonville Prison, England, on Aug. 15, after unsuccessfully feigning insanity.

SEPT. 24

Mary Sophia Money is found dead in the Merstham Tunnel on the London, Brighton & South Coast Railway; a coroner's jury decides she has been murdered, beaten to death; but this classic mystery will never be solved.

DEC. 11

Mrs. E. Stevens is found with her throat slit in her Wadhurst, Sussex, England, cottage, where she has lived with her son James; since they live in dire poverty, robbery is ruled out, and James Stevens is charged with the killing when it is learned that he is the sole beneficiary of his mother's life insurance. Though the case against him is weak, Stevens will be condemned to death, later commuted to life imprisonment.

ROBBERY

FEB. 11

Butch Cassidy, the Sundance Kid and others rob the bank at Loudres in Argentina, taking several sacks of gold.

MARCH 23

Robert Butler, a 60-year-old professional burglar who has spent more than 30 years in prison, robs merchant William Munday near Tooringa, Queensland, Australia, shooting his victim to death. Butler, one of the great rogues of the 19th century, will be executed for the robbery-murder.

MAY 8

Bank robber Bill Rudolph ("The Missouri Kid") is hanged in St. Louis for killing Pinkerton agent Charles Shumacher; a throng of witnesses, particularly admiring young women who have sent bouquets to his death cell, watch the desperado strangle to death.

ORGANIZED CRIME

JAN. 18

Joseph Bonanno ("Joe Bananas"), who will later become one of the Mafia family chiefs of New York City before moving into so-called retirement in Tucson, Ariz., is born in Sicily. Bonanno will also become the subject of many books, TV programs and articles that, incredibly, attempt to soften his image when, in truth, he was one of the czars of the ruling council of the Mafia syndicate.

AUG. 9

Host of the notorious 1957 Mafia conclave at Apalachin, N.Y., Joseph Barbara, Sr., who will become a N.Y. kingpin in labor racketeering and gambling, is born in Sicily.

WHITE-COLLAR CRIME

FEB. 18

Charles Ponzi, who will later become a multimillionaire con artist in a Peter-to-Paul investment swindle that causes thousands to lose their life savings, is arrested in Montreal, Que., for check forgery, is convicted, and serves a short prison term.

MISCELLANEOUS

JUNE 25

Murderer and thief Henri Languille is guillotined in Paris; a Parisian physician, Dr. Beaurieux, holds an on-the-scaffold experiment by lifting the severed head and calling out Languille's name to it; the head responds by opening its eyes and staring. This bizarre act is repeated three times before the head "dies."

JULY 7

Youthful Carl Panzram, who will go on to become a mass killer in the 1920s, burns down a warehouse in St. Paul, Minn., in a perverted search for thrills.

DEC. 30

In Caldwell, Idaho, IWW terrorist and bomber Harry Orchard plants a bomb on the front porch of Frank Stenuenberg, ex-governor of Idaho, who is killed when the bomb explodes. Orchard will later turn state's evidence against labor leaders such as Big Bill Haywood, admitting that he has planted scores of bombs in labor disputes, killing on one occasion 26 miners; Orchard will get life imprisonment; Big Bill Haywood, leader of the IWW, will be tried on May 9, 1907, for Stenuenberg's murder, and after a brilliant defense by Clarence Darrow, will be acquitted.

1·9·0·6

MURDER

JAN. 13

Chicago witnesses the last of a series of unsolved sex killings in which 20 women were molested either before or after death; the last victim is Mrs. Frank C. Hollister, wife of printing plant owner and social leader of Chicago's North Side, who had left her home to sing at a funeral; her mutilated body is found on a trash pile behind a fence on Belden Avenue.

JAN. 29

Mass killer Jeanne Weber is placed on trial in Paris, but forensic scientists are unable to prove her guilty, there being no witnesses to her strangulation of several children. She is pronounced not guilty as the parents of her victims scream in the courtroom: "There is no justice!" and "She will begin again!" (See "Murder" April 16, 1907.)

FEB. 23

Johann Otto Hoch, who has been found guilty of murdering Marie Walcker, is hanged in Chicago; Hoch has been marrying and murdering women for their money since 1885, his number of victims fixed at about 50, making him the all-time mass murderer in the U.S. in this century, and exceeded in U.S. history only by Herman Webster Mudgett (alias H. H. Holmes, also of Chicago), who killed more than 200 women in 1893–94 in an assembly-line murder-for-profit system.

MARCH 16

Morphine addict and thief Emma LeDoux is tried for poisoning her husband, A. N. McVicar, stuffing his body into a trunk and storing it at a warehouse in Stockton, Calif. She will be found guilty five days later and sentenced to death; later to be reprieved and finally paroled in 1925; Emma will be returned to prison for running a matrimonial scam in San Francisco and will die in Tehachapi Prison in 1941.

MARCH 17

William Carr, a black man accused of stealing a white man's cow, is hanged by 30 white vigilantes in Plaquemine, La.

MAY 7

George Michel purportedly murders mad prophet Joshua II over the power Joshua exercises on Michel's sister, Esther, in Corvallis, Ore. Michel is acquitted, but is murdered by Esther, who is sent to an asylum for life.

JUNE 25

Harry Kendall Thaw, Pittsburgh coke millionaire, shoots and kills famous architect Stanford White in

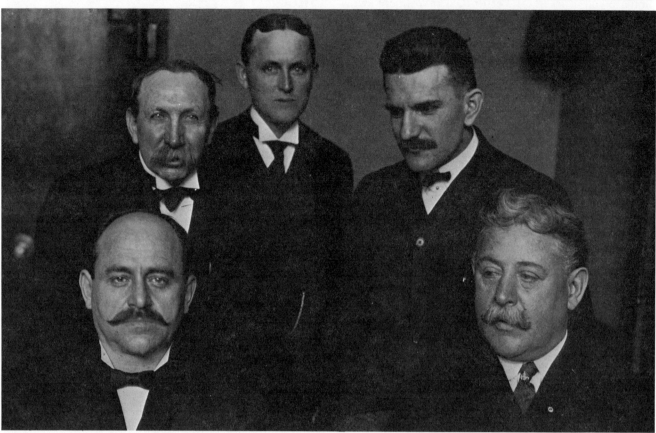

Johann Otto Hoch, killer of 50 women in matrimonial murder schemes, (shown left, seated with dark handlebar moustache), with his Chicago jailers. (Feb. 23, 1906)

front of hundreds of spectators watching a musical on the roof on New York City's Madison Square Garden; Thaw calmly tells arresting officers that White had ruined his wife, former showgirl Evelyn Nesbit. He is sent to an asylum.

JULY 11

Chester Gillette murders his girlfriend Grace "Billie" Brown as they are rowing on Big Moose Lake, N.Y., after she tells him that she is pregnant. Gillette's sensational trial will be attended by author Theodore Dreiser, who will use the story as material for *An American Tragedy*. Gillette will be electrocuted at Auburn Prison on March 30, 1908.

ROBBERY

JAN. 10

Elza Lay, top member of the Wild Bunch, is released from New Mexico State Prison after serving five years for an 1897 train robbery.

MARCH 2

Butch Cassidy, the Sundance Kid and others rob the bank at Via Mercedes in San Luis Province, Argentina, taking gold and bank notes.

APRIL 16

New York City detective Joseph A. Faurot arrests a British citizen named James Jones, whom he detects creeping shoeless and in evening wear from a Waldorf-Astoria hotel room; Faurot sends Jones's fingerprints to Scotland Yard in England, and within two weeks London reports that Jones is professional burglar Henry Johnson, alias Daniel Nolan, who has been convicted several times. Confronted with this information, Jones admits his identity and confesses to burglarizing rooms in the Waldorf. He receives a seven-year prison sentence, and the case becomes an early triumph for the fingerprinting system not yet adopted in the U.S.

APRIL 18

Hordes of looters ravage the earthquake- and fire-struck city of San Francisco; scores are shot to death on the spot by troopers under General Funston, who has declared martial law.

MAY 8

Old Bill Miner robs the Transcontinental Express of the Canadian Pacific near Furrer, B.C., taking several hundred dollars. Miner will be captured by Mounties and on June 1 will be sentenced to life imprisonment at the New Westminster Penitentiary at Victoria, B.C.

OCT. 16

Wilhelm Voight dresses in the uniform of an army captain and takes over the town of Kopeneck, Germany, ordering duped soldiers to arrest the town authorities and deliver the city funds, about 4,000 marks; to him. Voight then disappears.

ORGANIZED CRIME

FEB. 28

Benjamin "Bugsy" Siegel, who will become the syndicate's first West Coast boss of all rackets, is born in Brooklyn, N.Y.

APRIL 24

Vanished state game warden Seely Houk is found floating in the thawing Mahoning River in Pennsylvania, his head blown away by a shotgun blast; the murder is attributed to the Mafia.

APRIL 28

Anthony "Big Tuna" Accardo, who will later become head of the only Chicago Mafia family, is born in Chicago.

NOV. 22

Joseph Doto (or Dota), who will become the notorious "Joe Adonis" or "Joey A," New York City syndicate kingpin and friend of movie stars such as George Raft, is born in Sicily.

WHITE-COLLAR CRIME

JUNE 13

San Francisco's Mayor Eugene Schmitz and political boss Abe Rouf are arrested for graft, political pay-offs and kickbacks following an investigation led by ex-Mayor Phelan and a determined group of reform-minded citizens. Schmitz will be found guilty of extortion on June 13, 1907, and sentenced to five years in prison. Although the Board of Supervisors will appoint a new mayor, Schmitz will take the city seals with him and continue to conduct city business from his cell.

OCT. 1

Policy king Albert Adams, whose health has been wrecked by a short prison term, shoots himself to death in his suite in New York City's Hotel Ansonia.

MISCELLANEOUS

JAN. 6

In an early statistics-gathering effort it is shown that within one 24-hour period, Chicago's crime record includes four murders, seven suicides, and 10 deaths from bomb explosions and other forms of violence.

FEB. 11

The *Chicago Tribune* on this date describes "bloody Maxwell Street" as "the wickedest police district in the world."

JUNE 13

Freddie Muth, six-year-old son of a wealthy Philadelphia jeweler, is kidnapped by John Keene, black sheep of a prominent New York City family, and one-time bank bookkeeper (who had allegedly embezzled $30,000 from a New York City bank; he was released without prosecution) and now a stockbroker low on funds; he and the Muth boy, for whom Keene has demanded a $500 ransom, are found by police as they walk casually down a New York City street; Keene admits that he has unsuccessfully attempted to kidnap another child of a rich family before snatching the Muth child, pleads guilty and will be given 20 years of hard labor and solitary confinement.

JULY 4

Wealthy William V. McKeekin of Red Bank, N.J., disappears on his wedding day; foul play is suspected, but McKeekin will never be found.

DEC. 27

A federal court in Tombstone, Ariz., sentences Tomas Espinosa to two years for conspiracy to commit murder; Espinosa has plotted the deaths of several lawmen.

1·9·0·7

MURDER

JAN. 24

William Whiteley, founder of England's first department store, is shot and killed by Horace George Rayner, the tycoon's illegitimate son who has come to London's largest emporium to seek recognition and funds; Rayner then turns the gun on himself in an unsuccessful suicide attempt. He will be sentenced to death, but after 200,000 people petition for reprieve, the sentence will be reduced to life imprisonment; he will be released in 1919.

FEB. 3

Albert Soleilland is arrested for the murder of 11-year-old Martha Erbelding, whom he had abducted on Jan. 31 and taken to a Paris opera, where she disappeared (Soleilland later claimed that Martha went to the washroom and never returned); he will be tried on July 2, convicted and sentenced to death; later to be resentenced to life imprisonment.

FEB. 21

Dora Feldman McDonald, wife of millionaire con artist king and political fixer Big Mike McDonald, murders her young lover Webster Guerin in his Chicago offices over his affections for another woman. Mrs. McDonald, through her husband's influence, will be acquitted of the shooting in 1908; Big Mike will die bedridden in his mansion on Aug. 9, before the trial.

APRIL 16

Mass murderer Jeanne Weber, working as a maid with the alias of Moulinet, strangles nine-year-old Auguste Bavouzet, son of her employer, in Villedieu, France. (See ''Murder,'' May 4, 1907.)

APRIL 20

Carpenter Richard Brinkley, who has hoodwinked wealthy widow Johanna Maria Blume of Fulham, England, into signing her will over to him, attempts to poison the witnesses when the will is challenged after Mrs. Blume's death; he poisons by mistake Richard Beck and his wife, Elizabeth, who sample a bottle of doctored stout; Brinkley will be convicted of murdering the Beck couple, and he will be hanged on Aug. 13, at Wandsworth Prison.

APRIL 24

Alfred Packer, notorious Colorado cannibal who murdered a party of gold-seekers he guided into the mountains decades earlier, dies near Denver.

MAY 4

Jeanne Weber is arrested for the murder of the Bavouzet child in Villedieu, France. (See ''Murder,'' July 27, 1907.)

JUNE 8

Walter Lamana, seven-year-old son of a wealthy New Orleans undertaker, is kidnapped, then murdered after a $6,000 ransom note is ignored. Ringleader of the crime Leonardo Gebbia will be arrested, and hanged on July 16, 1909.

JULY 27

Mass murderer Jeanne Weber of France is released after Dr. Léon Henri Thoinot examines the Bavouzet child and mistakenly reports that the victim has died of fever. (See ''Murder,'' May 8, 1908.)

AUG. 5

Marie Vere Goolde and her husband, Otto, are arrested when a trunk that accompanies them from the Monte Carlo Express in Marseilles is discovered to contain the body of rich widow Emma Erika Levin, whom the Gooldes have murdered for her money; both will be quickly tried, convicted and sent to the French penal colony at Cayenne, French Guiana, for life, where Marie Goolde (née Marie Girodin) will die of typhoid fever in July 1908; her husband will commit suicide in September 1909.

SEPT. 12

A notorious 23-year-old prostitute known to customers as ''Phyllis'' (Emily Jane Dimmock) is found with her throat slashed in her London apartment. Artist Robert Wood, one of her customers, will undergo a sensational trial but will be acquitted; the murder remains a haunting mystery.

SEPT. 30

Sheriff Harvey K. Brown of Baker City, Idaho, scheduled to be a witness against union bombers of the IWW, is blown to bits by a bomb at the front gate of his house; his murder is never solved.

DEC. 17

John Lee, "the man they could not hang," is released from prison after serving 22 years. Lee had been a footman to wealthy spinster Emma Keyse (once a maid to Queen Victoria), who had been found with her throat slashed on Nov. 15, 1884; having a record for theft and known to be disgruntled over a wage cut, Lee had been convicted of the murder in London and sentenced to death; he had dreamed that he would not hang, and when he had been taken to the scaffold the trap failed to operate twice; Lee was removed to his cell and reprieved. After his release Lee moved to the U.S., where he died in 1933.

ROBBERY

FEB. 13

Bob Lee, Wild Bunch member and Kid Curry's cousin, is released from the Wyoming State Penitentiary after serving several years for robbery.

APRIL 20

Carl Panzram, future mass murderer, is court-martialed by the U.S. Army for stealing government property and is sent to Leavenworth to serve three years; he will be released in 1910 after 37 months.

AUG. 9

Train robber Old Bill Miner tunnels his way to freedom from the New Westminster Penitentiary at Victoria, B.C.

ORGANIZED CRIME

JAN. 29

Rosario Mancuso, later a New York labor racketeer of the national syndicate, is born in Buffalo, N.Y.

FEB. 22

Natale Evola, later an important subboss in New York labor racketeering and narcotics for the syndicate, is born in New York City.

MISCELLANEOUS

JAN. 28

Police lead widespread raids into the earthquake and fire ruins of the Barbary Coast in San Francisco, arresting hundreds of prostitutes working out of makeshift "cribs."

MARCH 7

Horace Marvin, Jr., four-year-old son of well-to-do Dr. Horace Marvin of Kittshammock, Del., is kidnapped but no ransom is ever demanded and the child is never found despite the intervention of President Theodore Roosevelt, who assigns Secret Service agents to investigate.

MAY 14

Five convicts escape, never to be seen again, from the penal colony at Cayenne, French Guiana; it is presumed that they have died in the near-impenetrable jungles or drowned at sea.

JUNE 20

Madame Garrity, a Chicago brothel owner in the red-light district of the First Ward, is convicted of white slavery for holding a 16-year-old girl for sex against her will and is sent to prison on a one-to-five-year sentence, the stiffest ever given a brothelkeeper in Chicago.

AUG. 1

Mrs. L. James, convicted for murdering her husband, is hanged at Cardiff, Wales; executioner H. A. Pierrepoint, amazed at the condemned woman's beauty, remarks after the hanging: "I was attracted and fascinated by the blaze of her yellow hair, and as she left her cell and walked in the procession to the scaffold the sunlight caused her hair to gleam like molten gold. I had hanged women before but never one so beautiful. . . ."

1·9·0·8

MURDER

FEB. 1

Mobs of revolutionaries surround the carriage carrying King Carlos I of Portugal, shooting and killing the tyrant and his son, Prince Luis, while the queen helplessly beats attackers over the head with a bouquet of flowers.

FEB. 20

The body of lady's maid Emma Sheriff is found on a cliff path in Southbourne, England, after an 18-year-old soldier, John Francis McGuire, tells police that she has disappeared; McGuire is charged with killing the older woman, with whom he had been having an affair, but he will be released for lack of evidence; the Southbourne Cliffs murder remains a mystery.

APRIL 28

Fire burns the home of Belle Gunness of LaPorte, Ind.; the bodies of her three children and a woman believed to be Belle are found; about 28 bodies, assumed victims of Mrs. Gunness, are then discovered on the Gunness farm; she is believed to have killed the gullible suitors for their money, chopped up the remains, fed part to her pigs and buried the bones. The woman's body in the smoking ruins was never positively identified, many claim, suggesting that Mrs. Gunness murdered her children and planted another female victim to pass as her own corpse before fleeing, never to be seen again.

Belle Gunness, LaPorte, Ind., farmwife believed to have murdered 28 gullible suitors before disappearing. (April 28, 1908)

Searchers digging in the smoking ruins of Belle Gunness's farmhouse. (April 28, 1908)

Some of the graves found on the Gunness farm. (April 28, 1908)

MAY 8

Mass killer Jeanne Weber is discovered in the act of strangling 10-year-old Marcel Poirot in Commercy, France; she is arrested and held for trial. (See ''Murder,'' Aug. 25, 1908.)

MAY 30

Six-year-old Mary Ellen Bailes disappears from her North London home, her hacked-up body later found wrapped in brown paper in a men's room; her killer is never found.

AUG. 24

Caroline Mary Luard, 58-year-old wife of retired 70-year-old Major General Charles Edward Luard, is found shot to death in the couple's summer home near their rural residence, Ightham Knoll in Kent, England; her killer is never found.

AUG. 25

Jeanne Weber, after murdering a half dozen children throughout France, is finally judged insane and locked up for life in an asylum in Mareville, where she will strangle herself to death in 1910.

OCT. 31

Teddy Haskell, 12-year-old crippled son of Mrs. Flora Fanny Haskell, an impoverished widow of London, England, is found with his throat slashed; Mrs. Haskell will be charged with his murder, it being claimed that she grew tired of supporting him or that she feared for his future; Mrs. Haskell will claim that a mysterious stranger killed her son and then raced past her; she will be freed for lack of evidence; the mystery man will never be found.

NOV. 27

Thomas Meade of Leeds, England, beats his mistress, Clara Howell, to death; he will plead that the charge be reduced to manslaughter, as he was drunk during the murder; all Mead's appeals will be denied, and he will be hanged on March 12, 1909.

DEC. 21

Spinster Marion Gilchrist is found in her Glasgow, Scotland, flat, her head battered; Oscar Slater will be convicted on May 27, 1909, of the murder and sent to prison for life, but through a decade-long investigation by author Arthur Conan Doyle and others, Slater will be proved innocent and released 18 years later with a sizable settlement.

ROBBERY

FEB. 5

Eugene Weidmann, who will become a terrorist killer-bandit plaguing Paris in the mid-1930s, is born at Frankfurt-am-Main, Germany.

MARCH 3

Butch Cassidy, the Sundance Kid and others are interrupted by Bolivian troops while robbing a pack train ten miles outside La Paz; following a running gunfight in which more than 20 soldiers are killed, Cassidy and the Sundance Kid are cornered in a corral in the village of San Vincente, Bolivia, where the Sundance Kid is killed and Cassidy reportedly commits suicide; it will later be claimed with some credence that Cassidy escaped the trap and returned to the U.S. to live out his life, using the alias William T. Phillips.

MARCH 13

Henry Starr and Kid Wilson rob the State Bank of Tyro, Kan., of $2,500; both men are apprehended a short time later.

MAY 25

Priceless church objects are taken, never to be seen again, from the Limoges Cathedral in Paris.

AUG. 5-16

Valuable church objects are stolen from the Cathedral of St. Viance in Paris and are never recovered.

OCT. 26

Jewel-encrusted statues, goblets, etc., are burglarized from the Church of St. Vaury, Creuse; the thieves are never caught.

DEC. 28

Hundreds of looters sweep over the earthquake-stricken town of Messina, Sicily, where thousands have been killed. Russian sailors from a passing warship land and shoot dozens of the brazen thieves, who refuse to stop stripping the dead even at gunpoint.

ORGANIZED CRIME

MARCH 17

Raymond L. S. Patriarca, who will become the Mafia

Chicago's notorious First Ward Ball, shown as it occurred for the last time, attended by hundreds of whores, pimps, thieves and crooked politicians. (Dec. 15, 1908)

Corrupt alderman Michael "Hinky Dink" Kenna, center, cosponsor of Chicago's infamous First Ward Ball. (Dec. 15, 1908)

syndicate kingpin of New England, is born in Worcester, Mass.

MAY 14

Louis "Louie the Lump" Pioggi, New York gangster, is forced to jump from a second-story window in Coney Island by Max "Kid Twist" Zwerbach and Vach "Cyclone Louie" Lewis, opposing mobsters; Pioggi will later beg Five Points gang chieftain Paul Kelly for help and will be sent 20 armed goons, who riddle Zwerbach and Lewis with bullets as they emerge from a Coney Island bar only hours later. Pioggi will later plead guilty to manslaughter and receive 11 months in jail.

MAY 24

Sam "Momo" Giancana, who will rise to supreme Mafia overlord of Chicago before being assassinated, is born in Chicago.

SEPT. 6

Anthony Joseph Biase is born in Omaha, Neb., the city he will later rule as the leading Mafia figure.

NOV. 30

Police chief of San Francisco William J. Biggy is found floating in the Bay shortly after a conference with a member of the Board of Police Commissioners; it is claimed that local gangsters have murdered Biggy because of his intentions to clean up the mobs still operating in the earthquake-devastated Barbary Coast.

WHITE-COLLAR CRIME

JAN. 27

Victor "The Count" Lustig, international con man who will sell the Eiffel Tower to duped scrap dealers in Paris decades later, is arrested for the first time, in Prague, Czechoslovakia, for a counterfeiting scheme.

JUNE 22

Master forger Courtney Townsend Taylor is born in

East Hartford, Conn.; he will later be described by the FBI as ''the most ingenious check-passer ever to operate in this country.''

SEPT. 3

Charles Ponzi, later a millionaire through a Peter-to-Paul investment scheme in Boston, is arrested in Atlanta, Ga., for smuggling aliens into the U.S.

MISCELLANEOUS

JULY 26

The Bureau of Investigation, precursor to today's FBI, is created, with little capital and manpower and minor federal authority.

DEC. 15

The last First Ward Ball in Chicago, sponsored by corrupt Aldermen ''Bathhouse John'' Coughlin and Michael ''Hinky Dink'' Kenna, is held, a traditional fund-raiser attended by hundreds of prostitutes, pimps, gamblers, thieves and gangsters, as well as scores of corrupt police officials; two days earlier, a bomb had gone off at the Chicago Coliseum, the Ball site, but the event takes place nevertheless; comments Hinky Dink: ''Some reformer planted that bomb to kill off our fun.''

1·9·0·9

MURDER

MARCH 15

Marks and Morris Reubens, London pimps, stab to death William Sproull, a sailor who refuses to pay one of their girls. Both men are later executed, despite Morris's claim that his brother did the killing.

JUNE 18

Elsie Sigel, errant granddaughter of Civil War Union General Fraz Sigel, is found dead in the New York City apartment of Chinese waiter Leon Ling; according to another boarder in the rooming house, Chon Sing, Miss Sigel had been strangled by Ling over an affair the young woman was having with another Chinese waiter; Ling will never be apprehended.

JULY 1

Indian student Madar Lal Dhingra, after obtaining a license to carry firearms and practicing target shooting, fires five shots into Sir William Hutt Curzon Wylie, onetime high official in India, at a London concert in the Imperial Institute; as another spectator, Dr. Cowas Lalcaca, an Indian from Hong Kong, moves to subdue him, Dhingra fires two more shots, killing the physician; he then turns one of the two pistols he carried on himself, but the weapon misfires; overpowered by raging spectators, Dhingra is arrested and tried for the double slaying; he claims he killed Wylie because ''English people don't have the right to occupy India and it is perfectly justifiable on our part to kill the Englishman who has polluted our soil.'' He will po-

litely salaam on hearing his death sentence and will be hanged on Aug. 17 at Pentonville Prison.

AUG. 15

An unknown hatchet man for one of the New York City tongs slips into the home of Bow Kum, a beautiful young Chinese woman, and stabs her through the heart, then chops off her fingers and slashes her body countless times before fleeing; it will later be explained that the killing is in retribution for Bow Kum's shifting her attentions from one tong member to that of a member of an opposing tong.

SEPT. 10

Wealthy contractor George Harry Storrs, of Yorkshire, England, is stabbed to death by an intruder in front of his wife and servants, who flee to fetch police; although several men will be arrested, no one will be convicted of this mysterious murder.

DEC. 30

Ah Hoon, a Chinese actor who had defied several New York City tong leaders, despite police protection, is found shot to death in his Chinatown room.

ROBBERY

JAN. 24

In one of London's rare armed robberies, Paul Hefeld and Jacob Meyer, Russian immigrants, rob Schurmann's Rubber Co. on Chestnut Road, Tottenham, taking 80 gold sovereigns and shooting several employees; Hefeld and Meyer are pursued on foot by several constables and citizens; the thieves shoot and kill 15-year-old Ralph John Joscelyn and Constable William Frederick Tyler; the running fight continues through the North of London as hundreds of armed police and citizens track the thieves; when the men reach a high fence topped by barbed wire, Meyer manages to crawl over but Hefeld falls back exhausted, committing suicide by sending a bullet into his own head; the bullet will later prove fatal. Meyer next breaks into a cottage owned by Charles Rolston and holds the family captive until three constables break down the door, exchanging fire with Meyer and mortally wounding him; the dying robber dances wildly about the cottage, laughing maniacally and grinning while blood spouts from his head wounds; he dies with a horrible grin on his face as dozens of witnesses stare down at him.

FEB. 16

Professional New York thief Leslie Coombs is sentenced to death in the electric chair for robbing and killing a man on a lonely road in St. Lawrence County, N.Y.

MARCH 24

Clyde Barrow, who will become one of the most notorious bandits of the 1930s in the American Southwest, is born to Henry and Cummie Barrow in Telice, Texas; he is one of their eight children.

MARCH 25

Church burglars in Paris continue their looting of shrines by breaking into the Church of the Soulerraine Creuse and taking priceless chalices. On April 27, they will loot a private museum of valuable artifacts.

JUNE 28

Henry Starr and Kid Wilson rob the bank of Amity, Colo., of $1,100; on July 11, Starr will be arrested in Bosque, Ariz., and returned to Colorado, when he will plead guilty on Nov. 30 and receive a seven-to-25-year sentence in the Colorado State Penitentiary at Canon City. Wilson will later be caught and sent to prison.

JULY 30

Old Bill Miner robs a Portland, Ore., bank of $12,000.

NOV. 11

British burglar William Butler kills 80-year-old Charles Thomas and his wife, Mary, while burglarizing their Monmouthshire cottage, going away with only £3 and overlooking the couple's savings box, which contains £150; Butler is quickly apprehended, tried and hanged.

DEC. 29

American bandits believed to be remnants of Butch Cassidy's South American band rob the Mercantile Company in Río Pescado in Chubut Province, Argentina, killing agent Lloyd Apjuan before escaping with a small amount of money.

ORGANIZED CRIME

FEB. 19

Police Commissioner Bingham forms a secret service branch to be used exclusively to check Black Hand/Mafia operations in New York City, placing police Lt. Joseph Petrosino at its head.

MARCH 12

New York City police Lt. Petrosino is shot to death in the main square of Palermo, Sicily, where he has traveled to compare photos of known New York City felons with wanted Sicilians who have fled to the U.S., so that they can be deported back to Sicily. The killing of Petrosino, which causes an international furor, is later attributed to Mafia chief "Don" Paulo Marchese (né Paul di Cristina), who later will become the Mafia chief of New Orleans.

APRIL 10

Roy Carlisi, later to become New York labor racketeer and narcotics trafficker for the syndicate, is born in Chicago.

WHITE-COLLAR CRIME

MARCH 15

Eddie Jackson, operator of Big Store con games and confidante to such lofty grifters as "Yellow Kid" Weil and Elmer Meade, is sent to Joliet Prison in Illinois on a green-goods conviction.

JUNE 3

Philip Musica, who under many aliases will go on to bilk giant American corporations out of millions in various schemes, is sent to Elmira (N.Y.) Reformatory for a year for an importing scam wherein Musica, using phony bills of lading through a bribed official, paid little or no duties on sausages and other foodstuffs that he resold to make a fortune.

MISCELLANEOUS

FEB. 8

Unknown persons abduct Tony Reddes from his father's meat shop in New York City; the child is never seen again; since no ransom is ever demanded, police conclude that someone wanted the four-year-old boy to raise as his or her own.

FEB. 9

Charles T. Skelly of the Board of Police Commissioners in San Francisco describes all nickel dance halls as dens of prostitution and insists they be closed down.

MARCH 18

James H. Boyle and his obese, alcoholic wife kidnap Willie Whitla, son of a wealthy lawyer in Sharon, Ohio; their ransom demand of $10,000 is met and the eight-year-old boy is released unharmed; the Boyles will soon be captured after throwing money about in a Cleveland bar and will receive long prison sentences.

JUNE 5

New York City vice squad raids net 3,145 prostitutes working out of hundreds of Manhattan brothels and cribs.

AUG. 29

Agents of the U.S. Department of Immigration raid The California, a notorious saloon-brothel on Chicago's Dearborn Street, where a half dozen immigrant women are found; all claim that they have been recruited from Europe to work in Chicago as whores; they are deported.

1·9·1·0

MURDER

JAN. 17

Dr. Hawley Harvey Crippen purchases five grains of hyoscine, a painless but deadly poison, with the intent of killing his henpecking wife, Cora, so that he can be with his mistress, Ethel Le Neve; Cora (born Kunigunde Mackamotski in New York City) will vanish from her home, 39 Hilltop Crescent off Camden Road, in North London on Jan. 31. (See ''Murder,'' March 12, 1910.)

FEB. 9

Dr. Bennett Clarke Hyde is indicted for murdering several members of the Swope family of Kansas City; Hyde's wife, Frances, is a member of the wealthy Swope clan, and by poisoning other members—Hyde gave them typhoid and other germs from stolen cultures—he intended to arrange for the family fortune to be inherited by Frances; following three trials with allegedly bribed jurors, the physician will be freed on a technicality in 1911.

MARCH 7

Infamous San Francisco poisoner Cordelia Botkin (who mailed arsenic-laced bonbons to the wife of her lover in 1898) dies in San Quentin.

MARCH 12

Ethel Le Neve, Dr. Crippen's paramour, moves into Crippen's fashionable North London home, ostensibly as a housekeeper, but is soon seen wearing Cora Crippen's clothes, which have been considerably altered for the petite Ethel. (See ''Murder,'' July 14, 1910.)

MARCH 25

Resenting the allegedly improper conduct of black man Judge Jones with a white woman, a mob of 40 white men drags Jones from the Pine Bluff, Ark., jail where he is being held on a minor charge and hang him.

JUNE 16

Thomas Weldon Anderson, a middle-aged actor, is found shot to death in the backyard of his mistress's London home; the murder is never solved.

JULY 14

Scotland Yard's Chief Inspector Walter Dew, who has suspected Dr. Crippen of murdering his wife, searches the physician's Hildrop home after Crippen and his mistress, Ethel Le Neve, leave on vacation for an unknown destination; Dew discovers chunks of a body wrapped in a man's pajamas beneath the basement cobblestones, the stomach still containing traces of the poison hyoscine. (Later, at the Crippen's trial, Cora Crippen's abdomen, bearing an identifiable scar, is passed in a soup tureen from hand to hand by queasy jurors ordered to examine the remains as an exhibit.) Dew will track down Crippen to Canada, where he has fled with Ethel, who is dressed as a boy, and return him to England to stand trial. (See "Murder," Oct. 18, 1910.)

AUG. 1

For no apparent reason, a mob of 200 whites shoot down about 20 blacks outside Palestine, Texas, as they emerged from a dance hall.

OCT. 15

A Navy deserter with a long criminal record, Walter Dipley, shoots and kills championship fighter Stanley Ketchel on a ranch near Conway, Mo., over the affections of the ranch cook, Goldie Smith; Ketchel, in training at the ranch owned by his friend Col. R. P. Dickerson, is shot while eating breakfast; when hearing the news, Wilson Mizner, Ketchel's onetime manager, first weeps, then quips: "That darling kid can't be dead. Start counting over him—he'll get up!"

OCT. 18

Dr. Crippen's five-day trial begins in London; he will be found guilty and be sentenced to hang for murdering his wife; his mistress, Ethel Le Neve, will be tried as an accessory after the fact but will be found not guilty and released; before Crippin is hanged at Pentonville Prison on Nov. 23, he requests that a photo of Ethel be placed in his casket; this last request will be granted.

NOV. 9

Frank Heideman kills nine-year-old schoolgirl Marie Smith with a hammer in Asbury Park, N.J.; the unrepentant murderer will go to the electric chair in May 1911.

ROBBERY

MARCH 18

John Alexander Dickman robs John Nisbet, a cashier en route to Widdrington Station, England, to pay miners' wages, as the train they ride continues toward Newcastle; Dickman will be convicted on circumstantial evidence and sentenced to death, despite a strong public outcry against the verdict; he will be hanged at Newcastle Prison on Aug. 10 while a crowd of more than 1,500 protests outside the prison walls.

SEPT. 17

George "Bugs" Moran, later to become a top North Side Chicago gangster, is sent to Joliet Prison for robbing a store; he will be paroled on June 18, 1912.

DEC. 16

A group of anarchists deported from Russia by Czarist police attempt to knock down a wall of the H. S. Harris Jewelry Co. store on Houndsditch Road in East London; a constable hearing the noise knocks on the door of the building adjoining the jewelers and is told that the owner will return later; the constable summons help, and nine officers burst through the door. The anarchists open fire, killing one officer outright and mortally wounding two others; the burglar gang flees with their wounded members. (See "Robery," Jan. 3, 1911.)

ORGANIZED CRIME

JAN. 1-MARCH 26, 1911

A Black Hand killer known only as "The Shotgun Man" (who openly cradles a shotgun in his hand in broad daylight as he patrols Little Italy in Chicago) is held responsible for at least 13 of the 38 Black Hand killings that take place between these dates at the intersection of Milton and Oak streets (known as Death Corner).

JAN. 28

Dominic Alaimo, future syndicate labor racketeer, is born in Pittston, Pa.

FEB 6

Carlos Marcello, who will become supreme Mafia syndicate overlord of New Orleans, is born in Tunisia.

FEB. 21

Carmine Galante, who will briefly rise to the position of supreme Mafia boss of New York City before he is murdered in 1979, is born in New York City.

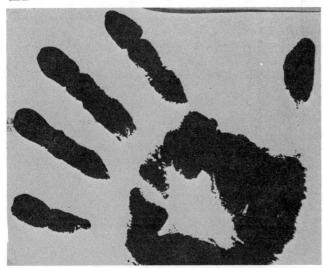

The Black Hand, symbol of the Italian terrorist-extortionist element of organized crime in the U.S. early in the century. (Jan. 1, 1910)

MARCH 5

The Chicago Vice Commission is created to combat the widespread prostitution and gambling infesting Chicago's First Ward; the Commission launches investigations into gangs controlling brothels; on Oct. 26, Chicago police will provide the Vice Commission with a list of gang activities, especially organized prostitution, listing 192 whorehouses and, by name, 1,012 inmates.

WHITE-COLLAR CRIME

JAN. 20-FEB. 15

Eugene and Shelton Burr deluge the New York market with enormous quantities of fake stock, which they print by the millions; they will net, according to postal inspectors, more than $50 million before they are arrested the following year.

JUNE 1–SEPT. 15

Cam Spears, notorious con man, gleans a fortune by selling sucker lists to New York City bucket shops.

NOV. 1

W. T. Wintemute, who has been selling bogus stock stince 1906 and is already a millionaire, is exposed and arrested. He will later be sentenced to prison for several years.

MISCELLANEOUS

OCT. 1

A unionist bomb explodes in the printing department of the *Los Angeles Times* building, killing 21 workmen; *Times* owner Harrison Gray Otis, who travels about in an armor-plated car, is an adamant foe of unions and publicly announces that organized labor has caused the bombing. A short time later Jim and John McNamara, union stalwarts, are arrested for the crime.

The *Los Angeles Times* Building, smoking and gutted after a union terrorist bomb exploded, killing 21 nonunion printers. (Oct. 1, 1910)

John (left) and Jim (right) McNamara, standing trial for the *Los Angeles Times* Building bombing. (Oct. 1, 1910)

1·9·1·1

MURDER

JAN. 1

Forty-eight-year-old widower Leon Beron is found dead on Clapham Common, in London's East End, stabbed repeatedly, his skull crushed, and a large "S" gouged into his forehead; Stinie (or Steinie) Morrison, who had borrowed money from Beron, will be tried on March 6, his felonious background revealed; he will be convicted on circumstantial evidence and sentenced to death; Morrison, whom to this day many feel was innocent, will die in Parkhurst Prison on Jan. 24, 1921, after fasting to death in a fit of pique.

FEB. 3

In Dalkeith, England, chemist's assistant John James Hutchinson poisons 17 people at the silver wedding anniversary party for his parents, slipping arsenic into the coffee he himself serves to guests; three die, including his father Charles; Hutchinson intends to collect £4,000 insurance money on his father's life, but when police interview Hutchinson on Feb. 20 at Newcastle-upon-Tyne, he will swallow prussic acid, committing suicide.

MAY 24

Frank Harold Henwood shoots and kills Sylvester Louis "Toney" Von Phul over the affections of Mrs. Sassy Springer, whose large ranch is outside Denver, Colo.; a man named Copeland is also killed by Henwood with a stray bullet; on June 28 Henwood will be found guilty of second-degree murder in the Copeland slaying but will not be convicted of murdering Von Phul until May 28, 1913, for which he will be sentenced to be hanged; Henwood, after many stays, will have his sentence commuted to life and will die in the Colorado Penitentiary in 1929.

JULY 18

Mrs. Louise Beattie is found in Richmond, Va., in the back seat of an auto, her head blown off; her murderer is never found.

AUG. 12

The caretaker of Lancaster Castle in England, James Henry Bingham, dies from poisoning; others in the Bingham family will also be poisoned, and Edith Agnes Bingham will be charged with murder but be acquitted; the mysterious "Bingham poisonings" will never be solved.

OCT. 10

In Agra, India, Mrs. Augusta Fullam and her lover, Henry Lovell William Clark, poison Mrs. Fullam's husband, Edward. Police later find a reminder note Mrs. Fullam has written to herself—"So the only thing is to poison the soup"—which leads to the arrest and conviction of the lovers; Clark will be executed on March 26, 1913; Mrs. Fullam will die in her cell of heat stroke on May 29, 1914.

NOV. 20

Rich spinster Eliza Mary Barrow dies in the London boardinghouse of Henry Frederick Seddon; though her death is attributed by doctors to "epidemic diarrhea," suspicious relatives will later order her remains examined and arsenic will be found; in a sensational trial, Seddon will be found guilty of poisoning the spinster for her money and will be hanged at Pentonville Prison on April 18, 1912.

NOV.28

Great circus showman "Lord" George Sanger, 85, is hatcheted to death on his East Finchley, England, farm by a jealous hired hand, Herbert Cooper. Before police can apprehend Cooper, he lies down on the railway track of the Great Northern Line between Highgate and Crouch End, where he is decapitated by a passing train.

ROBBERY

JAN. 3

London police surround a house at 100 Sidney Street after learning that several Russian anarchist jewel thieves (who have escaped after robbing the H. S. Harris Jewelry Co. store, killing three policemen on Dec. 16, 1910) have taken refuge there; a wild gun battle ensues and several officers are wounded; the Scots Guards are called in from their Tower post, and a full-scale battle erupts, which brings then Home Secretary Winston Churchill to the site "to watch the fun" (in the words of crime writer Colin Wilson); the battle lasts until 1:00 p.m., when the house bursts into flames; the two anarchists inside, Fritz Svaars and a man named Josef, shoot at the firemen, who are then ordered to withdraw while the house is allowed to burn to the ground, with one fireman killed by falling debris; Svaars and Josef are found dead in the ruins, the latter shot in the head, a possible suicide.

JAN 18

Old Bill Miner and others rob the Southern Railroad Express of $3,500 at White Sulphur Springs, Ga.; Miner will be tracked down and the 66-year-old train robber sent to the Georgia State Penitentiary for life, where he will die in 1913.

JUNE 11

Train robber and Wild Bunch member Ben Kilpatrick is released from the Atlanta Federal Penitentiary after serving time for robbery.

JUNE 15

Future super con man Robert Arthur Tourbillon (who takes great pride in his initials, ''R.A.T.'') robs New York's Roy Hotel of $160.

AUG 21

Laborer Vincenzo Peruggia removes Da Vinci's immortal *Mona Lisa* from the Louvre in Paris, smuggling the painting to his room, where he will keep it for almost two years until taking in to Florence, Italy, where he will be arrested (on Dec. 12, 1913) and the painting will be recovered intact; the *Mona Lisa* will be returned to the Louvre and Peruggia will serve a light sentence.

OCT. 31

Future bank robber and New York gunman Francis ''Two Gun'' Crowley is placed in a New York City foster home as an infant.

DEC. 9

William Wilson and Robert Evans, members of Butch Cassidy's South American bandit gang, are cornered by troopers in the Río Pico region of Argentina and are killed in a bloody shoot-out.

DEC. 21

In Paris Jules Bonnot leads a band of gunmen who shoot to death a bank messenger of the Société Général Bank, Saint-Ouen Branch, and rob him of 318,000 francs' worth of bonds, 5,500 francs in cash and 20,000 francs in notes and gold. The gang uses an auto, stolen on the night of Dec. 14, the first time an auto is used in a European robbery.

ORGANIZED CRIME

JAN 7

Future syndicate gambling boss Armand Rava is born in New York City.

MARCH 17

The *Chicago Tribune* lists 25 unsolved Black Hand killings that occurred in 1910.

JUNE 25

Charles Luciana, a 14-year-old boy, is committed to the Brooklyn Truant School for four months; he will grow up to become the notorious syndicate leader Charles ''Lucky'' Luciano.

AUG 20

Joseph Sica is born in Newark, N.J.; Sica's arrest record will date from 1928; the notorious syndicate subchieftain will later be charged with robbery, extortion, narcotics crimes and murder.

SEPT. 14

Future Syndicate gambling boss Frank Joseph Valenti is born in Rochester, N.Y.

SEPT. 23

Prosecutors investigating organized gambling in Chicago's Loop are warned by Big Jim Colosimo, the city's reigning crime czar, that they will be killed if they continue their campaign against widespread gambling, particularly in the First Ward, the red-light district known as ''The Levee''; investigations continue.

WHITE-COLLAR CRIME

FEB. 13

Con man Ernest J. Cox is arrested in Michigan for selling fake oil leases.

JUNE 1

Railroad czar E. H. Harriman spends a fortune on what he thinks are genuine European master paintings; but he has been bilked by a bunco ring in New York City, and the oils will prove to be worthless copies. Says Harriman: ''I'll let picture buying to someone else who knows pictures from now on.'' Though he does not disclose the amounts paid to the art hustlers, some estimate the loss to be $250,000.

OCT. 20

Stock tips publisher Cardenio F. King is arrested and later sent to the Charlestown Penitentiary in Boston for promoting fraudulent stocks.

MISCELLANEOUS

APRIL 4

Chicago's Vice Commission submits its report listing hundreds of wide-open brothels in the red-light district of the First Ward to the City Council; most Council members are on the local crime syndicate patroll and vote to shelve the report; officially the report is "placed on file."

AUG. 30

Responding to Black Hand kidnappings that have reached epidemic proportions in New York City's Little Italy, *The New York Times* editorializes: "Fathers and mothers never able to tell where the 'Black Handers' will strike next, live in dread that at any hour their child may be snatched up and carried off." A month earlier, the state of New York had put into law harsher penalties against the kidnapping Black Handers, making the minimum penalty from 10 to 50 years in prison.

OCT. 12

Mayor Carter Harrison of Chicago, after finding an expensively published brochure advertising the sexual delights of the Everleigh Club on his desk in City Hall, flies into a rage and orders all brothels closed down in Chicago's red-light district; the order is stalled by police who are receiving enormous kickbacks from brothel sponsors. On Oct. 24, Mayor Harrison, under great pressure from reform groups, will order his police chief to close down the Everleigh Club, the most expensive and notorious brothel in America; it will be padlocked the next morning after Minna and Ada Everleigh are allowed to remove all their furnishings; the sisters, whose real name is Lester, will retire with millions to New York, where they will become patrons of the arts, sponsoring exhibits and poetry readings, their true identities never learned by the social elite who attend the many galas at their 70th Street mansion; Minna will die on Sept. 16, 1948, age 71; Ada, at 94, will die on Jan. 3, 1960.

NOV. 13

Georgia Gov. Cole L. Blease delivers his gubernatorial address in Augusta before a huge throng, devoting most of his speech to the lynching of a black in Honea Path, Ga., a few days earlier; he states that he had refused to order state police to stop the lynch mob from "punishing that nigger brute [the victim]" and would have "resigned the office and come to Honea Path and led the mob myself" if the lynch mob had been prevented from hanging its victim.

Ada (left) and Minna (right) Everleigh, whose Chicago brothel was considered the most luxurious in the world. (Oct. 24, 1911)

MURDER

JAN. 23

Four blacks—Belle Hathaway, John Moore, Eugene Mamming and "Dusty" Cruthfield, all charged with killing wealthy white farmer Norman Haldey—are dragged from their cells in the Harris County jail in Hamilton, Ga., by a mob of more than 100 white men and are hanged en masse, their bodies riddled with gunfire.

MARCH 31

Winifred Marie Mitchell vanishes near the English village of Gussage, St. Michael; her body will be found on May 2, shot in the back of the head; Walter William Burton, a married man who had made Winifred his mistress, then grew tired of her and feared she was pregnant, will be convicted and executed at Dorchester Prison, the last man to be hanged there.

APRIL 9

Even after he is acquitted of writing "insulting letters" to a white girl in Shreveport, La., Tom Miles, a black, is seized by a mob and lynched.

JULY 13

Beatrice Constance Annie "Bessie" Mundy, wife of George Joseph Smith, is found dead in a bathtub in a boardinghouse at Herne Bay, England; her death is reported by her husband; Smith, who has murdered Bessie for insurance money, will go on to drown two more wives and collect insurance on them before relatives of his last wife turn him in as a bigamist; he will be convicted of killing Bessie Mundy and will be hanged at Maidstone Prison on Aug. 13, 1915; curiously, landladies who heard the three wives splashing about before their deaths also heard Smith later playing "Nearer My God to Thee" on the harmonium; he will forever be known as the "Brides of the Bath Murderer."

JULY 14

The body of a young woman, Dora May Gray, is found on the beach at Yarmouth, England, strangled with a bootlace that is still around her throat; this mysterious killing will never be solved.

SEPT. 28

Edward Hopwood, a married man in love with ac-tress Florence Dudley (real name, Florence Alice Bernadette Silles), rendezvouses with her; after she scorns him, he shoots and kills her while they ride in a London taxi, then tries to commit suicide but botches the job; Hopwood will be hanged for the crime.

DEC. 1

In Paris, Henri Girard, to collect insurance money on the life of Louis Pernotte, injects his friend with typhoid germs and kills him; Girard will unsuccessfully attempt to murder the entire Pernotte family, also for insurance money, by feeding them poisoned mushrooms *(Amanita phalloides),* but the Pernottes will recover without knowing they were intended murder victims; Girard will eventually be apprehended after poisoning a war widow, Mme. Monin, also for her insurance money; before his trial in 1921, Girard will commit suicide.

British killer of three wives, George Joseph Smith. (July 13, 1912)

ROBBERY

JAN. 3

The Bonnot gang of Paris begins a three-month robbery spree, murdering and robbing a wealthy old man and his servant; undisclosed sums are taken; on the night of Jan. 8–9, the gang will loot the Smith & Wesson gunshop on Boulevard Haussmann in Paris; the gang will steal three automobiles in the next ten weeks (one on Feb. 15 from manufacturer M. Malbec, one on Feb. 26 from a M. Buisson in Paris and on March 25, one whose occupants they will murder), using the vehicles in their robberies; on April 24, Bonnet will be trapped in a Paris apartment and, after killing one officer and wounding another, will escape; on April 29, Bonnet will be surrounded by police at Choisy-a-Roi, trapped in a barn with a confederate named Dubois; police will dynamite the barn, killing Dubois; when they rush inside they will find France's most feared bandit dead between two mattresses, a bullet in his head; his suicide note attempts to vindicate members of his gang and ends with the words ''I die.'' (See ''Robbery,'' Feb. 26, 1913.)

MARCH 12

Ben Kilpatrick (''The Tall Texan''), of the Wild Bunch, and Howard Benson board the Southern Pacific's Sunset Flyer at Dryden, Texas; while they are attempting to rob the express car, guard David A. Trousdale crushes Kilpatrick's skull with an ice mallet and shoots Benson to death with Kilpatrick's rifle; Trousdale will be given $1,000 reward and a week's vacation for his heroism.

MARCH 14

Floyd Allen and members of his gang are convicted of bank robbery in a Richmond, Va., courtroom; vowing he will never serve time, Allen and others produce guns smuggled to them and shoot up the courtroom, killing Judge Thornton L. Massie; deputies finally subdue them and all receive life sentences.

OCT. 9

George Mackay, alias John Williams, shoots and kills Inspector Arthur Walls, who interrupts his burglary of an Eastbourne, England, mansion owned by the Countess Sztarary (the countess, returning home late from a party, has seen Mackay prowling about and summons police); Williams is later turned in by confederate Edgar Powers, is convicted and hanged in 1913.

NOV. 22

Train robber ''Bub'' Meeks of the Wild Bunch, after several prison escape attempts, dies in the insane ward of the Wyoming State Hospital at Evanston, Wyo.

ORGANIZED CRIME

APRIL 6

Paul Castellano, who will become a prominent syndicate labor racketeer and brother-in-law to notorious Mafia chieftain Carlo Gambino, is born in New York City.

JUNE 8

George ''Bugs'' Moran, later a subchief of Chicago's North Side underworld boss Dion O'Bannion, is paroled from Joliet, Ill., prison after serving a short sentence for robbery.

JULY 15

Gambler and police informant Herman ''Beansie'' Rosenthal is shot to death by four assassins as he leaves New York City's Café Metropole, in full view of passersby; ''Billiard Ball'' Jack Rose will later inform police that Rosenthal has been ordered killed by New York City Police Lieutenant Charles Becker, head of a graft and kickback ring protecting gambling operations in Manhattan, because Rosenthal refused to kick back money to him; Rose will also name the killers— Gyp the Blood (Harry Horowitz), Dago Frank (Frank Cirofici), Lefty Louis (Louis Rosenberg) and Whitey

Crooked police lieutenant Charles Becker, who ordered the gang murder of gambler Herman Rosenthal. (July 15, 1912)

Lewis (Jacob Siedenshner), who will be quickly convicted and sent to the electric chair; Becker will also be found guilty, and he will be executed at Sing Sing on July 7, 1915.

AUG. 1

John Ormento, who will become a syndicate labor racketeer and narcotics overlord, is born in New York City.

SEPT. 18

John Sclish, future syndicate labor racketeer, is born in Cleveland, Ohio.

SEPT. 28

Reformers by the thousands march in torrential rains through Chicago's red-light district in an attempt to close up organized gambling dens; they will prove unsuccessful.

OCT. 5

New York City gangster Big Jack Zelig is shot and killed on a 13th Street trolley car by Red Phil Davidson in a gang feud.

NOV. 6

Owney ''The Killer'' Madden, New York City hoodlum who will rise to become a Prohibition crime czar, is shot by rival thugs at a 52nd Street dance; wounded six times, he will recover and eventually brag that he has killed all his attackers over the years.

WHITE-COLLAR CRIME

FEB. 1

Gustav Aufrecht and others begin selling phony Avalon Oil Land stock across the country; they will reap a fortune before they are exposed and arrested.

APRIL 14

The great liner *Titanic* strikes an iceberg and sinks; one of its passengers, Alvin Clarence Thompson, a con man, escapes in a lifeboat dressed as a woman and will later turn in phony insurance claims, collecting on *Titanic* victims he says are relatives; he will also collect large settlements on luggage and valuables he claims to have lost; he will henceforth be known by the moniker of ''Titanic'' Thompson.

JUNE 1-NOV. 1

Los Angeles sharper Clarence Hillman mulcts suckers of thousands through fraudulent land promotions.

MISCELLANEOUS

JUNE 14

General Pancho Villa is arrested on orders of Mexico City strongman Victoriano Huerta and is placed before a wall, about to be shot; Villa stalls the firing squad for almost 10 minutes, and just before the squad was about to shoot him down, a messenger arrives on horseback from President Madero with an order to stop the execution; criminal charges of failing to return stolen horses are dropped against Villa. (See ''Murder,'' July 20, 1923).

SEPT. 2

Murderer Reynold Forsbrey escapes his solitary-confinement cell in Sing Sing and almost escapes the prison but is detected on the wall and captured.

OCT. 3-5

Chicago authorities lead massive raids into the red-light district, arresting hundreds of prostitutes and closing down the Levee brothels.

OCT. 14

A boastful and somewhat demented New York City saloon owner, John Schrank, attends a political rally held in a Milwaukee, Wis., hotel for former President Theodore Roosevelt, who is organizing his Progressive Party (also known as the Bull Moose Party); as Roosevelt is leaving his hotel to address a large crowd, Schrank runs forward and fires a shot from a distance of six feet before he is subdued; the bullet plows through the bulky speech inside Roosevelt's coat before entering his chest.
Roosevelt insists on giving his speech, going before supporters to shout: ''It's all right, boys—they haven't killed me yet!'' He survives but will carry the bullet in his chest until he dies; Schrank will be sent to an insane asylum for life.

1·9·1·3

MURDER

FEB. 9

While a sheriff and two deputies stand by help-lessly, a mob of more than 1,000 persons conducts a mock trial in the yard of the courthouse in Houston, Texas, condemning a black, David Rucker, for the murder of Mrs. J. C. Williams; Rucker is then chained to a steel pump in the middle of the yard, soaked with oil and, with wood piled about him, is burned alive.

FEB. 12

Murderer Fredrick A. Pulin, the last person to be executed at Clinton Prison in Dannemora, N.Y., is electrocuted.

APRIL 14

Wealthy Julian Hall, pioneer airman, is shot and killed by his fiancée Jeannie Baxter, in London; Miss Baxter will be found guilty of manslaughter instead of murder due to the brilliant efforts of her attorney, Edward Marshall Hall.

APRIL 27

The body of 14-year-old Mary Phagan is found, strangled and beaten about the head, in the pencil factory of Max Leo Frank in Atlanta, Ga., where she worked; Frank will be convicted of her murder, largely upon the tesimony of an unreliable, drunken witness, Jim Conley, when Frank's death sentence is commuted to life in prison, a violently anti-Semitic mob will lynch Frank after dragging him, ill, out of the Milledgeville, Ga., jail on Aug. 16, 1915.

MAY 25

Peter Kurten, who will later be known as the "Dusseldorf Monster," rapes and kills an eight-year-old girl in Dusseldorf.

SEPT. 13

In Degerloch, near Stuttgart, Germany, Franz Wagner inexplicably becomes a homicidal maniac, killing his wife and children and nine other people in the street; running out of victims, Wagner next sets fire to many houses before police arrive to subdue him; he will be sent for life to an asylum, where he will die in 1938.

ROBBERY

FEB. 26

Surviving members of the bank-robbing Bonnet gang are found guilty of robbery and murder and sentenced to the guillotine; these include Callemin, Dieudonne, Soudy and Monier; only Dieudonne will later be reprieved.

MARCH 23

The city of Omaha, Neb., is struck by a devastating tornado, and only hours later, a mob of looters sacks the city; they are eventually driven off by National Guardsmen.

ORGANIZED CRIME

FEB. 8

Carmine Lombardozzi, future syndicate gambling boss, narcotics smuggler and labor racketeer, is born in New York City.

MAY 23

Vito Genovese, who will become one of the most feared members of the Mafia-syndicate hierarchy, arrives in the U.S., a 10-year-old immigrant from Sicily.

JUNE 24

Future counterfeiter and syndicate member Anthony Giordano is born in St. Louis, Mo.

WHITE-COLLAR CRIME

MARCH 1-APRIL 15

Ivar Kreuger, who has built a paper fortune while using forged Italian bonds as collateral, begins cornering the market on firms producing matches; he will later be known as "The Swedish Match King" and perhaps the most colossal con man of the 20th century.

OCT. 31

George Lester Below, who will become one of America's leading forgers, is born on a small farm outside Mountain View, Mo.

MISCELLANEOUS

AUG. 17

Murderer Harry K. Thaw escapes from New York's Matteawan State Prison Hospital for the criminally insane and seeks refuge in Canada; he will later be caught by William Travers Jerome, the man who prosecuted him for the murder of Stanford White, and returned to the asylum.

SEPT. 24

Henry Starr, noted western bandit, is paroled from the Colorado State Penitentiary with the governor's stipulation that Starr report monthly to his parole officer and never set foot outside the state; Starr ignores the edict and prepares for a sensational bank-robbing spree throughout Oklahoma.

SEPT. 29

Hundreds of blacks in Harrison, Miss., riot in what local lawmen describe as a "cocaine joy riot"; 10 are killed, 35 injured.

SEPT. 30

San Francisco's police commissioner decrees that no dancing, women or liquor will be allowed in the Barbary Coast, a criminal pesthole for decades.

Western outlaw Henry Starr, the first to use an auto in a bank robbery. (Sept. 24, 1913)

1·9·1·4

MURDER

FEB. 26

George A. Ball is hanged in Liverpool, England, for the murder of a 40-year-old spinster, Christina Bradfield, following a botched robbery of her shop in 1913.

MARCH 5

In Paris, novelist Hera Myrtel shoots and kills her husband, Paul Jacques, ostensibly to gain his fortune; she will be sent to prison for 20 years and will later joke that her real motive for killing her husband was because Jacques refused to read her books.

MARCH 12

Philadelphia boy Warren McCarrick vanishes; his body will be found three months later, but his murder will never be solved.

MARCH 13

Haughty Henriette Caillaux, wife of France's minister of finance, Joseph Caillaux, goes to the Paris offices of the newspaper *Le Figaro* and shoots to death its editor, Gaston Calmette; Mrs. Caillaux will later claim that Calmette had slandered her husband; a jury will acquit her on this flimsy excuse.

JUNE 28

Serbian separatist Gavrilo Princip shoots and kills Austria's Archduke Francis Ferdinand and his wife, Sophie, as they travel through Sarajevo, Bosnia (now Yugoslavia) in an open car; Princip is sent to jail, where he will later die of pneumonia; this crime sets off the bloodbath of World War I.

AUG. 9-JAN. 1, 1915

Frederick Mors, a deranged male nurse recently emigrated from Germany, kills 17 elderly patients in a Bronx, N.Y., nursing home; he will be sent to the Matteawan State Prison for the Criminally Insane, from which he will escape, never to surface again.

NOV. 11

Nurse Amy Gilligan, who operates a ramshackle nursing home in Hartford, Conn., feeds poison to Mrs. Amy Hosmer, one of her charges. Later Gilligan will be discovered to have murdered eight other patients in her care, whom she had convinced to turn over their property and savings to her. Nurse Gilligan will be exposed when relatives have the bodies of the Hosmer woman and others exhumed and the poison is found; Gilligan will be sent to prison for life.

DEC. 27

Thief Arthur Rottman, a German sailor working as a laborer in New Zealand, takes an ax to his employer, Joseph McCann, and McCann's family at the McCanns' Ruahine farm, killing three; when police will confront Rottman some weeks later he will blurt: "I am guilty. I know I'm done." He will be hanged at Terrace Jail in Wellington on March 8, 1915.

ROBBERY

FEB. 4

Jack "Legs" Diamond is arrested for burglary in New York City and given an indefinite term in the New York County Penitentiary; Diamond will become a New York City crime kingpin of the late 1920s and early 1930s.

MAY 7

After shoplifting a pair of cheap shoes in Groveton, Miss., a black named Charley Jones is taken from the custody of two officers and lynched by a mob.

JULY 14

Accused of stealing three mules near Lake Cormorant, Miss., a black man, James Bailey, is hanged by a mob of masked men.

SEPT. 30

Henry Starr and others rob the Kiefer Central Bank in Kiefer, Okla., of $6,400; they will commit a dozen other robberies in quick succession: Oct. 6, the Farmers' National Bank in Tupelo, Okla., of $800; Oct. 14, the Pontotoc Bank in Pontotoc, Okla., of $1,100; Oct. 20, the Byars State Bank in Byars, Okla., of $700; Nov. 13, the Farmers' State Bank in Glencoe, Okla., of $2,400; Nov. 29, the Citizens' State Bank in Wardville, Okla., of $800; Dec. 16, the Prue State Bank in Prue, Okla., of $1,400; Dec. 29, the Carney State Bank in Carney, Okla., of $2,853. (See "Robbery," Jan. 4, 1915.)

ORGANIZED CRIME

JULY 16
Chicago detectives raid a local syndicate gambling and brothel operation known as The Turf; gansters shoot it out with the cops, killing Sgt. Birns before escaping.

JULY 17
State's Attorney Maclay Hoyne tells the press that Chicago's First Ward is controlled by organized crime boss Big Jim Colosimo, claiming that the Levee is "worse than ever before, infested by the worst criminals in Chicago, a segregated district of pickpockets, gunmen, robbers and burglars."

JULY 26
Police Capt. Max Nootbaar notifies Chicago brothel-owners and gambling den operators in the Levee that if they don't close up he will shut them down with his flying squads; boss Big Jim Colosimo, in league with his sponsors, Aldermen Michael "Hinky Dink" Kenna and Bathhouse John Coughlin, will arrange to transfer Capt. Nootbaar to an unimportant station some months later.

AUG. 24
Ike Bloom, a subchief of Big Jim Colosimo in Chicago, has the liquor license of his club revoked; it will be quickly restored.

NOV. 15
Santo Trafficante, who will become syndicate kingpin for Florida, is born in Tampa, Fla.

NOV. 28
Owney "The Killer" Madden, leader of New York City's feared Gopher Gang, inveigles Patsy Doyle, a police informer and leader of the rival Hudson Dusters gang, to a back room of an Eighth Avenue saloon and shoots him to death; Madden is turned in to police by the two women he has used to entice Doyle to his death, and he will be sentenced to serve 10 to 20 years in Sing Sing.

WHITE-COLLAR CRIME

MARCH 9
Super New York City con man Charley Gondorff is convicted of running a wire store in Manhattan and is sent to Sing Sing for a short term.

JULY 20
Henri Desire Landru, who will become the notorious "Bluebeard" of France, is convicted in Paris of swindling and is sent to prison for four years.

OCT. 25
Thomas "Mournful" Meeker is convicted in a death scam—attending the funeral of a stranger, claiming the deceased owed him money, and collecting from bereaved survivors—and is sent to prison to serve a short term.

MISCELLANEOUS

FEB. 7
The notorious Brientown district in Washington, D.C., where hundreds of harlots freely mug drunken politicians, is closed down by an act of Congress.

FEB. 13
Alphonse Bertillon, creator of the Bertillon identification system, dies in Paris shortly after discovering that his "evidence" in the sensational Dreyfus case is wrong. (He had identified a signature as Dreyfus's when it was actually another's.)

AUG. 7
Katherine C. Larkin, a 13-year-old Bronx girl, is kidnapped by George Webb, a black janitor of her school, who repeatedly rapes her, then places her in an underground area in the boy's lavatory, where she is found four days later by police searching for her; Webb will be convicted of kidnapping and sent to Sing Sing for 40 years.

DEC. 18
San Francisco police make massive raids on brothel-opium dens, arresting scores of Chinese harlots.

MURDER

MAY 1

Henry Desire Landru, released from prison after serving a short term for swindling, begins his career as a mass murderer, killing women in matrimonial schemes for their wealth; he takes out his first lovelorn ad on this date in the Paris newspaper *Le Journal*. It reads: ''A gentleman, 45 years old, single with 4,000 francs and house, wishes to marry a lady of about his own age. Reply, C.T. 45.'' On June 12, Landru will take out another ad in a Paris newspaper, attracting a Mme. Heon; soon after she will meet with Landru and disappear. On June 26, Mme. Laborde Line, who has answered one of Landru's ads, will become his mistress and disappear, never to be seen again; she is the second of 10 known victims who are never found. (See ''Murder,'' Dec. 16, 1916.)

SEPT. 8

Mallie Wilson, a black, accidentally enters the hotel room occupied by a white woman in Dresden, Tenn. Wilson is jailed over the protests of the woman and her husband, and is lynched on this date by a large mob.

DEC. 8

Lt. Georges Codere, a 22-year-old French-Canadian officer stationed in London, takes $1,000 in Canadian currency to change into British currency from Sgt. Henry Ozanne, who is in charge of regimental funds; Codere instead goes on a spree, giving parties at the Hotel Savoy; then, to cover up his theft, he murders Sgt. Ozanne; when he tries to implicate two batmen (military valets), he is turned in to authorities; Codere will be convicted of murder and sentenced to death but will be reprieved.

Mass killer Henri Desire "Bluebeard" Landru, who found his victims in the lovelorn ads of Paris newspapers. (May 1, 1915)

DEC. 13

The body of Daniel J. McNichols is found in the basement of an abandoned Philadelphia building; police will prove that the victim has been murdered by his former partner, Edward Keller, who swindled McNichols, then turned to murder when his partner discovered the fraud; Keller will be convicted of voluntary manslaughter and given a 10- to 12-year sentence in Eastern State Penitentiary in 1916; Keller will be released in 1924 and will die the following year of a heart attack while robbing a Philadelphia bank.

DEC. 15

A Mme. Collomb answers another of Landru's advertisements in a Paris newspaper and vanishes. (See "Murder," Dec. 16, 1916.)

DEC. 17

Dozens of white men abduct an attractive black woman, Cordella Stevenson, from her home after knocking her husband senseless; after raping her repeatedly, they lynch her, leaving her naked body swaying from a telephone pole outside the Mobile & Ohio Railroad train station in Columbus, Miss.; the body is seen by many thousands of passengers for two days before it is cut down.

ROBBERY

JAN, 4

Henry Starr and his gang continue their robbery spree begun the previous autumn. On this date they rob the Oklahoma State Bank in Preston, Okla.; the outlaws blow open the vault, causing $1,200 in damages, but most of the currency is burned up in the blast and the robbers flee as lawmen arrive; in Jan. Starr and his gang will commit four more bank robberies: Jan. 5, the First National Bank in Owasso, Okla., of $1,500; Jan. 12, the First National Bank in Terlton, Okla., of $1,800, and the Garber State Bank in Garber, Okla., of $2,500; Jan. 13, the Vera State Bank in Vera, Okla., of $1,300.

APRIL 17

Caesar Sheffield, a black awaiting trial for stealing meat from a Valdosta, Ga., smokehouse, is taken out of the Valdosta jail by a mob and shot to death near the train station.

ORGANIZED CRIME

MARCH 5

Patsy Sciortino, who will become a syndicate gambling subboss, is born in rural Sicily.

MAY 25

Increased activities by Chicago's Black Hand organizations cause the *Daily News* to report that 55 bombs have been exploded within a year by extorting Black Hand members in Chicago.

JUNE 2

The Chicago *Record-Herald* reports that the Black Hand has murdered 40 persons in Chicago in 1911; 33 persons in 1912; 31 persons in 1913; 42 persons in 1914; and, in the first five months of 1915, six persons, with 12 bombs exploded.

WHITE-COLLAR CRIME

FEB. 15-20

Joseph "Yellow Kid" Weil and his partner, Fred "Deacon" Buckminster, a onetime Chicago vice cop, open a Big Store con in Chicago, selling phony stocks that net them more than $200,000.

Joseph "Yellow Kid" Weil, who became America's dean of con men. (Feb. 15, 1915)

Fred "Deacon" Buckminster, onetime Chicago vice cop who joined with "the Yellow Kid" to scam millions of dollars in fabulous confidence games. (Feb. 15, 1915)

JUNE 23

Fred Gondorf is arrested and his Big Store operation in New York City is padlocked; Gondorf will later be convicted of fraud and sent to Sing Sing, where his brother Charley will already be serving time.

MISCELLANEOUS

MARCH 21

Charles E. Stielow, who has been convicted of murder years earlier and has narrowly missed being executed several times, is proved innocent through a simple early-day ballistics experiment in N.Y.; Stielow is set free with apologies from the state.

JULY 5

German spy Robert Rosenthal is exposed as he sails on an outbound ship from England; before the ship reaches the three-mile limit—beyond which Rosenthal would have been safe from execution under the British espionage laws of World War I—the spy is executed on deck.

SEPT. 8

Henry Goddard Thomas, a drug dealer known as "The King of Cocaine," is arrested while his high-society clients in New York City panic.

NOV. 26

Baltimore playboy Dwight Mallory vanishes on a hunting expedition; his disappearance is used by sharpers to bilk large sums for his return.

1·9·1·6

MURDER

JAN. 30

Dr. Arthur Warren Waite, a dentist who intends to wipe out his in-laws to gain a family fortune, poisons his mother-in-law, Mrs. John Peck, in New York City; on March 12, Waite will kill her husband. In both instances Waite serves as a family doctor treating illnesses; he will later admit in court that he has administered diphtheria and influenza germs to Mrs. Peck and given her husband a nasal spray loaded with tuberculosis bacteria and chlorine gas; not a penny of the more than $1 million left by Peck to his children will go into Waite's pockets; the murderous dentist will sit down on Sing Sing's electric chair on May 1, 1917, asking calmly, "Is this all there is to it?"

MARCH 26

Robert Stroud, who will later be known as "The Birdman of Alcatraz," and who is serving a life term in Leavenworth for murder, enters the prison mess hall and stabs to death Andrew F. Turner, a guard with whom Stroud has been arguing; he will be sentenced to death but will receive through the intervention of his mother, who visits Mrs. Woodrow Wilson, a presidential reprieve with the proviso that he never receive parole.

MARCH 31

Jeff Brown, a black man who is running to catch a freight train pulling out of Cedar Bluff, Miss., accidentally bumps into the daughter of a white farmer; a quickly formed mob chases after Brown, jerks him from his perch in a boxcar, and lynches him on the spot.

Confident killer Dr. Arthur Warren Waite (center), flanked by two New York City detectives, on his way to court, where he was convicted of murdering his in-laws with doses of lethal bacteria. (Jan. 30, 1916)

SEPT. 28

Frederick Small murders his wife for insurance, then sets a slow-burning fire to his house outside of Mountainview, N.H.; standing in his doorway, within earshot of a friend waiting in a car, he wishes his wife good-bye, then drives to Boston where, also in the company of his friend, he will mail her a postcard to establish what he thinks is the perfect alibi; authorities, however, will find the corpse and the wounds made in her skull by the poker Small has wielded, and when Small returns from Boston he will be asked by the coroner what he wants done with the body. "What— is there anything left to be buried?" Small will reply; the fatal slip, along with the head wounds on the body and other overwhelming circumstantial evidence, will convict Small of the murder; he will go to his death by hanging at the state prison at Concord on Jan. 15, 1918, after bowing to spectators from the scaffold.

DEC. 16

Mme. Pellat, sister of Mme. Colomb, who has earlier begun an affair with Henri Landru in Paris and has disappeared, goes to police, insisting that Landru has murdered her sister; she is ignored. (See "Murder," March 9, 1917.)

DEC. 29

Gregory Rasputin, Russia's "Mad Monk," who has virtual control of the country through his power to hypnotize the Czar's hemophiliac son Alexis and stop his chronic bleeding, is marked for death; Rasputin has encouraged a war Russia cannot win, has sold high offices and is draining the treasury through his sway over the Romanoffs; Prince Felix Yusupov and others entice Rasputin to Yusupov's luxurious St. Petersburg palace on the promise that the lusty monk will meet Yusupov's attractive wife, Princess Irene; Rasputin is stalled in a lower den of the palace, where he is given wine and cakes containing enough cyanide to kill 20 men, but he does not die; Yusupov then stabs the monk and ties him hand and foot before going to get his fellow conspirators; returning, they find Rasputin free and charging at them; they fire several bullets into him, and he finally falls; he is then bound with chains and taken to the frozen River Neva, where a hole is cut and the body is thrown into the water; Rasputin is found the next day; he has survived poison, stabbing and gunfire and broken through the ice only to die on the riverbank of drowning. Yusupov flees Russia and will die in New York City in 1967.

Gregory Rasputin, Russia's "Mad Monk." (Dec. 29, 1916)

ROBBERY

MAY 12

Jack "Legs" Diamond is arrested in New York City for assault and robbery; he is discharged; on May 27, Diamond will be arrested in New York City for theft and again discharged; on July 15, he will be arrested for assault and released within an hour.

SEPT. 3

Wealthy lawyer Dwight Dilworth is stranded in Van Cortlandt Park, New York City, when his car stalls; three robbers take his wallet at gunpoint, shooting him to death when he resists; the holdup men are never found.

ORGANIZED CRIME

JUNE 10

Syndicate lieutenant-to-be Peter Joseph LoCascio, later known as "Mr. Bread," with an arrest record that will date from 1935 for conspiracy, narcotics and liquor violations, is born in New York City.

JUNE 26

Salvatore Charles "Lucky" Luciano pleads guilty to unlawful possession of narcotics in New York City. He is sentenced to one year at Hampton Farms Penitentiary and is paroled in six months.

OCT. 31

Future gambling and labor-racketeering syndicate subboss Gabriel Mannarino is born in New Kensington, Pa.

WHITE-COLLAR CRIME

FEB. 3

William Rickson is convicted of fraud and sent to prison in Maryland for two to 10 years; Rickson has pretended to be a private investigator to earn the $500 reward posted by the family of Dwight Mallory, missing heir who is never found.

APRIL 11

Louis Enricht cons reporters in Farmingdale, N.Y., by demonstrating his so-called new solution, which he claims will replace gasoline at a penny a gallon; the solution, which Enricht attempts to sell to gullible manufacturers, really is gasoline.

MISCELLANEOUS

JULY 22

An anarchist's bomb explodes at the corner of Market and Stuart streets in San Francisco during a mammoth Preparedness Day Parade attended by tens of thousands; the bomb kills nine and injures another 50 spectators; labor leader Tom Mooney is selected by police as the most likely suspect, despite the fact that he produces a photo showing him with his wife, Rena, watching the parade more than a mile from the site of the explosion; in the photo a large clock next to Mooney shows the exact time of the explosion; Mooney and his assistant, Warren K. Billings, are railroaded by antiunion elements who pay perjurer Frank C. Oxman to testify against Mooney; Oxman will claim that he saw the labor leader and Billings leave the bomb at the site of the explosion and will quote Mooney as saying to his cohort: "We must run away; the cops will be after us." Oxman, it will be proved, was 90 miles from San Francisco at the time of the explosion, but Mooney and Billings will be sent to jail, and despite the protestations of President Woodrow Wilson, they will both serve 22 years until released in 1939, in one of America's most shameful miscarriages of justice.

AUG. 31

Sheriff Sherman Ely of Lima, Ohio, refuses to turn over to a mob of more than 3,000 a black prisoner named Charles Daniels, who is being held on a charge of assaulting a white woman. Ely, who will not tell mob leaders where he has hidden the prisoner after they break into the jail, is slashed, kicked, beaten and almost lynched.

SEPT. 5

Rudolph Valentino, who will become the great Latin lover of the silent screen within a few years, is arrested by vice squads in New York City for conducting a badger game in a Manhattan whorehouse run by Mrs. Georgia Thym; all details of this arrest will later be mysteriously expunged from New York City Police Department records.

MURDER

MARCH 9

Parisian mass murderer Henri Desire Landru places another lovelorn advertisement, which is answered by Madame Jaume, who will become another victim. (See ''Murder,'' April 12.)

MARCH 10

In London, Alice Wheeldon is sentenced to a short prison term for plotting to murder British Prime Minister David Lloyd George.

MARCH 29

British Sgt. Leo George O'Donnell is hanged at Winchester Prison for murdering an officer of his company in an attempt to steal army funds; O'Donnell is hanged in civilian clothes, since it is thought that by wearing his army issue to the gallows he would degrade the King's uniform.

APRIL 12

André Babelay, another of Landru's vicitims, disappears in Paris. (See ''Murder,'' Aug. 10.)

APRIL 26

Kansas City killer Joseph P. Redenbaugh, 19, with two others, shoots and kills Alice McQuillan Dunn while she sleeps with her sister in her St. Paul, Minn., home, on the orders of her husband, Frank Dunn, a mail hauler; Redenbaugh, Dunn, and the others will be convicted and sent to prison for life; Redenbaugh will be released on May 9, 1962, considered at age 64 to be totally rehabilitated.

MAY 30

Kidnapped from his father's Springfield, Mo., home, Lloyd Keet, 14 months old, is held for $6,000 ransom, the baby abductors informing the father (a wealthy Missouri banker, the son of a millionaire) by letter that unless the money is paid the child will be tortured and killed; Mr. Keet drives into the Ozark Hills on June 1, 1917, depositing the money at the site indicated by the kidnappers, but they and the child fail to appear according to arrangements; a severe storm at the time has prevented their arrival, police conclude; the child's battered body is found at the bottom of a well at an abandoned farm near Springfield a few days later. By that time, authorities have arrested five men and a woman who have admitted planning the kidnapping of a St. Louis munitions manufacturer but claim they abandoned the plan and have nothing to do with the Keet boy; the six suspects are loaded into the sheriff's car on June 10, 1917, to be delivered to the state prison at Jefferson City; but thousands of people, having heard of the boys's death and the suspects in custody, almost riot in downtown Springfield, then send scores of vengeance-seeking men in fast cars after the sheriff's auto; the sheriff and his prisoners are overtaken about 40 miles northwest of Springfield; the primary suspect, a man named Piersol, is dragged to a tree and asked to confess; he screams his innocence but is hauled up; he is lowered to the ground and still insists upon his innocence as well as that of the other five suspects cowering in the car awaiting the justice of the lynch mob; Piersol is hauled up again, but Sheriff Webb begs for his life. Piersol is spared, and the sheriff and his party are allowed to continue on to Jefferson City; Piersol will be convicted of the Keet kidnapping and given 35 years in prison, but he will never be indicted for the child's murder.

AUG.10

Mme. Buisson, another of mass murderer Henri Desire Landru's victims in Paris, withdraws her savings of 12,000 francs from the bank on Landru's advicc, then disappears; her sister, Mme. Lacoste, tells police that Landru has taken her sister to his country retreat at Gambais, but no investigation is begun. (See ''Murder,'' Nov. 25.)

OCT. 31

Louis Voisin, a French butler in London, finds both his mistresses, Berthe Roche and Émilienne Gerard, battling in his rooms, ironically during a zeppelin raid on the city; Voisin, making an on-the-spot choice, batters in the head of Gerard, then, using his skills as a butcher, cuts up her body; a road sweeper working near Regent Square discovers the torso and arms in a sack, also containing a laundry mark and a note upon which is written the words ''Blodie Belgium.'' Gerard, who is later reported missing, is identified through the laundry mark, and her known lover, Voisin, is brought in for questioning; asked to write the words ''Bloody Belgium''—Gerard is from Belgium—Voisin makes the same spelling errors, writing ''Blodie Belgium.'' He will be convicted and sent to the gallows at Pentonville Prison on March 2, 1918.

NOV. 25

Mme. Jaume leaves Paris with Landru for Gambais and is never seen again. (See ''Murder,'' Jan. 13, 1918.)

ROBBERY

JUNE 1

Vernon C. Miller, future embezzler, bank robber and bootlegger in the Kansas City area, joins the U.S. Army, serving with distinction in France, where he becomes an expert with a machine gun; he will later use one at Kansas City's Union Station to slaughter lawmen in ostensibly trying to release bank robber Frank Nash from custody in 1933.

AUG. 28

A Brink's truck delivering a $9,100 payroll from Chicago's Corn Exchange National Bank to the Winslow Bros. ironworks is ambushed; guard Barton Allen, carrying the cash in a bag from the truck, is shotgunned to death and the bag taken; the driver of the truck also is killed and another guard wounded; four bandits roar away with the cash in a maroon touring car; police receive a tip from a jealous girlfriend of one of the robbers, and a man named Carraro is picked up; he quickly names "Blackie" Wheed as the ringleader of the bandits, along with two others, Asciutto and Therien; Wheed will be tracked by police to a cottage on Thomas Street, where he will shoot it out with the cops in a three-hour gun battle; out of ammunition, he will finally surrender; Therien is traced to Ottawa, Kan., where he will be arrested; Wheed, the leader of the holdup gang and killer of the guard and driver, will be executed; Carraro and Therien will be given long prison terms; the fourth gang member, Asciutto, will never be captured, presumed to have returned to his native Italy; half the loot is recovered from the captured bandits.

DEC. 12

Petty crook Johnny Lazia, who has ingratiated himself to political powers in Kansas City, Mo., is sentenced to 12 years in the Missouri State Penitentiary for robbing a store. He will be paroled after serving only eight months and seven days, at the request of high-ranking Kansas City citizens, including the prosecuting attorney of his case, who later becomes president of a bank that has the accounts of Lazia and his political sponsors; Johnny Lazia will go on to become the enforcer for Kansas City's boss Tom Pendergast, a position of great power, until Lazia is shot to death on July 10, 1934, at the hands of unknown gangsters.

ORGANIZED CRIME

FEB. 13

Charless Dion O'Bannion, petty thief and one time altar boy, forms a burglary gang made up of Earl "Hymie" Weiss, George "Bugs" Moran and others, which will become, in the 1920s, the nucleus of the gang that will control all underworld activities on Chicago's North Side.

JULY 29

New York City rackets boss Johnny Spanish (Joseph Weyler) dines in a Second Avenue restaurant after his bodyguards are paid to disappear by rival gangster Nathan "Kid Dropper" Kaplan; as Spanish leaves the restaurant, Kaplan and two of his men follow the racketeer down the street, then shoot him to death; Kaplan becomes the top criminal boss of New York City.

AUG. 1

Brooklyn-born Alphonse Capone becomes a sub-boss for Paul Kelley's Five Points Gang in N.Y.

WHITE-COLLAR CRIME

JULY 15

Onetime private detective Gaston Bullock Means bilks lumber heiress Maude King out of $150,000; she is later killed when "playing" with Means's pistol, or so he will tell a coroner's jury; Means will not be prosecuted and a short time later will be hired by William J. Burns as an agent for the Bureau of Investigation.

OCT. 7

Dr. John R. Brinkley, who will enact a host of medical cons that will make him a millionaire, arrives in Milford, Kan., which he will use as his base of operations.

MISCELLANEOUS

JAN. 21

In a marathon oratory session, 39 clergymen deliver fiery sermons in the Barbary Coast of San Francisco, blasting prostitution and other forms of vice rampant in this area; hundreds of prostitutes, gamblers, pimps and holdup men listen patiently, then resume operations the following day; on Feb. 14, clergymen in San Francisco will lead a food blockade against the Barbary Coast to stop wide-open prostitution, but the effort will collapse within a week.

FEB. 13

Mata Hari, an exotic dancer whose real name is Gertrude Zelle, is arrested in Paris and charged with espionage; she will be tried in a closed-door semimilitary hearing, found guilty of spying for the Germans during World War I, and will be shot by a French firing squad outside Paris on Oct. 15, 1917.

SEPT. 9

Bolsheviks break out of jail in Laishev, Kazan, Russia, torching the town; 20 of the Bolsheviks are lynched when caught.

1·9·1·8

MURDER

JAN. 13

Henri Desire Landru meets a Mme. Marchadier in Paris and takes her to his country home in Gambais, where she disappears; the woman's three dogs, which accompany them, are also killed by Landru. (See "Murder," April 5.)

FEB. 9

In London, 16-year-old Nellie Trew is found raped, beaten and strangled; next to her body police find a bone button with a piece of wire hooked to it and a military badge; newspapers publish photos of the badge and button, and it is soon learned that the badge, in the shape of a tiger, is that of the Leicestershire Regiment; a machinist tells police that such a badge has been worn by a fellow employee, David Greenwood; the suspect is picked up, wearing a coat with no buttons; he claims to have sold his regimental badge and lost the buttons, but his explanation and alibi are weak; moreover, the wire found on the button is identical to that manufactured by the firm for which Greenwood works; Greenwood will be found guilty and sentenced to death, but the sentence will be commuted to life imprisonment.

FEB. 12

In Estill Springs, Tenn., a mob of 1,200 greet a train carrying black man Jim McIlherron, who has shot and killed two white men; McIlherron is dragged from the train, tied to a stake, and burned alive, his body charred to the bone; none of the killers is ever brought to justice.

APRIL 5

Mme. Pascal, who has met Landru in Paris through one of his newspaper "lonely hearts" ads, vanishes, later presumed to have gone off with the mass murderer to his Gambais retreat—and her death at his hands. (See "Murder," Jan. 13, 1919.)

MAY 21

Earle Leonard Nelson, later to be known as "The Gorilla Murderer" (because of his apelike ability to escape capture by police) of 22 women from coast to coast, is charged in San Francisco with an assault on a child and is sent to an asylum from which he later escapes.

MAY 23

Joseph Maggio, New Orleans grocer, and his wife, are slaughtered by an intruder in their home, the mysterious "Ax Man of New Orleans"; Louis Besumer and his common-law wife, Harriet Lowe, will be attacked by the same fiend in their home on June 28, and Harriet Lowe will later die. On Aug. 10 the Ax Man will enter the home of Joseph Romano and crush his skull with an ax; in all instances, witnesses described the fleeing killer as being a tall, heavyset white man, but he will never be apprehended.

MAY 27

Schoolteacher Grace Lusk, who has fallen in love with horse doctor David Roberts in Waukesha, Wis., confronts Mrs. Roberts, asking her to divorce him; when the wife snarls that spinster Lusk is "a bitch, a slut whom the dogs follow down the street," Grace shoots her dead; she will be sent to the Waupun Penitentiary on June 19 and pardoned in 1923.

JULY 16

Czar Nicholas II and his entire family are executed by Bolsheviks under the command of Jacob Yurovsky, a murderous thug, under the orders of Lenin; the slaughter occurs in the home of N. N. Ipatiev in Eka-terinburg, Russia (in the western Urals); it will later be claimed that the Czar's youngest daughter, Anastasia, survives the mass execution, but this never be substantiated, nor will a wilder claim that the entire Romanoff family survives.

SEPT. 16

Charles Chapin, editor of the *New York Evening World,* who is drowning in gambling debts, murders his wife, Nellie, in the Hotel Cumberland; he will claim that he wanted her dead rather than to live in poverty; Chapin will be sent to Sing Sing for life, where he will become a model prisoner and be allowed to create magnificent gardens in and outside the prison; he will die on Dec. 13, 1930 and be known as "Sing Sing's Rose Man."

ROBBERY

JAN. 20

Joseph and Helen Holbach, an elderly German couple running a roadhouse near South Ozone Park, N.Y., are murdered in a particularly brutal robbery, and several hundred dollars and family jewels are taken; undercover New York City detective Michael Fiaschetti travels through several states, tracking Italian migrant truck farmers who have been working near the Holbach place at the time of the robbery, and discovers Mike Casalino, who confides to Fiaschetti that he and three others committed the robbery-murder; Casalino and Giuseppe Zambelli will be sent to the electric chair, and the other two robbers given 16 years in prison.

JAN. 29

Charles "The Ox" Reiser, one of America's most infamous safecrackers since the turn of the century, who has been in retirement, recruits fledgling hoodlums Dion O'Bannion, Bugs Moran and Hymie Weiss to form a safe-blowing burglary unit; they explode a safe at the Western Dairy Company in Chicago and take $2,000. (See "Robbery," Sept. 2.)

MARCH 13

Jack "Legs" Diamond is arrested in New York City for trying to rob a jewelry store; the charge is dismissed.

MARCH 28

Frank "Jelly" Nash, who is serving a life term in the Oklahoma State Penitentiary for murder (Nash has been a member of the old Henry Starr bank-robbing gang), impresses the warden with his reformed char-acter and has his sentence reduced to 10 years; Nash begs the warden to support his pardon, saying all he wants to do is join the army and fight in France for his country; he will be pardoned on Aug. 16 and immediately embark upon a robbing spree.

APRIL 16

Jack "Legs" Diamond is arrested for attempted robbery in New York City; the charge is dismissed.

APRIL 24

A Mme. Dreyfus is found dead in her Paris rooms on the Rue de Flandre, a robbery victim of the La Villette gang, who have taken the woman's savings, 94,000 francs.

MAY 24

George "Bugs" Moran is captured by Chicago police in the act of burglarizing a safe and is sent to prison; he will be paroled on Feb. 1, 1923, through the efforts of his cohort, Dion O'Bannion, whose North Side gang he joins.

JULY 4

Arthur "Dock" Barker, whose most infamous robberies will be commited with his brother Fred in the early 1930s, is arrested by police in Tulsa, Okla., for auto theft; Barker will escape while being brought to court.

SEPT. 2

Charles Reiser, Dion O'Bannion, Hymie Weiss and others slug the watchman at the Standard Oil Company in Chicago, take his keys, go into the paymaster's office, blow the safe with nitroglycerine (safecrackers using nitro were then called "petermen") and take $2,060. On the next day the Reiser gang will enter Schaeffer Brothers in Chicago through a coal chute and blow the safe, taking $1,400. (See "Robbery," Nov. 5.)

SEPT. 24

Margie Dean (born Margie Celano in Paris), one of America's early female bandits, is trapped by Kansas City police; Dean has been robbing banks in the Midwest with Frank "Jumbo" Lewis, Dale Jones and others. (The gang is the first to use an idling car outside a bank; Margie is the driver.) While Margie and Dale Jones escape, Roscoe Lancaster holds back the lawmen and is shot to death.

NOV. 5

The Reiser safecracking gang in Chicago sneak into the Prudential Life Insurance Company via a fire escape and blow the safe, taking $3,865. (See ''Robbery,'' Dec. 2.)

NOV. 24

Bank robbers Margie Dean and Dale Jones are cornered in Arcadia (Los Angeles), Calif., when they pull their big Marmon touring car into a gasoline station; Dean and Jones pull automatic weapons and begin shooting officers, killing several before they are riddled with gunfire from more than 20 policemen.

DEC. 2

The Reiser gang enters the Borden Farm Products Company in Chicago, blows the safe and takes $594.61.

ORGANIZED CRIME

APRIL 22

A Mafia hoodlum who will rise to syndicate power, Vito Genovese, fires four bullets into a man in Queens, N.Y.; the victim lives but refuses to testify against Genovese, who is set free.

APRIL 28

Joseph Paul LoPicolo, who will become a syndicate subboss in narcotics smuggling, is born in Chicago.

OCT. 24

In New York City, youthful Meyer Lansky and Lucky Luciano, founders of the crime syndicate some 15 years later, are arrested for assault and battery (against each other).

NOV. 15

Meyer Lansky is arrested and fined $2 for disturbing the peace; he will be arrested again on Nov. 25 and charged with a felony, but this will be dismissed.

WHITE-COLLAR CRIME

FEB. 10-MARCH 25

During the Oklahoma oil boom, the *Oklahoma City News* begins an editorial campaign to rid the city of oil-land swindlers leasing nonexistent property to suckers; as a result, the local police make several raids against sharpers, arresting scores.

JULY 18

Charles Aycock begins a nationwide mail-order con of selling his useless ''Tuberclecide'' as a sure-fire cure for TB; Aycock's operation will not be closed down until 1928.

AUG. 1-NOV. 1

Corrupt Bureau of Investigation agent Gaston B. Means hires himself out to both German and British spy masters, promising invaluable espionage information to them; he takes enormous amounts of money but delivers nothing.

MISCELLANEOUS

JAN. 21

Race hatred in Chicago culminates with more than 30 bombs being thrown into the homes of blacks.

1·9·1·9

MURDER

JAN 13

Lt. Col. Norman Cecil Rutherford shoots his friend Maj. Miles Seton to death in the mansion of Sir Malcolm Seton in the London suburb of Holland Park; Rutherford calmly surrenders to police and is judged insane and sent to Broadmoor, to be released after several years as cured; Rutherford's motives are vague; it was suggested by his lawyer that he thought that Seton was trying to steal his wife.

Mme. Marchadier, Henri Landru's last known victim, accompanies "Bluebeard" from Paris to his Gambais retreat and is never seen again. (See "Murder," April 12.)

FEB. 27

Dr. Walter K. Wilkins calls authorities to his home in Long Beach, N.Y., where his wife lies dying near the back porch; he points to her body and his own superficial head wounds and says that an intruder escaping his house has murdered his wife; it will be proved that Dr. Wilkins has murdered his wife for her money and he will commit suicide in his cell in the Mineola, N.Y., jail.

MARCH 10

The Ax Man of New Orleans hatchets to death the two-year-old daughter of Mrs. Rose Cortimiglia, while wounding Mrs. Cortimiglia and her husband; the distraught woman mistakenly identifies a neighbor, Frank Jordano, as the Ax Man, and Jordano, on her testimony, will be condemned to death, but before he is executed, Mrs. Cortimiglia will rush to authorities stating that she was mistaken, and Jordano will be released; on March 13, the *Times-Picayune* will receive a letter ostensibly written by the Ax Man, who threatens to come to New Orleans and kill at random but promises to pass over all homes where jazz music can be heard; the entire city of New Orleans will rock with jazz on March 19, the day stipulated in the letter for the visit, but no Ax Man killings will occur. (See "Murder," Oct. 27.)

APRIL 3

Ex-soldier William Little, a black, is beaten to death by a white mob outside Blakely, Ga., because he continues to wear his uniform after being mustered out of the army, even though he explains that he has no other clothing.

APRIL 10

Emiliano Zapata, the great Mexican revolutionary leader, is enticed to the hacienda of San Juan Chiameca outside Cuautla Morelos, Mexico, on the promise of a half-breed Yaqui, Col. Jesús Guajardo, that he will turn over his troops and supplies to the impoverished Zapatistas; Zapata goes before Guajardo's troops to receive their salute, and instead they shoot him and his followers to death; Guajardo is given $50,000 and promoted to Brigadier General by General Alvaro Obregon, who, with Venustiano Carranza, has plotted Zapata's assassination.

APRIL 12

A sister of one of Landru's many victims who have disappeared recognizes the mass murderer on a Paris street, follows him home, then brings police to his door, where he is arrested. (See "Murder," February 25, 1922.)

APRIL 28

In Forest Gate, London, Henry Perry, a veteran of the Egyptian war against the Turks, goes berserk in the home of his stepaunt, Mrs. Alice Cornish, axing her to death, along with her two young daughters and her husband, Walter. He will later be found with Mrs. Cornish's wedding ring, which he has chopped from her hand; he will be quickly condemned, and hanged on July 10.

APRIL 29

George Holden, a black who has survived two previous lynching attempts, is taken from the baggage car of a Vicksburg, Shreveport & Pacific train outside Shreveport, La., and lynched; Holden was accused of writing an improper note to a white woman.

JUNE 16

Mabel Greenwood of Kidwelly, Wales, dies of what doctors describe as a "valvular heart disease"; after her husband remarries, Mrs. Greenwood's body will be exhumed in 1920, and arsenic will be found; Harold Greenwood, a solicitor, will be tried for murdering his first wife, the prosecution stating that he has dosed a bottle of wine from which she drank; Greenwood's brilliant lawyer, Marshall Hall, will have Greenwood's daughter Irene take the witness stand and state that she, too, drank from the same bottle; Greenwood will be set free, and his wife's murder will never be solved.

JUNE 23

Djang Djing Sung, a factory worker in Birmingham, England, crushes the head of coworker Zee Ming Wu and steals his savings book containing £240; when confronted by police, Sung first attempts to throw the blame onto other Chinese workers but finally confesses; Sung will convert to Christianity before he is hanged in Worchester Prison.

JULY 5

Annie Bella Wright, 21-year-old factory worker, is mysteriously shot while riding her bicycle in Leicestershire, England; a male seen cycling with the victim is identified as Ronald Vivian Light, a teacher; Light first denies having owned a green bicycle—the color of the bicycle Miss Wright's companion was reportedly riding—then admits to owning one; he will be defended by Marshall Hall, who proves that the gun owned by Light, a .45, would have made a larger exit hole in the victim than the one found; Light will be judged not guilty, and the Green Bicycle Case will remain unsolved.

JULY 18

Wealthy Cleveland, Ohio, publisher Daniel Kaber is found in his bedroom stabbed 23 times; it will later be learned that his wife, Mrs. Eva Catherine Kaber, has hired, through Mrs. Erminia ''Big Emma'' Colavito, two killers to murder her husband so she can collect his fortune; the killers, Salvatore Cala and Vittoria Pisselli, will be tracked down and sent to prison for life, as will Mrs. Colavito and Mrs. Kaber, who will both die in prison.

OCT. 27

The Ax Man of New Orleans strikes again, killing Michele Pepitone as he lies sleeping in his bed; this is the last known killing of the Ax Man; he is never apprehended.

DEC. 2

Millionaire theatrical magnate Ambrose Small vanishes from his Montréal, Canada, home and is never found; he is thought to be a murder victim, but is this never proved. John Doughty, Small's secretary, disappears on the same day as his employer; investigators find that more than $100,000 in negotiable bonds belonging to Small have been taken, Doughty will be found in Nov. 1920 in an Oregon lumber mill and will be returned to Canada to face trial for the bonds theft; he will be found guilty in Toronto and sentenced to five years in prison.

DEC. 25

The body of Kitty Breaks is found on the sandhills of St. Anne's, near Blackpool, England, with several bullet wounds; the gloves of her lover, Frederick Rothwell Holt, are found nearby, along with footprints that match Holt's; the ex-British Army officer will be found guilty and sent to the gallows on April 13, 1920.

ROBBERY

JAN. 18-19

During this night the notorious La Villette robbery gang of Paris blows open the safe inside the Bank of Blache & Gravereau, taking only 510 francs; they overlook the larger safe in another vault. (See ''Robbery,'' Aug. 10, 1920.)

FEB. 10

Wilbur Underhill, later to be known as the ''Tri-State Terror'' robber, is arrested for burglarizing a Joplin, Mo., store; he will receive a light sentence.

Onetime British officer Frederick Rothwell Holt, who murdered his sweetheart and left his gloves behind. (Dec. 25, 1919)

MARCH 15

Bruno Richard Hauptmann, who will be executed in 1936 for the kidnapping-murder of Charles A. Lindbergh, Jr., is convicted of breaking and entering with the intent to rob the home of the mayor of Kamenz, Germany, receiving a short prison sentence.

OCT. 18

Frank ''Jelly'' Nash is arrested in Cordell, Okla., on charges of robbing the local bank of several thousand dollars a week earlier, but charges are dropped.

DEC. 30

Knowing Prohibition will go into effect within two weeks, small-time Chicago hoodlum Dion O'Bannion steals a truck full of liquor in Chicago's Loop, cold-cocking the driver and delivering the stolen truck and booze to the warehouse of Samuel J. ''Nails'' Morton; O'Bannion fences the booze and sells the truck with Morton, establishing himself as leading bootlegger on Chicago's North Side.

ORGANIZED CRIME

JAN. 1

The Chicago Crime Commission is organized by

concerned citizens to record the city's vice operations and pressure for police action.

APRIL 9

Michael James Genovese (a cousin to future syndicate boss Vito Genovese), who will become a syndicate labor racketeer, is born in Pittsburgh, Pa.

DEC. 26

Rosario Borgio, incensed with police interference with his numerous rackets in Akron, Ohio, offers a $250 bounty on every policeman killed by his henchmen; several officers are shot to death before the gang members are rounded up; Borgio, Paul Chiavaro, Lorenzo Bionde and Vito Mezzano will go to the electric chair.

WHITE-COLLAR CRIME

MAY 30

Col. Bermondt, a military swindler, manipulates Berlin and London banks to fund his takeover of Latvia to keep the Bolsheviks out of the tiny country; he assumes dictatorial leadership, then loots the country's treasury in Riga before Allied warships land troops; Bermondt escapes in a peasant smock and later writes a book mocking his gulled financial supporters entitled, *My War Against the Bolsheviks.*

DEC. 20

Charles Ponzi opens his Boston bank, offering to double depositors' money within a few months; he does, in a simple Peter-to-Paul swindle that at first earns him millions.

MISCELLANEOUS

MARCH 10

The U.S. Supreme Court upholds the conviction of Eugene V. Debs, Socialist presidential candidate, for violating the Espionage Act in statements he has made in a speech at Canton, Ohio, the previous June; Debs, while in the federal prison at Atlanta, will draw 915,302 Socialist votes for the presidency in 1920 as inmate No. 9653.

MARCH 24

Jack ''Legs'' Diamond is arrested for deserting the

army and stealing money from company funds; he is sent to the Disciplinary Barracks at Leavenworth to serve a five-year sentence.

JUNE 2

An anarchist places a bomb on the front steps of the home of Attorney General A. Mitchell Palmer in Washington, D.C., but the bomb explodes prematurely, blowing the anarchist to pieces (one of his feet lands on the front lawn of Under Secretary of the Navy Franklin Delano Roosevelt, who lives across the street). Palmer, incensed, will order his notorious 1920 ''Red Raids'' in retaliation, in which hundreds of dissidents will be arrested across the country and released after much harassment from federal marshals. (Also embarrassed will be the young lawyer in the Justice Department who has prepared the briefs on the raids and encourages Palmer to enact them, J. Edgar Hoover.)

JULY 28-30

A 17-year-old black youth swims into waters reserved for whites off the 31st Street Beach on Chicago's South Side; a fight breaks out and, some later

Chicago White Sox great pitcher Eddie Cicotte, who, with seven other teammates threw the 1919 World Series, a scam that prompted the press to dub the club "The Black Sox." (Oct. 1, 1919)

claim, white youths stone the black youth, who drowns. Brawling, then open warfare between blacks and whites ensues as thousands flee the beach; hot weather and racial tensions, which have been mounting for months over blacks buying into white neighborhoods, fuel the race war that breaks out all over the South Side of Chicago, leaving 22 blacks and 14 whites dead, with more than 500 others wounded by stabbings, beatings, stonings and shootings; Mayor William Hale Thompson, on July 30, orders militia into the vast area, and peace is slowly restored; four days later, Judge Robert R. Crowe attributes the racial war to anarchists.

SEPT. 9

Unionized policemen in Boston go out on strike, and the city is thrown open to hundreds of underworld gunmen, rapists, burglars and looters; citizens arm themselves and take up police duties with awful results—many are shot; hundreds of shops are brazenly looted in broad daylight; Governor Calvin Coolidge calls in troops, and new policemen are hired before the city returns to normal; Coolidge will later tell AFL president Samuel Gompers: "There is no right to strike against the public safety by anybody, anywhere, any time," a line that becomes famous and propels Coolidge into the limelight and the vice presidency under Warren G. Harding.

OCT. 1

Eight players on the Chicago White Sox—Joseph Jefferson "Shoeless Joe" Jackson, Charles "Swede" Risberg, Oscar "Happy" Felsch, Arnold "Chick" Gandil, George "Buck" Weaver, Fred McMullin, Eddie Cicotte, and Claude "Lefty" Williams—take small bribes from emissaries of New York gambler Arnold Rothstein and throw the World Series; the players will admit the plot the following year and all will be barred from baseball forever, giving the team the sobriquet "the Black Sox"; the blatant fixing of the 1919 Series ushers in Judge Kennesaw Mountain Landis as the game's first commissioner, who keeps a stern eye on players and managers for years to come.

1·9·2·0

MURDER

JAN. 11-12

Farm laborer Albert Edward Burrows kills his mistress, Hannah Calladine, and her two small children in Glossop, Derbyshire, England, throwing the bodies down a country well; Burrows will not be exposed until March 4, 1923, when a small boy from the area, earlier seen in Burrows's company, disappears and is found dead, sexually assaulted, in the same well; the impoverished farmhand will be convicted, and hanged in Nottingham on Aug. 8, 1923.

JAN. 12

Florence Nightingale Shore, a nurse like her namesake, is found at Polegate on the London-to-Hastings train, her skull crushed under a large hat that hides her faces as she sits dead, riding in the coach; doctors state that she has been beaten to death with a gun butt; her murder is never solved.

APRIL 8

The severed torso of a man is found in the Seine in Paris packed in a sleeping bag of waterproof linen and marked "A. Bill." The remaining parts of this obvious murder victim are never found, and the case remains unsolved.

MAY 1

Arthur Andrew Clement Goslett, a onetime West African diamond smuggler who immigrated to England in 1914, crushes the skull of his wife Evelyn (his third or fourth bigamous wife, it is not known which), as they walk next to the River Brent in Hendon, England; the tire iron Goslett has used as the murder weapon will be traced to him, and he will be quickly picked up, explaining that he has murdered Evelyn so that he can be with another common-law wife, Daisy Holt, who has just given birth to his child. "I am going to have the rope," he sighs; and he does, being hanged on July 27.

MAY 8

Henry Scott, a black pullman porter on the Atlantic Coast Line, train No. 82, is pulled off the train and shot 60 or more times outside of Tampa, Fla., by a mob of angry whites who have learned that he asked a white woman to wait until he finished making up a berth before preparing her bed.

MAY 11

Bridge expert Joseph Browne Elwell is found shot to death in his New York City mansion at 244 West 70th Street by his housekeeper; the millionaire womanizer sits in the front parlor, a bullet in his forehead, with the windows wide open to thousands of passersby, not one of whom comes forward with information regarding his killer; the case baffles police and remains unsolved.

JUNE 2

In Norristown, Pa., Blakely Coughlin, 13-month-old child of a wealthy family, is stolen from his crib; the father calls the local police, the Burns Detective Agency and other private detectives, offering rewards for the return of his son. After the press learns of the kidnapping, the Blakely home is swamped with crank letters. By June 16, Coughlin has paid the kidnappers $12,000, but nationwide interest is created when the child is not returned; Secret Service agents and postal authorities join the search for a ''foreign-sounding'' kidnapper (the father has heard his voice but did not see him clearly in the dark when making the payment); two months later, August Pascal, a Frenchman, is arrested; he admits taking the child, but for the next four months he cruelly plays a plea-bargaining game, claiming that the child is dead, then alive, saying that he will tell authorities where the child is if he is given immunity from prosecution; when the deal is turned down, Pascal states that the child was accidentally smothered to death during the abduction and that he threw the body into the Schuylkill River; a body some time later does wash up on the river bank, a badly decomposed child about the age of the Coughlin child, but the Coughlins refuse to identify it; believing their child still alive; they will continue fruitlessly to search for the infant; in Nov. Pascal will plead guilty to second-degree murder, kidnapping and other charges and be sent to prison for life.

JUNE 16

Three black circus roustabouts—Elmer Jackson, Isaac McGhie and Nate Green—are lynched by a howling mob of 5,000 whites outside Duluth, Minn., after being accused of raping a 17-year-old white girl.

JUNE 21

War hero Carl Otto Wanderer shoots to death his wife, Ruth, and an unknown tramp in Chicago; he tells reporters that the ragged stranger had accosted him and his wife, shooting his wife in an attempted holdup while Wanderer shot the stranger in self-defense; reporters Ben Hecht and Charles MacArthur learn Wanderer has set the whole thing up, paying the bum to pretend to rob them supposedly so that Wanderer can chase him away and appear a hero to his wife; Wanderer will later admit to committing the crime so he could develop homosexual liaisons; he will be hanged on March 19, 1921.

JULY 30

San Francisco murderer Emma Le Doux is paroled from San Quentin after serving 10 years.

AUG. 13

George Karl Grossman, a hulking mass killer living in Berlin, Germany, murders a woman named Sasnovski; he will not be exposed until 1921, when his landlord hears a struggle coming from his third-floor walkup apartment and finds the trussed-up corpse of a girl on Grossman's kitchen table, ready for dissection; the names of more than 50 women victims, with dates going back to 1913, will be found in Grossman's diary, an account of horror showing how he has murdered scores of women after sleeping with them, then butchered their bodies and sold the remains as fresh meat; Grossman will laugh when hearing his death sentence, and he will commit suicide in his cell before his scheduled beheading.

AUG. 19

Jack Alfred Field and William Thomas Gray murder 17-year-old Irene Munro, an attractive office worker, at the Crumbles in Eastbourne, England, enraged when she refuses to have sex with them; both are quickly arrested, having been seen with the victim only hours before the murder; the men will accuse each other of the murder at their trial, and both will be sent to the gallows at Wandsworth Prison on Feb. 4, 1921.

NOV. 30

Charles E. Davis, of Raleigh, N.C., is arrested on suspicion of murdering his wife, despite his claims that she has been killed by ''a lecherous-looking black''; Davis commits suicide in his cell.

ROBBERY

MARCH 23

Harvey Bailey, who has been robbing small southwestern banks for almost a decade, is arrested for hijacking and burglary in Omaha, Neb. and given a suspended sentence.

APRIL 15

The Slater and Morrill shoe factory in South Braintree, Mass., is held up by four men, who shoot and kill paymaster Frederick Parmenter and guard Alexander Berardelli, escaping with payroll boxes containing $15,776.51. Nicola Sacco, a shoemaker, and Bartolomeo Vanzetti, a fish peddler, will be picked up in the area on May 5 in a car similar to that used in the robbery; they will be charged with the theft and murders, and their subsequent trial will be highly controversial, with only circumstantial evidence presented against the two of them; they will be convicted on July 14, 1921, principally because of their anarchistic views and through the prodding of the presiding magistrate, Webster Thayer, a rigid, 64-year-old Back Bay judge who is highly prejudicial in the case; in his address to the jury in another robbery case, Thayer will lambaste Vanzetti, saying: ''This man, although he may not actually have committed the crime attributed to him, is nevertheless morally culpable, because he is the enemy of our existing institutions . . . the defendant's ideas are cognate with crime.'' Judge Thayer will later gloat at a Dartmouth game: ''Did you see what I did to those anarchist bastards?'' Thayer will refuse a new trial and will eventually sentence Sacco and Vanzetti to death on April 9, 1927; despite worldwide sentiment against their execution, one of the century's greatest judicial *causes célèbres,* both men will be executed at the Charlestown Prison on Sept. 23, 1927, culminating what many feel is a horrible miscarriage of justice. Charged with Sacco and Vanzetti is Celestino F. Madeires, who will later confess that he was present at the scene of the crimes but that Sacco and Vanzetti were not with him.

APRIL 25

Percy Toplis, a British bandit who has robbed stores and motorists and burgled scores of houses in Wales, England and Scotland, holds up a taxi driver in Andover, England, killing him when he resists; Toplis flees to Penrith, Scotland, where he is killed shooting it out with police.

AUG. 4

Southwest bandit Frank ''Jelly'' Nash receives 25 years in the state penitentiary at McAlester, Okla., for burglary with explosives, after being caught red-handed trying to blow up a vault in a small-town bank; he will be pardoned within a few years.

AUG. 10

Four members of the dreaded La Villette robbery gang hold up a cashier of the banking firm of Lesieur in Paris, escaping by car with more than 30,000 francs; the thieves later are identified as the brothers Leon and Georges Allard, Adam and Millot; on Oct. 5, Allard will steal a Citroen from the Avenue de Villers in Paris, and on Oct. 11, the car will be used by René Jean,

Nicola Sacco (right) and Bartolomeo Vanzetti (center). (April 15, 1920)

leader of the La Villette gang, in the robbery of a bank messenger carrying 225,000 francs on a Paris street; the messenger, who will be temporarily blinded by pepper thrown into his eyes, will still resist, and gang members will flee as police arrive; on Oct. 21, René Jean and others will rob wealthy Mme. Dessene in Paris, crushing her skull with a hammer and taking thousands of francs.

NOV. 5

Wilbur Underhill is sent to the state prison at Jefferson City, Mo., for robbery, to serve a five-year-sentence.

ORGANIZED CRIME

FEB. 2

In Chicago, Maurice "Mossy" Enright, who has murdered a half-dozen men in the newspaper circulation wars under the command of the Annenberg brothers who worked for the Chicago *Tribune,* including the daylight shooting of Dutch Gentleman in a State Street bar, is murdered by "Sunny Jim" Cosmano, Michael Carozza, Timothy Murphy and James Vinci; only Vinci is convicted, and he is sentenced to 25 years.

FEB. 25

Louis Coticchia, who will become a syndicate minion and have many arrests for robbery, assault, rape and grand theft, is born in Cincinnati, Ohio.

MAY 11

Al Capone, who has come from Brooklyn to serve as a bodyguard to Johnny Torrio, murders the crime boss of Chicago, Big Jim Colosimo, in Big Jim's elegant cafe on South Wabash Avenue; although Big Jim's murder is never officially solved, Capone is seen running from the restaurant in broad daylight shortly after the murder; he becomes No. 2 man under Torrio in controlling all illegal rackets on Chicago's South Side.

AUG. 15

Meyer Lansky is arrested in New York City for "breach of peace"—slugging pushcart vendors reluctant to pay protection—and is fined two dollars before being released.

SEPT. 28

The first bomb in the Chicago feud between the Powers and D'Andrea gangs is set off, killing no one but destroying a restaurant on the South Side.

DEC. 26

Monk Eastman, once-feared New York City gangster who had more than 1,000 hoodlums under his command at the turn of the century, is shot by a rival gangster while eating in the Bluebird Cafe.

The first known photograph (c. 1913) of gangster Johnny Torrio (right) shown with his sponsor in crime, Big Jim Colosimo (left), the crime boss of Chicago from 1911 to 1920. The man in the middle is Colosimo's father. (May 11, 1920)

WHITE-COLLAR CRIME

JULY 23

Swindler Charles Ponzi, whose fake Boston bank is taking in millions in a double-your-deposit scheme, goes to publicity agent William McMasters, asking him to create good press for the bank. Ironically, McMasters learns of Ponzi's Peter-to-Paul scam and writes a story on Aug. 2 for the *Boston Post* exposing the scam and explaining how Ponzi is using one man's deposit to pay off another's principal and interest. Ponzi is arrested as his paper empire crumbles and thousands run on his bank and receive little or nothing from their investment. Ponzi is sentenced to four years in prison.

MISCELLANEOUS

JAN. 16

The Volstead Act—Prohibition—goes into affect

across the United States, one of the most unpopular laws ever created and one that will be responsible for the lawless decade of the Roaring Twenties and the establishment of organized crime on a national scale.

JAN. 17
A federal warehouse storing liquor is raided by bootleggers in Chicago only hours after the Volstead Act is enacted.

JULY 20
Federal agents inspecting cracked paint on the side

of the Chinese mail liner *Nilo* find $40,000 in smuggled opium. There are no arrests.

SEPT. 16
A horse-drawn wagon is parked in front of the U.S. Assay Building at Broad and Wall streets and explodes moments later, at 11:59 a.m., killing as many as 100 people (the bodies are so mutilated that an exact count is impossible), while the anarchist who spent months building the cart into a massive bomb escapes unharmed; the offices of J.P. Morgan are destroyed, along with many others; though $100,000 in reward money is offered for the bomber's arrest, the mass killer is never found.

1·9·2·1

MURDER

FEB. 6
The body of Freda Burnell, an eight-year-old schoolgirl who has disappeared the day before, is found near a seed shop where she had been sent to purchase some items; Harold Jones, who had waited on the girl, will be arrested for the murder and will be acquitted, with courtroom spectators cheering him; two weeks after the trial, the body of 11-year-old Florence Irene Little will be found in Jones's attic, and he will confess to murdering both Freda Burnell and the Little girl; he will be tried for the Little murder and given a long prison term, saved from the death penalty because he is under age 16.

FEB. 18
Henry Starr, who has taken several years' hiatus from robbing banks and has appeared in several Hollywood-produced films about oldtime western bad men (Starr was the first outlaw to use an auto in a bank holdup), returns to his criminal profession by attempting to rob singlehandedly the Peoples Bank at Harrison, Ark., holding a gun on bank president W. J. Meyers, who shoots the bandit with a shotgun as he moves toward his parked car in front of the bank; Starr will die from his wounds on Feb. 22.

MAY 15
Con man Robert Arthur Tourbillon is arrested on suspicion of killing John R. Reid, a wealthy New York

City man, over the affections of a woman, but he is released for lack of evidence; Reid's killer will not be found.

AUG. 18
Jerome Withfield, a black suspected of raping the wife of a white farmer outside Winston, N.C., is tracked down and driven to the woman's home; she tells the mob of close to 2,000 white men that Withfield is not the man, but mob leaders insist that he is, saying that the proof is in the fact that the bloodhounds have tracked him down. "Please don't hang him on my front lawn then," the woman asks; her request is granted—the mob takes Withfield down the road and hangs him in some woods.

AUG. 21
Father Patrick E. Heslin is kidnapped from the rectory of Holy Angels Church in Colma, near San Francisco, and later is found murdered; the culprit is William Hightower, an entrepreneur who fails to collect a ransom for the priest and kills him and buries the body on a beach; Hightower will be sent to San Quentin for life.

SEPT. 5
Roscoe "Fatty" Arbuckle, the highest-paid comedian in films and Paramount's greatest asset, gives a wild, drunken party in Suite 1219–21 at the St. Francis Hotel in San Francisco and reportedly rapes in a locked bedroom one of the guests, Virginia Rappe, a rising starlet who has appeared in several films; Miss

Rappe dies days later of a ruptured bladder and other complications; several party guests, chiefly Bambina Maude Delmont and Alice Blake, insisted that Arbuckle had led the girl into the bedroom, locked the door, and refused to open it when guests responded to Virginia's screams; several authorities later claim that Arbuckle, who finally opened the door to reveal a disheveled Virginia Rappe in agony, had simply crushed her bladder by his enormous weight; the comedian will be tried three times on murder charges and finally acquitted; the last trial is still in debate today, many claiming that Arbuckle's Hollywood bosses, to save their moneymaking star, bought the jury; Fatty's career, however, was ruined, and he would die while trying to make a comeback in 1933.

OCT. 11

More than 500 whites tie black man Wylie McNeely to a buggy axle outside Leesburg, Tex., and burn him alive for allegedly insulting a white woman, drawing lots for the parts of the victim's anatomy regarded as choice souvenirs.

NOV. 11

Mrs. Annie Black, who runs a sweetshop in Tregonissey, England, dies of what doctors term "gastroenteritis," but a suspicious physician later exhumes the body and finds arsenic; the victim's husband, insurance salesman Edward Black, is later tracked down to a Liverpool hotel room, where constables find him alive but with his throat cut; at the trial, in Bodmin, a chemist will state that Black purchased arsenic from him shortly before his wife's death; Black will be found guilty, and hanged on March 24, 1922.

DEC. 23

Irene Wilkins, daughter of a London lawyer, is found murdered outside Bournemouth, England, after traveling there from London to begin a job as a cook; police will later find the telegram that lured Miss Wilkins to Bournemouth:

> Morning Post. Come immediately. 4:30 train Waterloo Bournemouth Central. Car will meet train. Expense no object. Urgent. Wood, Beech House.

Several similar telegrams sent to other women will be found and traced to Thomas Henry Allaway, a 36-year-old chauffeur working for a wealthy employer in Bournemouth; his handwriting, despite clumsy attempts to disguise it, matches that on the original telegrams; Allaway will be hanged at Winchester Prison on Aug. 19, 1922.

ROBBERY

JAN. 15

Arthur "Dock" Barker is caught burglarizing a bank in Muskogee, Okla.; he gives his name as Claude Dale and is sent to the state penitentiary at McAlester, Okla., on Jan. 30 as Bob Barker, another alias; Barker will be released on June 11 by court order and vanish before standing trial.

MARCH 7

John Mahoney, protégé of safecracker Charles "The Ox" Reiser, is caught blowing the same safe for the ninth time in two years in Chicago's West Side Masonic Temple; in exchange for leniency in court, Mahoney informs on Reiser's operations and burglaries; Mahoney is allowed to post bond, and his body will be found on April 30, riddled with bullets. (Mahoney has made a point of telling prosecutors that Reiser always kills witnesses against him.)

JUNE 1

Charles Dion O'Bannion, Charles "The Ox" Reiser and Earl "Hymie" Weiss are caught red-handed blowing the safe in Chicago's Postal Telegraph offices by a lone policeman, John J. Ryan; O'Bannion meekly hands over his pistol, and all the burglars are found with singed bills and nitro in their pockets. (O'Bannion later laughingly states that he did not shoot the cop for fear of blowing up himself and his friends.) Later, in court, O'Bannion will take the stand to explain to a grinning jury that he and his friends heard a loud explosion and they went into the Postal Telegraph office to investigate. "Whoever was blowing the safe must have heard us coming," O'Bannion will say from the witness stand. "They got away. We stepped off the fire escape through the window and were just looking at the safe when the policeman came in. I always carry a gun in the course of my work. At first I thought it might have been the thieves coming back. But when I saw it was a policeman, I put my gun down, and we gave ourselves up like good citizens." O'Bannion and the others are acquitted and all adjourn—burglars, jury, judge and prosecuting and defense attorneys—to Diamond José Esposito's Bella Napoli Cafe to celebrate.

JULY 25

Shortly after midnight, the Express No. 5 train, just out of Paris, is held up by five bandits, who rob many wealthy passengers and shoot and kill an officer attempting to stop them; French police will later track down the train robbers—Breger, who will be sent to prison, and Thomas and Bertrand, who will be killed in a gun battle with gendarmes in Paris on July 30.

OCT. 10

Charles "The Ox" Reiser kills Steve Pochnal, a watchman at the Cooke Cold Storage Company in Chicago, after Pochnal interrupts him blowing the firm's safe; Reiser is wounded and taken to Alexian Brothers

CRIME CHRONOLOGY • 1921

Hospital, where his wife, Madeline, will visit him a few days later and, according to police theory, fire 10 bullets into him so that she can have the 43-year-old burglar's sizable estate; emerging from the hospital bedroom, she tells the policeman on guard that Reiser has committed suicide; a coroner's jury incredibly comes to the same conclusion some days later, and Mrs. Reiser is given the master burglar's estate, valued at more than $100,000.

OCT. 14

Gerald Chapman and Charles Loeber stop a mail car on Leonard Street in New York City's financial district and take several sacks of mail containing more than $2,400,000 in negotiable securities; on Oct. 24, Chapman and others will rob a mail truck on Park Row in New York City for unknown amounts of securities; on Oct. 27, Chapman and two others will rob a mail truck in New York City, taking $1,424,199 in cash and securities.

OCT. 15

"Terrible Tommy" O'Connor is found guilty of murdering a guard during a holdup of the Illinois Central offices in Chicago a year earlier; he is sentenced to be hanged—the last man to be so sentenced in Illinois, the state going over to the electric chair soon thereafter—but O'Connor will escape the Criminal Courts Building jail on Dec. 13, only two days before his scheduled hanging; he will never be found, but a court order still in effect at this writing preserves the dismantled gallows upon which O'Connor was to hang until his whereabouts, dead or alive, are determined.

OCT. 27

Jack "Legs" Diamond, under the alias of John Hart, is arrested for burglarizing a New York City store; the charge is dismissed; on Nov. 18, Diamond will be arrested for burglarizing a New York City jewelry shop and will be discharged the following day by Judge Mancuso.

NOV. 9

"Big Tim" Murphy, onetime Illinois state representative, is found guilty of taking part in a $360,000 mail robbery earlier in the year and is sent to prison.

ORGANIZED CRIME

FEB. 7

In Chicago's Powers-D'Andrea political feud a bomb explodes in a Blue Island dance hall, injuring several D'Andrea adherents holding a rally.

MARCH 28

Gangster Angelo Genna and three henchmen waylay uncooperative union leader Paul A. Labriola on a Chicago street, emptying their pistols into him; Genna straddles the man and fires three shots point blank into Labriola's face, killing him, and saying as he saunters away: "He's done." On August 27, Angelo and Tony Genna, with others, will murder Dominick Guitillo, a rival Chicago gangster, and on Nov. 24 they will shoot to death another rival, Nicola Adams.

NOV. 20

Joseph Michael Valachi, later a top informant on La Cosa Nostra, is arrested in Jersey City, N.J., for carrying a concealed weapon; he is fined $100 and put on probation.

WHITE-COLLAR CRIME

JAN. 17-20

Marcus Garvey organizes the Negro Improvement Association and African Communities League, signing up tens of thousands of blacks and charging members one dollar in monthly dues on the promise that he would create a new African state for all American blacks, who would emigrate to Africa as soon as he could purchase enough steamships; Garvey's scam is believed by many, and he will even address the League of Nations later in the year; years later Garvey will be exposed as nothing more than a showy con man who has bilked his people of millions.

MAY 3

Con man Joseph "Yellow Kid" Weil sells phony oil stocks to the millionaire Albright sisters of Chicago for $180,000.

DEC. 12

Future imposter and con man Ferdinando Waldo Demara is born in Lawrence, Mass.

MISCELLANEOUS

SEPT. 8

Federal agents raid S.S. *King Alexander,* docked in

New York Harbor, confiscating opium, heroin and cocaine worth hundreds of thousands of dollars after a wild shoot-out with crew members.

Gordon Duffield, heir to a Chicago fortune, is abducted from his private school in New Jersey and is never seen again; his kidnapper will never be found.

1·9·2·2

MURDER

FEB. 2

Film director William Desmond Taylor is found in his luxurious Hollywood home by his servant, a bullet in his heart; his murder will unleash one of Hollywood's great scandals; letters to the amorous Taylor from Mary Miles Minter and Mabel Normand will wreck their careers, and Normand's wild drug addiction will later be revealed; Taylor's killer will never be found.

FEB. 25

Henri Desire Landru, who has been convicted of the murder of 11 lovelorn Parisian women, after a long and sensational trial in Paris, from Nov. 7 to Nov. 30, 1921, is executed by the guillotine; the infamous "Bluebeard," a bald, unimpressive 52-year-old, is sent to his death strictly on circumstantial evidence; throughout the trial, the mass killer, who has probably chopped up and and burned his victims at his Gambais country retreat, shouted to the prosecutor: "Produce your bodies!" When the executioner arrives for him, Landru refuses the last rites, calmly brushing past the priest and saying: "I am sorry, but I must not keep this gentleman waiting." These are his last words; Bluebeard goes to his death without confessing.

MARCH 4

Samigulla and Khatir Ziazetdinov, Russian peasants turned murdering cannibals in the village of Flyakulvin, are sent to forced labor for life.

MAY 31

Retired British Maj. Herbert Rouse Armstrong, who has poisoned his wife with arsenic because of her nagging and has attempted to poison rival solicitors, is hanged at Gloucester Prison.

JUNE 22

A onetime military adviser to Protestant forces in Belfast during the Irish Civil War, Sir Henry Wilson, is shot to death as he arrives at his home by IRA gunmen Reginald Dunne and Joseph O'Sullivan; both assassins will be executed at Wandsworth Prison on Aug. 10.

JULY 6

Los Angeles housewife Clara Phillips, who has discovered that her husband, Armour, is having an affair with 22-year-old Alberta Meadows, gets drunk with a friend, then intercepts Meadows in a department store parking lot; pretending to talk it out with her as they drive in Clara's car, Mrs. Phillips produces a hammer and, stopping the car, crushes her rival's skull; she later confesses the murder to her husband, who urges her to flee; when she does, he calls police; Clara is sentenced to San Quentin for life, branded "The Tiger Woman," but she will be released in 1935 from Tehachapi and fade into oblivion.

AUG. 13-14

Mrs. William Giberson of Lakehurst, N.J., murders her husband, owner of a taxicab firm, then fakes a robbery, tying up both herself and the corpse of her husband, then screaming for help; shrewd detectives, learning that she has purchased funeral clothes a week earlier and that she has expressed her hatred for her husband, trap her in various lies; she confesses and is sent to the penitentiary in Trenton for 20 years.

AUG. 22

A black man, Parks Banks, is lynched near Yazoo City, Miss., after he ignores warnings to leave town after a verbal disagreement with KKK leaders.

SEPT. 16

The bodies of Rev. Edward Hall and his leading choir singer, Mrs. Eleanor Mills, are found under a crab apple tree in De Russey's Lane near New Brunswick, N.J., their throats cut and their secret love letters strewn about their bodies; Mrs. Hall and her two brothers will be indicted for murder and go through two sensational trials before being acquitted; the Hall-Mills case will never be solved.

OCT. 3

Percy Thompson is murdered in London; his wife, Edith, and her lover, Frederick Bywaters, will be convicted of the killing and hanged on Jan. 9, 1923; Bywaters will attempt to assume all responsibility for the murder to save Edith Thompson, who probably was innocent despite the incriminating letters she had written to Bywaters before the murder.

DEC. 11

A mob unable to run down a black man accused of attacking the wife of the sheriff of Streetman, Tex., lynches the uncle of the man instead.

DEC. 27

In a feud over water rights, James A. Magnuson mails a bomb to neighbor James A. Chapman of Marshfield, Wis.; the bomb kills Chapman and his wife; part of the package, with Magnuson's writing on it, will be found and traced to the sender, and Magnuson will be sent to prison for life.

ROBBERY

FEB. 10

Arthur "Dock" Barker is sentenced to Oklahoma State Penitentiary at McAlester for life for bank robbery and murder; he will be paroled on Sept. 10, 1932, and will join with his brother Fred and others to form the dreaded Barker gang.

APRIL 16

Jack "Legs" Diamond, using the alias of John Higgins, is booked as a material witness in a New York City robbery and is released the following day.

APRIL 19

The Paris post office is robbed of an unrecorded sum by the notorious La Villette gang; by Nov. 28 all the members of this robbery gang, led by René Jean, will be rounded up and sentenced to death.

ORGANIZED CRIME

APRIL 22

Roger "The Terrible" Touhy opens his bootlegging operations in Chicago's northwestern suburbs, reaping a fortune.

DEC. 5

New York City gangster Benjamin Levinsky is shot to death by rival gangster William Lipshitz at 715 Broadway; Lipshitz receives a long prison term.

WHITE-COLLAR CRIME

FEB. 15

Con man Jackie French scams more than $300,000 from several businessmen in a Miami Big Store operation, convincing the suckers to place bets on sure horse-race winners that lose big in a phony gambling den French has set up.

JUNE 1-OCT. 1

Chicago flimflammer Leo Koretz sells more than $1 million in phony oil leases to several Windy City tycoons.

MISCELLANEOUS

MAY 21

Federal agents in New York Harbor seize a fortune in hard drugs being smuggled from the steamship *China*.

SEPT. 20

Thief Émile Courgibet, lifer at Camp Colbert in Dutch Guiana, makes good his jungle escape.

1·9·2·3

MURDER

MARCH 15
Dorothy "Dot" King, Broadway showgirl, is found murdered in her New York City flat by her maid; several wealthy sugardaddies who have kept her in the past are investigated, along with her scheming con man boyfriend Alberto Santos Guimares, but no one is arrested; the sensational case will never be solved, although most investigators believe that Guimares was guilty.

MAY 11
John Leonard Whitfield, while being picked up in Cleveland, Ohio, by two officers for questioning on a forgery charge, shoots and kills patrolman Dennis Griffin and escapes; he eludes officers in Wisconsin but will later be apprehended in Detroit while working for a lumber company under an alias; Whitfield will be convicted, but the jury will recommend mercy and he will receive a life term in the Ohio Penitentiary; the cop-killer will be shot to death while escaping on March 9, 1928.

MAY 20
Pleasant Harris, a thief, beats his girlfriend Katherine Wilson to death because she criticizes his manners (clucking her tongue when he belches as they walk down a New Orleans street); Harris will eventually be tracked down in New Jersey in 1926 and sent to prison for life.

JUNE 16
Carl Panzram, by his own later admission, strangles a man in Kingston, N.Y., for "the fun it gave me." Panzram will go on to murder 20 to 30 more people before he is executed in 1930.

JULY 20
Revolutionary leader Pancho Villa is ambushed by several gunmen in his hometown of Parral, Mex.; he and his bodyguards are shot to pieces; Villa's grave will be violated in 1926, his head decapitated and stolen.

OCT. 10
Mrs. Susan Newell is hanged at Duke Street Prison in Glasgow, Scotland, for the murder of a 13-year-old newsboy, John Johnstone; Mrs. Newell has admitted at her trial that she murdered the boy in June 1923 because he asked too much—a few pennies—for the papers he delivered.

NOV. 7
The Ku Klux Klan of Eufala, Okla., tries Dallas Sewell, a black man, in a barn and finds him guilty of "passing for white"; he is hanged in accordance with the Klan "Kode."

NOV. 11
In London, Nanny Dora Sadler, jealous of the wealthy children in her charge, turns on the gas in the nursery, murdering Jean and Sonia Katzman; she is condemned to death, but her sentence will be commuted to life in prison.

NOV. 23
Mrs. Dora Hunt, a wealthy 59-year-old spinster, is found strangled to death in her hotel bed in Cannes, France; the killing of this British vacationer baffles French police, who never solve the crime.

ROBBERY

FEB. 14
Wilbur Underhill is sentenced to five years in the Jefferson City, Mo., Prison for bank robbery; he will escape two months later.

JUNE 12
An unknown professional jewel thief switches bags with a diamond broker, taking jewels worth 800,000 francs. Detective Sgt. Rousselet begins looking for an infamous jewel thief named Booter who robbed a diamond broker in 1914 and was sent to prison for five years; Rousselet will track down Booter, whose real name is Kleinberg and who has committed a similar robbery with an accomplice named Finkelstein in Antwerp; the pair are arrested in Antwerp on July 29 and given a long prison term.

JULY 21
Twenty-year-old John Dillinger impulsively steals a car in Mooresville, Ind., his first criminal offense; he

drives it 17 miles north to Indianapolis, where he abandons it, fearing arrest; he is not detected.

AUG. 20

Al Spencer, onetime member of the Henry Starr gang, who has robbed banks on horseback, joins with Frank Nash, Earl "Dad" Thayer, Grover Durill, George Curtis, Curtis Kelly and Wilbur Underhill to hold up a crack train, the *Katy Limited,* outside Okesa, Okla.; the bandits take $20,000 in Liberty bonds in a mail sack and valuables from passengers; Spencer will be sought by posses throughout Oklahoma and will die in a shoot-out with police near Bartlesville on Sep. 20; $10,000 in Liberty bonds will be found stuffed into his overalls.

OCT. 11

Hugh, Roy and Ray D'Autremont attempt to rob train No. 13 of the Southern Pacific Railroad between Portland and San Francisco (near the town of Siskiyou, Ore.); they kill four of the train's crew members in the process and flee with nothing; they will be tracked down and sent to the Oregon Penitentiary for life.

NOV. 28

Jack "Legs" Diamond is arrested for robbing a New York City store; he will be discharged four months later for "lack of evidence."

ORGANIZED CRIME

JUNE 5

Charles "Lucky" Luciano is arrested, under the name Luciana, with heroin in his pocket; charges are dropped against the future Mafia syndicate boss because he leads police to a larger stash of heroin that belongs to rival gangsters who later "take him for a ride," slashing his throat and leaving him for dead; Luciano miraculously survives, earning the sobriquet "Lucky."

AUG. 17

Mafia strong-arm Joseph Valachi is arrested for burglary in New York City and is sentenced to one to two years in Sing Sing; he will be paroled on Oct. 23, 1924.

AUG. 28

Louis Cohen, alias Louis Kushner, an apprentice gangster, is encouraged by Jack "Legs" Diamond to murder rival bootlegger Nathan "Kid Dropper" Ka-

plan as he emerges from a New York City court; Kushner fires several shots into a police car, wounding a driver, shooting a hole through the hat of Police Capt. Cornelius Willemse and sending a bullet into Kaplan's head. "They got me," Kaplan says to his wife, Veronica, in true gangster style and dies in her arms as she screams: "Nate! Nate! Tell me that you were not what they say you were!" Kushner meekly surrenders to the police, saying with a shrug: "I got him—can I have a cigarette?" He is sent to Sing Sing for life, a willing dupe to Diamond and his plan to eliminate a bootlegging rival of the Little Augie Oren gang, for which he is a lieutenant.

The diminutive Louis Kushner, moments after he killed Manhattan crime boss Nathan "Kid Dropper" Kaplan. (Aug. 28, 1923)

SEPT. 7

On Chicago's South Side Frankie McErlaine and Danny McFall attempt to murder rival bootleggers Spike O'Donnell and his brothers, killing Jerry O'Conner with a submachine gun that McErlaine wields, spraying an entire block from a moving car; this is the first time the Thompson submachine gun is used in gang warfare.

DEC. 17

Johnny Torrio, boss of Chicago's South Side, is released on bond for illegally brewing beer.

Capone gangster Frankie McErlaine (center) being questioned by Chicago police; McErlaine was the first to use a submachine gun during the bootleg era. (Sept. 7, 1923)

WHITE-COLLAR CRIME

FEB. 28

Louis Enricht is sentenced to three to seven years in Sing Sing for attempting to sell a phony formula that supposedly changes water into gasoline.

MAY 18

Con man Philip Musica sets up a dummy company, Girard & Co., in Mount Vernon, N.Y., buying up large amounts of raw alcohol ostensibly to make hair tonic but instead selling it to bootleggers for bathtub gin and reaping enormous profits.

AUG. 24

J. Frank Norfleet, a wealthy rancher who has been fleeced by Lou Blonger's powerful army of confidence men, tracks down Blonger and many others to Denver, where they are arrested and given long prison terms.

MISCELLANEOUS

JAN. 18

Film star Wallace Reid, hooked on drugs, dies in a California asylum; it is later claimed that certain movie moguls, to save the industry embarrassment, have ordered Reid be given a fatal dose of morphine; no charges are ever brought in the actor's death.

JULY 1

''Big Raoul,'' the wealthy king of Paris's largest cocaine ring, receives a short prison term.

MURDER

FEB. 4

Catholic priest Hubert Dahme steps into a Bridgeport, Conn., street and is shot dead; the crime will be attributed to hobo Harold Israel, but a young prosecutor, Homer S. Cummings (later U.S. Attorney General), will prove that Israel has confessed out of hunger, exhaustion and harsh police questioning; Israel will be released, and Dahme's killer will never be found.

FEB. 8

Gee Jon is sent to the Nevada gas chamber for murdering his wife; Jon is the first man so executed.

APRIL 12

In a cottage near Eastbourne, England, on the Sussex coast, Patrick John Mahon, a married businessman, murders and dissects his mistress, Emily Beilby Kaye; a satchel containing the victim's bloody clothing will be found by his wife, leading to Mahon's arrest and conviction; though he claims that Miss Kaye fell and accidentally killed herself during an argument, Mahon cannot explain why he chopped up her body and hid the pieces all about the love cottage (her head is never found); Mahon will be hanged at Wandsworth Prison on Sept. 9.

APRIL 24

Chicago flapper Wanda Stopa, part-time artist and onetime mistress to advertising executive Y. K. Smith (a friend of Ernest Hemingway), goes to Smith's luxurious suburban home in Palso Park, Ill.; and attempts to shoot Mrs. Smith so she will have Smith to herself; her aim is bad, and she kills caretaker Henry Manning instead, then flees; detectives will trace Wanda to Detroit, where they will break down her hotel door to find her dead from swallowing an entire bottle of poison.

MAY 17

Some boys playing on the banks of the River Leine in Hanover, Germany, find human bones and skulls; police spy Fritz Haarmann will be arrested while prowling among the hundreds of homeless young boys in the train station, looking for victims; his attic rooms will be found to be covered with blood, and he will admit that he has slain scores of youths after enticing them to his rooms and seducing them, then butchering

their bodies and selling the remains in the street as "fresh meat." He cannot recall the number of his victims, stating at his trial: "It might have been 30, it might have been 40, I don't remember." He will be beheaded in Jan. 1925 after enjoying a last meal of coffee and cheese followed by cigars.

MAY 21

Chicago playboy intellectuals Richard Loeb and Nathan Leopold, both honor students at the University of Chicago, kidnap and kill 14-year-old Bobbie Franks, sending a ransom note to his father; both Loeb and Leopold are the sons of millionaires, and the killing is performed as a ritual slaying in an attempt to commit "the perfect crime." Leopold's glasses are found near the culvert where the killers have dumped the body; and the typewriter used to type the ransom note is traced to the pair; Loeb implicates himself by actually helping the police search for the killer; Loeb and Leopold are brilliantly defended by Clarence Darrow, who manages to get them life sentences in a bench trial;

Nathan Leopold (left) and Richard Loeb (center). (May 21, 1924)

Loeb will be murdered in 1936 in Joliet State Prison by inmate James Day after attempting to press a homosexual relationship; Leopold, thanks to the efforts of his lawyer, Elmer Gertz, and supporters such as Carl Sandburg, will be released on March 13, 1958, dying in Puerto Rico of a heart attack on Aug. 30, 1971.

JUNE 7

A drunken hallboy, Arthur Henry Bishop, seeking revenge for his dismissal, steals back into the London home of Sir Charles Lloyd and axes Frank Edward Rix, the butler who has fired him, while Rix is sleeping; at Bishop's trial his defense counsel will plead intoxication, trying for a manslaughter conviction; the eighteen-year-old, however, will be found guilty of first-degree murder and will be hanged on Aug. 14.

AUG. 13

Kid McCoy (Norman Selby), onetime welterweight champion of the world, runs amuck in Los Angeles when his lover, Mrs. Theresa Mors, refuses to divorce her husband; McCoy shoots and kills her, then holds up a store while drunk, shooting several bystanders before he is chased down on foot and arrested; McCoy will be sent to San Quentin for life, but he will be released in 1932 when given a job by Henry Ford in Detroit, where McCoy will commit suicide eight years later.

NOV. 19

Sir Lee Stack, British commander of the Egyptian Army, is assassinated in Cairo as his car moves slowly through a congested street; two Egyptian nationalists, Enayat and Mahmoud Rashid, brothers, will be traced through several pistols found in a basket of fruit they are carrying on a train when apprehended; they will be executed in Cairo in June 1925.

DEC. 21

Elderly Carl Denke, thought to be a kindly old man and whom everyone calls "Papa," is arrested in Munsterberg, Silesia (Now Ziebice, Poland) for the cannibal murders of at least 30 people between 1921 and 1924; the dissected, pickled remains of several bodies are found in barrels stored in Denke's rooms; Denke will hang himself with his suspenders in his prison cell before facing trial.

ROBBERY

JAN. 5

Brooklyn housewife-turned-bandit Cecilia Cooney and her husband, Ed, begin their robbing spree, taking $688 from a Brooklyn store; Cecilia will become notorious as the "Bobbed-Haired Bandit"; after several more robberies, the Cooneys will flee to Florida, where they will be captured; they will be sent to prison and released in 1931.

JUNE 28

Looters by the score invade Lorain, Ohio, after a vicious tornado destroys the town; several of the looters are shot by local police.

SEPT. 6

John Dillinger attempts to rob a local grocer in Martinsville, Ind., but the man puts up a struggle and calls for help; Dillinger, captured, will throw himself on the mercy of the court as a first offender but will be given a severe sentence by stern Judge Joseph Williams, concurrent sentences of two to 14 years for attempted robbery and 10 to 20 years for conspiracy to commit a felony (the grocer and the judge are Masonic brothers); this sentence undoubtedly will make a hardened criminal out of Dillinger, who later will become the most hunted man in the world.

OCT. 24

Three bandits snatch a Brink's bag containing several thousand dollars while Otis Elevator men are being paid in New York City at 40th Street and Broadway; they shoot guards Franklin Good (who later dies) and John Callanan; Callanan, though shot in the face, chases the bandit with the money bag and retrieves it; the robbers escape and are never captured.

NOV. 26

Joseph "Doc" Stacher, later a high-ranking syndicate gambling boss in Las Vegas, is arrested in New York City for breaking and entering a store, but the charge is dismissed the next day.

ORGANIZED CRIME

MARCH 14

Vito Genovese is charged with attempted vehicular homicide—trying to run over a rival gangster in Prospect Park, Brooklyn—and is found with a knife and loaded pistol; he will be released, stating as his occupation "truckman"; on April 25, Genovese will be picked up on New York City's Lower East Side carrying a loaded revolver for which he produces a permit; he will claim to be a "grocer" and will be released.

MAY 8

In Chicago, Al Capone, hearing that petty bootlegger "Ragtime Joe" Howard has manhandled Capone's bookkeeper, Jake Guzik, goes to Heinie Jacobs' South Wabash saloon and grabs Howard, who shouts: "Go back to your girls, you dago pimp!" Capone jerks out a pistol and puts it to Howard's head, emptying all six rounds and killing Howard on the spot; although a dozen customers witness the execution, all either disappear or lose their memories before Capone is brought to trial; the coroner's jury will report that Howard has been "killed by parties *unknown*"; Capone will never be prosecuted for the killing.

MAY 19

On the pretext of selling Sieben's massive brewery in Chicago to Johnny Torrio, rival Dion O'Bannion collects $500,000 from Torrio, then arranges for police to raid the place while Torrio, O'Bannion's lieutenant Earl "Hymie" Weiss and others are inspecting the premises; Torrio is booked as a bootlegger and bails himself out, refusing to bail out O'Bannion's men, who will later be released through their own lawyers; Sieben's brewery is padlocked and guarded night and day; O'Bannion laughs about the "dumb dagos" he has hoodwinked, but his ruse will bring about his own execution. (See "Organized Crime," Nov. 10.)

JUNE 14

Jack "Legs" Diamond is arrested in New York City for violating Prohibition laws and is dismissed the next day.

NOV. 10

In the feud between the Torrio and O'Bannion crime organizations, Charles Dion "Deanie" O'Bannion is executed in the flower shop he runs on Chicago's North State Street by three unidentified men (probably Frankie Yale, a Capone ally from New York City, and Capone hired killers John Scalise and Albert Anselmi); the three men greet him, pretending to pick up a floral arrangement for an underworld funeral, then grabbing O'Bannion's hands—he carries three pistols at all times—and shooting him to death in the first gangland "handshake" murder; O'Bannion's funeral is lavish, the first of the "big time" gangster funerals; his successor, Earl "Hymie" Weiss, vows revenge, and the bootleg wars in Chicago go into full swing, leaving, before the decade is out, more than 1,000 gangsters dead. (See "Organized Crime," Jan. 20, 1925.)

WHITE-COLLAR CRIME

FEB. 14

Davis Rowland MacDonald supposedly drowns himself in the Allegheny River near Pittsburgh—his clothes are found on the riverbank; his wife quickly collects the insurance money and, after having MacDonald declared dead, remarries. MacDonald turns up 14 years later as John Edgar Davis, saying that he faked his own death so that his unhappy wife could have some money and marry the man she loved; he is not prosecuted.

JULY 2

Stock manipulator and con man Lee T. Brooks is arrested in New York City for receiving phony stocks from racketeers and listing them on the Exchange; he will be sentenced to a long prison term.

NOV. 1

Alves Reis begins to counterfeit Portuguese money after discovering that the Bank of Portugal does not keep an inventory of old serial numbers of its currency; he is able to pass off millions before he is convicted on May 3, 1930, and sentenced to 80 years' imprisonment and 12 years' banishment from Portugal.

MISCELLANEOUS

JUNE 14

Criminal lawyer William Fallon is arrested for jury bribing and is jailed in New York City's Tombs; he posts a $100,000 bond and is released; in a subsequent trial he will be acquitted with the greatest lawyer of his day presenting his case—himself.

JULY 25

Federal agents seize on a New York City pier 809 cans containing raw opium worth $100,000.

AUG. 8

Manhattan financier Aaron A. Graff disappears from his luxurious mansion; he will later be found dead under mysterious circumstances, his abductors never apprehended.

1·9·2·5

MURDER

JAN. 1

Because her mother and other relatives make fun of Martha Hazel Wise, a 43-year-old farm woman, and her love for a younger man, the spinster feeds arsenic to 11 family members; three die near Medina, Ohio; when Miss Wise is interrogated by local authorities she will finally shriek: "Yes, I did it! But it was the devil who told me to do it!" She will be branded the "Borgia of America" and be sent to prison for life.

MARCH 29

Mrs. Mary Jones kidnaps three-year-old Raimonde von Maluski during a Salvation Army parade in New York City in revenge for charges by the Maluski family that she has stolen items from their home; the boy is never found, and Mrs. Jones is placed on trial, the presiding judge stating: "I believe you have killed that child." She is sent to prison for 25 years.

DEC. 13

French murderer Lazaire Teissier, who has killed a businessman for money, is condemned to 10 years penal servitude, convicted on circumstantial evidence.

DEC. 19

A mob in Clarksdale, Miss., lynches Lindsay Coleman, a black, who only minutes earlier was found not guilty of murdering wealthy plantation store manager Grover C. Nicholas.

ROBBERY

MARCH 20

Three youths rob a Paris post office, rifling the cash drawers and killing a postman before fleeing; a young girl will later identify the leader of the gang as Marcel Pierson, who will be tracked down to a furnished room in the Rue Fontaine; he and two accomplices will be condemned to death but their sentences later changed to life imprisonment.

APRIL 9

Joe Valachi is arrested for burglary in New York City. He is sent to Sing Sing for three years.

SEPT. 3

Looters in Ava, Ohio, dash to the site of the crash of the dirigible *Shenandoah,* stripping the dead.

SEPT. 16

Charles Arthur "Pretty Boy" Floyd is arrested for a St. Louis payroll robbery; he will be sent to the state penitentiary in Jefferson City, Mo., for five years.

ORGANIZED CRIME

JAN. 12

Earl "Hymie" Weiss, Bugs Moran and others attempt to machine-gun Al Capone to death at State and 50th streets in Chicago but miss the gangster.

JAN. 17

Vito Genovese and others are arrested for looting a cigar warehouse on Mulberry Street in New York City; charges will later be dropped; Genovese identifies himself as a "builder."

JAN. 20

Earl "Hymie" Weiss, Bugs Moran and others shoot down Johnny Torrio in front of the rival gangster's Chicago home as he emerges from his car with packages in his arms after shopping with his wife; police respond to the daylight fusillade, and Bugs Moran, leaning over the wounded Torrio, finds his gun jammed when trying to administer a fatal shot to the head; he flees; however, the murder attempt so unnerves Torrio that he quits the bootlegging racket, turning over all Chicago operations to the 25-year-old Capone, a $50 million-a-year racket.

MAY 26

Weiss, Moran and other North Side gangsters belonging to the O'Bannion mob chase Angelo Genna, a Capone ally, through the streets of Chicago, exchanging fire from their speeding autos, until Genna's car crashes into a telephone pole; the North Siders riddle his car with machine-gun bullets until it explodes and Genna is roasted to death.

JUNE 13

In Chicago, Michael Genna, John Scalise and Albert Anselmi fire from a moving car on Michigan Avenue at Bugs Moran and Vincent "The Schemer" Drucci, two O'Bannionites, who are on foot; Moran is wounded, but the two drive off their attackers with murderous return fire; Genna, Scalise and Anselmi are later driving down a Chicago street when a carful of policemen attempts to pull them over; they fire at the cops, killing one, but return fire blows out their tires, causing them to flee on foot; Genna hides in a basement but is flushed out and killed by police in an exchange of gunfire; Scalise and Anselmi escape; they will later be arrested but released.

JULY 8

Tony Genna is shot to death on Chicago's Grand Avenue by Giuseppe "The Cavalier" Nerone, Albert Anselmi and John Scalise, his own men who have gone over to Capone.

OCT. 10

Vito Genovese kills rival New York City hoodlum Gino Scioto; Genovese is arrested while running from the scene of the murder; he will eventually be released after telling officers that he is in the "produce business."

Al Capone in 1925 when he took over Torrio's crime empire in Chicago. (Jan. 20, 1925)

NOV. 11

O'Bannionite Vincent "The Schemer" Drucci murders Capone ally Samuzzo "Samoots" Amatuna on a Chicago street.

WHITE-COLLAR CRIME

JULY 30

Charles Henry Schwartz attempts to burn down his bankrupt factory in suburban San Francisco, substituting the body of a tramp named Barbe, whom he has murdered, for his own, so that his wife can collect life insurance; Barbe, however, will be identified through dental records, and Schwartz will be tracked down to an Oakland rooming house, where he will commit suicide before police can break down the door.

NOV. 26

A Rochester, N.Y., real-estate broker, Charles A. Lee, fakes his own death so that he can run away with another woman—he is married with three children; he will be found three months later in Louisiana and charged with defrauding insurance firms of $22,000, receiving a short sentence.

MISCELLANEOUS

MARCH 15

David C. Stephenson, Ku Klux Klan Grand Dragon, abducts attractive Madge Oberholtzer from her Irvington, Ind., home; Stephenson and two henchmen put Miss Oberholtzer on a train, where the KKK leader rapes her repeatedly, then gives her drugs before returning her home, where she dies of internal injuries; Stephenson will be convicted of second-degree murder on Nov. 14 and sent to the Michigan City, Indiana, Prison for life on Nov. 21.

APRIL 20

The great British explorer Percy Harrison Fawcett vanishes into the vast jungles of Brazil's Matto Grosso in search of the lost city of "Z"; he is believed murdered by the unfriendly Kalapolos Indians who cannibalized his party.

1·9·2·6

MURDER

FEB. 20

Earle Leonard Nelson, the "Gorilla Murderer," strangles his first victim, San Francisco landlady Mrs. Clara Newman, whose corpse he then rapes; Nelson has told Mrs. Newman that he is a Bible student looking for a cheap room; when she shows him a room, he attacks her; this is a *modus operandi* that will not change as Nelson goes on to murder at least 19 more females from coast to coast and in Canada; Earle Leonard Nelson will strangle Mrs. Laura Beale, a 60-year-old landlady, in San Francisco on March 2. (See "Murder," June 10.)

APRIL 27

Antoinette Scieri, a self-styled nurse who has poisoned six people out of sadistic joy, is sent to prison for life in Paris, the trial judge stating: "You have been called a monster, but that expression is not strong enough. You are debauched. You are possessed of all the vices."

JUNE 2

Black man Albert Blades stumbles into a picnic area and accidentally frightens some young white girls; he is lynched outside Osceola, Ark.

JUNE 10

Earle Leonard Nelson strangles and rapes 63-year-old Mrs. Lillian St. Mary, a San Francisco landlady; on June 26 Nelson will strangle and rape Mrs. George Russell, a landlady in Santa Barbara; on Aug. 16 Nelson will strangle and rape Mrs. Mary Nesbitt, an Oakland landlady. (See "Murder," Oct. 19.)

OCT. 6

Nurse May Daniels mysteriously disappears in Paris; her murdered body is found at the outskirts of Boulogne in Mar. 1927; the murder remains a riddle.

OCT. 19

Earle Leonard Nelson strangles and rapes Mrs. Beta Withers, 35, a Portland, Ore., landlady; he stuffs the body in a trunk, where it is later discovered by Mrs. Withers's 15-year-old son; Nelson will murder 59-year-old Mrs. Virginia Grant, another Portland landlady, on Oct. 20, hiding her body behind the furnace of her rooming house. On Oct. 21, also in Portland, Nelson will strangle and rape Mrs. Mabel Fluke, who is later found in the attic of her rooming house; on Nov. 10 Nelson will strangle and rape Mrs. William Edmonds, a San Francisco landlady. (See "Murder," Nov. 15.)

NOV. 11

John T. Bibeau shoots his best friend, Alfred Elliot, at a ranch outside Seattle, claiming that he has committed the murder because Elliot kept a black cat on the premises, the symbol of evil; he will be sent to prison for life.

NOV. 15

Earle Leonard Nelson strangles and rapes landlady Mrs. Blanche Myers in Portland, Ore.; on Dec. 23, Nelson will strangle and rape landlady Mrs. John Bernard in Council Bluffs, Iowa; he appears to be moving eastward, riding the rails, according to police tracking him; on Dec. 28 Nelson will strangle and rape Kansas City, Mo., landlady Mrs. Germania Harpin and her eight-month-old child. [See "Murder," April 27, 1927.]

DEC. 15

Mrs. Gladys Houck, wife of a distinguished Washington, D.C., physician, vanishes; although her body will be found floating in the Potomac on March 23, 1927, an obvious kidnap victim, the police will never solve her mysterious death.

ROBBERY

FEB. 25

Future bank and train robber Alvin Karpis is sent to the reformatory at Hutchinson, Kan., to serve five years for burglarizing a store.

APRIL 5

Bank and mail robber Gerald Chapman is executed in Hartford, Conn. He and two others have attempted to rob the largest department store in New Britain, Conn., but were interrupted by police and fled as Chapman shot and killed a pursuing officer; before going to his death, Chapman states: "Death itself isn't dreadful, but hanging seems an awkward way of entering the adventure."

APRIL 21

Joseph "Doc" Stacher is arrested for robbery in Newark, N.J., but is released the next day.

JULY 11

Lester Gillis, who will later be known among 1930s bankrobbers as "Baby Face" Nelson, receives his third parole for robbery in Illinois.

AUG. 24

A robber enters the Farmers' National Bank of Pittsburgh and demands $2,000, threatening to drop his bag, which he says contains a bomb, and blow up the bank—which he does when a teller kicks an alarm; 23 are injured, the bank is destroyed and the robber and a guard are killed in the blast.

DEC. 3

Fifteen-year-old Clyde Barrow steals a car in Dallas, Tex., and is arrested for auto theft within six blocks of the theft; he is dismissed as a first-time offender.

ORGANIZED CRIME

JAN. 10

In Chicago, Henry Spingola, ally of the Genna Brothers, is shot and killed by Capone gunmen. (The Gennas, at first Capone allies, thought to kill Scarface and then take over his bootleg empire, a decision that sealed their fates and that of their associates.)

FEB. 15

Urazio Tropea, a Genna ally, is shot to death by gunners firing from a speeding auto as he walks down a Chicago street.

FEB. 23

Edward "The Eagle" Baldelli, a Genna associate in Chicago, is "taken for a ride," and his bullet-ridden body is found in a ditch.

APRIL 22

Members of Chicago's South Side O'Donnell bootleg gang are ambushed by Capone gunners, with several wounded; Spike O'Donnell will almost be killed when a Capone gunner sprays the front of the Pony Saloon four days later; O'Donnell will tell the press: "I can lick this bird Capone with my bare fists any-time he wants to step out in the open and fight like a man." O'Donnell will then quit the bootlegging racket.

APRIL 27

Chicago Assistant State's Attorney William H. McSwiggin is machine-gunned to death by Al Capone from a speeding car in Cicero, Ill.; the many witnesses who see Scarface murder the man who is attempting to send him to jail will lose their memories in forthcoming weeks, and Capone will never be indicted.

MAY 21

In St. Louis, Mariano Deluca, who refuses to pay tribute to a Mafia-type organization known as "The Green Ones," is shot to death on his front doorstep by three gunmen.

MAY 30

Citizens of Forest View, Ill., form a vigilante group and burn down the Capone-owned Maple Inn; Capone gunmen call local firemen, who arrive and stare at the blaze; when the gunmen beg the firemen to save the inn, the chief replies: "We can't spare the water." The inn burns to the ground.

JUNE 7

Al Capone is arrested in Chicago and charged with violating the National Prohibition Act; he will be released with apologies the next day.

JUNE 27

The Green Ones in St. Louis beat and shoot Harvey J. Dunn to death when he refuses to turn over his distillery to them.

JULY 28

Al Capone is arrested in Chicago for murder, charged with ordering the death of John Conlon, a Moran gangster; the charge is dropped within one hour.

AUG. 10

Capone gunners miss killing Earl "Hymie" Weiss in a shoot-out on a Chicago street; on Aug. 15 Capone killers will again miss killing Weiss.

AUG. 21

The Green Ones in St. Louis shoot and kill Joseph Schamora, a rival gangster competing for the control of bootleg booze.

SEPT. 5

Pete Webbe, a member of the Cuckoos mob in St. Louis, is shot and killed by a carload of Green Ones, their mortal enemies.

SEPT. 9

Jack "Legs" Diamond is arrested for smuggling narcotics in Mount Vernon, N.Y.; he is discharged within hours.

SEPT. 20

Earl "Hymie" Weiss, Bugs Moran, the Gusenberg brothers and other O'Bannionites in Chicago, eight carloads of them, slowly drive past the Hawthorn Hotel and Restaurant in Cicero, Capone's headquarters, in broad daylight, spraying the street with machine-gun fire; Vincent "The Schemer" Drucci calmly alights from one of the cars, stands at the hotel entrance and empties his machine gun into the hotel lobby, wounding Capone gunman Louis Barko; Capone is hiding on the floor of the Hawthorn Restaurant, his bodyguard on top of him as the O'Bannionites fire more than 1,000 rounds into the hotel before slowly driving away.

SEPT. 22

Joseph Corsiglio, an associate of the Cuckoos gang in St. Louis, is murdered by The Green Ones. On Sept. 23 the Cuckoos will strike back, spraying the Submarine Bar and killing Green Ones associates Frank Christian and Anthony Dattalo; an innocent newspaper dealer, Joseph Rubino, will also be killed in the attack.

OCT. 1

Al Capone is arrested in Chicago for violating the National Prohibition Act and is dismissed within the hour.

OCT. 11

Earl "Hymie" Weiss is shot and killed as he alights from his car in Chicago in front of Holy Name Cathedral on North State Street; also killed is one of his henchmen, Paddy Murray; three others are wounded when two machine-gun nests stationed in the second-floor window across the street open up; the Capone hired killers, who flee out a back doorway, are later reported to be Frank Diamond, Frank "The Enforcer" Nitti, John Scalise, Albert Anselmi and Tony "Joe Batters" Accardo, the latter of whom is the patriarch of Chicago's Mafia family at this writing.

OCT. 15

Kustandy Ajilonny, a Green Ones ally in St. Louis, is murdered by members of the rival Cuckoos.

OCT. 21

Capone meets with Bugs Moran and other rival gangsters in Chicago's Hotel Sherman and agrees to peace terms, dividing the city once again and giving himself the lion's share of the spoils; before they leave the hotel room, Vincent Drucci urges Bugs Moran, the new leader of the O'Bannionites, "to shoot that bastard dead now." Moran declines.

WHITE-COLLAR CRIME

JAN. 24

In New York City, the Democratic Club is raided by police and closed down for gambling. (See "White-Collar Crime," Jan. 1, 1927.)

APRIL 27

Patrick Henry "Packy" Lennon begins mulcting tycoon A. J. Cunningham in a clever series of stock cons; Lennon will milk Cunningham, a naïve dupe, out of millions before he is exposed in 1929.

AUG. 18

Charles Ponzi, the sensational Peter-to-Paul investment con artist from Boston, is arrested and sent to jail for selling bogus deeds to Florida property during the land boom.

MISCELLANEOUS

FEB. 23

Earl Carroll, producer of the racy *Vanities* shows in New York City, holds a party for Countess Vera Cathcart in his theater, at which 17-year-old Joyce Hawley takes a naked bath in a tub of champagne, guests dipping into the tub with their glasses for a drink and a peek. Carroll, who reneges on paying the girl for her "performance," is sued by Hawley, who later testifies that he has broken the Prohibition laws; Carroll insists that the tub contained only ginger ale, but he will be convicted of perjury, fined $2,000 and sentenced to the federal penitentiary in Atlanta, Ga., for a year, but he will serve only three months.

MARCH 17

Ronald Chesney is found not guilty of murdering his mother in Edinburgh, Scotland; he will be found dead, an apparent suicide, on Feb. 16, 1954, by his girlfriend, who will tell police that he had admitted to her that he had murdered his mother.

AUG. 18

Joseph "Doc" Stacher is arrested for assault and battery in Newark, N.J., and dismissed.

1·9·2·7

MURDER

JAN. 17

The bodies of millionaire Augustin Martelletti and his wife are found in their luxurious apartments above the banking institution of Cores, Martelletti, Hermanosa Cia. in Mercedes, Argentina; both have been repeatedly stabbed, their bedroom splashed with blood; police find a cap at the scene and later learn that a pair of trousers covered with blood has been sent to a local cleaners; these are traced, along with the cap, to Felix Tellos, a former employee of the financial firm; he admits the killings, saying that he intended to rob the family safe and that when the Martellettis woke up he killed them; Tellos is given a 20-year sentence, the maximum punishment, Argentina having no capital punishment.

FEB. 11

Albert Fish molests and kills four-year-old William Gaffney in the Georgetown area of Washington, D.C.; Fish, later known as "The Cannibal," will claim to have molested, murdered and eaten scores of young children before he is executed on Jan. 6, 1936.

MARCH 19

Ruth Brown Snyder, a housewife, and Henry Judd Gray, a corset salesman, murder Mrs. Snyder's husband, Albert, a successful editor in Queens, N.Y., hammering his skull with a sash weight while he sleeps; when confronted by police, the lovers turn on each other, and their subsequent trial will capture headlines across the country in what Damon Runyon terms "The Dumbbell Murder," because the killers are "so dumb." Both are convicted and sent to the electric chair at Sing Sing on Jan. 12, 1928; an enterprising newsman smuggles a tiny camera into the execution room and photographs Mrs. Snyder as the current charges through her; the photo runs the full length of the front page of the New York *Daily News* the following day, becoming the most famous tabloid picture of the era.

APRIL 27

Earle Leonard Nelson murders and rapes Mary McConnell, a landlady in Philadelphia; on May 1 Nelson will murder and rape Jennie Randolph in Buffalo, N.Y.; Nelson, always on the move, on June 1 will murder and rape two sisters, Minnie May and Mrs. M. C. Atorthy both landladies, in Detroit; from Chicago on June 3 Nelson will flee to Winnipeg, Canada, where he will abduct a blind flower girl, Lola Cowan, murdering and raping her on June 8; on the following day in Winnipeg, Nelson will wait until Mrs. Emily Patterson is left alone in her house by her husband, then strangle and rape her; Nelson will become the subject of one of the greatest manhunts in North America, with thousands of lawmen and vigilantes searching for the "Gorilla Murderer." (See "Murder," Nov. 14.)

The celebrated photo of Ruth Snyder being electrocuted in Sing Sing's death chamber for the murder of her husband. (March 19, 1927)

JULY 1

Paddling a canoe on Lake Palourde, Fla., Dr. Tom Dreher and his lover, Ada LeBout, drop the body of Ada's husband into the lake; they will later confess to the murder, and they will be hanged on Feb. 1, 1929.

JULY 9

A policeman in Battery Park, New York City, finds bags containing the dissected body of a Miss Brownell; her brutal murder is solved on July 10 when Ludwig Lee, a tenant in Miss Brownell's boardinghouse, will admit to the killing; he will also confess to murdering a Mrs. Bennett, and will be sent to the electric chair in 1928.

AUG. 21

Jesse Watkins of San Francisco kills his former employer, Henry Chambers, and later admits to the police that he has murdered Chambers "because he was too content." Watkins will be sent to McNeil Island Prison for life.

SEPT. 30

In a pub fight in Cardiff, Wales, Edward and John Rowlands, Daniel Driscoll and William Joseph Price attack and kill David Lewis, a famous Welsh rugby player, cutting his throat on a well-lit street; all will be hunted down; Price will be acquitted; John Rowlands will receive a life term in Broadmoor Prison, a lunatic asylum for the criminally insane; and Driscoll and Edward Rowlands will be hanged at Cardiff Prison on Jan. 27, 1928.

OCT. 19

Petty thief Pete McKenzie shoots and kills Chief of Detectives Sam Street in San Antonio, Tex.; McKenzie, as the result of one of the greatest manhunts in the state, will later be found hiding in the attic of his brother's home; he will be sentenced to death, but a question of his sanity will arise, and his sentence will be changed to life imprisonment.

NOV. 14

Earle Leonard Nelson is captured in the small town of Killarney, Canada, by an army of police, who close in on him; the mass killer is taken to Winnipeg, where he will be convicted, and hanged on Jan. 12, 1928.

NOV. 15

In Omar, Del., Mrs. Mary Carey and her son Howard murder Mary's brother, Robert Hitchens; they will not be exposed as the killers until years later, and they will be executed in 1935.

DEC. 29

Frederick Edel, a cat burglar with several murders to his credit, kills 39-year-old actress Mrs. Emeline Harrington in her Manhattan apartment, stealing her jewelry; he will be caught in Jan. 1928 when skipping out of a New Haven, Conn., hotel with some of Mrs. Harrington's jewelry in his suitcase; Edel will be tried in New York City and will be executed the following year.

ROBBERY

JAN. 7

Wilbur Underhill attempts to rob a Tulsa, Okla., bank; he steals a car and murders its driver; captured, Underhill will be sent to the Oklahoma State Penitentiary at McAlester for life, but he will escape on July 14, 1931.

MARCH 11

Nine members of the Flathead Gang, led by ex-choirboy Paul Jawarski, mine a road with pipes full of high explosives 20 miles outside Pittsburgh and blow up a Brink's armored car as it passes; the car is tossed onto its top, and the bandits break through the exposed wooden floor with sledgehammers, scooping up valises containing payrolls amounting to more than $104,000; all the guards are knocked unconscious by the blast and miraculously escape serious injury; the weaknesses of the car's construction, as demonstrated by this sensational robbery, cause Brink's to modernize completely its armored cars; Jawarski and others in his gang will eventually be captured, and several, including the ex-choirboy, will be sent to the electric chair for the murder of guards during other robberies.

AUG. 15

Joseph "Doc" Stacher is arrested for burglarizing a store in Newark, N.J., and is given a short prison term.

SEPT. 27

Frederick Guy Browne and William Henry Kennedy, professional British thieves, steal a car in Essex, England, and are stopped by Constable Gutteridge, whom Browne shoots to death; Browne stands over the dead officer and shouts: "What are you looking at me like that for?" Browne then shoots out the constable's eyes (he will later admit that he believes the superstition that his image can be traced on the dead man's eyes) and flees with Kennedy; both will be caught, and hanged at Pentonville Prison on May 3, 1928.

ORGANIZED CRIME

APRIL 4

Vincent "The Schemer" Drucci, lieutenant of Bugs Moran, is arrested and, while being driven to headquarters in Chicago for questioning on a gangland murder, attempts to take a gun away from Detective Sgt. Danny Healy; Drucci is shot four times and killed.

APRIL 5

Big Bill Thompson is again elected mayor of Chicago, largely because of Capone backing; Thompson has run on a slogan of "a wide-open city" and will prove to be the city's most corrupt mayor in modern times.

JUNE 10

Capone sends hit man James DeAmato to New York City to investigate the bootleg operations of Frankie Yale, whom Scarface thinks is hijacking his liquor; DeAmato will be found shot to death in Manhattan four days later.

JULY 1

New York City rackets boss and head of the powerful Unione Siciliane Frankie Yale (Uale) has his car curbed by a black sedan as he drives toward his Brooklyn home on 44th Street; his car crashes into a house as rival mobsters rake his car with machine-gun fire (the first time such a weapon is used in New York City), killing Yale before he can draw his revolver and struggle free of the wreckage; the killing has been performed by gangsters sent by Al Capone; Scarface has taken revenge for Yale's murder earlier that summer, of one of his emissaries, James DeAmato.

JULY 8

Charlie Birger, southern Illinois bootleg kingpin who has invented such astounding gangland tactics as making a tank out of an oil truck to invade the domains of rival gangsters as well as bombing his enemies from the air, goes on trial for ordering the execution of Mayor Joe Adams of West City, Ill., a supporter of the rival Sheldon gang; Birger will be found guilty, and he will be hanged on April 21, 1928, laughing and cracking jokes with his executioner up to the moment the noose is slipped over his head.

AUG. 9

Anthony F. "Shorty" Russo and Vincent Spicuzza, gunmen working for the Green Ones in St. Louis, are lured to Chicago by rival Cuckoo gangsters and shot to death; on Aug. 24, Benny "Melonhead" Giamanco will announce in St. Louis that he will avenge the deaths of his friends Russo and Spicuzza; he will be found shot to death three hours later, another Cuckoos victim.

OCT. 13

Big Joe Lonardo is shot to death in Cleveland, Ohio, by members of the Porellos gang, rivals for bootleg control of the city.

New York City gangster lies dead after being ambushed, probably by Capone gunmen. (July 1, 1927)

OCT. 15

Little Augie Orgen (Orgenstein) and Jack "Legs" Diamond, his lieutenant and bodyguard, are shot down in a New York City street; their assailants are said to be Louis "Lepke" Buchalter, Jacob "Gurrah" Shapiro and Hyman "Little Hymie" Bernstein, who have been attempting to take over Little Augie's rackets; Orgen is killed, Diamond will recover.

OCT. 27

Wealthy St. Louis merchant Charles Palmisano is shot to death for refusing to continue paying extortion to The Green Ones mob.

NOV. 10

Singer Joe E. Lewis, who refuses to sing in a nightclub owned by "Machine Gun Jack" McGurn, has his throat slashed by McGurn goons; he will survive to become one of America's highest-paid nightclub comedians.

NOV. 15

Benedetto Amato, a Green Ones leader in St. Louis, is shot in the back while he walks down a city street; he dies.

DEC. 22

Al Capone is arrested in Chicago for carrying a concealed weapon; he is fined $10 and released.

WHITE-COLLAR CRIME

JAN. 1

A police raid on New York City's Democratic Club reveals that more than $100,000 has been wagered there the previous week; the club is padlocked.

FEB. 13

Walter Hohenau emigrates from Germany to Houston, Tex., where he sells several useless machines he claims will turn water into gasoline; he will later flee to Mexico when his absurd scam is exposed.

MAY 15-JULY 25

A con clan called the Williamsons, who sell flimsy roofing and siding and other useless household repair materials, invade Cleveland, bilking hundreds of suckers in home-repair scams.

OCT. 1

Robert Boltz sets up a Peter-to-Paul investment scam in Philadelphia; he will reap millions before being exposed 13 years later.

MISCELLANEOUS

MARCH 9

Virginia Jo Frazier, two-year-old daughter of a Chattanooga (Tenn.) city commissioner, is kidnapped and released a short time later, left at a minister's home naked and drugged but unharmed and unmolested, after a ransom of $3,333 is paid; the kidnapper, a 17-year-old, is later given a long prison term.

JUNE 27

Joseph "Doc" Stacher is arrested on two counts of assault and battery in Newark, N.J. He will be arrested twice again this year on similar charges, all of them dismissed.

SEPT. 19

Herman Barker, of the terrible Barker Brothers, is trapped after committing a robbery in Newton, Kan.; as police close in on his stalled car, Barker puts his pistol to his head and commits suicide.

DEC. 15

William Hickman, an egocentric college student, kidnaps Marian Parker from her Los Angeles home—she is the twin daughter of wealthy lawyer Perry Parker—and holds her for ransom; Parker pays Hickman $7,500 on a lonely road and is handed what he thinks to be his sleeping 12-year-old child wrapped in a blanket; as Hickman drives off, Parker discovers that his daughter has been strangled to death and her legs chopped off; an intense manhunt for Hickman begins, and he will later be tracked down in Echo, Ore; returned to California, he will quickly be tried, then hanged at San Quentin on Feb. 4, 1928; Hickman will spend a half hour combing his thick, wavy hair before going to his death.

1·9·2·8

MURDER

FEB. 2

Businessman Cecil Campbell and his wife take a room at New York City's Grand Central Hotel, where Campbell crushes his wife's head with a hammer; he tries to throw himself out of a window but cannot commit suicide; apprehended, Campbell will later state that he has committed the murder because he and his wife, both elderly, are stone broke and starving and that he wanted to save her further anguish; he will be given a 20-year prison sentence.

MARCH 23

In Gladbeck, Germany, bloodstains are used for the first time to prove a man innocent of murder; the accused, a man named Hussman, is released in a triumph of forensic scientific exhibits.

MAY 1

Near Riverside, California, perverted 20-year-old Gordon Stewart Northcott and his equally unbalanced mother begin waylaying teenage boys, seducing them, then murdering and burying their bodies—the count is never known but will later be estimated to exceed 20—until Northcott's nephew discovers the killings and informs police; Mrs. Northcott will be sent to prison for life, and Northcott will be hanged at San Quentin on Oct. 2, 1930.

MAY 19

Wealthy British vacationer Elizabeth Wilson is murdered near an exclusive golf course in Le Touquet, France; her murder baffles French police—some say the married woman has been killed by a secret French lover; the case remains unsolved.

JUNE 3

Mass child-killer and cannibal Albert Fish abducts 12-year-old Grace Budd in New York City and strangles and butchers her in White Plains, N.Y.; Fish will begin writing the parents of his subsequent victims, which will eventually lead authorities to him; he will admit to countless murders over an 18-year period and to cannibalizing his victims "by the light of a full moon." When Fish goes to the electric chair at Sing Sing on Jan. 16, 1936, he will be called "The Moon Maniac" by the press.

JULY 17

General Alvaro Obregon, who has just become president-elect of Mexico, is sitting in a San Angel cafe a few miles outside Mexico City when 26-year-old José de Leon Toral, a political opponent, asks to sketch his portrait; Obregon agrees and says: "I hope you make me look good, kid." Then Toral empties a pistol into Obregon's face, killing him on the spot; Toral later will be executed.

DEC. 6

Miao Yi Chung, who has murdered his wife for her jewelry—they were married in New York City and honeymooned at the Borrowdale Gates Hotel in Grange, England, the previous June—is hanged at Strangeways Jail in Manchester, England

ROBBERY

JAN. 17

Wilbur Underhill is arrested for hijacking and murder in Okmulgee, Okla., and sent to the state prison for life.

MAY 23

Four bandits rob the First National Bank of Lamar, Colo., of $218,000; the bank president, A. N. Parrish, and the cashier, N. J. Parrish, his son, are killed; the bandits kidnap Dr. W. W. Weininger as a hostage, later killing him and abandoning his car, which the bandits had used to escape; a fingerprint on the car is photographed and proves to be that of William Harrison Fleagle, better known as Jake, a small-time crook who has served time in Oklahoma for robbery as early as 1910; lawmen quickly determine that the four bandits are Jake and his brother Ralph Emerson Fleagle; Howard Royston, a bank robber from San Andreas, Calif; and George Johnson Abshier, a former bootlegger; Jake will be chased down in Bramson, Mo., where he will be killed in a gun battle with police; the other three men will be captured and later hanged in the Colorado State Penitentiary at Canon City.

JUNE 15

Joseph Valachi is paroled from Sing Sing after serving a term for burglary.

AUG. 16

Mass killer Carl Panzram is arrested for house-breaking in Washington, D.C., and given a short jail term.

ORGANIZED CRIME

MARCH 3

In New York City, Meyer Lansky attempts to kill his own gunman, Daniel Francis Ahern, who is cutting in on his rackets; on March 9 Lansky will be arrested for felonious assault on John Barrett, a rival gangster; Lansky will be released a short time later.

MARCH 21

"Diamond Joe" Esposito runs for Republican ward committeeman in Chicago against Capone's wishes; a labor racketeer and political boss since 1910, Esposito is shot to death in front of his home while his horrified wife watches from an open window; his killers are never found, but insiders know Capone gave the orders for the execution.

JUNE 26

"Big Tim" Murphy, who opposes Capone and Mayor Thompson in labor racketeering, is shot to death in front of his Chicago home; his killers are never apprehended.

SEPT. 7

Antonio Lombardo, head of Chicago's powerful Unione Siciliane, and his bodyguard Joseph Ferraro are shot to death at State and Madison streets; his killers, thought to be Joseph Aiello and his brothers, who covet the Unione for themselves, shoot Pasqualino Lolordo, Lombardo's successor, on Jan. 8, 1929, while drinking wine with Lolordo in his parlor.

SEPT. 27

Meyer Lansky becomes a naturalized U.S. citizen in New York City.

NOV. 4

Arnold Rothstein, known as New York City's "Big Bankroll," the man who is worth untold millions and reportedly finances most of the East Coast rackets, is shot in the Park Central Hotel; he is rushed to a hos-

pital, where he tells police: "I won't talk about it. I'll take care of it myself." He will die on Nov. 6 without naming his murderers; it is claimed that Rothstein welched on more than $300,000 in gambling losses to George "Hump" McManus, Nathan "Nigger Nate" Raymond, Meyer Boston and other gamblers and that one of these men has killed him; McManus will be indicted but not tried for lack of evidence, and Rothstein's murder will never be solved; however, it is quite likely that he has been murdered by rising members of the new crime cartel because he controlled so many rackets.

Arnold Rothstein, rackets financier, super gambler and fixer known as "the Big Bankroll," mysteriously murdered. (Nov. 4, 1928)

DEC. 5

Two dozen Sicilians from Chicago, New York, Detroit, Tampa, St. Louis, Buffalo and Newark meet in Cleveland's Hotel Statler to form the national crime syndicate; Joseph Guinta represents Capone (a non-Sicilian); from New York comes Joseph Magliocco, Charles "Lucky" Luciano, Joseph Profaci and others.

WHITE-COLLAR CRIME

AUG. 1-SEPT. 10, 1930

Samuel Insull, Chicago utilities czar, and his associates flood the market with public securities valued at $650 million, helping to cause the great stock market crash of 1929; Insull will later be prosecuted but acquitted.

MISCELLANEOUS

MAY 18

The New York City residence of Robert G. Elliott, executioner at Sing Sing, is mysteriously bombed; no one is injured; and the bombing is never solved.

NOV. 19

Wealthy Dr. Charles Brancati, whom police later claim is connected with bootlegging gangsters, steps into a New York City subway and is never seen again; Brancati is thought to be a victim of kidnappers.

1·9·2·9

MURDER

FEB. 4

Kate Jackson, a promiscuous, blackmailing housewife in Kenilworth, England, is found at the back door of her cottage by her husband and neighbors in answer to her screams; she dies of head wounds in a few hours without regaining consciousness; her husband, Thomas Jackson, will be tried but acquitted, and the murder will never be solved.

FEB. 6

In Columbus, Ohio, James Howard Snook, a veterinary professor, slashes Theodore Hix to death in a professional argument; Snook will be electrocuted in 1930.

MARCH 3

James Bell of Newark, N.J., inexplicably goes berserk and, running through the city streets with a pistol and a shotgun, shoots five people, killing Charles Ramperger and Julius Rabinowitz; he will be sent to prison for life.

MARCH 15

Mrs. Violet Emelia Sydney of Croydon, England, becomes ill; and doctors discover that her medical prescription is dosed with arsenic; attending physicians are cleared, and other deaths in the family going back more than a year are investigated; exhumed bodies will prove two other members of the Duff and Sydney households have been poisoned, but the killer will never be found.

APRIL 26

Eva Rablen of Tuttleton, Calif., a flapper tired of her lame husband, Carroll, who has been wounded in World War I, enters a dance hall, then returns to the car where Carroll Rablen sits, giving him a cup of coffee laced with strychnine; following Rablen's agonizing death, detectives prove that Eva has purchased the poison from a local druggist; she will be sent to prison for life.

APRIL 28

Eccentric British painter Edith May Olive Branson is murdered in her villa at Les Baux, France; several lovers, a caretaker, even competing artists in the area are briefly held as suspects, but in the end the French police will mark the case unsolved.

MAY 24

Mamie Shoaf, destitute, kills her three children in Lebanon, Ky., then commits suicide in a local cemetery.

JUNE 20

Carl Panzram, an inmate at Leavenworth, crushes the skull of the prison's laundry foreman, Robert G. Warnke, a man with whom he has had no apparent quarrel; On Sept. 5, 1930, Panzram will be hanged in Leavenworth's yard for the killing, dragging the hangman up the scaffold stairs as he rushes to his own death.

JULY 1

In Nagyrev, Hungary, a choir director goes to the local police to claim that Mrs. Ladislaus Szabo, a woman he hardly knows, has attempted to serve him poisoned wine; a routine investigation reveals that the village of Nagyrev is peopled by dozens of female bluebeards who have been poisoning their husbands to take young lovers for almost 20 years; leader of this murder-love cult is Mrs. Julius Fazekas, who will commit suicide when officers break into her cottage; another mass killer, Juliane Lipka, will confess to poisoning seven persons from 1914 to 1929; Mrs. Lipka and seven others will be hanged and their bodies put on display.

JULY 2-3

Detroit religious cultist and real-estate broker Benny Evangelista, his wife and his four children are found hacked to pieces in their home; Benny is found sitting at his desk, decapitated, his head on the floor beside his body; these gruesome killings are thought to be part of some sort of religious rite or a Mafia assassination, but they are never solved.

DEC. 10

Harry Grew Crosby, madcap playboy, literary posturer, sun-worshipper and nephew of J. Pierpont Morgan, leaves his wife, Caresse, at New York City's Savoy-Plaza Hotel and meets with his mistress, Josephine Rotch Bigelow, who is also married, trysting in the studio apartment of a friend, artist Stanley Mortimer, at the Hotel des Artistes; hours later both are found dead by Mortimer and police; lawmen, after studying the positions of both corpses, conclude that Crosby, 31, has killed Mrs. Bigelow, 22, whom he has called "The Sun Goddess," and then committed suicide with a .25 Belgian automatic; the murder-suicide shocks the literary world, Crosby having been the publisher of such giants as James Joyce, Hart Crane, Ezra Pound and Ernest Hemingway; in weird commemoration of this homicidal event, e.e. cummings wrote:

> 2 boston
> Dolls; found
> with
> Holes in each other
>
> 's lullaby

ROBBERY

MARCH 9

Charles Arthur "Pretty Boy" Floyd is arrested in Kansas City for robbery, but the charge is dismissed; he will be arrested in Kansas City three more times during the year, always on suspicion of robbery but

nothing will be proved against him and he will be released each time.

MARCH 14

Joseph Valachi is arrested for armed robbery in New York City but is released the following day for lack of evidence.

OCT. 13

Clyde Barrow is found running from the scene of a burglary in Dallas and is arrested, but he will be released a few days later for lack of evidence.

ORGANIZED CRIME

FEB. 14

The St. Valentine's Day Massacre occurs in Chicago at 2122 North Clark Street at the S.M.C. Cartage Company, a garage front for the Bugs Moran mob; five men, three in policemen's uniforms, draw up before the garage late in the morning in a Cadillac touring car similar to that used by detectives and enter the garage, where seven men are lined up against the brick wall; they have gathered to receive an out-of-town shipment of booze; with their backs to the so-called police officers, the seven are suddenly shot down in a hail of machine-gun and shotgun fire; those slaughtered are Adam Heyer, bootlegger and owner of the garage; Al Weinshank, the mob's accountant, a one-time safecracker; Dr. Reinhardt Schwimmer, an optometrist friend of Weinshank's; and Moran's top gunmen—John May, James Clark and the deadly brothers Pete and Frank Gusenberg; Moran, with two bodyguards—Willie Marks and Ted Newbury—barely miss being killed when they spot the Cadillac parked in front of the garage and duck into a coffee shop, thinking the place is being raided; when the bogus police leave, May's German shepherd begins howling and brings curious neighbors, who discover the carnage; only Frank Gusenberg survives for even a few hours, but he refuses to name his murderers; a badly shaken Bugs Moran later blurts: "Only Capone kills like that!" Chicago police frantically attempt to pinpoint the killers but fail; "Machine Gun Jack" McGurn has masterminded the operation and undoubtedly wielded one of the machine guns, but he provides Louise Rolfe, the "Blonde Alibi" who insists that McGurn has been with her during the shooting; others accused are Fred "Shotgun Ziegler" Goetz and Claude Haddox; only one man—Fred R. "Killer" Burke—is positively linked with the mass murder, when police match slugs from the machine guns fired at the killing site to a machine gun found in Burke's home; the "Killer" flees to Michigan, where he shoots and kills the first cop he sees, knowing the state has no death penalty; Burke will go behind bars for life; the other killers are never found.

APRIL 6

Joseph "Crazy Joe" Gallo is born in Brooklyn, N.Y.

MAY 8

After returning from Miami, Al Capone invites one-time henchmen Joseph "Hop Toad" Guinta, Albert Anselmi and John Scalise to dinner at his Cicero, Ill., hotel headquarters; after a lavish meal, Capone rises from the long dinner table, surrounded by goons, and goes into a blistering rage, informing his guests that he knows they have been operating behind his back to take over his Chicago rackets and bootleg empire and have planned to kill him; Capone takes a baseball bat from beneath the table and, one by one, crushes the skulls of Guinta, Scalise and Anselmi, who sit paralyzed with fear, silently awaiting their executions. Their bodies are later found at the outskirts of Chicago, dumped in a ditch, naked.

MAY 16-17

Al "Scarface" Capone, who has absented himself from Chicago during and after the St. Valentine's Day Massacre, fearing Moran will make an all-out effort on his life, goes to Philadelphia and arranges with local police to be arrested for carrying a gun without a permit; he is given a year sentence, a private suite of jail rooms, catered meals, a private telephone and is allowed visitors at all hours; "Al's safer in jail," says Moran with a sneer; in the next six months Eliot Ness, leading his "Untouchables" Prohibition agents, will raid two dozen Capone distilleries and breweries, destroying $1 million in equipment and supplies; Capone will be paroled on May 16, 1930.

JUNE 13

Charles "Lucky" Luciano is arrested in New York City on suspicion of murdering William "Red" Cassidy and Simon Walker, rival racketeers, whom Luciano reportedly shot in Legs Diamond's Hotsy Totsy nightclub; Luciano will be released for lack of evidence; and the real killers will be discovered to be Diamond and his enforcer, Charles "Charlie Green" Entratta, who are never prosecuted for the crime.

SEPT. 29

Joe Valachi is arrested in New York City for assault and battery; he is released.

OCT. 17

Lucky Luciano is reportedly ordered to murder his

chief, Joe "The Boss" Masseria, by La Cosa Nostra leader Salvatore Maranzano and refuses; Luciano will be badly beaten by Maranzano thugs days later, an act that will seal Maranzano's fate. (See "Organized Crime," April 15, 1931.)

NOV. 18

Capone's bookkeeper, Jake Guzik, is found guilty of tax fraud and will later be sentenced to five years in prison.

WHITE-COLLAR CRIME

APRIL 26

Robert Arthur Tourbillon, who has recently been released from the New Jersey State Prison after serving a term for fraud, is arrested for swindling an apple farmer out of his property in New York and receives a three-year sentence.

JUNE 1

Russian-born Serge Rubinstein begins to use funds of the Banque Franco-Asiatique in Paris, where he holds a position, to buy up a restaurant chain worth $450,000; he takes $60,000 of depositors' money and returns it after gutting the chain and making a $250,000 profit.

DEC. 1

From London, flimflammer Oscar Hartzell cables thousands of American suckers involved in his Drake Inheritance scam to send more money to him to fight President Hoover, who he says has caused the stock market crash to prevent billions in settlement dollars from being disbursed to them.

MISCELLANEOUS

JULY 10

In New York City, the wife of Yin Kao, former Chinese consul, admits to federal agents that she has smuggled into the U.S. more than $600,000 worth of opium "for friends." She is deported.

AUG. 9

New York City theater magnate Alexander Pantages is accused of raping 17-year-old Eunice Pringle;

he will be judged not guilty thanks to the brilliant courtroom maneuvers of young criminal attorney Jerry Geisler; the case makes Geisler famous, and he will become the top attorney in the entertainment field.

NOV. 30

Professor F. Kockel in Leipzig, Germany, runs blood tests on what is thought to be the body of Erich Tetzner, apparently killed when his Opel car crashed near Regensburg and burned; police are suspicious when Mrs. Tetzner immediately claims large insurance monies; also the body, charred and unrecognizable, appears to be too small for Tetzner, a large man; Professor Kockel confirms police suspicions when he reports that blood samples prove negative for carbon monoxide, showing that the victim has been murdered before being put into the car; Mrs. Tetzner is watched and, in December, she will make a call to Strasbourg, France, where Tetzner is discovered and arrested; he will be tried for murdering the man found in the car and convicted, beheaded in Regensburg on May 2, 1931.

1·9·3·0

MURDER

JUNE 27

Amarillo, Tex., lawyer A. D. Payne plants a bomb in the family car, which blows up his wife when she goes on a shopping trip and horribly wounds his young son; Payne, a newsman learns, has several mistresses and has killed his wife to be with one of them; while awaiting trial for murder, Payne will explode a small charge in his cell—he will have strapped to it his chest—and kill himself.

JULY 22

Detroit radio newscaster Jerry Buckley, who has waged a war over the airways against local corruption, is shot dead in the lobby of the LaSalle Hotel; bystanders will later identify Ted Pizzino, Angelo Livecchi and Joseph Bommarito, members of The Purple Mob, as the killers; incredibly, a jury will find the trio not guilty, and the Buckley killing will never be officially solved.

AUG. 4

In Spokane, Wash., Joseph Mines batters to death 74-year-old John Karakinikas, a total stranger; Mines will later claim that he has smoked two marijuana cigarettes before the murder and did not know what he was doing; he will be found guilty of only manslaughter and sent to prison for 20 years.

SEPT. 12

Newark, N.J., businessman Louis Balducci is shot to death on the street after an argument with a man in a car; the license of the car is traced to George Segro, who will later admit that he has had a business feud with the victim for years; Segro will be convicted of manslaughter and be sent to prison for 15 years.

SEPT. 20

Elderly Margery Wren, the proprietor of a sweet-shop in Ramsgate, England, is found by constables, horribly battered about the head; she will linger for five days in a hospital, at first babbling that no one has attacked her; but before her death on Sept. 25, she will tell officers that her attacker is "a man with a red face." Her murder will never be solved.

OCT. 12

Avis Wooley, a 17-year-old baby-sitter, answers a Kansas City ad, meeting Paul Kauffman, who tries to get her drunk and seduce her; when she resists, Kauffman strangles her with silk stockings he has bought for her; Kauffman, traced through his advertisements appearing in the *Kansas City Star,* will confess, telling police that he has killed the Wooley girl not for sexual reasons but for the 70 cents she had in her pocket; he will be hanged for the crime.

ROBBERY

MARCH 2

Clyde Barrow, using the alias of Elvin Williams, is arrested in Waco, Tex., as he flees a store he has burglarized; he is convicted and given 14 years, but he will escape from the local jail on March 11, cutting the bars with a saw smuggled to him by his new girl-friend, Bonnie Parker; Barrow will be recaptured on March 18 in Middletown, Ohio, and returned to Texas, where he will begin serving his term in the Texas State Penitentiary at Huntsville; he will be paroled on Feb. 2, 1932, and begin one of the worst crime waves in the Southwest, with waitress-turned-gun moll Bonnie Parker at his side.

MARCH 11

Charles Arthur "Pretty Boy" Floyd, Jack Atkins and Tom Bradley rob the bank in Sylvania, Ohio, taking several thousand dollars; police on motorcycles chase the bandits out of town, one of the officers, Harlan F. Manes, being shot dead from the rear window of the bandits' car; the bandits crash into a telephone pole and are captured; Bradley will be sent to the electric chair for killing Manes; Atkins will receive life imprisonment but Floyd will escape en route to the penitentiary, kicking out a window and jumping from a speeding train, then hiding out in Toledo until moving southward toward Oklahoma's Cookson Hills, his sanctuary, where residents think of him as a modern-day Robin Hood. (Floyd goes out of his way to burn unrecorded mortgages when robbing banks in Oklahoma.)

MARCH 23

Thief Alvin Karpis is arrested for burglarizing a Kansas City store and stealing a getaway car; he is sent to the state reformatory, from which he escapes.

SEPT. 10

Oliver Curtis Perry, 1890s train robber, dies in his Clinton Prison cell at Dannemora, N.Y., after blinding himself.

SEPT. 17

Three men pretending to be bank examiners walk into the Lincoln National Bank & Trust Company in Lincoln, Neb., and hastily loot the vault of $2,702,796 in cash and securities, then calmly walk outside, where armed guards escort them to a waiting car; three men named O'Connor, Lee and Britt are arrested, with O'Connor and Lee being sent to prison for the robbery for 25 years; however, they will be released 10 years later as innocent; other men, their identities unknown to this day, are the real perpetrators of the largest bank robbery in American history to this date.

OCT. 28

Willie "The Actor" Sutton, with Marcus Bassett, robs M. Rosenthal & Sons Jewelers in New York City (Sutton, typical of his *modus operandi,* dresses up as a telegraph messenger to gain access to the locked establishment); the pair get away with gems valued at more than $30,000; Bassett will be caught on Nov. 28 and will confess to police that he and Sutton have pulled eight stickups in recent months, netting the pair $214,000.

DEC. 16

Herman K. Lamm, who had been a German officer cashiered for cheating at cards during World War I and who has established the time method of bank robbing in America since 1917, enters the Citizens State Bank of Clinton, Ind. (Under Lamm's system each bandit is assigned a post, one at the wheel of the car outside the bank, one going through the cages, one going into the vault, and one guarding everyone inside the front door and holding a stopwatch, calling out the required time to rob the bank.) With Lamm are G. W. "Dad" Landy, James "Oklahoma Jack" Clark and Walter Dietrich; they scoop up $15,567 and walk outside to their waiting Buick, but the driver panics and takes a sharp U-turn, hitting the curb and blowing a tire; the gang commandeers another car but it cannot go faster than 35 miles per hour, having a secret governor on it; the gang transfers to a truck, but this breaks down, its radiator empty, as they approach the Illinois border; the last car the gang steals has only a gallon of gasoline, and, just inside the Illinois border, the gang is surrounded by more than 200 possemen and deputies from Illinois and Indiana; they shoot it out for several hours; the driver and Herman Lamm are shot to pieces; Clark and Dietrich surrender with empty guns; "Dad" Landy, age 71, rather than go to prison, sends his last bullet into his brain; Walter Dietrich will be sent to the Michigan City, Indiana, Prison, where he will meet John Dillinger and carefully explain Lamm's precision bank robbery system, which Dillinger will later employ to great effect.

ORGANIZED CRIME

FEB. 26

A campaign to rid New York City of the "Moustache Petes," elderly Mafia dons, by ambitious younger men commanded by Salvatore Maranzano, is begun with the killing of Tom Reina, an old-time Mafia don; Vito Genovese blows off the top of Reina's head with a shotgun.

JUNE 9

Alfred Jake Lingle, street reporter for the *Chicago Tribune,* is murdered in the congested tunnel leading to the Illinois Central train terminal in Chicago's Loop while en route to a racetrack; his killer, dressed as a

Corrupt Chicago newsman Alfred "Jake" Lingle lies dead in a train underpass, executed gangland-style. (June 9, 1930)

priest, calmly walks up behind Lingle and shoots him in the back of the head, then runs from the tunnel and up the stairs to street level, where he disappears into dense crowds; at first Colonel Robert R. McCormick of the *Tribune* offers enormous rewards for the apprehension of his reporter's killer, but it will later be learned that Lingle, a $65-a-week newsman, had a fortune in the bank, several cars and three houses and had been in the pay of Capone for years, feeding Scarface vital information from his friend Police Commissioner Russell; Russell will resign; it will then be learned that when Capone went to prison in Philadelphia Lingle went to work for Capone's archenemy, Bugs Moran, which was the reason Lingle was killed; Leo Vincent Brothers, an out-of-town killer, will eventually be identified as Lingle's assassin and will receive 14 years in prison. "I can do that standing on my head," he will say with a sneer; he will be paroled in eight years. On the same day, in Chicago, Capone personally kills Joey Aiello, the killer of Scarface's ally and friend Patsy Lolordo.

JUNE 11

Abe "Kid Twist" Reles is arrested for the first time, on a murder charge, and is released a short time later;

Reles and others have already begun killing anyone, anywhere, for profit and on assignment as members of a killers-for-hire group that will later be known in New York City as Murder, Inc.

AUG. 15

Albert Anastasia and Frank Scalise shoot Pete Morello, a Moustache Pete, in his East Harlem, N.Y., loansharking office, as part of the Mafia purge instigated by Maranzano.

SEPT. 9

Thomas "Three-Finger Brown" Lucchese murders another Moustache Pete, Joe Pinzolo, in New York City.

OCT. 23

Chicago gangster Jack Zuto, who has informed police about Capone operations, is tracked down by Scarface's gunners in a Delafield, Wis., resort and shot to death as he slips nickels into a jukebox; as Zuto lays dying with dancers gathering about him, his first selection plays—"Good for Me, Bad for You."

NOV. 5

Joseph "Doc" Stacher is arrested in Newark for assault and battery and is released.

In the Bronx, N.Y., Maranzano gunmen shoot to death Steven Ferigno and Al Mineo, other members of the Mafia old guard marked for eradication; they just miss Joe "The Boss" Masseria.

WHITE-COLLAR CRIME

JUNE 19

Vito Genovese is indicted for conspiracy to violate counterfeiting laws; he has been caught with $500,000 in counterfeit currency; he will be released a short time later.

JULY 17

France deports Serge Rubinstein because of his speculation with francs, which ruins several banking institutions.

DEC. 15

Abram Sykowski purportedly suckers several financiers into advancing funds to him, saying that he controls Capone millions in American banks and needs heavy capital to bribe banking officials into releasing the gangster's money to his care. He is never convicted of the crime.

MISCELLANEOUS

FEB. 10

Chicago authorities arrest 158 corporation employees, charging them with selling 7 million gallons of alcohol to local bootleggers—a $50 million-a-year racket. Only a few receive light sentences.

FEB. 17

Wealthy Granite City, Ill., banker Charles Pershall is kidnapped and ransomed for $40,000; his kidnappers are never caught.

APRIL 21

A cellblock fire intentionally started by some unknown inmate in the Ohio Penitentiary claims the lives of 322 prisoners.

MAY 10

A race riot in Sherman, Tex., sees mobs of whites burn down several blocks of homes of blacks.

JULY 5

Reginald Arthur Lee, the British acting consul-general in Marseilles, France, mysteriously disappears; he is later thought to be a murder victim of drug smugglers he was personally investigating; Lee's body is never found.

AUG. 6

Judge Joseph F. Crater vanishes on a Manhattan street after he gets into a cab; he is presumed the murder victim of blackmailers knowing of his corrupt practices.

OCT. 19

Frank "Jelly" Nash, notorious Oklahoma bandit doing a long stretch in Leavenworth for bank robbery, and who has been made a trustee for exemplary behavior, is sent on an errand by Warden Tom White (Nash has been cooking gourmet meals in the warden's home outside the prison walls for the warden and his family) and never returns; oddly, the bank robber has stolen a three-volume set of Shakespeare from the prison library; Nash will disappear into the underworld, first working with the Johnny Lazi mob (under Boss Pendergast) in Kansas City, then robbing banks in the Southwest; Nash will be arrested in Hot Springs, Ark. (a notorious "open city" for wanted criminals) and returned to Kansas City en route to Leavenworth, where he will die in the Kansas City Massacre of June 17, 1933.

DEC. 5

An enormous shipment of morphine is uncovered by U.S. Customs agents on board the S.S. *Alesia*, a Turkish freighter docked at a Brooklyn, N.Y., pier.

DEC. 16

Nell Quinlan Donnelly, a millionaire clothing firm owner in Kansas City, is abducted with her chauffeur, $75,000 being demanded for their safe return; the kidnappers in their ransom demands inform Mr. Donnelly that his wife will be blinded and the chauffeur murdered if the money is not paid; Donnelly and his close friend U.S. Senator James A. Reed attempt to negotiate the ransom, but newsmen learn of the kidnapping; Reed announces that if Mrs. Donnelly is harmed he will "spend the rest of his life, if necessary, to run down the kidnappers and send them to the gallows"; within 34 hours, Mrs. Donnelly and the chauffeur are released unharmed with no ransom paid. The kidnappers are not found.

1·9·3·1

MURDER

JAN. 6

Wealthy recluse John Albert Drinan, 83, is found in his luxurious apartment in Paris, his skull crushed and a broken pitcher next to his bed; his murder is never solved.

Evelyn Foster, 29, a taxi driver in Otterburn, England, is hired to drive a stranger to a nearby town; she is later found battered and burned, her car smoldering, alongside a dark road; half conscious, Evelyn is brought home and tells her parents that the stranger has attacked her and then tried to burn her alive in the car; after she dies local police botch the investigation, and all clues are obliterated; Miss Foster's killer is never found.

JAN. 19

Mrs. Julia Wallace is found dying in her Liverpool home by her husband, William Herbert Wallace, and neighbors; a small amount of money is taken, but Mrs. Wallace's killer is not discovered; Wallace, a mild-mannered insurance broker, will be put on trial with no real evidence against him, and he will be acquitted; he will claim that he was lured away from his home by someone calling on the phone who identified himself as ''R. M. Qualtrough,'' an obvious alias; ''Qualtrough'' is never located.

JAN. 23

A lone maniac attacks and strangles house servant Louisa Maude Steele in Lewisham, England, when the young woman goes to purchase some cough syrup for her employer; her body is found hours later near Blackheath Woods; there are bite marks on her neck, which creates the myth that Miss Steele has been attacked by a ''vampire killer''; the murderer is never found.

FEB. 26

Call girl and blackmailer Vivian Gordon is found strangled to death in Van Cortlandt Park in the Bronx, N.Y. She has had many affairs, and some of her sponsors are investigated, but no evidence will be found to bring indictments; the case remains open to this day.

JUNE 8

Showgirl Starr Faithfull is found dead on the sands of Long Beach, N.Y., and is first thought to be a drowning victim; but sand found in the girl's lungs means that she was suffocated on the beach; rumor and speculation run high in this sensational case, but no one is ever convicted of the mysterious murder.

Starr Faithfull, whose strange death remains unsolved. (June 8,1931)

JUNE 21

Lt. Hubert George Chevis of Aldershot, England, dies of eating poisoned partridge; his murderer is never found.

JULY 2

Peter Kurten, who has murdered at least 15 people from 1913 to 1930 and has been turned in to authorities as the ''Monster of Dusseldorf'' by his wife, is executed; over breakfast, Kurten, a meek-mannered 47-year-old factory worker, had told his wife that he was the monster who had been plaguing several German cities and suggested that if she wished to obtain a reward, she inform the police. Kurten had been tried in Dusseldorf for nine murders and was convicted, despite his lawyer's plea of insanity; before Kurten's execution he has a double helping of wiener schnitzel, sauerkraut and mashed potatoes; he is then led out to the axman; "I hope I hear my own blood gurgle," he says as he mounts the scaffold; he is beheaded a moment later in the courtyard of Klingelputz Prison in Cologne, Germany.

Patrolman William Kohler is shot to death on an Oakland, Calif., street by two young hoodlums, Lewis Hurschel Downs and Joseph Gasparich; when they are later caught, both admit the killing, saying they did it "for kicks." Downs and Gasparich will be given life sentences in San Quentin and will be paroled on Sept. 24, 1943.

AUG. 14

On board the steamship *Belgenland,* en route from Tokyo–Yokohama to New York City, Hisashi Fujimara, a wealthy Japanese silk merchant carrying a large amount of money for his firm, suddenly vanishes from his stateroom along with the suitcase of money he has been carrying; he is presumed murdered, his body dumped into the sea; the money is never found, although the ship and passengers are thoroughly searched when docking.

SEPT. 14

Joseph Kahawawai is brought before American Navy Lt. Thomas Massie in Hawaii by two seamen, E. J. Lord and A. O. Jones; Massie accuses Kahawawai of being one of five men who have raped his wife, Thalia, when she went swimming a few nights earlier; "We done it," says Kahawawai, and Massie goes into a blind rage, killing him; Jones and Lord help Massie drag the body to the family car, and Massie's mother-in-law, Mrs. Granville Fortesque, drives the car, with the men and the body in the back seat, to the top of a mountain to bury the corpse, but they are discovered; all are charged with murder; Clarence Darrow, hired as their defense lawyer, will manage a conviction of second-degree murder in a bench trial; they will be sentenced to spend only one hour in the dock before being released, a sentence that will bring the local population to near riot.

NOV. 9

While drunk, William Lester Scott of Sasakwa, Okla., crushes his wife's head, then places her in the family car, which he parks on a railroad track; a passing train crushes the car but fails to obliterate Mrs. Scott's murder wounds; Scott will be tried twice and will not be convicted until April 18, 1935; he will be sent to the state prison at McAlester, Okla., for life.

DEC. 15

Vera Page, a 10-year-old schoolgirl, is abducted in Kensington, London, England; she is found the next day in some bushes, strangled and sexually abused; police arrest Percy Orlando Rush and build a solid case of circumstantial evidence against him, but a coroner's jury will fail to indict him.

DEC. 17

Richard Wall, a wealthy American with a mysterious background—he likes to tell people he is a retired Chicago gangster—is found with his head crushed as he sits in his expensive roadster parked on a Paris street; French police will later track down Guy Davin, a friend of Wall's, and Davin will admit cockily that he has killed Wall for the considerable cash in his pockets; Davin will be sent to Devil's Island for life.

ROBBERY

JAN. 15

Baby Face Nelson robs a Chicago jewelry store and escapes with only a few gems.

FEB. 23

"Iron Irene" Schroeder, who has robbed a number

Thomas Massie (left) with Clarence Darrow and Mrs. Fortesque and seaman A. O. Jones; a murder conviction with a sentence that shocked the world. (Sept. 14, 1931)

of banks across the country in a sudden crime wave with her lover, Walter Glenn Dague (and her small son, who witnesses the robberies), is electrocuted in Pennsylvania's Rockview Penitentiary for killing a policeman in one of her many escapes; Dague will be executed a few days later; as "Iron Irene"—thus dubbed by the press for her cool nerves during her trial—sits down in the electric chair, she turns to the matrons and says: "Tell them in the kitchen to fry Glenn's eggs on both sides—he likes them that way." These are her last words.

MARCH 25

Pretty Boy Floyd shoots and kills William and Wallace Ash, sons of a brothel owner, when they tell the much-wanted bank robber that they intend to turn him in—Floyd has been hiding out at Mother Ash's Kansas City whorehouse. (It was Mother Ash who once approached Floyd and said: "I want you all to myself, pretty boy," thus giving Floyd his unforgettable sobriquet, which he hated.)

MAY 2

Alvin Karpis is discharged after serving a term in the Kansas State Penitentiary for robbery.

JULY 17

Baby Face Nelson is sent to the Illinois state prison at Joliet as Lester Gillis, to begin serving a 1-year-to-life term for robbery.

JULY 21

Pretty Boy Floyd kills Prohibition agent Curtis C. Burks, who stumbles upon his Kansas City hideout; on Dec. 12, Floyd and George Birdwell, an ex-preacher, after robbing a dozen small banks, rob *two* banks in Paden and Castle, Oklahoma, taking a few hundred dollars from each.

ORGANIZED CRIME

APRIL 1

The Maranzano-Masseria gangland feud, called the Castellammarese War in New York City (after Castellammare, the Sicilian birthplace of Salvatore Maranzano), shifts into high gear, with Mafia dons in America such as Steven Magaddino in Buffalo sending thousands to Maranzano, along with guns and cars to battle Joe "The Boss" Masseria.

APRIL 15

Realizing that his chief, Masseria, is losing the Mafia war in New York City, Charles "Lucky" Luciano secretly goes over to Maranzano; Luciano drives Joe "The Boss" to Coney Island to eat at the Nuova Villa Tammaro, which is owned by Gerardo Scarpato, a friend to both of them; at 3:30 p.m. sharp, Luciano excuses himself to go to the washroom, and moments later, four men—Bugsy Siegel, Joe Adonis, Albert Anastasia and Vito Genovese—rush up to Joe "The Boss" and empty their pistols into him; he falls face forward into a plate of linguine, dead; the hit team has been provided by Meyer Lansky, who becomes Luciano's closest confidant.

MAY 13

Jack "Legs" Diamond is arrested for violating the National Prohibition Act—serving booze in his New York City Hotsy Totsy Club—but he is released hours later.

JULY 30

Police in New York City arrest eight gunmen lying in wait to kill Legs Diamond outside his club; they are Dutch Schultz's men.

SEPT. 10

Salvatore Maranzano, who claims to be *capo di tutti capi* ("boss of bosses") now that Masseria is dead, is himself shot and stabbed to death inside his offices at the Eagle Building at 230 Park Avenue; his killers, Thomas Lucchese and three others, flee before police arrive.

OCT. 24

Al Capone, who has earlier in the year pleaded guilty to tax evasion, expecting a short prison term, is sentenced to 11 years; the stunned Capone will later be sent to Atlanta Federal Penitentiary, then Alcatraz, where paresis of the brain, contracted from the many whores he has slept with over the years, will eat away at his mind and turn him into a drooling idiot.

NOV. 11

Benjamin "Bugsy" Siegel, "Doc" Stacher, Louis "Lepke" Buchalter, Jacob "Gurrah" Shapiro and others are arrested in a Jewish gangster enclave at New York City's Hotel Franconia; all are booked on suspicion, then released; it is reported that this meeting is designed to organize non-Sicilian New York City gangsters under the Luciano banner.

DEC. 18

Jack "Legs" Diamond is shot and killed by Dutch Schultz's gunmen in an Albany, N.Y., rooming house;

Diamond and Schultz have been warring for years over disputed bootleg territory.

DEC. 21

In Chicago, Robert G. Fitchie, president of the Milk Wagon Drivers' Union, is kidnapped by Murray ''The Camel'' Humphreys and others and held for $50,000 ransom, which is paid; Fitchie is released and, incredibly, Humphreys declares the ransom money on his tax return, paying taxes on it.

WHITE-COLLAR CRIME

OCT. 3

Peter C. ''Paddy'' Barrie runs a ringer horse at Havre de Grace in France and gleans more than $1 million in bets.

MISCELLANEOUS

JAN. 5

Film star Alma Ruben is arrested for smuggling drugs; she will never go to trial, dying of an overdose on Jan. 21.

JAN. 26

Millions of dollars in losses result from arson fires set by revolutionaries in Buenaventura, Colombia.

MARCH 14

Inmates at the state prison at Joliet, Ill., riot over what prisoners claim is ''goat stew'' fed to them in the mess hall.

MARCH 15

Thomas E. Dewey is sworn in as assistant U.S. attorney in New York City. He will become the nemesis of organized crime in New York.

APRIL 20

Fred Blumer, brewery owner in Monroe, Wis., is kidnapped from his offices at gunpoint by several abductors, who will take him to Freeport, Ill., where he will be held until a large ransom is paid; the kidnappers will demand $150,000, but apparently this sum will be arbitrated; Blumer will be released unharmed and his kidnappers will never be detected.

JUNE 27

Garment tycoon Sam Sapphine burns down the Wonder Apparel Shop in New York City because, he states, his partner, Sol Cohen, has not paid for his share of the business.

SEPT. 23

Shanghai customs officials seize an enormous shipment of heroin on the docks. No arrests are made.

NOV. 30

Berlin police arrest August ''Little Augie'' Del Gracio as the Simplon Express arrives; they find 250 kilos of morphine in his luggage.

DEC. 11

Frank ''Jelly'' Nash, who has earlier escaped from Leavenworth, finances a break engineered by Monk Fountain, who has just been paroled from the penitentiary; Fountain ships a box of shoe paste to the prison shoe factory (he knows the shoe paste boxes are never inspected by guards) and secrets five pistols inside, along with a dismantled rifle and sawed-off shotgun and some dynamite bombs, marking the box with a symbol certain convicts will recognize; these weapons are recovered by seven prisoners, who force their way out of the penitentiary, using warden Tom White as a hostage; within 24 hours Tom Underwood, Charles Berta, and Stanley Brown are recaptured, and Whitey Lewis is shot while running through a cornfield; Bill Green and Grover Durrill shoot themselves as posses close in; Earl ''Dad'' Thayer is the last to surrender; it marks the end of the old Al Spencer holdup gang.

DEC. 28

The S.S. *Ceres*, from Istanbul, docks in Hamburg, and customs officials seize 1,513 kilograms of raw opium in a consignment of gum. No arrests are made.

MURDER

JAN. 5

A hopeless drunk named Michael Malloy is selected by five men in the Bronx, N.Y., to die so they can collect large sums of money from insurance policies they have taken out on him; they poison him with horse liniment and turpentine; one of the conspirators runs him over with his taxi; however, Malloy appears indestructible; the killers strip him while he is in a stupor, dump him at the Bronx Zoo, spray him with water and leave him to freeze; Malloy appears the next day in a Bronx bar complaining of a headache; disgusted, the killers finally gas Malloy to death and put in for the insurance money; all five are detected and turn on each other, Harry Green exposing the plot first and gaining immunity; the four others—Tony Marino, Dan Kreisberg, Joe Murphy and Frank Pasqua—will be electrocuted in Sing Sing in 1934.

MARCH 5

Rhodes Cecil Cowle, the 20-year-old son of Mrs. Daisy Louisa Cowle de Melker, who lives in Germiston, a suburb of Johannesburg, South Africa, dies in agony; doctors quickly determine that he has been poisoned by arsenic; his mother is identified by a local pharmacist as having bought the poison; Mrs. de Melker, investigators learn, has been married three times, her first two husbands dying under mysterious circumstances; their bodies will be exhumed and found to be loaded with poison; Mrs. de Melker will be found guilty of killing William Cowle in 1923 and Robert Sproat in 1927; she had collected considerable insurance money on both and murdered her son when he began blackmailing her, threatening to inform authorities how she murdered her first two husbands unless she gave him most of her savings; Mrs. de Melker will be found guilty in a speedy trial and will be hanged on Dec. 30.

MARCH 7

A trunk delivered to a Philadelphia rooming house is opened by suspicious police because of its strange odor; it contains the body of a white-haired woman who has been strangled; she is identified as the wealthy Mrs. Mamie Schaaf of Atlantic City, N.J., who owns a boardinghouse; police discover that one of her tenants, Louis Fine, has disappeared; in his rooms they find an express receipt for the trunk, which has been sent to a man named Henry Miller; other documents reveal that Fine and Miller are one and the same; Fine returns to the Atlantic City rooming house, where he is arrested; faking a heart attack, he is sent to a hospital, where he is shown Mrs. Schaaf's will, which names him as sole beneficiary; displaying amazing recuperative abilities, Fine leaps from his hospital bed to examine the document, blurting: "The old fool! I wanted her to give me some money—it was the only way I could get it." Fine will be sent to the electric chair later in the year.

MARCH 18

Herman Drenth of Clarksburg, W. Va., is hanged for murdering five women, but the toll of this American Bluebeard may be as high as 50; Drenth roamed the country for 20 years, pretending to be a used-furniture salesman, marrying well-to-do widows for their money in Washington, Massachusetts, Illinois and other states, returning with his victims to Clarksburg, where he had a concrete blockhouse rigged up to gas his victims to death; he often took a hammer or an ax to them; when police finally inspected this "operations room," as Drenth called it, they found it coated with blood; Drenth's own wife knows nothing of her husband's double life; he was captured because the black smoke periodically belching from his blockhouse with its terrible odor finally drew the attention of police, who found the bodies of Mrs. Asta Buick Eicher and her three children and those of four other women buried in shallow graves near the blockhouse; Drenth merely shrugged when confronted, saying: "You've got me on five. What good would 50 more do?"

APRIL 30

Will Carter, who owns a roadhouse restaurant outside Rochingham, N.C., opens his front door to loud knocking late at night and is shot dead by two men; Mrs. Carter rushes in to scream: "Why did you shoot him?" They flee, and Mrs. Carter later picks out from police photos a picture of Clay Fogelman, who escaped prison some months earlier with another bootlegger, Jimmy Napier; deputies later will kill Napier in a gunfight and capture Fogelman, who will be tried for killing Carter; it will be learned that the motive for the murder is revenge—Carter, having years earlier informed police that Fogelman was a bootlegger, was repsonsible for his imprisonment; Fogelman will be executed at the state prison at Raleigh, N.C., on Sept. 10.

JULY 5

Zachary Smith Reynolds, heir to a more than $30 million tobacco fortune, is shot to death at his palatial estate at Winston-Salem, N.C.; his wife, Libby Holman, onetime torch singer, will be charged with the crime and claim that he shot himself out of "despondency." She will be acquitted when the family drops all charges, but the death of the tycoon remains unsolved.

AUG. 29

Frank J. Egan, San Francisco's public defender, orders two ex-convicts in his employ to run over wealthy widow Mrs. Jessie Scott Hughes so that he can gain her inheritance; police grill Verne Doran, Egan's chauffeur, who admits that he and Albert Tinnin have murdered the widow on Egan's orders; all three men are sent to San Quentin for life.

SEPT. 16-17

Donald Ross, a British businessman living in a villa at Maison Lefitte in Paris, is found brutally murdered, his skull crushed; French police first think that Ross has been the victim of spies because he has served in British Intelligence during World War I; the case will not be solved until Dec. 1932, when three burglars—Adolphe Guillemenot, René Anchisi and Serge Sauvageot—are arrested; while in their cell, one of them passes a loaf of bread to another in such a way that a guard becomes suspicious and grabs the loaf, finding inside a note that reads: "Don't forget you were not in Paris September 16." Backtracking, police realize that this is the date of Ross's death; the burglars are interrogated and confess the murder, saying that they had met the victim on a train; he was drunk and invited them to his villa for more drinks; when he went to sleep they looted the place, and they killed him when he stirred to "keep him quiet"; all three are sent to French Guiana to serve 20 years; they will be released in 1955.

OCT. 23

Winnie Ruth Judd flies into a rage at her friends Mrs. Agnes Leroi and Miss Helwig "Sammy" Samuelson and kills both, chopping up their bodies and shipping them from Phoenix, Ariz., to Los Angeles. When she comes to pick up the trunk in Los Angeles, suspicious freight handlers ask why the trunk is seeping blood; Winnie panics and flees but soon is picked up by police; she will be tried for the ax murders on Nov. 12 and will go to prison for life; she will be paroled, after many escapes, in 1971.

DEC. 9

Patrolman Frank Lundy is shot dead when he interrupts a Chicago holdup; despite weak evidence, Joseph Majczek is found guilty and sent to prison for 99 years; his scrubwoman mother takes out a newspaper ad in 1944 offering a reward for the identification of the real killer of Officer Lundy; James McGuire of the *Sun* begins to investigate, and he proves that the evidence against Majczek has been rigged; he is released, later to be profiled in the motion picture *Call Northside 777*. The actual murderer is never discovered.

ROBBERY

FEB. 2

Clyde Barrow is paroled from the Texas State Penitentiary at Huntsville after serving a term for burglary.

FEB. 11

Pretty Boy Floyd escapes a police trap in Tulsa, Okla.

FEB. 17

Baby Face Nelson escapes from the Illinois State Prison at Joliet, going to Los Angeles to work for local bootlegger Joe Parente; here Nelson will meet John Paul Chase, who will remain with the psychotic bank robber until his violent death in 1934.

MARCH 9

Adam Richetti, sometime bankrobbing partner of Charles "Pretty Boy" Floyd, is arrested for bank robbery as he walks down a street in Sulphur, Okla.; he will be taken to the state penitentiary at McAlester, where his lawyers will later be able to free him on a $15,000 bond; he will promptly jump bail and join up with Floyd once again on a bank-robbing spree.

MARCH 25

Clyde Barrow robs the Sims Oil Company offices in Dallas, Tex., of $300.

APRIL 7

Pretty Boy Floyd kills a special investigator for the State of Oklahoma, Erv A. Kelley, while evading police near Bixby, Okla.

JUNE 17

Fred Barker, Alvin Karpis, Phil Courtney, Larry Devol, Tommy Holden and Harvey Bailey rob the Fort Scott (Kan.) Bank of $47,000 in cash and bonds.

JULY 7

FBI agents acting on a tip arrest Tommy Holden, Francis Keating and Harvey Bailey, all notorious bank robbers, as they play golf at the Old Mission Country Club outside Kansas City; all are prison escapees and will be returned behind bars, Bailey making several additional escapes before he will be finally recaptured and sent to Leavenworth for life, erroneously blamed for the 1933 kidnapping of Charles F. Urschel of Oklahoma City (a job engineered by George "Machine Gun" Kelly; his wife, Kathryn; and Albert Bates).

JULY 25

Fred Barker, with Alvin Karpis, Frank Nash, Larry Devol, Earl Christman and Jess Doyle, rob the Cloud County Bank in Concordia, Kan., taking more than $250,000.

AUG. 5

Clyde Barrow kills Sheriff C. G. Maxwell and Deputy Sheriff Eugene Moore at a barn dance in Atoka, Okla., after the lawmen recognize him.

AUG. 8

Fred Barker, with Volney Davis and Larry Devol, robs the Citizens Security Bank at Bixby, Okla., of $1,000.

AUG. 12

Bonnie Parker, recently released from jail for harboring Clyde Barrow, rejoins Barrow and takes Sheriff Joe Johns of Carlsbad, N.M., hostage, finally releasing him in San Antonio, Tex.

SEPT. 27

Arthur "Dock" Barker is paroled from the Oklahoma State Penitentiary by Governor William H. "Alfalfa Bill" Murray; Barker immediately joins his mother and his brother Fred in planning bank robberies and kidnappings that will capture headlines across the country.

OCT. 8

Bonnie Parker and Clyde Barrow, his brother Buck Barrow (who escaped from Eastham Prison in Texas on March 2, 1930), Ray Hamilton and W. D. Jones rob the Abilene State Bank of $1,400 in Abilene, Tex.

NOV. 1

Pretty Boy Floyd, Aussie Elliott and George Birdwell rob the Sallisaw Bank in Sallisaw, Okla., of $2,530. Floyd calmly parks his getaway car at the end of the one-street town and, cradling a machine gun, walks down the street to the bank; several farmers sitting on chairs recognize him and wave. Says one: "Howdy, Chock [Floyd's nickname]. Where you headed?" "Goin' to rob the bank," replies Floyd. "Give 'em hell, Chock!" shouts another farmer.

NOV. 7

Pretty Boy Floyd, Aussie Elliott and George Birdwell rob the bank at Henryetta, Okla., taking $11,352.20.

NOV. 9

Bonnie Parker, Clyde Barrow and others rob the bank in Orenogo, Mo., taking $200.

NOV. 30

Pretty Boy Floyd, Aussie Elliott and George Birdwell rob the Citizen's State Bank of Tupelo, Miss., of $50,000.

DEC. 16

Arthur "Dock" Barker, Fred Barker, Alvin Karpis, Jess Doyle, Bill Weaver, Verne Miller and Larry Devol rob the Third Northwestern Bank of Minneapolis, Minn., taking $20,000 and killing two policemen in pursuit of their speeding cars.

DEC. 23

In Temple, Tex., Clyde Barrow steals a car, killing its owner, Doyle Johnson.

ORGANIZED CRIME

FEB. 20

Bootlegger Abe Wagner, an ally of Dutch Schultz, is fired upon by several members of a youthful gang led by Vincent "Mad Dog" Coll; Wagner escapes.

FEB. 25

Abie Loeb and Al Gordon, bootleggers, are shot and killed by two men in St. Paul, Minn., near a speakeasy; two men are picked up running two blocks away and give their names as Joe Schaefer and George Young; some hours later, two guns are found, and the prints on them match those of John Newman and Albert I. Silverberg, hit men wanted for murdering federal Prohibition agent John G. Finiello on Sept. 9, 1930, during a raid on a brewery in Elizabeth, N.J.; both Silverberg and Newman are convicted and sent to prison for life.

MARCH 16

Antonio Lonzo and Gerard Vernotico, two Old Guard Mafia leaders, are gunned down on orders of Vito Genovese in Manhattan.

APRIL 19

Meyer Lansky and Lucky Luciano are arrested on suspicion at the Congress Hotel in Chicago, among many Chicago and out-of-town gangsters; all are released, and it is reported that this is the first meeting of the crime cartel in Chicago, an organizational meeting at which it is decided Chicago will function under the direction of Frank "The Enforcer" Nitti (who is Capone's right-hand man) while Capone serves time for income-tax evasion; Nitti will sit on the national board of the newly formed crime syndicate.

SEPT. 1

Samuel Seabury's investigation into New York City corruption leads to the resignation of Mayor James J. Walker, the town's leading playboy.

Jimmy LaFontaine, leading gambling club operator in Washington, D.C., is kidnapped by Philadelphia gangsters and held for $100,000 ransom; the amount is delivered and the gambler is released unharmed.

NOV. 25

Joe Valachi and three others murder Michael "Little Apples" Reggione in Manhattan.

WHITE-COLLAR CRIME

MARCH 4

William Elmer Mead, using his Magic Wallet scam (whereby a sucker finds a wallet loaded with important papers, letters from the President, etc., and comes to believe that the owner is an important man, a millionaire whose schemes are genuine), bilks a financier in St. Louis, Mo., for more than $200,000.

OCT. 19

Forger Charles J. Drossner is sent to the Wisconsin State penitentiary at Waupun, where his fingerprints are routinely sent to Washington and Scotland Yard; his prints, the Yard later reports, match that of José de Braganca, a notorious international forger and swindler wanted in Paris and Rome; after serving his short sentence in Wisconsin, de Braganca will be sent to Europe to serve a life sentence.

MISCELLANEOUS

JAN. 19

Wealthy banking firm owner Benjamin Bower is kidnapped and then ransomed for $50,000 in rural Colorado by unknown kidnappers.

MARCH 1

Charles A. Lindbergh, Jr., 20-month-old son of the legendary American flier, is kidnapped from his home in Hopewell, N.J., by Bruno Richard Hauptmann, who demands $70,000 in ransom after he has killed the child; he collects $50,000 in a series of meetings with go-between Dr. John F. Condon; the body of the Lindbergh baby will not be found until May 12.

JUNE 30

Haskell Bohn, 22-year-old son of a rich St. Paul, Minn., manufacturer, is kidnapped and held for $12,000 ransom. He will be released unharmed and his kidnappers will never be apprehended. (The kidnappers originally demanded $35,000, "haggling like fishmongers," but settled for less than half of that amount.)

DEC. 12

Willie "The Actor" Sutton and John Eagan break out of Sing Sing, sawing through bars and wriggling into a corridor, picking the lock on the prison's mess hall and going into the mess hall's cellar, then out a cellar doorway to the yard and, using a homemade ladder, over the wall, where a waiting auto takes them to New York City.

1·9·3·3

MURDER

FEB. 6

Ernest Brown, a 35-year-old groom working for Frederick Ellison Morton on a Yorkshire, England, farm, shotguns his employer to death, then sets fire to the victim as he sits in his car inside his garage; officers inspecting the remains of Morton, dead by accidental fire they are told by Brown, find the shotgun wounds and arrest the groom, who has been carrying on a torrid affair with Mrs. Dorothy Morton; Brown will be hanged at Armley Prison, in Leeds on Feb. 6, 1934, uttering moments before his death either the words "ought to burn" or "Otterburn." If the latter words were spoken, Brown may have been referring to the burning death of Evelyn Foster and may have been her mysterious murderer in 1931.

FEB. 15

President-elect Franklin D. Roosevelt is almost killed when Giuseppe Zangara, an unemployed millhand from New Jersey, fires at his open touring car as it slowly moves through dense, cheering crowds in Miami, Fla.; two of the bullets fired by Zangara strike Chicago Mayor Anton J. Cermak, who will die from these wounds on March 6; Zangara, an illiterate, embittered anarchist, intended to kill Roosevelt, not Cermak, although some will later claim that Zangara was in the pay of the Chicago mob, which Cermak was vigorously attempting to wipe out; however, he will say, minutes before going to the electric chair on March 21, concerning FDR: "If I got out I would kill him at once."

MARCH 17

Police in Covington, Ky., stop a car to check on an expired license, and the driver, Charles Burke, suddenly slashes his wrists; he is dead before arriving at a hospital; in his car police find the dismembered body of his wife, Ella, packed in small jars; Burke, police later will learn, murdered and chopped up his wife in their luxurious New York City apartment after she sued him for divorce and began to see a younger man; he drove from New York City, throwing out her remains in the jars along his route.

AUG. 7

A trunk arriving in Kobe, Japan, on board the *Shanghai Maru* and labeled "Q. T. Man," who is not on the passenger list, is opened; authorities find the murdered corpse of a young Eurasian girl jammed in-side; Shanghai police are notified, and they quickly backtrack the shipment of the trunk to two brothers, Joseph and Patricio Remedios; in the brothers' Shanghai, China, home police will find the name "Q. T. Man" written on a blotter and in the same handwriting as on the trunk; Patricio Remedios will break down and admit killing the young woman, Choy Ling, known also as Mary Chin, his mistress, after a violent argument; Remedios will be sentenced to 20 years' hard labor in the penal colony on the island of Timor in the Dutch East Indies.

SEPT. 2

Kenneth Neu, a young, unemployed singer, is picked up in Times Square by wealthy Lawrence Shead, whom he kills in his New York City hotel room, stealing Shead's money and slipping on his best suit, then fleeing to New Orleans, where he kills hardware store owner Sheffield Clark, Sr.; with Clark's money and car, Neu attempts to drive to New Jersey but is stopped and arrested; he almost gleefully admits to the two murders and proudly tells officers that he is wearing Shead's suit, the one in which he will be hanged on Feb. 1, 1935, after singing a song on the scaffold that he has written for his own execution: "I'm Fit as a Fiddle and Ready to Hang."

OCT. 16

Mrs. Christobel Bayly is found dead in a duck pond on her farm 60 miles from Auckland, New Zealand; she has been raped and strangled, and her husband, William Alfred Bayly, is missing; a neighbor, Samuel Pender Lakey, tells police that the couple were always quarreling—an untruth, according to other neighbors; Lakey even suggests that Bayly has murdered his wife; suspicious police find human hair, bone and bits of flesh in Lakey's house, then discover Bayly's watch and cigarette lighter in Lakey's possession; Lakey will be tried and convicted of killing the Bayleys, and hanged in Auckland on July 20, 1934.

NOV. 21

Dr. Alice Wynekoop of Chicago kills her daughter-in-law, Rheta Gardner Wynekoop; Dr. Wynekoop, who has never approved of her playboy son's wife, claims that she examined her for surgery in her own home for abdominal pains and gave her too much chloroform; to cover this error, Dr. Wynekoop then claims, she fired a bullet into the young woman to make it appear that she has been killed by intruders; she will be sent to prison for life at age 63, will serve 14 years and be paroled in 1949, dying two years later.

May 8, the Barrow gang will rob the Lucerne State Bank in Lucerne, Ind., of $300; on May 16, they will rob the First State Bank of Okabena, Minn., taking $1,500.

Killer Kenneth Neu, still wearing one of his victim's suits, listens to his death sentence; he will be hanged after composing a song for the occasion. (Sept. 2, 1933)

Bonnie Parker playfully "gets the drop" on Clyde Barrow in a snapshot taken by Clyde's brother Buck somewhere in rural Texas. (Jan. 6, 1933)

DEC. 6

Ernest D'Iorio strangles Jennie Zablecki in Detroit because, he later tells police, she has told his girl-friend not to marry him.

ROBBERY

JAN. 6

Clyde Barrow and Bonnie Parker narrowly escape a police trap in Dallas, killing Deputy Sheriff Malcolm Davis. On April 13 the Barrow gang escape a police trap in Joplin, Mo., after a wild shoot-out in which Clyde and Buck Barrow shotgun to death policemen Wes Harryman and Harry L. McGinnis, as the gang crash their car through a garage door, smash into several police cars blocking their way and speed off; on

MAY 22

John Herbert Dillinger, inmate 13225, is paroled from the Michigan City Prison in Indiana, thanks to a petition signed by hundreds of his townspeople in Mooresville, Ind., including the judge who originally sentenced him for attempted robbery in 1924; on June 10, Dillinger, Paul "Lefty" Parker and William Shaw will rob the National Bank of New Carlisle, Ind., taking $10,600.

JUNE 16

FBI agents and local police arrest Frank "Jelly" Nash in the White Front Poolhall in Hot Springs, Ark., spiriting the bank robber to a waiting car before he can signal confederates; Nash has been caught wearing an expensive red wig (he is bald and asks agents not to manhandle the toupee—"It cost me two hundred bucks!").

JUNE 22

The Barrow gang robs the Alma State Bank in Alma, Tex., taking a few hundred dollars; on the following day, Bonnie Parker and Clyde Barrow will rob a Piggly Wiggly store in Fayetteville, Tex., obtaining about $50, then will kill Marshal H. D. Humphrey when he pursues them.

JULY 6

James "Fur" Sammons (so named because of his penchant for robbing expensive furs from stores and warehouses) is arrested by Sheriff Tom Bash and six FBI agents in a rented Kansas City house; more than $8,000 is found on Sammons, who is wanted for robbing International Harvester Company of $85,000 in Chicago in 1926 and for a $47,000 fur robbery in Baltimore, Md.; he is one of the "big fish" caught in the dragnet thrown out for the machine gunners of the Kansas City Massacre; Sammons will receive a long prison sentence.

JULY 17

Dillinger and Harry Copeland rob the Commercial Bank of Daleville, Ind., taking $3,500.

JULY 18

The Barrow gang robs three gasoline stations in Fort Dodge, Iowa, getting less than $100. Dillinger, when reading of these Barrow robberies, says to his gang members: "They're punks—they're giving bank-robbing a bad name."

JULY 24

The Barrow gang is surrounded by a 200-man posse in a picnic grounds outside Dexter, Iowa; in an incredible three-hour gun battle, Buck Barrow is wounded six times, dying five days later; Blanche Barrow is captured with him, while W. D. Jones, Bonnie Parker and Clyde Barrow, all wounded, escape.

AUG. 4

Dillinger and Harry Copeland rob the First National Bank of Montpelier, Ind., taking $10,110; on Aug. 14, Dillinger, Harry Copeland and Sam Goldstein will rob the Citizens National Bank in Bluffton, Ohio, taking $2,100.

AUG. 15

Arthur "Dock" Barker, his brother Fred, Larry Devol, Alvin Karpis and Charles J. Fitzgerald rob the Swift Company payroll in St. Paul, Minn., taking $30,000; on Aug. 22, Dock and Fred Barker, Monty Bolton, Fred "Shotgun Ziegler" Goetz, and Bill "Lapland Willie" Weaver will rob a Federal Reserve mail truck in Chicago, getting several sacks of useless

canceled checks and killing policeman Miles A. Cunningham in the process.

SEPT. 6

Dillinger, Harry Copeland and Hilton Crouch rob the Massachusetts Avenue State Bank of Indianapolis, Ind., taking $24,000; on Sept. 22, Dillinger will be arrested in the Dayton, Ohio, apartment of his girlfriend, Mary Longnaker, and taken to Lima, Ohio, to stand trial for the Bluffton bank robbery of Aug. 14.

SEPT. 26

Ten of the toughest bank robbers in Michigan City, Ind., State Prison break out, a break engineered weeks earlier by John Dillinger, who has smuggled guns into the prison inside a specially marked thread box; escaping are Dillinger's close prison friends and seasoned bank robbers Harry Pierpont, Charles "Fat Charley" Makley, John "Three-Finger Jack" Hamilton, Russell Clark and other prisoners, including James "Oklahoma Jack" Clark, Walter Dietrich, James Jenkins, Joseph Burns, Joseph Fox and Edward Shouse; once in hiding, Pierpont, Makley, Clark and Hamilton make plans to free Dillinger from the Lima, Ohio, jail; on Oct. 3, Harry Pierpont, John Hamilton, Charles Makley, Russell Clark and Edward Shouse will rob the First National Bank in St. Mary's, Ohio, taking $14,000, which will be used to finance Dillinger's release from the Lima jail; on Oct. 12, Dillinger will be freed from the Lima jail by Pierpont, Makley and Clark, who first pretend to be officers coming from Indiana to interrogate Dillinger; Sheriff Jess Sarber demands credentials and Harry Pierpont produces a gun, saying, "These are our credentials." When Sarber tries to shove the gun away from his face, Pierpont shoots him twice and Makley hits him on the head with the butt of his gun; Dillinger is released minutes later from his cell by Pierpont; Dillinger pauses to see Sarber dying on the floor and asks Pierpont, "Did you have to do that?" Pierpont does not answer as they all flee; Sarber dies a few minutes later. On Oct. 20, Dillinger, Pierpont and others visit the police arsenal in Peru, Ind., saying they are reporters inspecting weapons that might be used against the Dillinger gang; custodian Ambrose Clark happily shows them the arsenal and is promptly held at gunpoint while the gang takes submachine guns, shotguns, pistols, rifles and many bags of ammunition. On Oct. 23, Dillinger, Pierpont, Hamilton, Clark and Makley rob the Central National Bank of Greencastle, Ind., taking $75,346; the technique employed is the time system established by Herman K. Lamm, with Makley standing guard at the door with a stopwatch, calling "time" after five minutes, and Dillinger, leaping over the six-foot-high tellers' cages, cleaning out the tellers' drawers, Pierpont emptying the vault, and Hamilton, Clark and Edward Shouse waiting at the wheel of the getaway car parked in front of the bank; during this robbery Dillinger spots a farmer with $50 in his hand and asks: "Is that your money or the banks's?'' ''Mine,'' replies the farmer. ''Keep it,'' Dillinger says cavalierly, ''we only want the bank's.'' (This Robin Hood-like act will later be wrongfully attributed to Bonnie Parker and Clyde Barrow.)

NOV. 2

Wilbur Underhill, Ford Bradshaw and others rob the Citizens' National Bank at Okmulgee, Okla., taking $13,000.

NOV. 15

A U.S. mail truck carrying $100,000 in old $5 bills is stopped a few blocks from the train depot in Charlotte, N.C., by four bandits wielding submachine guns and is looted; Charlotte police find the hideout of the holdup gang and identify the bandits through fingerprints left on a beer bottle; Basil ''The Owl'' Banghart and ''Hill Billy'' Costner will be arrested on Feb. 11, 1934, in Baltimore for the robbery, carrying $13,000 of the stolen bills, and will be sent to prison to serve long terms; ''Dutch Louie'' Schmidt will be captured 10 weeks later and sent to prison for 32 years; Charles ''Ice Wagon'' Connors, who has left his prints on the beer bottle, is found in late spring in a Chicago suburb, shot to pieces gangland style.

Two Chicago police detectives spot Dillinger and his new girlfriend, Evelyn ''Billie'' Frechette, driving down Irving Park Road and give chase, shooting at the bandit; Dillinger outdistances them in his souped-up Terraplane and escapes. On Nov. 20, Dillinger, Pierpont, Makley, Clark and Hamilton rob the American Bank & Trust Co. of Racine, Wis., taking $20,736.

NOV. 22

Bonnie Parker and Clyde Barrow narrowly escape a pursuing posse near Grand Prairie, Tex.

ORGANIZED CRIME

APRIL 12

Dutch Schultz gunmen burst into a bedroom of the Carteret Hotel in Elizabeth, N.J., and shoot to death Maxey Greenberg and Mandel Gassell as they sleep; their boss, Waxey Gordon (Irving Wexler), with whom Schultz has been carrying on a bottleg war in New Jersey, is in the next room; hearing the shots, Gordon flees.

APRIL 24

Gunmen working for Louis ''Lepke'' Buchalter in-

vade the New York City headquarters of the Fur & Leather Workers Union, where one gunman and a union worker are killed; the union has resisted coming under the domination of Lepke.

JUNE 27

Chicago gangster Murray ''The Camel'' Humphreys flees to Mexico after being indicted for income-tax evasion; he will be returned to Chicago 16 months later, fined $5,000 and sent to prison for 18 months.

JUNE 29

Mob-controlled giant without a punch Primo Carnera, who has been ballyhooed as unbeatable in the ring and who has racked up an impressive list of winning fights, all staged by the mob, allegedly knocks out heavyweight champion Jack Sharkey with a phantom punch in the sixth round of the championship fight in Long Island City, N.Y.; sports experts insist to this day that Sharkey took ''a dive''; After milking Carnera, who thought he had legitimately won the crown, the mob will put him into the ring with Max Baer, who will beat him to a pulp the following year, taking the championship; mobsters will then siphon off all of Carnera's fabulous winnings and send him home to Italy where, at Sequals on June 29, 1967, he will die without a dime.

AUG. 12

Ferris Anthon, a lieutenant of Joe Lusco, who has been trying to take over the bootleg territory controlled by Johnny Lazia in Kansas City, is shot to death in broad daylight as he is about to enter his home at the Cavalier Apartments; his killers, Sam Scola and Gus Fascone, Lazia gangsters, are caught by police arriving on the scene and both are killed as they attempt to flee.

SEPT. 4

Fulgencio Batista takes over Cuba, cementing relationships with Meyer Lansky, who will be given all gambling concessions on the island, kicking back $1 million a year to the dictator.

NOV. 20

Al Silverman, a wealthy businessman, is found dangling from a fence in Somers, Conn., his throat cut, his face battered, a victim of New York City's Murder, Inc.

NOV. 25

Abe ''Kid Twist'' Reles, Frank ''The Dasher'' Abbandando, Harry ''Happy'' Maione and Harry ''Pittsburgh Phil'' Strauss murder Alex ''Red'' Alpert in New York City, another ''hit'' for Murder, Inc.

NOV. 29

The naked, bullet-ridden body of Vern Miller, one of the machine gunners at the Union Station in the Kansas City Massacre, is found in a roadside ditch outside Detroit; it is speculated that Miller was killed because he took money to free Frank ''Jelly'' Nash from the custody of officers at the station and instead killed him and fled; Miller's body bore burn marks indicating that he had been tortured before his death with hot irons and cigarettes; police officials credit the murder to the notorious Purple Gang of Detroit.

WHITE-COLLAR CRIME

MARCH 12

Ivar Kreuger, the ''Swedish Match King,'' is exposed, along with the Italian bonds he has forged many years earlier and which he has used as collateral to take out enormous loans to buy match companies; Kreuger, who may be the most colossal swindler of the 20th century after bilking more than $200 million from government and personal investors in his bogus corporation stock, uses a dueling pistol once owned by Napoleon Bonaparte to commit suicide in his lavish Paris apartment.

DEC. 24

Serge Alexandre Stavisky, an international con man who has bilked the French government and private investors of millions of francs in phony stocks, is exposed and disappears; several highly positioned officials commit suicide or are murdered, and the Chautemps cabinet collapses in the financial scandal; Stavisky, French police later will report, has committed suicide in a Chamonix resort hotel on Jan. 8, 1934, but many will believe that he has been murdered so as not to expose other French cabinet members and financiers who have been in collusion with his schemes.

MISCELLANEOUS

FEB. 12

Charles Boettcher II, a millionaire broker in Denver, Colo., is kidnapped from his home but quickly released after a ransom of $60,000 is paid; Verne Sankey, who heads a robbery gang with Gordon Alcorn, and others are later tracked down and sent to prison, given long terms for the kidnapping.

Ivar Kreuger, "the Swedish Match King" and colossal swindler, committed suicide when his scams were exposed. (March 12, 1933)

MAY 27-28

Mary McElroy, 25-year-old daughter of the city manager of Kansas City, Judge H. F. McElroy, is kidnapped from her home at gunpoint by Walter McGee and Clarence Stevens, pretending to be deliverymen; Miss McElroy, chained to the inside of the speeding delivery truck, is taken to the farmhouse of Clarence Click, where McGee, his brother George, Click and Stevens provide their victim with clean sheets, a radio and serve her meals on a tray, apologizing for the crude cuisine; they demand $60,000 ransom be paid by Judge McElroy, who eventually pays $30,000; Miss McElroy is driven to the outskirts of Kansas City and given $1 by the courteous Walter McGee for bus transportation (the kidnappers have not even bothered to look in her purse, which contains several hundred dollars). All four kidnappers will be caught; three will be given long prison terms, and Walter McGee will be sentenced to death; according to James Henry ''Blackie'' Audett, in interviews with the author, he drove Mary McElroy to the state prison several times, (his job being a courier and bagman for the Pendergast-McElroy-Lazia combine), where Mary poured out her love for her kidnapper Walter McGee. She later pressured her father into begging for McGee's life in a special conference with the governor; this was granted and McGee's sentence was commuted to life imprisonment; following the death of her father and the collapse of the Pendergast Machine, Mary McElroy will go into seclusion, shooting herself on Jan. 20, 1940, apparently still pining for Walter McGee, who had no hope of prison release; her suicide note read:

> My four kidnappers are probably the only people on earth who don't consider me an utter fool. You have your death penalty now—so—please—give them another chance.
> Mary McElroy

MAY 31

Harvey Bailey escapes from the Kansas State Penitentiary with Wilbur Underhill, Big Bob Brady, Jim Clark and Ed Davis; Bailey splits from the Oklahoma bandits, who vanish into the Cookson Hills; he hides out at the broken-down ranch owned by R. G. ''Boss'' Shannon, at Paradise, Tex.; Shannon is stepfather to Katherine Kelly, wife of the infamous George ''Machine Gun'' Kelly; Bailey will be captured on the ranch by FBI agents on Aug. 12 and mistakenly charged with kidnapping Oklahoma oil man Charles Urschel, a crime committed by the Kellys, and sent to Leavenworth for life; Bailey will be paroled in 1965 and will die in 1979 as a retired 91-year-old cabinetmaker in Joplin, Mo.

JUNE 15-18

Arthur ''Dock'' Barker, his brother Fred, Alvin Karpis, Monty Bolton, Fred ''Shotgun Ziegler'' Goetz and Charles J. Fitzgerald kidnap millionaire brewer William A. Hamm, Jr., in St. Paul, Minn., collect $100,000 ransom and release their captive unharmed three days later; the Barker brothers and their ma then plan another series of bank robberies and kidnappings.

JUNE 16

Pretty Boy Floyd and Adam Richetti capriciously kidnap Sheriff Jack Killingsworth of Bolivar, Mo., dropping off the lawman days later near Kansas City, Mo., unharmed.

JUNE 17

Federal and state lawmen escorting Frank ''Jelly'' Nash back to Leavenworth are attacked by four machine gunners at Kansas City's Union Station; one of the gunmen, a heavyset man standing on the running board of a car parked opposite the police cars where lawmen stand (some have gotten into one car with their prisoner, Nash, who is wearing a red wig), shouts: ''Up! Up! Get 'em up!'' One of the lawmen fires a pistol at the gunman, and the machine gunner shouts: ''Let 'em have it!'' A withering fusillade is opened up on the lawmen from two directions in the parking lot behind the depot; killed in the murderous crossfire are FBI agent Raymond Caffrey; Otto Reed, police chief of McAlester, Okla., who has captured Nash in Hot Springs, Ark., a notorious ''safe'' city for gangsters on the run; and Kansas City police detectives W. J. ''Red'' Grooms and Frank Hermanson; FBI agents F. J. Lackey and R. E. Vetterli are wounded; one of the machine gunners is wounded, but all four attacking

gangsters escape; also killed is Frank ''Jelly'' Nash who, it is later claimed, is not recognized because of the red wig agents compelled him to wear; the Kansas City Massacre slayers are identified by the FBI as Adam Richetti and Charles Arthur ''Pretty Boy'' Floyd, but this is in error; the real killers, as stated to the author by eyewitness James Henry ''Blackie'' Audett years later, are Verne Miller, William ''Solly'' Weissman and the brothers Maurice and Homer Denning. (The FBI will relentlessly hunt down Floyd for the mass slaying and, will hang Richetti.)

JULY 11

Jake ''The Barber'' Factor, a Capone ally, is allegedly kidnapped by Roger Touhy and his gang; Touhy later will be convicted of this apparently phony kidnapping and sent to prison for life in Illinois for a crime he never committed.

JULY 14

Forty Chicago millionaires are put under 24-hour police guard because of the kidnapping epidemic raging throughout the nation.

JULY 22

Katherine and George ''Machine Gun'' Kelly and Albert Bates kidnap millionaire oilman Charles F. Urschel in Oklahoma City, holding him for $200,000; when it is collected, Urschel is released unharmed; agents will arrest Bates in Denver, and he will be sent to prison for life; the Kellys will be captured in Memphis on Sept. 26 by local police; Memphis Detective Sgt. W. J. Raney, not the FBI, will arrest Kelly, and Kelly will never shout: ''Don't shoot, G-Men!'' as FBI Director J. Edgar Hoover will later claim; Kelly will die in his Leavenworth cell in 1954; Katherine Kelly, the real brains behind the gang, will be released in 1958 and will disappear.

NOV. 9

Thomas Harold Thurmond and John Maurice Holmes kidnap Brooke Hart, 22-year-old son of a wealthy hotel and department store owner in San Jose, Calif.; they kill Hart when unable to collect the ransom and later are captured and placed in the Santa Clara County Jail in San Jose, which on Nov. 26 will be stormed by more than 15,000 irate citizens; Thurmond and Holmes will be lynched, with the governor of California, James ''Sunny Jim'' Rolfe, applauding the action of the mob, stating: ''I would like to parole all kidnappers in San Quentin and Folsom to the fine, patriotic citizens of San Jose.''

NOV. 18

New York City businessmen Dr. Jerome Garber and Sam Berliner are arrested for burning down buildings they own to collect insurance money; both are sent to prison to serve long terms.

1·9·3·4

MURDER

MARCH 3

Six persons—Mrs. and Mrs. Flieder and their guests, Mr. and Mrs. Cehovert, a man named Jordan and Bert Balcom—are tied up in their cottage in Erland Point, Wash., by Seattle thug Leo Hall, who robs the house, then crushes the skulls of all six persons before firing a bullet into each victim's head; Hall later will be turned in for the mass slaying by a distraught girlfriend and will be executed in 1935.

Eddie McDonald and Mickey Fallon rob a couple parked on New York City's Riverside Drive, shooting the man, Joe Arbona. They are dubbed "The Show-Off Killers" by the press and are quickly captured after their girlfriends turn them in; Fallon gets 35 years in prison, McDonald 25 years.

APRIL 21

Mrs. Jeannie Donald beats eight-year-old Helen Pristly to death in Aberdeen, Scotland, molesting her after death, then putting the corpse into a sack and throwing it down the stairs of her apartment building; she is quickly convicted and sentenced to hang, but her sentence is commuted to life imprisonment, and she will be released in 1944.

MAY 23

Ethel Lillie Major, after repeated attempts, finally succeeds in poisoning her husband, Arthur, in Kirkby-on-Bain, Lincolnshire, England; when police rountinely interview her, Scotland Yard's Chief Inspector Hugh Young asks: "Do you think your husband might have been poisoned?" "I didn't know that my husband died of strychnine poisoning," replies Mrs. Major, a fact otherwise known only to the pathologist working on the body, Inspector Young and the murderer; Mrs. Major, for this fatal slip, will be hanged at Hull Jail on Dec. 19.

JULY 16

A mob in Bolton, Miss., lynches James Sanders, a 25-year-old black accused of writing abscene letters to a 16-year-old white girl.

JULY 25

In a Nazi attempt to take over Austria, Otto Planetta and other SS thugs rush into the Chancellory in Vienna and shoot Chancellor Englebert Dollfuss, who takes several hours to die, begging for a physician; the Nazi coup fails, and Planetta and other assassins are hanged, shouting "Heil Hitler!" from the scaffold.

JULY 30

Robert Allen Edwards, wanting to marry another woman, kills his fiancée, Freda McKechnie, when he discovers she is pregnant, insisting that she take a swim with him at night in Harvey's Lake, Pennsylvania (near Edwardsville); he crushes her skull with a blackjack as they swim, and she is dead before sinking; Edwards' clothes and blackjack later are found on the beach, and he is quickly convicted and executed the following year.

AUG. 13

Patrick "Paddy" Carraher, a drunken bully and brawler who has been in trouble with Glasgow, Scotland, police since 1923, gets into an argument with a young soldier, James Sydney Emden Shaw, stabbing Shaw to death; Carraher will plead drunkenness at his trial and will be found guilty of "culpable murder" (manslaughter) and sent to prison for only three years; in 1943 Carraher again will be arrested, for razor slashing and assault and battery; on Nov. 23, 1945, Carraher, again drunk, will kill another young soldier, John Gordon, this time paying with his life, at Barlinnie Prison, Glasgow, on April 6, 1946.

OCT. 9

King Alexander I of Yugoslavia is shot to death by Vlada Cheenozamsky, a Croation nationalist in the employ of Ante Pavelic, underground Croation leader, as his car slowly makes its way through crowds greeting him in Marseilles, France; shot with the king is Louis Barthou, the French foreign minister, who also dies hours later; the assassin is thrown to the ground immediately after firing into the car by policemen and shot in the head.

NOV. 5

In Kelayres, Pa., 50 persons are shot down from ambush as they march in a political parade; five are killed; the culprits are discovered to be members of the political opposition, led by John J. "Big Joe" Bruno, his brother Philip, his sons Alfred and James, and Tony Orlando, another relative; they are all given long prison terms.

NOV. 10

Following a boozy, aimless life, Elza Lay, onetime member of the Wild Bunch and western train robber, dies in El Paso, Tex.

NOV. 11

Charles Manson is born in Cincinnati, Ohio, to unwed mother Kathleen Moddox of Ashland, Ky.

ROBBERY

JAN. 1

Wilbur Underhill marries and moves into a honeymoon cottage in Shawnee, Okla., which is surrounded on New Year's Day by scores of FBI agents and local police, who open up a barrage that tears the house to pieces; Underhill fires rifles and pistols in return, diving out a window and, though wounded several times, staggers down the street and vanishes; agents find the bank robber lying on a display bed in a furniture store hours later; the "Tri-State Terror" will die on Jan. 6.

JAN. 16

Three on-and-off Barrow gang members, Raymond Hamilton, Joe Palmer and Henry Methvin, escape Eastham Prison in Texas.

JAN. 19

Big Bob Brady, who has escaped from the Kansas State Penitentiary and who has been robbing many banks over four months with James Henry "Blackie" Audett, is killed by a large posse near Paola, Kan.

JAN. 20

Clyde Barrow and Bonnie Parker rob the State Bank of Lancaster, Tex., getting only a few hundred dollars.

JAN. 25

Dillinger, Pierpont, Makley and Clark are arrested in Tucson, Ariz., by local police while vacationing; Dillinger is returned to Indiana to stand trial for murdering a policeman in a bank robbery in East Chicago, Ind., on Jan. 15, a robbery Dillinger could not have committed; Makley, Pierpont and Clark are sent to Ohio to face murder charges over the killing of Sheriff Jess Sarber when the mob broke Dillinger out of the Lima, Ohio, jail. (See "Robbery," March 3, 1934.)

FEB. 14

Willie "The Actor" Sutton is found guilty of bank robbery in Philadelphia and is sent to Eastern State Penitentiary to serve a 25-to-50-year sentence.

FEB. 17

More than 1,000 state police, local officers, FBI men and special deputies invade Cookson Hills, Okla., to clean out the many bandits hiding there; Bonnie Parker and Clyde Barrow blast their way through the ring of lawmen; Aussie Elliott and Raymond Moore are shot to death in a gun battle near Sapulpa; Ed Newt Clanton is trapped near Chelsea and is riddled; Pretty Boy Floyd and Adam Richetti escape the dragnet, slipping across the Arkansas line; Ford Bradshaw is

America's most notorious bank robber, John Dillinger, in 1934. (Jan. 25, 1934)

cornered near Arkoma and shoots it out toe-to-toe with Sheriff Will Harper, who shoots him through the head; it is the finish of the anachronistic outlaw bands of Oklahoma.

MARCH 3

John Dillinger carves a wooden gun from the top of a washboard and blackens it with boot polish to make it appear real in his Crown Point, Ind., jail cell where he is awaiting trial for murder and bank robbery, and cows guards into releasing him; he escapes the "escapeproof jail" with murderer Herbert Youngblood, using Sheriff Lillian Holley's car, the fastest in the state, and drives across the Illinois line; thus Dillinger commits interstate auto theft, his first federal offense, which the FBI uses to make Dillinger Public Enemy No. 1.

MARCH 5

Harry Wells robs the Citizens' State Bank of Luling, Tex., taking $2,482; FBI agents and local lawmen surround Wells' hideout in Gladwater, Tex., on March 15 and smoke him out; he is sent to prison for 99 years.

MARCH 6

Dillinger, with Baby Face Nelson, John Hamilton, Eddie Green, Tommy Carroll and Homer Van Meter, robs the Security National Bank in Sioux Falls, S.D., taking $49,000.

MARCH 13

Dillinger, Carroll, Hamilton, Nelson, Green and Van Meter rob the First National Bank of Mason City, Iowa, taking $52,000; Dillinger is wounded in the arm, Hamilton in the shoulder, when a retired cop fires at them from an open window (Meredith Willson, composer of *The Music Man,* is a young man on the street watching the robbery); all escape, but Hamilton later dies of his wounds and is secretly buried in a remote quarry by the gang, Dillinger pouring quicklime over him to disguise his identity.

APRIL 1

Clyde Barrow kills two state motorcycle policemen, E. G. Wheeler and H. D. Murphy, who interrupt a picnic he is having with Bonnie Parker's family near Grapevine, Tex.

APRIL 22

Melvin Purvis, agent in charge of the FBI office in Chicago, leads an abortive raid against the Little Bohemia Lodge at Manitowish Waters, Wis., to capture Dillinger and other gang members; agents shoot three CCC workers getting into a car in front of the lodge, one of whom, Eugene Boiseneau, will die later as a result (this slaying is subsequently and wrongly attributed to Dillinger), and shoot up the lodge's façade while the gang members slip out the back way and make good their escape; in his flight, Baby Face Nelson will shoot FBI agent W. Carter Baum to death the following day while commandeering his car near the Little Bohemia Lodge.

APRIL 28

Evelyn "Billie" Frechette, Dillinger's girlfriend, is captured at Little Bohemia Lodge; she will be fined $1,000 and sent to prison for two years for harboring Dillinger. (The lodge proprietor, Emil Wannatka, Sr., is not charged, having been an unwilling host to the gangsters, he later claims.)

MAY 23

Bonnie Parker and Clyde Barrow are betrayed by their own henchman, Henry Methvin, who sets up a police trap with Texas Ranger Frank Hamer and his men outside Gibsland, La.; the possee, using submachine guns, B.A.R.'s, shotguns and rifles, rake the bandit's car with hundreds of bullets, killing the notorious outlaws; Bonnie dies with a half-eaten sandwich in her mouth; Clyde is shoeless; he had been driving in his socks.

JUNE 30

Dillinger allegedly robs the Merchants National Bank of South Bend, Ind., with Pretty Boy Floyd and others, taking $18,000. (This is the last robbery, according to FBI officials, committed by Dillinger, although James Henry "Blackie" Audett has informed the author that he and Dillinger robbed at least a dozen banks in the Midwest from May 1 to June 15, gleaning more than $250,000.)

JULY 22

FBI agents under the command of Melvin Purvis in Chicago claim to have killed John Dillinger as he emerges from the Biograph Theater, but all evidence unearthed by the author and published in previous works points to the fact that Dillinger has not been killed and that another man, James Lawrence, has been set up by Anna Sage ("The Woman in Red"), Louis Piquett (Dillinger's lawyer) and members of the corrupt East Chicago, Ind., Police Deptartment, who have easily duped a too-eager Melvin Purvis; salient evidence here includes the autopsy of the man shot, the only copy of which was later given to the author, in which the dead man's eyes are clearly stated to be brown, while Dillinger's were blue; the dead man was also shorter and heavier than Dillinger would have been, and did not have any of Dillinger's known scars or recently received wounds; Dr. J. J. Kearns, Cook County chief pathologist, performs a flawless autopsy with another physician checking all his information and two medical assistants writing it all down in front of more than 40 other doctors in a classic irrefutable examination; on July 26, after giving his father $15,000 to have concrete mixed with scrap iron poured around the body buried in his name in an Indianapolis cemetery, Dillinger, with James Henry ''Blackie'' Audett, according to information supplied to the author by Audett in 1979, drives west to Klamath Falls, Ore., where Dillinger, with more than $200,000 from recent robberies, settles down, marrying an Indian girl from the reservation near Beatty, Ore. Audett will later claim, ''The last time I saw John was in 1972, when he was living in northern California.''

AUG. 21

Four bandits stop an armored car of the U.S. Trucking Corp. as it is making a payroll stop at the Rubel Ice Plant in Brooklyn and take $427,950; the bandits are later caught and given long prison terms but the money is never recovered.

OCT. 22

Charles Arthur ''Pretty Boy'' Floyd is killed by FBI agents in a gun battle outside East Liverpool, Ohio; with his dying breath, Floyd tells Melvin Purvis that he was not at the Kansas City Massacre.

NOV. 27

Baby Face Nelson kills two FBI agents, Sam Cowley and Herman Hollis, in a running gun battle outside Barrington, Ill.; Nelson is mortally wounded, and his wife, Helen, and John Paul Chase dump his naked body on the road some miles away before fleeing; Helen Gillis will be captured in Chicago on Nov. 29 and sent to prison for one year, John Paul Chase will be tracked down to a hideout on Mount Shasta, Calif., on Dec. 27 and sent to Alcatraz for life.

ORGANIZED CRIME

JULY 10

St. Louis underworld boss Johnny Lazia is murdered, some say on orders of Boss Tom Pendergast, who has learned that Lazia, recently convicted of tax evasion, is about to expose Pendergast.

OCT. 9

Vito Genovese orders the murder of old Mafia don Ferdinand ''The Shadow'' Boccia in New York City; Genovese will be indicted for the murder on Dec. 4 but will be released.

WHITE-COLLAR CRIME

FEB. 3

Joseph ''Yellow Kid'' Weil bilks a greedy financier of $50,000 while posing as the bank president of a deserted bank he has rented and resurrected for the scam in Chicago.

JULY 4

William J. Cressy, who will make millions through phony mail-order schemes, begins offering rare Indian head pennies that are actually fakes.

MISCELLANEOUS

JAN. 6

''Handsome Jack'' Klutas, a college graduate who leads a kidnapping gang in Chicago specializing in kidnapping underworld figures, is shot dead by Chicago police in the suburb of Bellwood.

JAN. 17

Arthur ''Dock'' Barker, his brother Fred, Alvin Karpis and others kidnap millionaire banker Edward G. Bremer, holding him for a $200,000 ransom and releasing him after receiving the money a few days later.

APRIL 25

June Robles, six-year-old daughter of a wealthy Mexican-American ranching family in Tucson, Ariz., is kidnapped and held for a $15,000 ransom. The child, with thousands searching for her, is found 19 days later in a pit dug out of the desert floor outside Tucson, chained to a wooden beam, half starved to death, eating scraps thrown to her by her kidnappers as one might throw bones to a dog. The kidnappers, who have collected no ransom, are never found.

MAY 9

Retired oilman and millionaire William F. Gettle is kidnapped from his Arcadia, Calif., home and is held for $80,000 ransom. Before this sum is paid the kidnappers' hideout is located and Gettle is rescued. Three men plead guilty to the kidnapping and are sent to San Quentin for life.

OCT. 10

Wealthy Mrs. Alice Speed Stoll is kidnapped by

mental defective Thomas Robinson, Jr.; Mrs. Stoll returns home in a few days; no ransom is paid, and Robinson is convicted and sent to prison for life.

NOV. 26

Outlaw Arthur Gooch, stopped for routine questioning near Paradise, Tex., by two officers, wounds one lawmen, then forces both men to drive him across the state line into Oklahoma. Gooch later will be caught, charged with kidnapping and be executed under tough new laws, the first person to be executed (hanged on June 19, 1936) for such an offense.

1·9·3·5

MURDER

MARCH 24

Francis Rattenbury, 67, a successful, semiretired architect living at the Villa Madeira in Bournemouth, England, is attacked in his sleep, his head crushed with an ice mallet by his 19-year-old chauffeur, George Stoner, who is having an affair with his employer's wife, Mrs. Alma Rattenbury, 31, mother of two; Mrs. Rattenbury, onetime lyric writer and a heavy drinker, has hired Stoner as a lover; when police are summoned by house servants, Mrs. Rattenbury is hysterical, playing jazz records, weaving about the sumptuous villa in a drunken state, alternately kissing embarrassed detectives and screaming, especially when she steps on and crushes her husband's dental plate, which has slipped from his mouth as he is carried to an ambulance en route to the hospital, where he dies; to shield her lover, Mrs. Rattenbury insists that she has committed the murder; her lover, meanwhile, in a police station, states that he alone killed Rattenbury, and Stoner will be tried, convicted and sentenced to death; when Mrs. Rattenbury hears that Stoner will be executed, she commits suicide, stabbing herself six times next to a small Bournemouth stream; Stoner, ironically, does not die, his sentence later being commuted to life imprisonment.

APRIL 8

Smuggler James Smith disappears in Sydney, Austraila; his arm, bearing an identifying tattoo, is disgorged by a shark swimming in an aquarium outside Sydney 10 days later; police conduct a spectacular investigation among Australian smugglers but never pinpoint Smith's killer; it is speculated that Smith has been murdered, his body jammed into a trunk not large enough to hold his entire body, and when the trunk is dumped into the sea, the arm, dangling from the trunk, is eaten by the shark later captured and put on display in the aquarium.

MAY 11

Irving Latimer, onetime pharmacist from Jackson, Mich., who has crushed his mother's head on Jan. 24, 1889 (and later offers a mythical prostitute named Trixy as his alibi, saying he was sleeping with her in a Detroit hotel room at the time of the murder), is paroled after serving 46 years in prison, one of the longest terms in the state's history; Latimer is picked up for vagrancy a few days later and sent back to jail; he will die in an old-age home in 1946.

JUNE 16

Peoria, Ill., machinist Gerald Thompson, a meek-mannered 25-year-old who lives with his mother, rapes and murders Mildred Hall, his 16th rape victim in 10 months; a massive manhunt unearths the killer, who admits the murder. His clothes, stained with his victim's blood, are found along with dozens of photos he has taken of his rape victims (all bound and gagged, naked before his car's headlights), including Mildred Hall; also found is a diary Thompson has kept that details his crimes; he will be sent to the electric chair on Oct. 15.

JUNE 28

Eva Coo, onetime madame of a Cooperstown, N.Y., whorehouse, is sent to the electric chair for murdering her handyman, Harry Wright, whom she has gotten drunk and run over with her car on June 15, 1934, to collect insurance on his life; Eva Coo sits down in Sing Sing's electric chair with a wide smile, saying her last words to prison matrons standing nearby: "Good-bye, darlings."

AUG. 15

Los Angeles barber Robert James, who runs a successful six-chair shop he has purchased from insurance money on the life of a nephew whom he has driven over a cliff, insures his wife, Mary, and, with the help of handyman Charles Hope, gets her drunk, then sticks her foot into a boxful of rattlesnakes Hope has brought for the occasion; though bitten repeatedly, Mary survives, the alcohol in her system working as an antidote; James and Hope finally drown her in the bathtub, then place her body in a lily pond behind James's home, passing her death off as accidental; however, the snakebites arouse the curiosity of inspecting officers, who grill Hope; he breaks down, testifies against James for immunity, and James is quickly convicted; he will be hanged on May 1, 1942, the last man to be hanged in California, the state converting to the gas chamber following his death.

SEPT. 8

Senator Huey Long of Louisiana, the dictatorial "Kingfish" who has run the state with an iron hand since becoming governor in 1928 and later U.S. senator, is shot in the state capitol building by Dr. Carl Austin Weiss, who is, in turn, riddled with bullets by Long's bodyguards and is dead before hitting the floor; Long dies of his wounds on Sept. 9, asking with his last breath, "Why would anyone want to shoot me?" The answer is unclear; some speculate that Weiss has murdered Long over family insults, the rape of a relative or death threats to his father-in-law, Judge Benjamin Pavy, an opposition leader; Robert Penn Warren will later profile the case in *All the King's Men*.

SEPT. 14

Dr. Buck Ruxton of Moffat, Scotland, an Indian from Bombay, inexplicably murders his wife, Isabella; when a maid, Mary Rogerson, comes upon the murder scene, Ruxton also strangles the maid to death; to cover the murders, the doctor dismembers the corpses and tosses them into the River Annan, but the remains are found and identified; Ruxton will be quickly convicted, and hanged at Stangeways Jail in Manchester on May 21, 1936.

SEPT. 16

Film star Thelma Todd is found in her blood-splashed

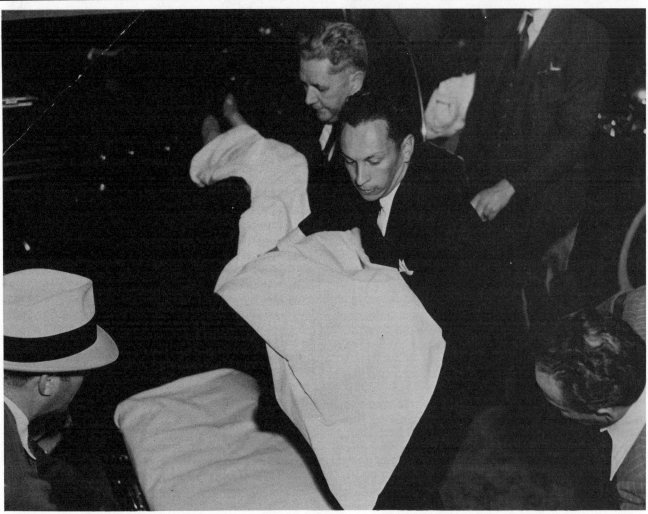

The body of film actress Thelma Todd being removed from her car in Pacific Palisades, Calif.; only the police didn't call it murder. (Sept. 16, 1935)

The first of a dozen bodies that will be attributed to the never-found "Mad Butcher of Cleveland" are dug up. (Sept. 23, 1935)

car inside a garage overlooking her famous roadhouse restaurant on the Pacific Highway between Malibu and Santa Monica, Calif.; her death is never solved, although suspicion is cast upon a former husband, Pat DiCicco; it is rumored that gangsters have murdered the actress after she has refused to let them open a gambling room above her popular restaurant.

SEPT. 19

Wealthy contractor Augusto Okonski is found shot to death in his Buenos Aires, Argentina, home, his wife, Ana, standing nearby, terrified, holding a gun; she quickly states that a hobo with bushy eyebrows and a fierce expression has run into the Okonski home and killed her husband, wiping off the gun and thrusting it into her hand; she is locked up, but police later discover Okonski's diaries and expense ledger in which he states he has given money to the poor and, only a few days before his death, 20 pesos to a young unemployed man named Ernesto Pesce; the murder gun

is traced to a pawnshop, where the proprietor states it has been stolen by a young hobo with busy eyebrows; police send out a wanted poster, and Pesce is found in Córdoba, northwest of Buenos Aires; he will admit the killing and be sent to prison for 25 years.

SEPT. 23

The first two of a dozen victims of the killer who will later be called the "Mad Butcher of Cleveland" are found in the city's run-down industrial section, Kingsbury Run, chopped up corpses of two men, one identified as Edward Andrassy, a petty thief and child-molester; most of the victims killed through 1937 will be prostitutes, hobos and small-time crooks; the "Mad Butcher of Cleveland" will never be apprehended.

DEC. 2

Murderer Albert Kessel is the first man to die in California's new gas chamber.

DEC. 22

Charlotte Bryant poisons her husband, Frederick, with arsenic in Coombe, England, so she can be with a lover; Mrs. Bryant's notorious affairs will lead authorities to inspect the corpse and find the poison, and she will be quickly found guilty of murder, to be hanged July 15, 1936.

ROBBERY

JAN. 8

Arthur "Dock" Barker is captured in Chicago by FBI agents as he leaves his apartment; he is frisked, one agent asking, "Where's your gun?" "Home," answers Barker, "and ain't that a helluva place for it?" Barker will be sent to Alcatraz for life for the Bremer and Hamm kidnappings; on June 13, 1939, he will be shot to death while trying to escape The Rock.

JAN. 16

Following a terrific gun battle with FBI agents and local police, Fred and Ma Barker are killed in a hideout cottage at Lake Weir, Fla.; their close ally Alvin Karpis goes into hiding (briefly) when he hears of their deaths.

MARCH 22

Five bandits attempt to hold up cashiers and guards at Chicago's Wilson & Co., a meatpacker, but are driven off by fire from Brink's guards. The would-be thieves are never identified.

APRIL 25

Alvin Karpis, Harry Campbell and Joseph Rich rob the Youngstown Sheet & Tube Plant payroll in Youngstown, Ohio, taking $70,000.

JUNE 7

William Schweitzer robs New York City lawyer Howard Carter Dickinson of $135, shooting him in his car; he later carps to his girlfriend after finding so little in his victim's wallet: "That's a helluva little bit of money to kill a man for." He leaves Detroit and later will be picked up in Chicago while buying souvenirs; Schweitzer will be sent to prison for life.

JULY 7

Alvin Karpis, Harry Campbell, Fred Hunter, Ben Grayson and another man identified only as "Brock" rob Erie Mail Train No. 622 in Warren, Ohio, getting $34,000.

DEC. 5

A bank car of the Hull Branch of the Banque Provinciale de Canada is waylaid by another car in Québec, Canada; $16,000 is stolen, and the guard, Armand Nadeua, is killed; several Québec criminals are grilled but the thieves are never pinpointed.

ORGANIZED CRIME

JAN. 25

Chicago union leader Tommy Maloy is indicted on income-tax-evasion charges; he has failed to report $350,000 of income for the years 1929–32; before he can be tried, killers sent by Frank Nitti (who is fearful that Maloy will implicate him) will shoot Maloy to death on Feb. 4.

FEB. 25

A Brooklyn refining "plant" processing heroin from opium and owned by Lansky, Buchalter and others is blown up by rival gangsters.

AUG. 21

Jimmy LaCapra, onetime associate of Kansas City crime kingpin Johnny Lazia and who has been hunted for more than a year by Lazia gunmen who suspect that he has murdered their boss, is found dead, his body ripped to pieces by dozens of bullets, on a roadway outside New Paltz, N.Y.

SEPT. 30

Bugsy Siegel murders Joey and Louis "Pretty" Amberg, loansharks who have been waging war against the Bug and Meyer mob, in Brooklyn.

OCT. 23

Dutch Schultz (Arthur Flegenheimer), top bootlegger in New York City during the 1920s, is shot down with three henchmen—Bernard "Lulu" Rosenkrantz, Abe "Misfit" Landau and Otto "Abbadabba" Berman—in the Palace Chophouse in Newark, N.J., by Emmanuel "Mendy" Weiss and Charlie "The Bug" Workman, sent on orders of Charles "Lucky" Luciano and other crime cartel leaders; Schultz, who has been a member of the syndicate board, went against the will of other members by planning to murder New York City District Attorney Thomas E. Dewey; Schultz, shot in the restaurant washroom, dies hours later in the hospital after raving incoherently; Weiss will go to the electric chair in Sing Sing with Lepke Buchalter and

Louis Capone for other murders in 1944; Charlie "The Bug" Workman will serve 23 years in the New Jersey State Prison; when released, Workman will go to work as a "salesman" in New York City's garment district.

White-Collar Crime

MARCH 1

Sharper Ralph Marshall Wilby is arrested for embezzlement in Norfolk, Va.; he will receive a short sentence.

JULY 18

William Elmer Mead is arrested in New York City and sent to prison for fraud.

SEPT. 1

Victor "The Count" Lustig, who has sold the Eiffel Tower *twice* to gullible scrap dealers, escapes from the FBI detention center in Washington, D.C. Treasury agents will recapture Lustig later.

Miscellaneous

MARCH 2

Convict René Belbenoit escapes from the penal colony in French Guiana; he will later write a book about his criminal exploits entitled *Dry Guillotine*.

MARCH 5

Notorious New York City madam Polly Adler is arrested in her Manhattan brothel in a vice crackdown that will lead many prostitutes to testify against prostitution kingpin Charles "Lucky" Luciano, who will receive a long prison term and be profiled by Eduardo Cianelli in the movie *Marked Woman*.

MAY 24

Nine-year old George Weyerhaeuser is kidnapped from his Tacoma, Wash., home by William Mahan, who holds the boy for $200,000, then releases him on June 1, unharmed; Mahan will be captured when passing some of the marked ransom money and will go to prison for 60 years.

SEPT. 8

Movie choreographer Busby Berkeley is arrested and charged with manslaughter after three persons are killed in an accident involving his car; he will be tried three times before being acquitted.

OCT. 15

John Favorito, who has held up and killed a gasoline station attendant, is electrocuted in the New Jersey State Prison in Trenton; the executioner is almost knocked down by a powerful shock after touching the dead man's arm seconds after sending the current into the killer.

Murder

JAN. 16

Albert Fish, "The Cannibal," is electrocuted in Sing Sing for the murder of 12-year-old Grace Budd, whom Fish has claimed to have chopped up and eaten; the 66-year-old killer tells authorities before he dies that he has murdered and killed scores of children over the past decades and that he looks forward to sitting down in the electric chair. "What a thrill that will be," he coos, "the only one I haven't tried."

FEB. 15

Floyd Horton of Bedford, Iowa, and his mistress, Mrs. Anna Johnson, poison Horton's wife, Elta, but the strychnine they feed her is detected and both will go to prison for life.

FEB. 27

Ralph Jerome Von Braun Selz is picked up for stealing a car in San Francisco; police soon learn from him that he has killed 58-year-old Ada French Rice, the estranged wife of the mayor of Nome, Alaska. Selz admits murdering the woman for her money and leads police to her mountainside grave, doing clog dances and singing strange songs for accompanying reporters as the body is dug up. A smile clings to Selz's face and he is dubbed the "Laughing Killer" before being convicted of murder on March 13 and sent to prison for life.

APRIL 16

Nurse Dorothea Waddingham is hanged in Nottingham, England, for poisoning several patients in her care; she has murdered these helpless invalids for their savings.

MAY 23

Adolf Seefeld, who has admitted to molesting and murdering 12 young boys between 1908 and 1935, is executed in Berlin, Germany.

JUNE 15

Mildred Mary Bolton, a housewife jealous of his secretary, fires six shots into her lawyer husband Joseph W. Bolton, Jr., while he sits in his Chicago office, then watches him crawl to a corridor elevator, leaving a trial of blood. "He's putting on an act," Mrs. Bolton tells horrified witnesses with a wide smile; she will be sent to prison for life, committing suicide with a pair of scissors in her cell at the women's penitentiary at Dwight, Ill., on Aug. 29, 1943; her suicide note will read: "I wish to die as I have lived, completely alone."

JUNE 17

Woman-hater Albert Walter goes to San Francisco police headquarters to admit he has murdered Blanche Cousins, a college student he has picked up. "I always knew I would kill a woman someday," Walter says unfeelingly as he lights a cigarette; he will be hanged within a year.

JULY 16

Mrs. Mary Creighton and Everett Applegate are electrocuted at Sing Sing for poisoning Applegate's wife because she has complained of her husband's immoral sexual relations with Mrs. Creighton's teenage daughter.

OCT. 2

Police in Liège, Belgium, receive an anonymous letter telling them that a 56-year-old widow named Marie Petitjean Becker has poisoned at least a dozen people, including Mrs. Jean Perot; Mrs. Julia Bossy; Mrs. Aline-Louise Damoutte; Mrs. Yvonne Martin; Mrs. Anne Stevart; Mrs. Matilda Bulte; her husband, Charles Becker; and her landlord, Lambert Beyer, all for insurance money or savings left to her in wills; all

the bodies will be exhumed and the lethal drug digitaline found in all the corpses; Mrs. Becker will be arrested carrying the poison; in her apartment police will find a veritable warehouse of cheap woman's jewelry, all taken from the homes of her victims; on July 8, Mrs. Becker will be found guilty of committing all the murders and will be sent to prison for life.

OCT. 5

A woman is found slashed to death in her compartment as a passenger train pulls into Sofia, Bulgaria; later she will be identified as 41-year-old Elena Milanoff, a wealthy widow; police later will capture her murderer, Pau Goluneff, a friend of the victim's daughter who will admit killing Mrs. Milanoff for money; he will be sent to prison for life.

DEC. 27

Wealthy Charles Mattson of Tacoma, Wash., is kidnapped; his murdered remains will be found on Jan. 11, 1937, but the kidnappers will never be identified, even though they have collected $27,000 in ransom money.

ROBBERY

JAN. 13

Joseph Valachi is arrested for robbery in New York City and is released a short time later "for lack of evidence."

JAN. 25

Emil Haye, a French-Canadian jewelry salesman, is thrown from a speeding car at Hertfordshire, on the outskirts of London; Haye has been murdered for his gems, Scotland Yard detectives will later learn, killed by an international jewel thief named André Cartier; by the time Cartier is tracked down to Paris he will already have been sent to prison for 20 years on another recent robbery.

MAY 1

Bank robbers Alvin Karpis and Fred Hunter are arrested in New Orleans by J. Edgar Hoover and an army of FBI agents; both will be sentenced to Alcatraz for life, but Karpis will eventually be released and will die in Europe in 1979.

ORGANIZED CRIME

JAN. 13-FEB. 1

Special prosecutor Thomas E. Dewey orders

hundreds of prostitutes and pimps arrested in a New York City vice crackdown, closing 40 brothels and causing the collapse of Lucky Luciano's vice empire.

FEB. 13

"Machine Gun" Jack McGurn is shot to death in a Chicago bowling alley by two Bugs Moran machine gunners avenging the St. Valentine's Day Massacre.

APRIL 16

George Browne and Willie Bioff extort $1 million from Hollywood movie moguls, threatening to close down theaters across the country through their control of the powerful Motion Picture Projectionists' Union. (They give the moguls a sample by having operators in New York City run films without sound.) Both men later will be killed on orders of the syndicate after they turn informants against many Chicago hoods.

APRIL 22

Johnny Torrio is arrested in White Plains, N.Y., on charges of income-tax evasion; Torrio, many times a millionaire from his bootlegging rackets in early 1920s Chicago, will post $100,000 bond and drag his case through the courts for years, finally receiving in 1939 a 2½-year sentence and an order to pay $86,000 in back taxes; he will be paroled on April 14, 1941.

JUNE 7

Charles "Lucky" Luciano is found guilty on several counts of racketeering, prostitution and smuggling and is sentenced to 30 to 50 years in Sing Sing; the smug gangster has outdone himself by insisting on taking the witness stand, where prosecutor Thomas E. Dewey has picked his lies to pieces.

JULY 7

In New York City, Frank Costello is convicted of racketeering and sent to Dannemora Prison to serve 30 to 50 years.

JUNE 12

Harry "Pittsburgh Phil" Straus and "Buggsy"

Goldstein, notorious "Murder, Inc." assassins (Straus had been arrested 27 times for murder in 19 years without a conviction) are executed in Sing Sing for the 1939 strangling and cremation of Brooklyn gambler Irving "Puggy" Feinstein.

SEPT. 12

Joseph Rosen, who is about to testify that he had once seen Louis "Lepke" Buchalter murder a man years earlier, is shot to death in his New York City candy store by Lepke's enforcer Mendy Weiss.

WHITE-COLLAR CRIME

FEB. 5-MARCH 1

Sulun Osman, a Turkish con man in Istanbul, sells the *Orient Express* for $75,000 to a gullible financier; Osman will be caught within a month and sent to prison for two years.

APRIL 13

Samuel Sapphire, one of New York City's most experienced forgers, is acquitted for forging $10 bills.

MISCELLANEOUS

FEB. 8

Carl "Cowboy" Fisher of St. Joseph, Mo., is convicted of attempted rape and sent to prison for two years; three years earlier, Fisher led a mob that lynched Lloyd Warner, a black accused of raping a young girl.

MARCH 21

Harry Gee, No. 1 racketeer of New York City's Chinatown, is arrested with a huge cache of opium; he will receive a long prison term.

MURDER

JAN. 17

At a union meeting in the Manhattan Opera House, Frank Cicero is stabbed to death by Gabriel Klar and Joseph Berger for singing a song too loudly; each killer will be given a 10-year sentence.

FEB. 6

Powerful union leader Norman Redwood is shot to death outside his Teaneck, N.J., home; union boss Sam Rosoff will be accused of ordering Redwood's murder, but little evidence will be mounted against him, and the killing remains unsolved.

FEB. 11

Wenzel Cerny is found guilty of murdering Judge Jan Velgo in Beno, Czechoslovakia; Cerny claims that Velgo's young wife, Mrs. Marie Havlick Velgo, has paid him to murder her elderly spouse, but his accusation does not hold up, and Mrs. Velgo is released after her first trial; however, she will be tried again, convicted of conspiracy and sent to prison for 12 years; Cerny will be sent to prison for life.

Albert E. Volckman, who has murdered a minister's young daughter in New York City, is executed in Sing Sing.

MARCH 27

New York City sculptor Robert Irwin murders two women out of frustration at not getting a job; later he will be caught with some household items taken from his victims' apartment and blurt: "To kill is one thing, but to be a sneak thief!" Irwin will be sent to prison for life despite a brilliant insanity defense mounted by Samuel S. Leibowitz.

MAY 12

During the day of coronation of King George VI at Westminster Abbey, four Irishmen explode in the Sportsman Club in London when a pianist plays *God Save the King;* the Irishmen beat many patrons and stomp a woman to death; Terrence McDonagh, who has killed Edith Gertrude Elizabeth Watson, will be sent to prison for 12 years; the other three drunkards will draw minor sentences.

JUNE 1

Self-styled Anna Marie Hahn poisons 68-year-old Jacob Wagner in Cincinnati after taking care of him for a few weeks; she will soon thereafter poison 70-year-old George Opensdorfer; when poison is found in both bodies, Mrs. Hahn is confronted. "I have been like an angel of mercy to them," she says, but it will later be proved that she has collected insurance money on the slain men, has attempted to murder her husband, Phillip Hahn, for insurance funds and that she has forged physicians' signatures on prescriptions to obtain poison; Mrs. Hahn, after throwing a small party for local reporters in her cell, will go to the electric chair.

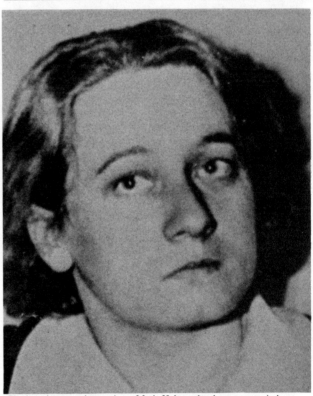

Cincinnati mass poisoner Anna Marie Hahn, who threw a party in her death cell the night before her execution. (June 1, 1937)

JULY 2

Arthur Perry murders his wife and plants evidence that implicates a New York City neighbor, Ulysses Palm, as the killer; Perry will be tripped up in his lies and later convicted and sent to the electric chair.

AUG. 7

Jean de Koven, a 22-year-old American dancer vis-

Eugen Weidmann, German-born kidnapper and killer of a half-dozen people, including American dancer Jean de Koven, with police after his capture in Paris. (Aug. 7, 1937)

iting Paris, is abducted from her hotel, and a ransom note demanding $500 for her release is received; her murderer, German-born Eugen Weidmann, will be tracked down to a remote villa and captured after a terrific battle with police; he will admit to killing a half-dozen people for their pocket money or small ransom amounts; Weidmann will be guillotined on May 18, 1939.

OCT. 16

North Arlington, N.J., police find 19-year-old Paul Nathaniel Dwyer asleep in a car with the battered bodies of Mrs. Lydia Littlefield and her husband, Dr. James Littlefield, beside him; he confesses killing the pair but later states that Sheriff Francis M. Carroll has murdered the couple, claiming that Carroll called Dr. Littlefield to check on his daughter—whom Dwyer has been seeing—to see if she is pregnant; the doctor mentioned something about incest (Carroll, according to Dwyer, has had an affair with his daughter Barbara), and the sheriff killed the couple, ordering Dwyer to

take them out to the car; Carroll will be tried and sent to prison for life for the Littlefield killings; he will be released in 1950 but Dwyer, oddly no more than an accessory to the murders, remains in jail at this writing.

ROBBERY

JAN. 7

Harry Linton Butler, prominent real-estate broker and president of the Pasadena, (Calif.) Realty Board, robs the Colorado-Mentor branch of the Bank of America, taking $4,000 from the tellers' cages; he is shot dead some blocks away by pursuing policemen; it will be learned that the 50-year-old Butler has robbed other banks after a $50,000 real-estate loss in Oregon prompted him to turn criminal.

JAN. 31

Bill Dainard and another bandit rob $5,000 from the Oakville State Bank in Oakville, Wash.; Dainard will be tracked down and sent to prison.

ORGANIZED CRIME

MAY 11

Abe "Kid Twist" Reles and other Murder, Inc., killers for hire strangle New York City businessman George Rudnick; on Oct. 1, New York City businessman Max Rubin will be shot in the head by Reles and other Murder, Inc., assassins, but Rubin will miraculously survive.

JULY 20

William Phillips dies in Spokane, Washington of natural causes; many believe Phillips to have been the notorious western bandit Butch Cassidy, who has allegedly survived a military ambush in Bolivia in 1908, where his close friend the Sundance Kid (Harry Longbaugh) was killed, and returned to the U.S. to live out a long life under the alias of Phillips.

DEC. 1

Special prosecutor Thomas E. Dewey launches a massive investigation into the criminal affairs of Vito Genovese in New York City.

WHITE-COLLAR CRIME

MARCH 24

International con man Serge Rubinstein arrives in Tokyo, Japan, and immediately sells all his stock in Korean mine property, then later smuggles out of Japan (which has forbidden any large amounts of currency to leave the country) millions in yen wrapped around his three mistresses in the form of obis (a traditional saronglike Japanese garment); Rubinstein will later dump the yen on the open market, reaping a fortune and causing the Japanese yen to drop fantastically in value.

MISCELLANEOUS

SEPT. 25

Carles S. Ross, a 72-year-old greeting-card manufacturer, is kidnapped at random in Chicago by John Henry Seadlund and James Atwood Gray and held for $50,000 ransom, which will be paid in Oct. 1937; Seadlund will then murder Ross and his partner, Gray, and flee to California, where he will be arrested (while placing a bet at Santa Anita racetrack) by FBI agents; the kidnapper-killer will be electrocuted in 1938.

NOV. 4

Arnett Booth, Orville Adkins and John Travis kidnap wealthy 79-year-old Dr. James Seder from his Huntington, W. Va., home, holding him for 12 days in a damp, abandoned coal mine and waiting for a $50,000 ransom to be paid. Lawmen track down the kidnappers before the money is paid and rescue Dr. Seder, who later dies from pneumonia contracted while in the mine shaft; Seder's death, caused by the kidnappers, results in mandatory death sentences under the new Lindbergh laws. Adkins, Booth and Travis are all hanged on March 21, 1938.

DEC. 16

Ralph Roe and Theodore "Sunny Boy" Cole make a break from Alcatraz and are never seen again; some believe they successfully swim San Francisco Bay and go into permanent hiding with $200,000 of secreted money taken from earlier bank robberies, but the FBI marks them as dead.

$1 \cdot 9 \cdot 3 \cdot 8$

MURDER

FEB. 21

London prostitute Dora Alice Lloyd is strangled to death by a customer, who is seen by a half-dozen people to leave her apartment building; he is never found.

FEB. 24

Peter Levine is kidnapped from his New Rochelle, N.Y., home; his dismembered body will be discovered on March 29, but his killer is never found.

APRIL 17

Twenty-three-year-old Sophie Kujat is fished out of the Passaic River at Newark, N.J.; she has been strangled to death, a rope still around her neck; a night watchman on the dock identifies Edward Holle, who was once engaged to the victim before marrying another woman, as having been on the docks with Miss Kujat some days before her body is found; Holle confesses that he has tried to break off the affair after his marriage but an argument broke out and he strangled his onetime girlfriend; he later will reenact the murder before police cameras, and the motion picture will be played before a jury that will convict him, the first such evidence ever presented; Holle will be sent to prison for 20 years.

APRIL 29

Harvey L. Rousch has his business partner, Homer T. Myers, receipt a personal note for $15,000 in Myers' Delaware, Ohio, home, after giving him a check for that amount; Rousch then shoots Myers and his wife to death, setting their house on fire to cover the murders; the bodies are found with the wounds and the police break down Rousch, who confesses; he will be sent to the electric chair.

AUG. 6

James Boyd Kirkwood enters a police station in Edinburgh, Scotland, to tell a desk sergeant: "I killed a woman last night." He leads officers to the estate of Sir William Thompson and a fresh grave containing the body of 35-year-old Jean Ronald Powell, a dairy worker Kirkwood says he has killed while undergoing a mental seizure; although it will later be proved that Kirkwood suffered an epileptic fit while committing the murder, he will nevertheless be sent to prison for life.

AUG. 14

Miss Pamela Raper, a 26-year-old sculptor from England, disappears in Paris; her body later will be found in a fisherman's net off Toulon; although she has been murdered, her killer is never found. (Despite evidence to the contrary, French police will inexplicably later rule the death accidental.)

SEPT. 24

Texas Rangers investigating the disappearance of many waitresses who have worked for Joe Ball enter Ball's tavern outside San Antonio, Tex.; Ball runs to the cash register, pulls out a pistol and blows out his brains; witnesses in recent weeks have told the Rangers that Ball has murdered many women, perhaps as many as 20, who have worked for him as waitresses, killing them to steal their savings, pay and tips, then chopping up their bodies and feeding the remains, heads and all, to the dozens of pet alligators living in a large pool behind his tavern; later police will find hundreds of human bones at the bottom of the alligator-infested pool.

OCT. 15

Martin "The Gymp" Snyder, estranged husband of singer Ruth Etting, shoots Miss Etting's accompanist, Myrl Alderman, as he is about to enter Miss Etting's Los Angeles home; Snyder will be convicted of attempted murder in his first trial but will be released in a second trial when an eyewitness dies; the case will be profiled in the motion picture *Love Me or Leave Me*.

NOV. 25

Future mass murderer Charles Starkweather is born in Lincoln, Neb.

DEC. 6

In his parked car, railway clerk Rodney Greig of Oakland, Calif.; repeatedly stabs his girlfriend, Leona Vlught, then slits her throat, later telling police that the victim asked to be killed because she felt she had no future; newsmen report that Greig has drunk the victim's blood, calling him a "vampire killer," a charge Greig denies up to the moment he enters the gas chamber at San Quentin the following year.

ROBBERY

JAN. 12

Anthony Bocchini, manager of the Guarantee Loan Society of Alton, Fla., is robbed of $125,000 in jewelry by two bandits; the holdup men, Joseph Bates and Robert Clement, are traced through a wire they have received from the mastermind of the robbery, William H. Connelly; Bates and Clement are sent to prison for life on March 14; Connelly evades police until March 26, 1940, when he is picked up in Shreveport, La.; he is sent to prison for 10 years.

MAY 24

Duncan Johnston, former mayor of Twin Falls, Idaho, calls police to report that his friend George L. Olsen, a jewelry salesman from Salt Lake City, is missing; Olsen is found by Twin Falls police shot dead in his car, his jewelry, valued at $15,000, missing; police put Johnston under surveillance, and he will eventually lead them to the stolen jewelry; owner of a jewelry store, Johnston will admit that he has killed Olsen to wipe out a debt of many thousands of dollars for previously purchased jewelry and to obtain the gems he had been carrying; Johnston will be sent to prison for life.

AUG. 25

Fifteen-year-old Estelle Mae Irwin and Bennie Dickson rob the Corn Exchange Bank of Lake Benton, Minn., of $2,174.64; on Oct. 31, Irwin and Dickson will rob the Northwest Security National Bank of Brookings, S.D., waiting for two hours for the time vault to open and lining up more than 50 persons under their guns; when the vault does open, the teenagers will take $17,529.99 in cash and $29,640.50 in securities; Dickson will be shot to pieces by FBI men in St. Louis on April 6, 1939, while buying hamburgers for himself and Estelle, whom he has married; she will be picked up in Kansas City, Mo., on April 7, 1939, and later go to prison for 10 years.

OCT. 7

After a prolonged trial and several stays of execution, bank robber and onetime partner of Charles Arthur "Pretty Boy" Floyd, Adam Richetti, is taken into the gas chamber of the Missouri State Penitentiary. He is strapped down in the chair, and, squirming and screaming madly, he yells out his innocence of any participation in the Kansas City Massacre of 1933 at the Union Station in which five men were killed by underworld machine gunners ostensibly attempting to free bank robber Frank "Jelly" Nash from custody, and killing Nash. FBI officials determined that Vern Miller, Floyd and Richetti were the killers, but an eyewitness, James Henry "Blackie" Audett, later refuted this claim. Richetti dies within three minutes after inhaling the lethal fumes. He is the first man to be executed by gas in the state.

DEC. 21

Onetime Wild Bunch member and train robber Matt Warner dies of natural causes near Salt Lake City, Utah; the western bandit has been a bootlegger during the 1920s but is a respected justice of the peace at his death.

Super conman Philip Musica, who took his own life rather than go to prison. (Dec. 16, 1938)

ORGANIZED CRIME

APRIL 14

Jacob "Gurrah" Shapiro, partner of Louis "Lepke"

Buchalter and who is wanted for labor racketeering, turns himself in to police and is sent to prison, where he will die in 1947.

AUG. 21

Hyman Yuran, onetime partner of Louis "Lepke" Buchalter, is murdered by Murder, Inc., goons and thrown into a lime pit near Lack Sheldrake, N.Y., on Lepke's orders; Lepke fears that old associates might inform on him and result in his being sent to prison.

NOV. 10

Leon Sharff and his wife are murdered in New York City on Lepke's orders to silence them concerning his racketeering activities.

WHITE-COLLAR CRIME

NOV. 8

In its war on New York gambling, the state Assembly adopts an amendment to the New York State Constitution that makes wiretapping evidence admissible in state courts.

DEC. 16

Master swindler and stock manipulator Philip Musica is exposed, and when lawmen enter his New York mansion, the sharper runs to his bathroom and shoots himself.

MISCELLANEOUS

OCT. 7

Comedians George Burns and Jack Benny are arrested in New York City and charged with gem smuggling; they state that Nathaniel Chapereau, a notorious smuggler, convinced them that they would save a fortune on duty charges for imported jewels for their wives if they paid him directly; Chapereau is sent to prison for five years; Benny and Burns plead guilty and receive one-year suspended sentences; Burns pays an $8,000 fine and Benny $10,000.

1·9·3·9

MURDER

FEB. 24

Franklin Pierce McCall, 23-year-old son of a Princeton, Fla., minister, is hanged for kidnapping and murdering James Bailey Cash, five-year-old son of a Princeton businessman who paid $10,000 to have his son returned. (The body was found in some woods a half mile from the boy's home; McCall claimed that he had accidentally smothered the child to death when he held a handkerchief over his face when abducting him.) J. Edgar Hoover, who personally handled the case, said that he had interviewed McCall, who told him he had committed the kidnapping "for the better things of life for his wife and himself" and because he "had been unable to get steady employment."

MARCH 2

A young man and woman are whipped to death in a lover's lane outside Atlanta, Ga., for violating the "Moral Kode" of the Ku Klux Klan.

MARCH 6

Georgina Hoffman, also known as Mary Heath, a singer fans have dubbed "The Black Butterfly," is stabbed to death in her Dover Street flat in London; she has last been seen with a ship's steward, Arthur James Mahoney, who is traced to his home in Brixton; when Mahoney answers the door, his face full of lather, he jerks his head at the constables before him and says: "The knife's upstairs." Mahoney, who also stabbed a hospital maid and attacked a child in recent years, is adjudged insane and sent to Broadmoor Prison for the criminally insane, where he will die 16 months later.

MARCH 20

Earl Austin and Lacene McDowell are riding in Austin's car in Hardin County, Ill., when the auto suddenly blows up, killing both; parts of a dynamite bomb are found at the scene of the explosion by detectives, who immediately go to mechanic Ira Scott, who has last fixed the car; Scott breaks down and states that Alice Austin, Earl's estranged wife, and her lover, Ted Simmons, have paid him $50 to plant the bomb; all three are sent to prison for 14 years each.

ROBBERY

FEB. 6

The Mistele Coal Company in Detroit is held up by a lone bandit who takes $10,000 and then races to a car, wounding three civilians and two policemen who pursue him; the same bandit, pretending to be an FBI man, appears in a Milwaukee hotel on March 21, robbing several guests in their rooms; he is identified that night by detectives in the Chicago, Milwaukee & St. Paul railroad station; when they ask him to step into the washroom, he pulls a gun from his overcoat pocket and runs out; the bandit jumps into a taxi and orders the cabbie to drive north, out of the city; instead the cabbie drives downtown to Milwaukee police headquarters, racing into the police garage; the bandit jumps out, holding two guns, and forces a dozen cops to lie on the floor while he runs out of the building; several squad cars pursue him and, some blocks away, police shoot it out with the bandit, who gives up when out of ammunition; he is identified as Joseph Ricardo, wanted for robbery in several states; he will be sent to prison for 10 years for impersonating an FBI agent.

ORGANIZED CRIME

JAN. 28

Isadore Friedman and Louis Cohen, both witnesses to early-day crimes committed by Louis ''Lepke'' Buchalter, are killed in New York City on Lepke's orders.

JAN. 29

Allie ''Tick Tock'' Tannenbaum and ''Knuckles'' Mitzberg murder Albert ''Plug'' Sherman in New York City on Lepke's orders.

MARCH 29

Boss Tom Pendergast goes to prison for income-tax evasion.

MARCH 30

Joseph Miller, onetime union partner of Lepke, is murdered in New York City by Murder, Inc., killers on Lepke's orders.

APRIL 28

Abraham ''Whitey'' Friedman is murdered in New York City on Lepke's orders.

MAY 10

''Tootsie'' Feinstein, one of Lepke's closest friends, who has long ago decided to quit the rackets, is murdered in New York City on Lepke's orders.

MAY 25

Morris Diamond, office manager of Teamsters' Local 138, is killed in New York City on Lepke's orders.

AUG. 25

Gossip columnist Walter Winchell, who has received a phone call from Lepke a day earlier, arranges for Lepke to surrender personally to J. Edgar Hoover of the FBI on a New York City street.

SEPT. 6

Irving ''Puggy'' Feinstein is tied with ropes by Abe Reles and other Murder, Inc., killers and burned alive on orders from Lepke, who sends out the word from his prison cell.

NOV. 6

Johnny Torrio is sentenced to 30 months in prison for tax evasion; on the same day, his protégé, Al Capone, his brain wasted with paresis, is released from Alcatraz; he retires to his estate at Palm Island, Fla., where he raves for years, still thinking he is the crime overlord of Chicago; Jake Guzik and others pay honorary visits to him, pretending he is still their boss; privately, Guzik tells friends: ''Al's as nutty as a fruitcake!''

NOV. 8

Edward J. O'Hare, onetime Capone partner in his racetracks, who has served for years as an undercover agent, helping to provide information that sent Capone to prison, is shot to death while he drives his car down a Chicago street. (His son, Butch O'Hare, will become one of America's first Air Force aces during World War II.)

NOV. 22

Bugsy Siegel and others murder Harry ''Big Greenie'' Greenberg in Los Angeles; he has been killed on orders of Meyer Lansky, having stolen syndicate money years earlier in New York City, and recently trying to blackmail Lepke.

WHITE-COLLAR CRIME

APRIL 23

James McKay and William Graham, operators of

various Big Store con games, are arrested in Reno, Ariz., and sent to prison.

SEPT. 1

Embezzler, forger and swindler Ralph Wilby is arrested in Colton, Calif., for fraud under the name of James W. Ralston; he will receive a long prison term.

MISCELLANEOUS

AUG. 25

An IRA bomb goes off in Coventry, England, during a festival and kills five, injuring 50 more.

1·9·4·0

MURDER

MARCH 13

Udham Singh, a fanatical Sikh assassin, attends a London meeting of the Royal Central Asian Society and East India Association and charges the stage, firing two shots into Sir Michael Francis O'Dwyer, ex-governor of the Punjab (who has been in office during the 1919 Amritsar riots, when Singh's brother had been killed), killing him instantly and wounding three other dignitaries; attempting to flee up the aisle of the theater, the assassin is tackled by 60-year-old Claude Riches, a member of the audience; when police arrive they find Singh's pockets full of ammunition. "Only one dead?" he asks. "I thought I could get more. I must have been slow." He will be hanged at Pentonville Prison on June 25, 1940.

MARCH 15

While running for the office of sheriff in Okaloosa County, Fla., Les Wilson is shot to death while he sits in his Crestview, Fla., home with his family; his son, Ray Wilson, will become sheriff of the same county in 1956, despite numerous death threats, and will spend most of his time tracking down his father's assassins, his own boyhood friends, Jessie and Doyle Cayson, who have killed Wilson to keep lucrative contracts through existing political connections; the brothers will be sent to prison for life.

JULY 9

Florence Ransom, a middle-aged woman living with Lawrence Fisher of Piddington, England, visits Fisher's estranged wife in nearby Matfield, killing her, her daughter and a maid with a shotgun; Mrs. Ransom leaves a monogrammed white leather glove at the scene of the murders, which leads detectives straight to her door; she will be condemned to death but later sent to Broadmoor for the criminally insane.

AUG. 20

Exiled Russian revolutionary leader Leon Trotsky, who lives in a fortresslike villa outside Mexico City, is visited by a trusted aid, Frank Jackson, who pretends to discuss the publication of one of Trotsky's forthcoming articles; Jackson suddenly attacks Trotsky, driving a pickax into his skull before fleeing; he is arrested and identified first as Jacques Mornard, later as Ramon Mercades del Rio, a Moscow-trained assassin acting on orders from Stalin to murder his onetime revolutionary ally; Del Rio will serve 20 years in a cramped cell, kept in isolation from other prisoners, before being released in 1960 and given a Czechoslovakian passport before he disappears behind the Iron Curtain.

ROBBERY

MAY 30

James Henry "Blackie" Audett is released from Alcatraz after serving five years for bank robbery, having been arrested as an escaped fugitive on Aug. 18, 1934, only two weeks after, he claims, depositing John Dillinger (listed as officially dead by the FBI) in rural Oregon; on Aug. 30, Blackie and others will rob the State Bank in Omaha, Neb., taking several thousand dollars; he will be caught a short time later and sent to Leavenworth for 20 years, then shipped back to Alcatraz, where he will remain until The Rock is closed on May 5, 1963; Audett will be the last federal prisoner to step off Alcatraz's dock.

ORGANIZED CRIME

FEB. 2

Abe "Kid Twist" Reles is arrested in Brooklyn,

N.Y., along with several other Murder. Inc., killers and charged with numerous homicides; Reles will make a deal with prosecutor Burton B. Turkis and begin to talk nonstop, exposing Murder, Inc., and top syndicate chieftains such as Louis "Lepke" Buchalter.

APRIL 15

William Bioff is convicted of pandering and income-tax evasion in Chicago but will spend only a few months in jail because of legal loopholes.

MAY 13

The murder trial against Harry "Happy" Maione and his Murder, Inc., partner Frank "The Dasher" Abbandando opens in New York City; their former employee, Abe Reles, will testify against them.

JULY 31

Bugsy Siegel murders Whitey Krakower in Brooklyn to even an old score—Krakower had once informed on him.

SEPT. 9

Harry "Pittsburgh Phil" Strauss is put on trial for the many homicides he has committed for Murder, Inc., in New York City; Abe Reles will testify against him, and Strauss will be sentenced to the electric chair on Nov. 11.

WHITE-COLLAR CRIME

FEB. 10

George Ashley, a wiley con man, begins his national lonely hearts club, which submits photos of attractive young girls to lonely men, who write to Ashley, sending money for the girls' transportation; the women never arrive.

MARCH 31

New York State enacts a pari-mutuel law to discourage gambling through bookies.

1·9·4·1

MURDER

JAN. 24

Lord Erroll, wealthy 39-year-old playboy, is found dead in his car, a bullet in his head, near his luxurious estate in Kenya; suspected of the murder is Sir Henry John Delves Boughton, whose wife has been seeing Erroll and who was about to divorce Boughton to marry the victim; evidence against the jilted husband, however, is lacking, and his is released, only to commit suicide on Dec. 21, 1942 in a Liverpool, England, hotel, from barbiturates.

FEB. 27

Mrs. Harvey Collins of Memphis, Tenn., slips poison into a bottle of milk drunk by Walter Lewis "Daddy" Samples, her lover; both Mrs. Collins and her husband are later tried for the murder, but Mrs. Collins admits that she alone has murdered Samples to escape what she terms his "sexual hypnotic hold." She is sent to prison for 20 years.

APRIL 4

Samuel Morgan, an ex-soldier, is hanged at Walton Jail in England for having murdered 15-year-old Mary Hagan on Nov. 2, 1940.

MAY 1

Antonio "Babe" Mancini, operator of a Soho saloon in London, knifes to death underworld character Harry "Scarface" Distleman outside his club; this pedestrian murder will be turned into a *cause célèbre* when prosecuting attorneys debate with the presiding judge, who has repeatedly stressed manslaughter, not murder, to the jury; Mancini, however, will be convicted of murder and hanged.

OCT. 8

New Zealand stockbreeder Eric Stanley George Graham goes berserk after his business fails and kills four police officers, who arrive to quell an argument with neighbors near Graham's Koiterangi farm; the wounded Graham escapes, and the country's largest manhunt ensues, with troops called in to hunt down the killer. Graham will shoot and kill two guardsmen on Oct. 12 as he escapes, again wounded; he will be tracked down on Oct. 15 to a farm building, where he will be mortally wounded in a terrific gun battle with police; Graham will die in the hospital before he can be indicted for the six murders he has committed.

OCT. 14

Mrs. Theodora Greenhill, a London widow, is murdered, apparently for her money; detectives find a note on the desk at which the woman has been strangled and her head crushed: "Received from Dr. H. D. Trevor the s . . ." Trevor is no doctor, but a 62-year-old petty crook who is easily traced through fingerprints at the scene; Harold Dorian Trevor will be found guilty and later hanged.

NOV. 9

Child-molester and British soldier Harold Hill abducts, strangles and stabs to death six-year-old Kathleen Trendle and eight-year-old Doreen Hearne near Penn, Buckinghamshire, England; Hill is tracked down through a laundry mark on a khaki handkerchief found nearby, and his fingerprints are found to match those on a gas mask also left at the scene of the crime; Hill will be hanged the following year.

DEC. 6

Richard Franklin Speck, future American mass murderer, is born in Kirkwood, Ill.

ROBBERY

JAN. 14

Burglar Horace Blacock is arrested for a spectacular series of home robberies in Atlanta, Ga.; Blacock, who has victimized the homes of the wealthy, will later figure in one of Atlanta's most sensational murders. (See "Murder," Sept. 29, 1943.)

FEB. 24

French super thief Émile Buisson and two others rob two bank messengers in Paris of 4 million francs.

NOV. 21

Mrs. Ethel Leta Juanita "Duchess" Spinelli, leader of a terror-robbery gang in San Francisco during the 1930s, goes to San Quentin's gas chamber for ordering the death of a gang member, Robert Sherrard, fearful that Sherrard would tell police that she and others have killed Leland Cash, a robbery victim.

ORGANIZED CRIME

APRIL 14

Johnny Torrio is sent to Leavenworth to serve a short term for tax evasion.

MAY 24

William Bioff, George Browne and Nick Cicella are indicted for racketeering in New York; they have been extorting millions from Hollywood moguls through the gangster-controlled projectionsts' union. Bioff and Browne will be found guilty, Bioff being sentenced to 10 years and given a $20,000 fine, Browne given eight years and a $20,000 fine.

JUNE 12

Murder, Inc.'s leading killer in New York City, Harry "Pittsburg Phil" Strauss, is found guilty of murder and sentenced to death, largely through the testimony of Murder, Inc.'s Abe "Kid Twist" Reles, who has turned informer to avoid prosecution for murder.

Mrs. Ethel "Duchess" Spinelli, the first woman executed in San Quentin's gas chamber. (Nov. 21, 1941)

SEPT. 15

Louis "Lepke" Buchalter, leader of Murder, Inc., and one of the directors of the national crime syndicate, goes to trial; testimony by Reles and Albert "Allie" Tannenbaum, members of his hit-man troop, convicts him and two henchmen, Louis Capone and Mondy Weiss, of murdering Joseph Rosen years earlier; all three receive death sentences.

NOV. 12

Killer-turned-informer Abe "Kid Twist" Reles "falls" from the window of his sixth-story room in the Half Moon Hotel in Coney Island, where he is being held in protective custody; it is claimed by the six cops guarding Reles, all of whom were supposedly preoccupied while the gangster went out the window, that Reles fell while trying to escape.

WHITE-COLLAR CRIME

MARCH 1

High-rolling con man Serge Rubinstein, who has bragged about entering the U.S. with a fake passport, is investigated in New York City by immigration authorities attempting to oust him from the country; they will be unsuccessful.

MAY 10

Mrs. Marie Fuller of Detroit begins to sell fake Ford Motor Company stock to suckers who believe that Henry Ford is secretly liquidating his financial empire; she will realize more than $200,000 in nine years before being exposed and jailed.

OCT. 1

The U.S. Congress, in an attempt to curb widespread street gambling, imposes a new tax law on coin-operated amusement gaming devices.

MISCELLANEOUS

OCT. 28

Harlem's biggest drug dealer, known simply as Elias, is arrested and charged with drug smuggling, but the case against him is inadequate for a conviction.

OCT. 31

Robert Pitts is arrested in Austin, Tex., for not having a draft card; when police attempt to take his fingerprints, they are stunned to find that the suspect has no trace of the papillary lines on the tips of his fingers; inspecting Pitts' body, they discover skin grafts taken from his chest; after a laborious investigation, FBI agents locate Dr. Leopold William August Brandenburg of Union City, N.J., who has figured in several robberies and who has experimented with skin transplantation; Brandenburg admits to performing the skin grafts on Pitts, who turns out to be a professional thief named Robert J. Phillips; both Phillips and Brandenburg are sent to jail, the latter for harboring a fugitive.

MURDER

FEB. 9

Evelyn Margaret Hamilton, a chemist's assistant, is found strangled in a London air-raid shelter; the next night Mrs. Evelyn Oatley is found strangled in her Soho flat; detectives find prints on a can opener that has been used to mutilate the victim horribly; but the fingerprints on it match those of no known criminal in Scotland Yard files; as public panic spreads in war-torn, blacked-out London of a new Jack the Ripper, another victim, Mrs. Margaret Florence Lowe, is found on Feb. 14 in her apartment, strangled; the police, from marks found on the victims, deduce that the fiend is left-handed, but little more; the next victim, also discovered on Feb. 14, is Mrs. Doris Jouannet, wife of the night manager of the Paddington Hotel, who returns home to discover her strangled with her own stocking, her naked body horribly mutilated with a razor; again police have no clues, but a day later a man accosts a young woman leaving a pub, Mrs. Heywood, and attempts to kiss her; when she refuses, he attempts to strangle her, but she is saved by passersby; the masher escapes but leaves a gas mask; hours later another woman, Kathleen King, is accosted by the same man and almost strangled to death, but her screams bring the neighbors in her apartment building to her door, and the man flees out the window; police find an RAF cadet's belt; the gas mask and belt bear the same serial number, 525987, which is easily traced to Gordon Frederick Cummins, a 28-year-old RAF cadet living in North London; his fingerprints match those found on the can opener and other items left at the scenes of the murders; he is also left-handed, as the police suspected; Cummins, who has been raised in upper-class respectability and pretends to be the illegitimate son of a member of the House of Lords, will be convicted of three of the murders and hanged on June 25 during a terrible air raid on London.

APRIL 22

Married and with five children, religious fanatic Donald Fern entices Alice Porter to an empty church outside Pueblo, Colo., where he crucifies the young woman; he will be tracked down and sent to a prison for the criminally insane.

MAY 2

Ivy McLeod, of Melbourne, Australia, is strangled on her way home; Pauline Thompson is found strangled a week later; Gladys Hosking is found strangled on May 28 on a Melbourne Street; a fourth woman is threatened, apparently by the same killer, but he leaves when she warns him she will call police; an Australian sentry informs police that following the Hosking murder he allowed a bloodied American GI to pass his post; the sentry inspects every American soldier standing on parade in the nearby American camp and picks out Pvt. Edward Joseph Leonski, a heavyset Texan, who immediately confesses to all three murders; his bunkmates come forward to quote Leonski as having told them that "I'm a Dr. Jekyll and Mr. Hyde. I killed! I killed!" Leonski later tells police that his strange motivation for the killings is that he has been obsessed with soft female voices. "That's why I choked these ladies. It was to get their voices!" He explains that Pauline Thompson sang a song as he walked with her on a date. "Her voice was sweet and soft, and I could feel myself going mad about it." Despite an insanity plea, Leonski will be quickly convicted, and hanged on Nov. 9.

MAY 27

Reinhard Heydrich, chief of the Nazi security police and deputy chief of the Gestapo, is assassinated by Czech patriots Josef Gabcik and Jan Kubis, who fire at his open touring car as it speeds through Holesovice, a suburb of Prague, Czecheslovakia, on the Dresden–Prague Road; Kubis hurls a grenade at the car, which explodes; Heydrich, stumbling from the

wreckage, cursing and firing his pistol at his attackers, falls mortally wounded with springs from the car's seat driven into his stomach; he will die on June 4. In retaliation, the Nazis will wipe out the village of Lidice, killing 1,331 Czechs; Kubis and Gabcik are among the slaughtered victims, although the Nazis have never identified the assassins.

OCT. 7

The body of Joan Pearl Wolfe, who had run away to live in the woods near Godalming in Surrey, England, is found; one of the girl's letters to a Canadian soldier named August Sangret is discovered nearby; Sangret is located and blood matching that of the victim is found on his uniform; his bloody knife is also found near the murder site. Sangret, a full-blooded Indian, will be found guilty, and sent to the gallows at Wandsworth Prison on April 29, 1943.

OCT. 9

Mrs. Ellen Symes is found murdered on Brompton Farm Road in Strood, England; an army deserter, Reginald Sidney Buckfield, is picked up and held for four weeks as a suspect; he is then turned over to military authorities, but as he passes a detective he hands him a 10,000-word thriller he has written in jail called *The Mystery of the Brompton Road;* Buckfield, who is called "Smiler" by his fellow troopers because of his perpetual grin, is then arrested for the Symes killing, the very manuscript he has written being the evidence against him. "Oh, that's all fiction," he tells officers. "That's how I thought the murder might have been committed." The mystery story, however, proves that only the author and the killer knew the details of the killing, and Buckfield will be convicted and sentenced to death; later he will be reprieved and sent to Broadmoor Prison for the criminally insane.

DEC. 31

Derek Thayer Lees-Smith stabs his widowed mother to death in London during what doctors later term "a breakdown in his power to control," which is attributed to low blood sugar or hypoglycemia; the 20-year-old student is sent to a mental asylum for life.

ROBBERY

SEPT. 6

John Elbert and Phil Ferdinand, both in their early 20s, torture and kill hermit Giovanni Leonidas in his Sismundo Valley, Calif., hut in an attempt to obtain the gold he has reportedly hoarded; Mrs. Josephine Humphrey, who has accompanied the pair, later informs on them and both will be given life sentences.

OCT. 30

Burglar Jake Bird is arrested by Tacoma, Wash., police after a series of robberies in the city; Bird admits to having killed 10 robbery victims with an ax in Washington, Illinois and other states; he will be hanged in Washington in 1948.

ORGANIZED CRIME

FEB. 14

Meyer Lansky, to avoid prosecution, registers with the Selective Service Board, giving his age as 40.

FEB. 19

Frank "The Dasher" Abbandando and Harry "Happy" Maione receive death sentences in New York City for the many murders they have committed for Murder, Inc. They will be executed in Sing Sing.

WHITE-COLLAR CRIME

FEB. 15

Mildred Hill, a Washington, D.C., con artist, begins her mail-order matrimonial scam, sending out a newsletter and photos of her attractive daughter, mulcting would-be suitors for money in her name. She will later be apprehended and given a short sentece.

MAY 20-JULY 25

Embezzler Fred Wilby guts the William T. Knott Company, a department store corporation, out of $400,000; he will later flee to Canada but be caught and sent to jail for seven years.

MISCELLANEOUS

OCT. 9

Roger "The Terrible" Toughy, Basil "The Owl" Banghart and four others escape from Stateville Prison in Illinois; they hide in Chicago but are rooted out by police following a terrific gun battle, in which Gene O'Connor and St. Calir McInerney are killed. Toughy, Banghart, Eddie Darlok and Martlick Nelson are returned to prison.

OCT. 19

Actress Frances Farmer is arrested in Santa Monica, Calif., for drunk driving, an arrest that will lead to the ruination of her film career.

NOV. 18

Drug smuggler M. Elias is arrested with others and indicted in New Jersey, where proceedings for deportation to New York are begun, but the drug king escapes through legal loopholes.

1·9·4·3

MURDER

JAN. 1

Anti-Communist editor Carlo Tresca is shot to death on a New York City street; his murder is never solved, police speculating that he has been killed by spies or Mafia gunmen.

JAN. 27

Harry Dobkin is hanged at Wandsworth Prison, England, for murdering his wife, Rachel, a year earlier; Dobkin has stated that he has killed his wife, from whom he has been legally separated, because she nagged him about support payments; the murder would never have been detected had not a German bomb opened up the London grave where Dobkin hid the body.

JAN. 29

Mental defective Brune Ludke, who has been sterilized by the SS for sex assaults, is discovered in Berlin, Germany, having sex with the body of Freda Ros-

New York City editor Carlo Tresca, whose murder remains unsolved. (Jan. 1, 1943)

ner, a 51-year-old woman he has just killed; Ludke confesses to murdering 85 women and practicing necrophilia on most of his victims and will be sent for medical "experimentation" to Vienna, where he will be given a lethal injection on April 8, 1944.

FEB. 3

Estelle Evelyn Carey, Chicago mob girl and friend of gangster Nick Dean, is found horribly mutilated in her North Side apartment; though police speculate that Estelle has been killed because of her knowledge of hidden mob money, the murder is never solved.

JULY 8

Sir Harry Oakes, a flamboyant, self-made millionaire who owns most of the Bahaman island of New Providence, where Nassau is located, is found dead in the bedroom of his sprawling estate house, Westbourne, by his best friend, Harold Christie, who is an overnight guest; Oakes's head has been crushed by what police later term "a long, blunt instrument," and his body has been burned to a cinder, his corpse covered by feathers from a pillow, dumped in wild caprice by the killer; Oakes's playboy son-in-law, "Count" Mario Alfred Fouquereaux de Marigny, with whom Oakes

has been quarreling and who is an obvious sham in quest of Oakes's considerable millions, is arrested by police and later tried for the murder, but he will be released on Nov. 11, returning to his wife, Nancy, Oakes's daughter, who is fiercely loyal to de Marigny; the case will never be solved, although many will later speculate that Oakes was killed by mobsters on orders from Meyer Lansky, who had been blocked by Oakes from taking over gambling concessions on the island.

Bahaman multimillionaire Sir Harry Oakes, horribly murdered at his Nassau estate, a killing never solved. (July 8, 1943)

JULY 23

In London, Eric Brown places a land mine beneath the cushions of his tyrannical father's wheelchair, and when the invalid Archibald Brown sits down on the chair he is blown to pieces; the Hawkins No. 75 grenade mine is quickly traced to Eric Brown's army unit and subsequently to the killer, who admits the murder and is sent to an asylum for life.

SEPT. 29

Henry C. Heinz, powerful banker and one of Atlanta, Ga.'s, leading citizens, is shot to death by an intruder in his home; although police arrive at the scene within minutes—the Heinz home was recently burglarized—the killer has fled; the mystery will not be cleared up until 1945, when home burglar Horace

Blalock is arrested while burglarizing the Atlanta home of a wealthy lawyer and his fingerprints are found to match those left at the Heinz murder scene two years earlier; Blalock will confess to the killing and be given a life sentence; he will be paroled ten years later.

DEC. 30

Paula Wolfe unleashes a diatribe against her husband Lewis, in their rooms of the St. George Hotel in Brooklyn, N.Y., recounting scores of assignations she has kept with other men and then screaming: ''You're not a man, or you'd kill me for all this.'' When she falls asleep, Wolfe clubs her to death with a shoe, then turns himself into police; he will be sent to Dannemora State Prison for life.

ORGANIZED CRIME

FEB. 8

Lawyers for Lucky Luciano begin efforts to reduce their client's sentence of 30 to 50 years; Luciano appeals for parole from Clinton State Prison in Dannemora, N.Y.; it is denied.

MARCH 15

Edward J. ''Spike'' O'Donnell, onetime Chicago beer baron during Prohibition and powerful South Side boss, is shot in the back while entering his home by a lone gunman. O'Donnell survives.

MARCH 18

A federal grand jury indicts members of the Chicago syndicate for racketeering, including Frank Nitti, Phil D'Andrea, Paul ''The Waiter'' Ricca and John Roselli; the next day, Frank ''The Enforcer'' Nitti, Capone's top lieutenant during the bootleg era, unable to face another prison term, wanders along the railroad tracks of the Illinois Central line and then shoots himself.

JULY 8

Brooklyn District Attorney William D. O'Dwyer, later New York City Mayor, makes a personal appeal for the release of Louis ''Lepke'' Buchalter, but the state of New York, under advice of federal authorities, turns down O'Dwyer's plea; it is later stated that O'Dwyer's actions were dictated by Luciano and other syndicate leaders who had O'Dwyer and many others on their payroll.

OCT. 5

Paul ''The Waiter'' Ricca, Phil D'Andrea, Frank Maritote, Charles ''Cherry Nose'' Gioe, John Roselli and Louis Kaufman go to trial and will be found guilty on New Year's Eve of extorting millions of dollars from Hollywood moguls through the Bioff-Browne projectionists' union; each will be given a 10-year sentence and a $10,000 fine.

WHITE-COLLAR CRIME

APRIL 16

Pyramid con man Lowell Birrell takes over several firms owned by dying tycoon Cecil Stewart and begins looting the company treasuries, a scam that will stretch on for years.

MISCELLANEOUS

JAN. 18

Jazzman Gene Krupa is arrested in San Francisco for narcotics violations; although this arrest damages the drummer's career, Krupa later will reform.

JAN. 19

Theater actress Madge Bellamy is arrested in San Francisco for assault with a deadly weapon; she has fired three shots, missing socialite Stanwood Murphy, whom, she claimed, had jilted her for another woman. Her case will be won by Jake Ehrlich.

JUNE 3-8

Los Angeles is the scene of widespread rioting when Marines and other military personnel begin fighting with Mexican *pachucos* wearing zoot suits; scores are injured in the ''Zoot Suit Riots,'' and the zoot suit is officially banned by the City Council.

AUG. 16

Elizabeth and Andrew Toth, Hungarian immigrants in New York City who are violently anti-Nazi and suspicious of banks, keeping as much as $5,000 on their persons most of the time, vanish and are never again found; police believe they have either been killed by members of the Nazi-controlled German-American Bund or have been robbed and murdered by thieves; to this date, the disappearances remain a mystery.

MURDER

MARCH 26

A mob of white men, after learning that the 220-acre farm owned by black minister Rev. Isaac Simmons has oil deposits, take Simmons and his son Eldridge for a country drive, shooting the minister to death (and breaking his bones and cutting out his tongue after death) and beating the son mercilessly before running him out of the county; although Eldridge Simmons later will name the killers, a local coroner's jury in Amite County, Miss., will return a verdict that Rev. Simmons has been killed ''at the hands of unknown parties.''

JUNE 19

Antonio Agostini, an immigrant Italian worker who had moved to Sydney, Australia, in the late 1920s, is tried for the murder of his wife, Linda, whose body has been stored in a tub of formalin by authorities since September 1934; the woman's body, originally found burned, dressed in only pajamas (it will later be called ''The Pajama Girl case''), a bullet in the head, was discovered at the outskirts of New South Wales, Australia, and was identified by seven people after a new police commissioner put the corpse on display in early 1944; Agostini, who claimed in 1934 that his wife and he were separated, that he had not seen her since and that the dead woman is not his wife, changes his story in 1944; now stating that his wife attempted suicide and when he tried to stop her the gun went off and she was killed while lying in bed, wearing pajamas; after which he panicked and hid the body; this explanation does not explain why the woman had been struck several blows to the head, which were the causes of death; Agostini is convicted of manslaughter and will serve only six years in prison before being deported to Italy in 1950.

NOV. 8

Arthur Heys, an RAF enlisted man, gets drunk at a dance near Beccles in Suffolk, England, and, while making his way back to camp, rapes and murders Winifred Mary Evans, a 27-year-old WAAF; hair from the victim is found on Heys's uniform, and scratches are observed on his hands and face; he is also identified by a WAAF corporal, who has seen him in the female quarters on the night of the crime; Heys awkwardly attempts to throw the blame elsewhere by attempting to smuggle out of camp an anonymous letter addressed to the commanding officer that states that Heys is being wrongly accused; the letter, written in Heys' own hand, gives complete details of the murder, which will serve almost as a confession; Heys is convicted and will be hanged the following year.

ROBBERY

OCT. 7

Teenage stripteaser and runaway Elizabeth Marina Jones, after meeting GI Gustave Hulten in a London nightclub, robs cabdriver George Edward Heath on King Street; Hulten shoots Heath to death before the two flee in his cab, dumping the body near Staines; two days later, police arrest Hulten, who is still behind the wheel; Hulten is turned over to British authorities and quickly implicates Miss Jones, who tells police that she thought Hulten was the head of ''a Chicago mob that had moved into London.'' Hulten will be hanged on March 8, 1945; Elizabeth Jones will be sent to prison for life.

ORGANIZED CRIME

MARCH 4

After many ninth-hour reprieves, Louis ''Lepke'' Buchalter, one of the most dangerous men in America and the only board member and director of the national crime syndicate ever to pay the supreme penalty, goes to the electric chair in Sing Sing for the murder of Joseph Rosen; preceding Lepke are Louis Capone and Mendy Weiss, two of his hired killers; Lepke, who has offered to ''blow the lid off the country'' by ''singing'' to then New York Governor Thomas E. Dewey, tells New York City District Attorney Frank Hogan in his final hours nothing of importance, obviously disinclined to jeopardize his family. ''I am anxious to have it clearly understood,'' Lepke says only an hour before his death, ''that I did not offer to talk and give information in exchange for any promise of a commutation of my death sentence.'' Louis Capone is strapped into the electric chair before 36 newsmen witnesses and dies wordlessly; Mendy Weiss chews gum as he is strapped into the chair; he asks to make a statement and then says: ''All I want to say is, I'm innocent. I'm here on a framed-up case. Give my love to my family and everything.'' Lepke, boss to the end, strides defiantly into the death chamber, staring coldly at the newsmen, saying nothing, almost throwing himself into the chair; he has fought against this moment through his lawyers for two years and three months—the longest occupancy of anyone in the Sing Sing death house up to this time—and he is executed in less than three seconds with 2,200 volts sent through his 5-foot, 4¼-inch frame, sending his 165-pound body against the straps. One newsman later writes: ''You look at the face . . . you cannot tear your eyes away. . . . Saliva drools from the corner of his lips. The face is discolored. It is not a pretty sight.''

APRIL 22

Frank Abatte, crime kingpin of Calumet City, Ill., a notorious sin strip area, is found murdered, several shotgun bullets in his back, outside Hot Springs, Ark. The killer is never discovered.

JUNE 15

Ernest ''The Hawk'' Rupolo, a top Vito Genovese gunman now jailed in New York City, implicates Genovese in several 1930s murders, but corroboration of the story of Genovese's 1934 killing of Ferdinand ''The Shadow'' Boccia is eliminated when the other witness, Peter LaTempa, is poisoned in his cell (his killer is never found); Rupolo will be tortured and killed in 1964 before his body is dumped into New York's Jamaica Bay.

AUG. 27

Vito Genovese, who has fled to Italy with more than $2 million shortly before World War II, is arrested by CID agent Orange Dickey in Nola, Italy, and is returned to the U.S. to face charges of murder; with one of the two chief witnesses against him dead, authorities will be forced to release the mob chief on June 11, 1946, and he will promptly resumes his control of many New York City rackets and takes his place on the board of directors of the syndicate.

SEPT. 16

Political leader Girolamo LiCausi is attacked and beaten by mobs in Villaba, Sicily, for speaking out against the Mafia.

MISCELLANEOUS

MARCH 25-28

Pyromaniac George Holman sets fire to 11 San Francisco and Oakland, Calif., flophouses in which 22 persons are killed; he is spotted by a janitor running from one of the buildings and carrying a can of kerosene; Holman is promptly arrested, convicted and sent to San Quentin to serve 22 consecutive life sentences for arson-murder.

NOV. 1

Joseph Valachi is arrested in Brooklyn for peddling narcotics; the charges are later dismissed.

1·9·4·5

MURDER

FEB. 14

Laborer Charles Walton, 74, is found on Meon Hill, Lower Quinton, England, a pitchfork driven into his chest and a sickle blade in his throat, a killing similar to the ritualistic murders of the 16th century committed against those accused of witchcraft; Walton's killer will never be found.

APRIL 28

Italian dictator Benito Mussolini; his mistress, Clara Petacci; and several aides are executed by Communist partisans near Lake Como as they attempt to escape into Switzerland; the bodies are hanged upside down from the girders of a gutted gasoline station in Milan days later while thousands cheer; several Italian women will rush forward, shouting, ''Is there no decency?'' and tie Clara Petacci's skirts tightly to her legs.

MAY 29

A female skull and jawbone are found in Borley Rectory at Essex, England; these remains are claimed to be that of Marie Lairre, a nun abducted by a mad country squire named Waldergraves, who supposedly strangled Marie Lairre on May 17, 1667.

JULY 2

The bones of a white male are found at the bottom

of a well near Alexandria, Va.; police painstakingly reconstruct the murder of ex-Marine Brad J. Ellison, who disappeared in the area on Dec. 29, 1929; he was murdered by Raymond "Scissors" Saunders on orders of Frenchy Carney, whose wife in 1929 was about to run away with Ellison; the bones will be displayed in court, the first time in the history of the state when a skeleton serves as Exhibit A; Saunders, now a hopeless alcoholic, will be convicted by a tramp's testimony, that of eyewitness Robert B. Leitch, whose story was ignored in 1929 when he first accused Saunders; Saunders will be sent to prison for life.

OCT. 13

Mrs. Lydia Thompson, 47-year-old wife of wealthy Detroit car dealer Victor Louis Thompson, is found mutilated and decapitated in woods near Pontiac, Mich.; though her husband later is tried for the murder, prosecutors stating that he has killed his wife to marry his secretary, evidence is lacking and Thompson is released; the case remains unsolved.

DEC. 13

Irma Grese, known as "The Beast of Belsen," who has ruthlessly murdered countless inmates of the infamous SS concentration camp, is hanged in Hamelin, Germany.

ROBBERY

JUNE 3

Burglar William Heirens, 17 years old, who has been robbing Chicago homes for months, enters the apartment of Mrs. Josephine Alice Ross, having a sexual climax while looting the place and knowing she is present (he later admits), asleep in her bed; when she is awakened by his movements, he murders her; Heirens will go on to burglarize scores of houses, beating senseless Army Lieutenant Evelyn Petersen in her apartment on Oct. 5, then robbing and murdering Frances Brown soon after; he allegedly writes a message in lipstick on the wall of his last victim's apartment: "For Heaven's sake, catch me before I kill more. I cannot control myself." (Later police will state that this is a hoax perpetrated by newsmen.) On Jan. 7, 1946, Heirens will kidnap and kill six-year-old Su-

Nazi concentration camp killer Irma Grese, "the Beast of Belsen," shown with a male prisoner, will be hanged for her crimes. (Dec. 13, 1945)

zanne Degnan from her North Side home, demanding ransom for her return while all the while distributing pieces of her chopped-up body into Chicago sewers; he will be caught while attempting a burglary on June 26, 1946, and eventually will be sent to prison to serve three consecutive life terms for the murders, which he insists today he has not committed; at this writing, Heirens appears close to being released.

DEC. 15

William ''Treetop'' Turner, one of the most infamous burglars in America, is found guilty of five counts of burglary and murder, but the verdict will be overturned.

ORGANIZED CRIME

MAY 7

A petition for executive clemency to free Lucky Luciano is sent to New York Governor Thomas E. Dewey, who refuses to act.

MAY 15

Gun-happy Mickey Cohen shoots and kills Chicago bookie Max Shaman, whom he later claims has insulted him; Cohen flees to the West Coast to become a henchman for Bugsy Siegel and is never prosecuted for this shooting.

AUG. 8

Paul ''The Waiter'' Ricca and Louis ''Little New York'' Campagna, Chicago syndicate bosses serving time for extortion, arrange to have themselves transferred from Atlanta to Leavenworth so that they, according to some sources, can carry on their business with associate Cherry Nose Gioe, a Leavenworth inmate.

NOV. 21

All the reigning Mafia dons of Sicily meet in Palermo to decide how to set up international drug trafficking after World War II.

WHITE-COLLAR CRIME

JUNE 13

Francis Gross is convicted in Utica, N. Y., of ''selling stiffs,'' promising the relatives of slain servicemen that he will forward their personal belongings for a price; this insidious con man is given a stiff prison sentence.

AUG. 10-SEPT. 30

Cleveland sharper Norman D. Harris cons hundreds of real-estate suckers into buying scores of unconstructed six-room houses for bargain prices, but no buildings are put up and Harris eventually is arrested, convicted and sent to prison for nine years.

MISCELLANEOUS

MAY 7

Willie ''The Actor'' Sutton tunnels his way out of Eastern State Penitentiary in Philadelphia, only to pop up under the very noses of two beat cops, who promptly arrest him and return him to his cell.

SEPT. 10

Norwegian traitor Vidkun Quisling is sentenced to death in Olso for collaborating with the Nazis during World War II and later executed.

OCT. 4

Nazi collaborator and former French Premier Pierre Laval is put on trial for treason in Paris; he will be executed as a traitor on Oct. 15.

1·9·4·6

MURDER

MARCH 16

A male torso, its limbs missing, is found by children playing near Hamilton, Ont., Canada, and is identified as 39-year-old bus conductor John Dick; parts of Dick's body later are found in the basement of his home, along with the body of his wife's infant son, which is hidden in a suitcase; Mrs. Dick, the former Evelyn MacLean White, a widow who has refused to live with her husband, is charged with the murder; she states that her lover, steelworker Bill Bohozuk, has killed her husband and her son, Peter (from a former marriage); in her first trial Mrs. Dick will be convicted of murder; subsequently she will be acquitted of killing her husband but convicted of manslaughter in the death of her child; Bohozuk, through legal proceedings, will later be released; Donald MacLean, Evelyn's father, will be convicted of being an accessory after the fact and given five years; Evelyn Dick will go to prison for life.

APRIL 6

Habitual criminal Patrick Carraher, who has served three years for ''culpable homicide'' for stabbing a man in a Glasgow street brawl in 1938, is hanged at Barlinnie Prison in Scotland for murdering John Gordon in another street fight.

MAY 9

San Francisco housewife LaVerene Borelli enters her home drunk to shoot her husband, Gene, to death as he sleeps in bed; she later states that she has discovered his love affair with another woman, the reason for the *crime passionnel;* the case becomes a sensational courtroom battle wherein Jake Ehrlich skillfully manages to have the charges reduced to manslaughter; Mrs. Borelli will be sent to Tehachapi Prison for women and will be paroled on March 10, 1953.

MAY 26

Mass murderer Dr. Marcel Petiot, onetime army surgeon, burglar and Nazi collaborator, who has from 1941 to 1944 murdered 63 refugees attempting to flee Nazi-occupied France after promising to help them—he has injected them with poison, watched them die in agony, then stolen their meager belongings—is guillotined in Paris.

JUNE 9

King Ananda of Siam (now Thailand), recovering from a strange illness later claimed to be caused by poison, is shot to death in his Bangkok palace by unknown assassins.

JUNE 21

The body of film actress Margery Gardner, 28, is found mutilated in Room 4 of London's Pembridge Court Hotel; some days earlier Neville George Clevely Heath, posing as RAF Captain Rupert Brooks, has boldly gone to police to see a photo of Gardner when she was still only missing, which sets police on his trail after her body is found; Heath will be convicted, his insanity plea will be ignored, and he will be hanged on Oct. 16 at Pentonville Prison.

OCT. 20

Olive Balchin, 40, is found murdered at a Manchester, England, bombsite, her skull crushed by a hammer discovered nearby; descriptions of a man who has been seen with the slain woman lead police to Walter Graham Rowland, who has a conviction of child-murder; despite a claim by David John Ware, an inmate in a Liverpool jail, that *he* has killed Balchin, Graham will be convicted, and hanged at Strangeways Prison on Feb. 27, 1947; Ware later will be sent to an asylum for life for attempting to murder another woman, in 1951.

NOV. 30

The body of John McMain Mudie, a hotel barman, is found strangled and trussed in a chalkpit outside Woldingham, Surrey, England; witnesses report part of a license plate number on a car that had been seen near the pit a short time before the body is discovered; the car is traced through a leasing agency to Thomas John Ley, onetime minister of justice for New South Wales, Australia; Ley and a friend, Lawrence John Smith, are tried for the murder, Smith admitting to being an accessory; apparently Ley has killed Mudie over the affections of 63-year-old Mrs. Maggie Brook; both Ley and Smith will be condemned for the ''Chalkpit Murder'' but will be reprieved, Smith receiving a life sentence, Ley being sent to Broadmoor Prison for the criminally insane, where he will die of a stroke on July 24, 1947.

ROBBERY

MARCH 13-APRIL 18

War hero Erwin Walker goes on a Los Angeles robbing spree, sticking up dozens of stores; he is cornered several times but manages to shoot his way to freedom while wielding a submachine gun; he later kills patrolman Loren C. Roosevelt, who interrupts Walker in the act of robbing a grocery store; Walker will be convicted and sentenced to death but will later be judged insane and sent to an asylum for life.

JUNE 5

Dozens of looters are arrested when the LaSalle Hotel catches fire in Chicago.

JUNE 26

Onetime Chicago bootleg baron now down on his luck George "Bugs" Moran stoops to robbing a bank messenger in Dayton, Ohio, with Virgil Summers and Albert Fouts, taking about $10,000; Moran will be arrested the following month and will be sent to prison; he will die in Leavenworth in February 1957.

Onetime big shot bootlegger in Chicago George "Bugs" Moran is shown in custody after committing a bank robbery. (June 26, 1946)

AUG. 18

The first of a spectacular series of robberies is committed by Justin William McCarthy on Park Avenue in New York City (he will become known as "The Park Avenue Bandit") when he robs furs and jewelry from a limousine parked at curbside; his take will top $200,000 in similar robberies before he is caught and sent to prison.

ORGANIZED CRIME

JAN. 3

New York Governor Thomas E. Dewey announces that Charles "Lucky" Luciano will be released from prison but will be deported from the U. S., back to his native Italy; on Feb. 9, Luciano will sail for Italy onboard the *Laura Keene,* destination, Genoa; later it will be claimed that the notorious syndicate board director has been released for his cooperation in convincing partisans to help U.S. forces invading Sicily and mainland Italy three years earlier; others will say that his political connections effected the release; the real cause is shrouded in mystery to this day.

JUNE 24

James Ragen, who has operated the betting wire services for the syndicate in Chicago, is shot to death in his car at the corner of State Street and Pershing Road; his killers are never found.

DEC. 9

Vincent "Jimmy Blue Eyes" Alo and Joe Adonis, who have been deported, secretly return to the U.S. from Havana, Cuba, before being run out of the country once more.

DEC. 26

Benjamin "Bugsy" Siegel opens his fabulous gambling casino, The Flamingo, in Las Vegas, a city he will almost single-handedly develop into America's gambling capital; but Siegel will not live to enjoy its fruits; he will begin to argue with his East Coast and Chicago backers when the casino initially proves a flop.

WHITE-COLLAR CRIME

FEB. 1-JUNE 15

Serge Rubinstein, international swindler and con

Guards Fire Into Cellblock From This Catwalk

Main Cellblock, Where Convicts Are Barricaded

Gun Gallery Seized by Prisoners

Warden's Home

Gun Tower

Auditorium

Recreation Yard Where Marines Guard Prisoners

Lighthouse

Guards' Quarters

Guards' Quarters

Main Gate Leading to Arsenal, Cell Block and Radio Control Room

Old Army Parade Ground

Photo showing locations important in the bloodiest prison break in the history of Alcatraz. (May 2, 1946)

man, invests his mulcted millions from European flim-flams by buying up U.S. firms, then promptly gutting their treasuries and selling off the companies for profits; authorities fail to prosecute the con man successfully.

APRIL 25-AUG. 30

Samuel Mussman, a peg-legged con man, gleans a fortune from gullible foreign businessmen by leasing U.S. government buildings he claims will soon be vacated.

OCT. 1-DEC. 30

New Orleans con man Robert Lyman Seibert markets postwar nylons at a 35 percent discount, taking in $10,000 a week before it is discovered that he has no nylons to sell.

MISCELLANEOUS

MAY 2

Bernard Coy, Joseph Paul Cretzer, Clarence Carnes

and others lead the most bloody escape attempt ever at Alcatraz; Cretzer, Coy and two others are killed in the ensuing gun battle after murdering two guards. Carnes is recaptured and given life in prison.

SEPT. 30

An international military tribunal, established to investigate war crimes in Nuremberg, Germany, condemns 11 high-ranking Nazis to death; on Oct. 15, No. 2 Nazi Hermann Goering will commit suicide in his Nuremberg jail cell, taking cyanide hidden, it is later claimed, in a hollow tooth in his mouth (some will say that the poison has been smuggled to him by sympathizers); on Oct. 16, the 10 others—Foreign Minister Joachim von Ribbentrop, Field Marshal Wilhelm Keitel, Col. Gen. Alfred Jodl, Arthur Seyss-Inquart, Hans Frank, Wilhelm Frick, Julius Streicher, Alfred Rosenberg, Ernst Kaltenbrunner and Fritz Sauckel—will be hanged, as will Goering's corpse; Streicher shouts before falling through the trap: ''The Bolsheviks will hang you one day!'' Field Marshal Keitel yells: ''All for Germany!'' Martin Bormann was condemned to death *in absentia*.

1·9·4·7

MURDER

JAN. 15

The mutilated body of Elizabeth Short, known as "The Black Dahlia," is found in a vacant lot on Norton Street in Los Angeles; the letters "B. D." are carved on one thigh; as an army of detectives investigates this fiendish and mystifying murder, the killer mails the personal effects of the raven-haired would-be actress to a local newspaper, stating that he will send a follow-up message and then turn himself in; he does not surrender, stating in a subsequent letter, "I've changed my mind. You would not give me a square deal. Dahlia killing justified." Robert "Red" Manley, a married 24-year-old hardware salesman who has known Elizabeth Short, is a prime suspect, but he is·released for lack of evidence and later commits suicide; several copycat murders will follow the Dahlia slaying, which is unsolved to this day.

Elizabeth Short, "the Black Dahlia," whose shocking murder was never solved. (Jan. 15, 1947)

APRIL 11

Louise Peete becomes the second woman in California history to go to the gas chamber for murder; she has been released after serving 18 years for the 1920 murder of Los Angeles millionaire Jacob Charles Denton; her second murder conviction, for which she receives the death penalty, is for slaying Mrs. Margaret Logan (later taking over her house in Pacific Palisades, Calif., and burying the body in the backyard), who befriended Mrs. Peete while she served time and became her sponsor once she was released.

Louise Peete, the second woman to go to San Quentin's gas chamber (April 11, 1947)

MAY 2

Dr. Robert George Clements poisons his fourth wife, who dies the following day in a Southport, England, nursing home; her death is initially attributed to "mycloid leukemia"; morphine, however, is detected by physicians in a postmortem when they observe the dead woman's pinpointed pupils; when police reach Dr. Clements they find him dead, a suicide from an overdose of morphine; it is speculated that the doctor has also murdered his three previous wives; Dr. James Houston, who wrongly diagnosed the illness of the fourth Mrs. Clements, also will commit suicide.

OCT. 18

Eileen Isabella "Gay" Gibson, an actress, is reported missing on board the liner *Durban Castle* en route to London; charged with her murder is 31-year-old steward James Camb, who claims that he was having sex with Eileen Gibson when she suffered a fit and died; he goes on to state that he panicked, shoving her body through the porthole and into the sea; Camb will be convicted of murder on March 22, 1948, and sentenced to death but later will be reprieved and given a life sentence.

NOV. 18

Albert Welch, a railway linesman in Potters Bar, Middlesex, England, vanishes; his remains are later found on a local golf course; but his murderer is never found.

DEC. 18

Nina Housden of Highland Park, Mich., inveigles her estranged husband, Charles, to her home, where she strangles him to death, chops up his remains and wraps the pieces as "Christmas packages," which she puts into the family car; she then sets off for her native Kentucky but develops car trouble in Toledo, Ohio, where a mechanic checking over her auto finds the human remains and informs police; Mrs. Housden, who will admit having murdered her spouse out of jealousy, will be sent to prison for life.

ROBBERY

APRIL 29

Three gunmen robbing a jewelry store in London's West End shoot and kill Alec de Antiquis, father of six, who attempts to stop them; Superintendent Robert Fabian of Scotland Yard later leads investigators, who uncover a discarded raincoat belonging to professional thief Charles Henry Jenkins; two of Jenkins's friends, Terence Peter Rolt and Christopher James Geraghty, are also rounded up and confess to the robbery and shooting; Jenkins and Geraghty are sent to the gallows at Pentonville Prison on Sept. 17; Rolt, who is only 17, is sent to prison; the execution of the two robber-killers causes widespread protest from the anticapital-punishment faction.

SEPT. 3

Bank robber Émile Buisson escapes the Paris asylum where he has been confined for several years.

ORGANIZED CRIME

JAN. 25

Al Capone dies at his estate in Palm Island, Fla., age 48, succumbing to paresis of the brain, which has turned him into a raving lunatic; his body is shipped North and buried in Chicago.

Al Capone, shown at his Palm Island, Fla., retreat, just before his agonizing death; he died a raving lunatic. (Jan. 25, 1947)

APRIL 11

Lucky Luciano arrives in Genoa, Italy, and is taken into custody, warned that he is to avoid all criminal activity; upon his release on May 14, 1947, Luciano will take over the direction of worldwide drug trafficking controlled by the syndicate.

MAY 9

Mafia leader Nick DeJohn is murdered in San Francisco; although many suspects are arrested, the killing is never solved.

JUNE 16

Virginia Hill, Bugsy Siegel's paramour and bag-

ROBBERY

JAN. 23

Caryl Chessman is arrested in Los Angeles while driving a stolen car; later he will be identified as the notorious "Red Light Bandit," who has terrorized local lovers' lanes in late 1947, flashing a red light while robbing the occupants of cars and compelling females at gunpoint to perform sexual acts with him; on May 18, 1948, Chessman will be convicted of 17 charges of robbery-rape and be sentenced to death as an habitual criminal, a four-time loser; Chessman will fight the death sentence for 12 years before going to the gas chamber in 1960.

JAN. 26

Sadimacha Hirasawa, pretending to be a Dr. Jiro Yamaguchi, enters the suburban Shiinamaki branch of the Teikoku Imperial Bank in Tokyo, Japan, just as the bank closes, telling 14 employees that they must drink some medicine to prevent an outbreak of amebic dysentery then rampant in the district; the employees swallow teacups full of a liquid heavily laced with potassium cyanide, a deadly poison; 13 die on the spot, while Hirasawa loots the bank of more than 180,000 yen (about $600) and vanishes; Japanese police laboriously interview thousands of people who have received cards from a man pretending to be a physician and finally pinpoint Hirasawa, an artist, who later is identified by the lone surviving bank employee; Hirasawa admits his guilt and is imprisoned for life.

FEB. 13

Donald George Thomas, one of London's most notorious burglars, is stopped on the street by policeman Nathaniel Edgar and questioned about several recent robberies; Thomas shoots the officer and flees, but the dying Edgar tells other constables to check his notebook, which contains Thomas's name and address; the burglar is arrested in his Clapham rooms and will be sent to prison for life.

ORGANIZED CRIME

FEB. 23

Lucky Luciano is arrested in Cuba after sneaking into that country to have a summit conference with U.S. syndicate chiefs; he is returned to Italy.

JULY 16

Charles Yarnowsky, a leading syndicate head in Jersey City, N.J., is found murdered, his body chopped to pieces; John DiBiasio, his lieutenant, will be found shot to death in front of his Jersey City home 25 days later in another obvious syndicate murder.

OCT. 1

Chicago police mount a drive against syndicate gambling dens, arresting in the dragnet Johnny Ambrosia, a top mob man.

DEC. 12

Mob man Jimmy Velsco is murdered in a syndicate hit in Tampa, Fla.

DEC. 16

Meyer Lansky, who has undergone a prolonged divorce, marries his manicurist, Thelma Scheer "Teddy" Schwartz.

MISCELLANEOUS

MARCH 23

Joseph Valachi is arrested in New York City for narcotics violations; he is released for lack of evidence.

APRIL 5

Illegal-alien smuggler William Murphy is arrested in Florida; he and several others draw stiff prison sentences.

JUNE 15

Jazzman Charlie "The Bird" Parker is arrested in New York's Dewey Square Hotel for drug violations.

AUG. 3

Whittaker Chambers, an editor for *Time* magazine and admitted ex-Communist, names former State Department official Alger Hiss as a onetime important member of the Communist underground in Washington, D.C.; on Dec. 15, a federal grand jury in New York City will indict Hiss for perjury for denying that he gave Chambers secret government documents to be delivered to Soviet agents; on Jan. 25, 1950, Hiss will be sentenced to five years in prison.

AUG. 31

Actor Robert Mitchum and others are arrested

smoking marijuana in the Laurel Canyon cottage of Lila Leeds during a party. With famed criminal lawyer Jerry Geisler defending him, Mitchum is later sentenced to two years on jail, which is instantly reduced to 60 days. The actor will be photographed mopping floors and doing other chores at the Wayside Rancho, the county penal institution, and he will be released within 50 days, with time off for good behavior. His comment about the confinement to newsmen will be that the institution is "just like Palm Springs—without the riffraff, of course." His career will remain unharmed.

1·9·4·9

MURDER

FEB. 3

Millionaire miller Marcel Hilaire murders his 20-year-old mistress, Christiane Page, in Paris because, he later tells police, she caused him to neglect his business; he is sent to prison for life to serve hard labor.

FEB. 18

John George Haigh, 39-year-old engineer and well-mannered womanizer, inveigles wealthy 69-year-old widow Mrs. Olive Durand-Deacon from a London hotel, where they both live, to a storeroom in Sussex on the pretext that he will put into production her cosmetic creations; Haigh shoots the woman, strips her, takes her cash and valuables, then puts the body into a 40-gallon drum of sulphuric acid; Haigh, after going back to his "factory" several times to make sure Mrs. Durand-Deacon's body is utterly destroyed by the acid, goes to police to report the disappearance of the widow; his polished manner and glib answers to questions arouse suspicion, and detectives find that he has a police record; they inspect the Sussex storeroom, then charge him with murdering the widow. "Mrs. Durand-Decon no longer exists," Haigh says with a snort. "I've destroyed her with acid. You can't prove murder without a body." But the police do find enough remains to prove their case. Haigh then pretends to be insane, asking jailers: "What's it like at Broadmoor?" (the prison for the criminally insane, where he expects to be sent). Haigh then brags how he has murdered eight others in the past, destroying their bodies with sulphuric acid; he is dubbed by the press "The Acid Bath Murderer" and is quoted as having drunk his victims' blood as would a vampire; his ruse is apparent, and his insanity pleas will be denied; Haigh will be hanged at Wandsworth Prison on Aug. 10, 1949.

John George Haigh, England's infamous "Acid Bath" murderer. (Feb. 18, 1949)

mercial airliner, to collect insurance money on a relative; the bomb explodes in-flight on a Philippine plane en route to Manila, killing 13; Vergo later is caught, convicted and imprisoned.

MAY 7

Crispin Vergo plants the first bomb on board a com-

AUG. 12

With a hammer, London housewife Mrs. Nora Patricia Tierney inexplicably crushes the head of Marion Ward, a six-year-old child of a neighbor, then tries to throw the blame on her husband; she is found guilty and sent to Broadmoor Prison for the criminally insane.

AUG. 22

Mrs. Martha Beck and her lover, Raymond Fernandez, who have been running an interstate lonely hearts swindle in which Fernandez has played the role of stud and they have murdered several women for their money, are convicted in New York City for the murder of Mrs. Janet Faye; Mrs. Beck will eat two complete chicken dinners before she follows Fernandez to Sing Sing's electric chair on March 8, 1951.

SEPT. 6

War hero Howard Unruh, who has withdrawn into himself in recent months, expressing paranoia about neighbors, suddenly goes berserk in Camden, N.J., shooting 13 people in 12 minutes; he later barricades his house to shoot it out with police but is captured; the mass murderer is sent for life to an asylum for the criminally insane.

SEPT. 9

To get rid of his wife, Rita Morel Guay, so he can live with his mistress, waitress Marie-Ange Robitaille, Albert Guay of Québec City, Canada, plants a bomb on Flight 108 of Canadian Pacific Airlines; the bomb explodes 40 miles outside Québec City; killed with Mrs. Guay are 22 others, including three children; Guay also has taken out $10,000 in flight insurance on his wife; he and two others who have helped prepare and plant the bomb, Marguerite Pitre and her cretinous brother Genereaux Ruest, will all be hanged. Ruest will confess and name his accomplices.

OCT. 10

Advertising executive Daniel Raven batters his in-laws Leopold and Esther Goodman to death with a TV aerial in London, then races home to change his blood-soaked clothes; investigating police note his immaculate appearance late at night when they arrive to question him; then discover his half-burned, bloodied clothes in a boiler room; Raven will be found guilty, and hanged at Pentonville Prison on July 6, 1950.

ROBBERY

JUNE 25

The South Chicago Savings Bank is held up by five bandits; one of them, a machine gunner named Jakalski, sprays two Brink's guards, Joseph Den and Joseph Koziol, killing them instantly as they appear on the scene to make a delivery; the bandits take only $920 in cash and $377,000 in bank-endorsed, nonnegotiable checks; four of the bandits are caught within a month, Jakalski being extradited from Cheyenne, Wyo., where he is being held as a vagrant; Jakalski will be acquitted twice of murdering the guards, but will be sent to prison for 199 years for the robbery.

NOV. 7

Call girl Jean Lee; her pimp, Robert David Clayton;

Mrs. Martha Beck (left) and her lover, Raymond Fernandez (second from right), the notorious "lonely-hearts killers." (Aug. 22, 1949)

and a thug, Norman Andrews, rob wealthy bookmaker William George Kent in a Carlton, Australia, hotel, torturing him with a broken bottle until he tells them where he has hidden his money; the trio are arrested in a Sydney bar while celebrating the theft and are told that Kent has died of his injuries; all three will be hanged on Feb. 19, 1951, at Pentridge Jail.

ORGANIZ͟ CRIMl

JAN. 8

New York City c͟ agent Charles E. Wyatt announces the arrest of ͟eral wealthy importers in connection with a $300͟0 cache of opium that has been smuggled into the ͟.S.; Wyatt states that Lucky Luciano is behi͟ dope-smuggling ring, but this claim is not p͟e͟

͟ansky and his wife sail to Italy on the *Italia*, ͟ on a honeymoon but in reality to set up a ͟ce between gangster Meyer Lansky and Lu-

AUG. 19

Salvatore Guiliano and his bandits, fighting for the Mafia in Sicily, kill seven *carabinieri* and wound 11 others in a wild gun battle near Palermo.

SEPT. 16

Philip "Little Farfel" Kavolick, a Meyer Lansky confidant, is found dead on a suburban road in Valley Stream, N.Y., with six bullets in his head.

WHITE-COLLAR CRIME

JAN. 1

In an effort to rid the community of all gambling, Twin Falls, Idaho, cancels all licenses for slot machines; other municipalities in the state follow suit.

JAN. 17

Salvatore Sollazzo, in an elaborate scheme, fixes the basketball game between Long Island University and North Carolina State, bribing players; Sollazzo will go on to fix innumerable other games with a host of confederates and involving many top players, a scandal that will not be made public until 1951.

MAY 24

Congress passes new legislation prohibiting the use of gambling ships off U.S. shores.

MISCELLANEOUS

JAN 9

B. Simonovich, one of the world's most notorious alien smugglers, is arrested in Florida and indicted but skips to Havana, Cuba.

SEPT. 3–4

Communist underground workers set fires all over Chungking, China, in widespread terrorist arson that leaves more than 100,000 homeless.

1·9·5·0

MURDER

AUG. 5

Attractive Jacqueline Richardson, 27, is murdered by her lover, Jean Liger, who buries her body in a shallow grave outside Paris; her body later is discov-

ered, and Liger will be arrested and tried in 1955, telling a French court: "She wanted to marry me, but it was not for a home or for children, but to have someone like me at her disposal. She thought of nothing else . . . I didn't want to marry a loving machine." Incredibly, Liger will be convicted only of manslaughter and will be given seven years' hard labor.

NOV. 17

Ernest Ingenito, a mentally disturbed malcontent, argues with his wife, Theresa, in Minotola, N.J., then grabs two Luger pistols, a carbine and a hunting knife and drives to the home of his in-laws, the Mike Mazzoli family, in Gloucester County, shooting and killing seven of the family members; he will be apprehended a short time later, will be convicted of five murder charges and will be sent for life to the New Jersey State Hospital for the Insane.

DEC. 31

William Cook, an itinerant vagrant, robs several motorists in Texas, then stops Carl Mosser's car near Tulsa, Okla., killing Mosser and his entire family, for which he will be executed on Dec. 12, 1952.

Mass killer William Cook in custody in Tijuana, Mexico. (Dec. 31, 1950)

ROBBERY

JAN. 17

Eleven men led by Anthony "Fats" Pino and Joseph F. "Big Joe" McGinnis rob the Brink's armored car service center in Boston of $2,775,395; one of the gang, Joseph "Specs" O'Keefe, who is cut out of his share of the loot, later will inform on the gang, and all of them will be rounded up and given stiff prison sentences.

Joseph "Specs" O'Keefe (right), one of the 11 men who robbed Brink's in Boston of millions; he then turned in the others. (Jan. 17, 1950)

ORGANIZED CRIME

FEB. 6

A dynamite bomb explodes the front of gangster Mickey Cohen's Los Angeles home, but the gunman escapes injury.

APRIL 6

Syndicate chief Charlie Binaggio and his bodyguard are shot to death in the First District Democratic Headquarters in Kansas City.

MAY 26

Senator Estes Kefauver begins hearings into the criminal career of Meyer Lansky in Florida.

JUNE 5

High-ranking Florida mobster Jimmy Lumia is murdered by Mafia hit men in Tampa.

JULY 4

Romantic Sicilian bandit chieftain Salvatore Giuliano, long a tool of the Mafia, and who has heard that he has been marked for death for kidnapping Mafia *capo di capi* Don Carlo and the archbishop of Monreale, is murdered near Portella della Ginestra by his lieutenant and cousin, Gaspare Pisciotta, as Giuliano sleeps in his bed. His body later is photographed in a town square, a carbine at his side, a fake death scene to support the claim that the bandit has been slain in a gun battle with police. Pisciotta later confesses the murder, stating that Guiliano has been killed because he actually intended to overthrow the Mafia in Sicily (where it still reigns supreme). In a later statement Pisciotta tells magistrates that the Mafia is integral with Sicilian society and culture: "We were a single body, bandits, police and Mafia, like the Father, the Son and the Holy Ghost."

SEPT. 16

Meyer Lansky, Vincent "Jimmy Blue Eyes" Alo and six others plead guilty to illegally operating three casinos in Broward County Fla.; they receive light sentences.

SEPT. 25

Chicago Police Capt. William Drury is shot to death while sitting in his car on Addison Street, an obvious syndicate killing (with shotguns); reportedly Drury has been on the mob payroll.

DEC. 11

Samuel L. Rummel, Mickey Cohen's lawyer, is shotgunned to death in Los Angeles. Two suspects in the killing, Tony Trombino and Tony Brancato, later are killed by shotgun blasts reportedly fired by Cohen.

DEC. 13

Willie Moretti, onetime syndicate boss of New Jersey, appears before a U. S. Senate subcommittee in Washington, D.C. to testify on organized crime. Moretti says little, but Luciano, Frank Costello and others believe he will later turn informer, so Moretti will be shot to death while eating dinner in Joe's Restaurant in Cliffside Park, N.J., on Oct. 4, 1951.

WHITE-COLLAR CRIME

MARCH 10-MAY 1

Joseph Levy, impersonating prison officials, orders huge quantities of supplies for Sing Sing, paying by personal checks that allow for surplus amounts to be paid to him in cash; the checks, of course, are worthless; later Levy will be apprehended and imprisoned.

DEC. 26

William Henry Waldron, Jr., a distinguished lawyer in Huntington, W. Va., embezzles $7,000 from a local bank and vanishes; he will turn up as Robert Coleman Johnson, a commercial fisherman in Madeira Beach, Fla., and be arrested on Aug. 21, 1966, after beating his wife, Phyllis, to death; he will be sent on Feb. 2, 1967, to the state prison at Raiford to serve 20 years for second-degree murder.

MISCELLANEOUS

SEPT. 24

Minneapolis drug dealer John Wong shoots a federal agent while Wong's rooms are being searched; Wong will go to prison for life.

1·9·5·1

MURDER

JAN. 12

Shopkeeper Frederick Gosling, 79, of Chertsey in Surrey, England, is found dead, tied to a chair, his head crushed and his shop looted; the victim is said to have hoarded thousands of pounds on the premises; schoolgirls later report having seen two men in the shop attacking the owner and identify Joseph Brown and Edward Charles Smith, who will be convicted, and hanged at Wandsworth Prison on April 25.

MARCH 17

Onetime medical student Pauline Dubuisson shoots her lover, Felix Bailly, to death in his Paris apartment after learning he intends to marry another; she will be sent to prison for life.

APRIL 10

San Francisco business executive Milton Morris is shot to death by his wife, Gertrude, who thinks he is transferring his affections to his secretary; brilliant attorney Jake Ehrlich rushes to defend her, but Mrs. Morris laughs at his attempts; she shouts to reporters in court: "I'm a criminal! I murdered someone! I owe society a life!" When Ehrlich manages to get her only a manslaughter conviction and an eight-year prison sentence, Gertrude Morris sneers before being led away by matrons and snaps at him: "Well, Master, I suppose this is one more feather in your cap!"

AUG. 9

Herbert Leonard Mills, a nineteen-year-old poet, calls a London newspaper to report finding the body of 48-year-old Mabel Tattershaw of Nottingham. He insists that he alone report the story, bragging of his writing prowess, and is paid to do so for *News of the World;* the story amounts to a confession, which editors turn over to police; Mills confesses the killing, saying that he has seduced his victim after she fell into a trance over his poetry and that he has killed her to commit the perfect murder; "The strangling itself was quite easily accomplished," he brags; Mills will be executed in December.

AUG. 26

Debauchee Michael Gelfand, onetime Paris playboy who has been living off various women for 15 years, shoots his mistress, Edith Tarbouriech, then himself; he survives, spending two years in jail awaiting trial; he has murdered his mistress, he will say, because she has insulted his honor; he will be sentenced to two years' imprisonment, or time served, and released following his trial; Gelfand will die 15 days later while walking down the Champs Élysées, his own bullet still lodged next to his heart finally killing him in what some term ironic justice.

DEC. 13

Film producer Walter Wanger attempts to murder Jennings Lang by shooting him in Beverly Hills, Calif., over the affections of Wanger's wife, Joan Bennett; Lang, who is Bennett's agent, survives, and charges against Wanger are dropped.

ROBBERY

JULY 8

A Brink's armored car is attacked by three bandits as it parks in front of the Bowman Dairy Company in Chicago to pick up receipts; the bandits attack driver Julius Blanchart, who is struck on the head with a shotgun butt; he remains conscious, pulls his pistol and kills one of the bandits, wounding another; his fellow guards rush forward to kill the wounded bandit, who is drawing another gun; the third bandit escapes; through Blanchart's courage, not a dime of the Brink's money is lost.

OCT. 20

In Chicago, more than $230,000 in jewels and furs are stolen by burglars from the Congress Hotel Jewel & Fur Shop owned by Mrs. Pearl Lowenberg Robinson; the furs and jewels will never be recovered.

ORGANIZED CRIME

MARCH 14

Frank Costello, known as "The Prime Minister" of the crime syndicate, appears before the Kefauver U.S. Senate crime committee in a New York City federal court; his testimony contributes little to their investigations.

JUNE 18

Mob henchman Leonard "Fat Lennie" Caifano is killed in Chicago while attacking Theodore Roe.

JUNE 20

Mickey Cohen, West Coast syndicate sachem, is sentenced to five years in prison and fined $10,000 for tax evasion.

WHITE-COLLAR CRIME

FEB. 17

Louis Rosenbaum of Cincinnati testifies before a U.S. Senate crime committee concerning his gambling operations, admitting to making bets and taking layoff bets from bookmakers.

FEB. 18

Salvatore Sollazzo is arrested for his basketball fix-

West Coast gangster Mickey Cohen (right) with bodyguard Johnny Stompanato; Cohen briefly inherited Bugsy Siegel's crime kingdom until ousted by the Mafia. (June 20, 1951)

ing; many of the game's stars, including All-American Sherman White for LIU; Connie "Crazy Shots" Schaff of NYU; Gene Melchiorre of Bradley; and Ralph Beard, Alex Groza and Dale Barnstable of Kentucky are arrested for taking bribes in the worst basketball scandal on record; Sollazzo will be indicted on Feb. 29, 1952.

MISCELLANEOUS

JAN. 23
Top New York City gambler Harry Gross pleads guilty to 66 counts of bookmaking and conspiracy to violate gambling laws.

FEB. 15
Saul Chabot attempts to smuggle $171,197 in gold hidden behind the fender of his 1950 Buick sedan, which is accompanying him and his wife on the *Queen Elizabeth* en route for Europe; Chabot is arrested by customs agents in his cabin before sailing and later will receive a five-year prison term.

APRIL 5
Julius and Ethel Rosenberg of New York City are sentenced to death for stealing atomic bomb secrets and giving these to the Soviet Union.

JULY 22
Pyromaniac Kenneth Skinner, 17, is sent to San Quentin for 10 years after setting fire to a San Francisco apartment building in which eight persons burn to death.

1·9·5·2

MURDER

FEB. 17

Leone Bouvier, a comely young woman in Saint-Macaire-en-Mauges, France, shoots her boyfriend, Émile Clenet, after he insults her, telling her that he is leaving her to live a new life in the U.S.; she will be sent to prison for life.

MARCH 24

The body of Hilda Rose Pagan, 16, is found beaten to a pulp in Mission Park, San Francisco; Ivan Rodriguez, her 18-year-old boyfriend, is questioned and he confesses that he has killed the girl because he could not bring himself to have sex with her and after she angrily called him ''a queer''; Rodriguez will receive a life sentence.

AUG. 4

Sir Jack Drummond, a noted British biochemist on vacation in France, is shot along with his wife and daughter at a campsite near the village of Lurs in Provence; Gaston Dominici is accused of the murders by his son Gustave and later admits that he made advances to Drummond's wife after he witnessed her undressing at the campsite; when Drummond intervened, Dominici shot the scientist, then the wife and daughter; the 75-year-old farmer will be sentenced to death, then have his sentence commuted to life imprisonment; he will be released in 1960, dying in 1965.

NOV. 12

Ian Hay Gordon attacks university student Patricia Curran, 19-year-old daughter of a Belfast, Ireland, judge; stabbing her 37 times when she resists his sexual advances. Gordon, an RAF serviceman stationed at Edenmore, near Belfast, gives himself away to other airmen when asking them to provide an alibi for him; he is arrested and confesses the murder but will be judged insane and sent to an asylum for life.

ROBBERY

JULY 16

Habitual criminal, housebreaker and burglar Leslie Green enters the home of wealthy 62-year-old Alice Wiltshaw in Barlaston, Staffordshire, England, taking more than £3,000 worth of jewelry, including rings from Mrs. Wiltshaw, whom Green murders; her body is found in a pool of blood by her husband; police conclude that the intruder knows the house well enough to make his move when the servants are off duty; witnesses describe a man on the premises at the time of the robbery-murder, and this leads police to arrest Leslie Green, a former chauffeur-gardener for the Wiltshaws; some of the stolen rings surface when Green's girlfriend admits Green has given them to her; denying his guilt to the end, Green will be hanged at Winson Green Prison outside Birmingham, England, on Dec. 23.

SEPT. 12

Jewelry salesman Fred Wasserman is slugged on Milwaukee Avenue in Chicago and his sample case taken, containing more than $30,000 in gems; though several suspects are taken into custody, the robber will not be found.

NOV. 2

Warehouse thieves Derek Bentley and Christopher Craig break into a London warehouse, when they are surprised by police; Craig, cornered on a rooftop; shoots and kills Constable Sydney George Miles before jumping from the roof and fracturing his spine; both youths are taken captive and charged with robbery-murder; Craig, who is only 16, is sent to prison for an indeterminate time, but Bentley is convicted of murder although he never fired the weapon; he was heard to shout to Craig: ''Let him have it!'' and therefore is held responsible for the shooting, although Bentley's lawyers insist what Bentley meant was that Craig was to turn over the pistol to Constable Miles; nevertheless, feebleminded Bentley will be hanged on Jan. 23, 1953, amid a violent storm of protest that, more than any other execution, leads to the ending of capital punishment in Great Britain.

NOV. 13

Two Brink's guards, Bud Murray and Al Pukay, enter the Canadian Bank of Commerce in Walkerville, Ont., Canada, to find two bandits robbing the vaults and tellers' cages, the bank's 22 employees all handcuffed and lying on the floor; the guards draw their guns and fire at the bandits, who flee without a dime; Pukay and Murray chase the bandits to the street, where the robbers commandeer a passenger car and make a successful escape, never to be captured.

Organized Crime

SEPT. 10

Meyer Lansky is arrested as a common gambler in New York City; he pleads guilty and serves 90 days.

SEPT. 20

Anthony Strollo, Mafia chieftain in New York City, orders Eugenio Giannini killed; Giannini is shot to death in East Harlem.

OCT. 21

Because of widespread arson and murder by berserk Mau Mau warriors in Kenya, a state of emergency is declared and troops are marshaled to fight what has become a near-army of thugs and killers, hundreds of whom have taken the secret Mau Mau oath. Jomo Kenyatta and 83 other Mau Mau suspects are arrested. Kenyatta will be tried in January 1953 and imprisoned until 1961 until the secret murder sect is stamped out. On Oct. 22 Chief Nderi approaches a crowd taking the Mau Mau oath in a Kenyan village and orders them to disperse; he and two tribal policemen are cut to pieces. Two days later, Eurpoean farmer Eric Bowyer and his two houseboys are slaughtered by Mau Maus. On Nov. 26 Tom Mbotela, a Nairobi City councilor who has denounced Mau Mau and is prepared to testify against Kenyatta, is slain. European deaths throughout the Mau Mau terror will number 32, but the savagery of attacks—in one instance Mau Maus who had been long-time servants on a European farm turned on the family, slaughtering them, disemboweling six-year-old Michael Ruck while still alive—arouses all Kenya (there are 45,000 Europeans living in the country and they will put together their own militia).

White-Collar Crime

NOV. 1

Authorities in New Orleans crack down on illegal gambling operations; more than a dozen gamblers are arrested in connection with a nationwide racetrack betting scheme involving AT&T employees who have been paid to rig betting results.

Miscellaneous

APRIL 29

Stephen Schrieber of New York City has made millions in smuggling gold to Europe and, with the proceeds, buying diamonds and smuggling these into the U.S. for sale at an enormous profit; he arranges for passage on the *Queen Mary* sailing for Europe, his "accompanying baggage" being a 1949 Pontiac with a specially built gasoline tank containing $110,000 in gold, which is found by customs agents after they strip the car in a service station; they replace the tank and wait at the gangplank to arrest Schrieber when he embarks on the *Queen Mary,* but apparently the master smuggler is warned and skips the country on a fake passport; he is never found, although he will be variously reported in Canada, Europe and South America.

SEPT. 8

In Toronto, four of Canada's toughest bank robbers, including Georges Lemay, break out of the local jail by sawing through the bars of their cells; all will be recaptured within weeks.

=1·9·5·3=

Murder

JAN. 17

Werner Boost shoots and kills a lawyer near Dusseldorf, Germany; the mass murderer will kill a young couple in November 1955, also near Dusseldorf, and will perform another "double murder" in 1956 by shooting another couple; Franz Lorbach, Boost's accomplice, is apprehended and he confesses, implicating Boost, who is not tried until 1959, when he is sent to prison for life, West Germany having no capital punishment.

MARCH 9

Barbara Graham murders elderly Mrs. Monohan

10 Rillington Place, London, the address of mass murderer John Christie. (March 24, 1953)

during a break-in of her Los Angeles home; Ms. Graham will go to San Quentin's gas chamber on June 3, 1953.

MARCH 24

A West Indian tenant at 10 Rillington Place, London, smells a powerful odor and, tearing down a thin-walled cupboard, discovers three women's bodies; police are summoned and find another body beneath the floorboards and two more female bodies buried in the small garden; the former tenant, John Reginald Halliday Christie, is arrested and readily confesses to murdering the females, including his wife; he is also responsible for the 1949 murders of upstairs neighbors Mrs. Evans and her daughter Geraldine, murders for which Timothy John Evans, the husband, was hanged (Evans was a mental defective and confessed to the murders under police pressure); Christie explains that he has strangled his victims while having sex with them, the only way he can have intercourse; this sexually inadequate fiend—he was called "Reggie No Dick" at school—is hanged at Pentonville Prison on July 15.

APRIL 11

Party girl Wilma Montessi is found almost naked; drowned at a beach outside Rome; later it will be determined that she has been murdered by an overdose of drugs; playboy Hugo Montagna, at whose lavish home Wilma has earlier indulged in sex orgies and

Italian party girl Wilma Montessi, found murdered on a beach near Rome. (April 11, 1953)

Crowds outside Strangeways Prison protesting the hanging of Mrs. Louise Merrifield in Manchester, England. (April 14, 1953)

drug parties, is accused of having drugged the party girl, but evidence is lacking; her murder will never be solved.

APRIL 14

Mrs. Louise Merrifield of Blackpool, England, poisons Mrs. Sarah Ann Ricketts, for whom she works as a housekeeper, in an attempt to obtain her modern bungalow and inheritance; Mrs. Merrifield has made several fatal slips, talking about obtaining a new house as an inheritance *before* slaying her victim and asking a physician to certify that Mrs. Ricketts is well enough to make out a new will in her favor long before she poisons her victim; after Mrs. Ricketts dies of obvious poisoning, Mrs. Merrifield is arrested; she will be hanged at Strangeways Prison, Manchester, on Sept. 18.

MAY 31

Barbara Songhurst and Christine Reed, teenagers in Teddington, England, vanish, their bodies found days

Mrs. Styllon Pantopiou Christofi, who strangled her daughter-in-law out of jealousy in London. (July 29, 1953)

later, both raped, battered about the head and stabbed to death; a month later Alfred Charles Whiteaway, a 22-year-old laborer and married man, is arrested for attacking two women and raping one on Oxshott Heath in Surrey; an ax belonging to Whiteaway is found with blood on it, and he signs a confession admitting the Songhurst and Reed killings, which he later tries to deny; he will be hanged at Wandsworth Prison on Dec. 22.

JULY 29

Mrs. Styllon Christofi strangles her daughter-in-law, Mrs. Hella Christofi, to death with her own scarf in their London home, then sets the body on fire, which brings passersby into the house; the murder is apparent, and Mrs. Christofi admits hating her daughter-in-law and being fearful that her son would soon abandon her; at her trial it is pointed out that Mrs. Styllon Christofi had been acquitted of murdering her mother-in-law in 1925 when someone jammed a burning torch down that ill-fated woman's throat; Mrs. Styllon Christofi will be hanged on Dec. 13, 1954, at Holloway Prison.

SEPT. 12

Shirley Collins, 14, is sexually assaulted and murdered at Mount Martha, outside Melbourne, Australia; although police round up dozens of sex offenders as suspects, her killer is never found.

SEPT. 28

Carl Austin Hall and Mrs. Bonnie Heady kidnap and kill six-year-old Bobby Greenlease, Jr., son of a wealthy car dealer in Kansas City, Mo., then collect $600,000 in ransom money; they go on a drinking binge—Hall is an alcoholic—and soon are discovered; both will be sent to the gas chamber on Dec. 18.

OCT. 16

Thomas Ronald Harries murders his adopted uncle and aunt, John and Phoebe Harries, on their farm near Carmarthenshire, England, and buries their bodies in a field; Scotland Yard detectives grow suspicious with Harries's explanation that his aunt and uncle have inexplicably gone to London and make a disturbance outside the farmhouse some nights later; Harries rushes

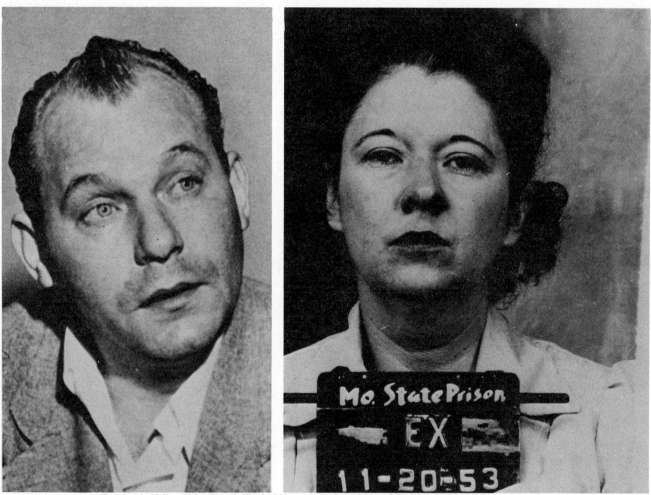

Carl Austin Hall and Mrs. Bonnie Heady, kidnappers and murderers of Bobby Greenlease, Jr. (Sept. 28, 1953)

Workmen removing the body of six-year-old Bobby Greenlease from a shallow grave behind Mrs. Heady's home in St. Joseph, Mo. (Sept. 28, 1953)

mass murders; firemen arrive quickly, put out the fire and discover the murder wounds; Ciucci will be quickly convicted and will be sent to the electric chair in 1962.

ROBBERY

APRIL 14

A pickpocket, in order to make his job easier while attending a Caracas, Venezuela, church ceremony at the beginning of Holy Week, begins to shout: ''Fire! Fire!'' Thousands stampede, trampling to death 53 persons; the pickpocket makes off with their wallets and purses and is not caught.

DEC. 4

Chicago robber Richard Carpenter, who has committed scores of holdups in recent months, shoots and kills Police Lt. Murphy and is later surrounded when taking refuge with local resident Leonard Powell, shooting it out with cops; Carpenter finally is subdued and taken into custody; he will go to the electric chair on March 16, 1956.

ORGANIZED CRIME

MARCH 26

A Mau Mau gang raids a police arsenal at Naivasha, Kenya, taking large stores of guns and ammunition. Later that night, the village of Lari in the Rift Valley is attacked by hundreds of Mau Maus, many of them high on drugs. They overpower Chief Luka, a long-time Mau Mau foe, and dissect him alive, throwing his remains in the faces of his eight wives. One woman has her arm chopped off, and her baby is decapitated; she watches in horror as crazed Mau Maus drink the infant's blood (she survives to identify later 50 of the killers who will be hanged). Most of the village's victims, 84 in all, are women and children. Before departing, the Mau Maus burn down 200 buildings and slaughter 1,000 cattle; only 31 persons, all mutilated, survive. The mass killing shocks the world.

JUNE 11

Clem Graver, 21st Ward Republican Committee-man in Chicago and a state representative, drives away with three unidentified men and is never seen again; Graver was mob-connected, according to some sources, and was marked for death.

outside and runs to the secret graves, leading police to the victims; later he will be hanged at Swansea Prison.

NOV. 30

Frederick Emmett-Dunne, a British sergeant serving in occupied Duisberg, Germany, quarrels with Reginald Watters, a fellow sergeant, and kills him with a single karate blow; he tells superiors that Watters has committed suicide, an explanation that is unquestioningly accepted; Emmett-Dunne will return to England and marry Watters' widow; the dead man's friends, however, insist that Watters would never commit suicide, and the case will be reopened; Dr. Francis Camps, an eminent pathologist, will examine the exhumed body of Watters and determine that he was killed by a karate chop to the throat; Emmett-Dunne will be convicted on medical evidence alone and given life imprisonment.

DEC. 1

Maniac Carl J. Folk is released from a mental institution and enters a camper at an Arizona rest area, where he overpowers Raymond Allen; he then rapes Allen's wife and murders her; Allen manages to break loose of his bonds and grabs a hidden gun, shooting Folk in the stomach; Folk will be sent to the gas chamber in March 1955.

DEC. 4

Vincent Ciucci, in order to live with his mistress, chloroforms his wife and three children, shoots them, then sets fire to his Chicago apartment to cover the

JUNE 19

According to his later nonstop revelations concerning New York City Cosa Nostra operations, Joseph Valachi, on orders of his boss, Vito Genovese, murders, with three others, police informant Stephen Franse in Greenwich Village, N.Y.

OCT. 1

The body of Chicago syndicate subboss Anthony Ragucci is pulled from a sewer, where it has been stuffed by unknown killers.

WHITE-COLLAR CRIME

MARCH 9

The U.S. Supreme Court upholds the constitutionality of the federal gambling tax.

JUNE 5

Con men Jean Berthier and Raymond Alberto, who have passed themselves off to French Riviera tycoon Baron Scipion du Roure de Beruyere as secret agents for the French government attempting to buy up caches of uranium for the West (and bilking Baron Beruyers out of millions of francs in the process), are sent to prison for four years; they laugh hysterically in the dock on hearing the sentence.

OCT. 1

International swindler Abram Sykowski, in custody of Paris police, escapes and vanishes forever.

MISCELLANEOUS

JAN. 11

A homemade bomb secreted by social malcontent George Peter Metesky, who will be known as New York City's "Mad Bomber," explodes in the Pennsylvania railroad station on 34th Street at the height of the rush hour, injuring several persons.

MAY 1

Sex deviate Clarence E. Watson lies in wait for attractive airline stewardess Althea Dixon as she enters her Washington, D.C., apartment, then brutally and repeatedly rapes her; he will later be identified and sent to prison for 13 years.

1·9·5·4

MURDER

JAN. 2

The Tuskegee Institute reports that not a single lynching has occurred in the U.S. in the past two years.

FEB. 3

Under the pretext of painting her portrait, William Sanchez de Pina Hepper rapes and strangles 11-year-old Margaret Spevick, whose mother has given her permission to travel to Brighton, England, to stay with Hepper and his daughter, her friend; the 62-year-old onetime American spy in Spain and BBC translator vanishes on Feb. 7 when Mrs. Spevick finds her slain daughter in his Brighton apartment; he will be located in Spain and extradited to England to stand trial; his defense will be paranoia, sexual impotency and loss of memory, but he will be hanged at Wandsworth Prison on Aug. 11.

FEB. 15

Christa Lehman of Worms, Germany, inexplicably poisons three neighbors to death by giving them chocolate truffles laced with a phosphorus compound known as E-605, as painstakingly determined by forensic scientist Kurt Wagner; Christa will confess and be sent to prison for life.

FEB. 16

Wanted murderer John Donald Merrett, alias Ronald Chesney, a playboy from an upper-crust Scottish family, is found dead, an apparent suicide with a bullet in his brain, near Cologne, Germany; Merrett, who

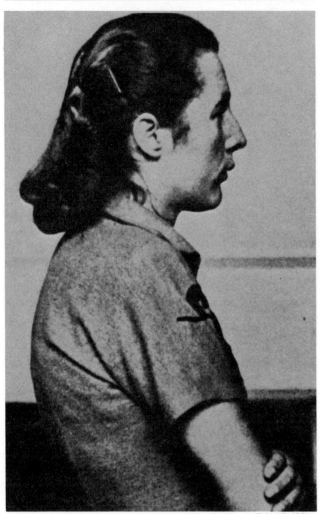

Mass poisoner Christa Lehman of Worms, West Germany. (Feb. 15, 1954)

was acquitted of murdering his mother in 1926–she was found shot in the head at her breakfast table, and Merrett claimed she had committed suicide—has drowned his wife, Vera, in her bathtub after getting her drunk and crushed the skull of his mother-in-law in Ealing, England, where she had been running a nursing home.

MARCH 4

In New York City, William Snyder Byers murders Mrs. Anna Gresch at the urging of her daughter, his girlfriend, Theresa Gresch, because Mrs. Gresch objects to Byers; he will go to the electric chair indifferent to his fate, chewing bubble gum; Theresa Gresch will be sent to prison for 25 years.

JUNE 2

Mrs. Lorraine Clark of Amesbury, Mass., angry because her husband, Melvin, objects to her flirting with several men during a party they give at their home, stabs him in the heart with darning needles, shoots him several times, then trusses up the body and drives to the Merrimack River, where she ties three 15-pound weights to the corpse and dumps it into the water; she next files for divorce, saying her "abusive" husband has left her; instead of washing out to sea, as Mrs. Clark expects, the body washes ashore and is identified; Mrs. Clark will be sent to prison for life.

JUNE 11

G. Edward Grammer is hanged at the Maryland Penitentiary for murdering his wife in 1952 for the sake of another woman; the successful salesman has beaten his spouse to death, then placed her body in a car then sent careening down a road; police, however, have found a rock fixed to the accelerator, a standard ploy used to propel a driverless car; this clue leads to Grammer's arrest and execution.

JUNE 22

Pauline Parker and Juliet Hulme murder Mrs. Honora Mary Parker, beating her to death in a Canterbury, New Zealand, park, because Mrs. Parker has refused to allow her daughter, Pauline, to accompany Juliet's family on their move to South Africa; both girls, lesbians, will be given short prison terms and will be released in 1958.

JULY 3–4

Dr. Sam Sheppard of Cleveland murders his wife, Marilyn, so he can be with another woman, according to a 1954 conviction; F. Lee Bailey will manage to win Sheppard a new trial 12 years later, in which he will be cleared of the killing, although many feel that Sheppard, who will die in 1970 of natural causes, was guilty.

SEPT. 9

When fellow workers in Elizabeth City, N.C., laugh at Robert William Jordan's fears about serving in the Army—he has just been drafted—the 22-year-old plant worker grabs a rifle from his locker and shoots four of them, killing three; he will be given a life sentence.

SEPT. 10

In a crude scheme to take over his employer's estate in Stinson Beach, Calif., Filipino houseboy Bart Caritativo murders wealthy Camille and Joseph Banks, forging an illiterate will that leaves everything to him; Caritativo will go to San Quentin's gas chamber on Oct. 24, 1958.

NOV. 8

Demented by love, 20-year-old Denise Labbe drowns her 2½-year-old daughter Catherine at Blois, France, at the instigation of her perverted lover, Jacques Algarron, who has demanded she kill the little girl to prove her love for him. "It was a love ritual," Denise tells police. She will go to prison for life; Algarron will receive a 20-year sentence.

ORGANIZED CRIME

FEB. 9

Gaspare Pisciotta, who is informing on the operations of the Mafia and is being held in police custody, is poisoned in his cell in the Palermo, Sicily, jail; an autopsy shows that he has been dosed with 20 milligrams of strychnine, enough to kill a dozen men.

APRIL 18

Waruhiu Itote, onetime corporal in the Royal African Rifles and railway fireman who leads more than 5,000 Mau Maus on Mount Kenya (he calls himself "General China"), is captured and is persuaded to inform on other leaders and help break up the secret society. He is placed in a prison camp with Jomo Kenyatta and later points him out, while wearing a hood to prevent retaliation (which became the widespread custom with all informers, who helped to identify more than 17,000 Mau Maus), as the leader of the criminal society. Thousands of the murderers are executed, many more thousands will be given long prison sentences.

WHITE-COLLAR CRIME

MAY 30–AUG. 1

Scores of hustling con clans, known as the "Williamsons" invade Iowa and Minnesota, working hundreds of home-repair cons that mulct tens of thousands of dollars from gullible citizens.

SEPT. 13

International swindler and con man Serge Rubinstein, who has been sent to prison in 1949 for draft evasion, is paroled.

MISCELLANEOUS

MARCH 1

Puerto Rican nationalist Lolita Lebron, 34, mother of two, and three male Puerto Ricans open fire on the assembled U.S. representatives from the House gallery in Washington, D.C.; five Congressmen are wounded, and Lebron and her companions are given life terms, which are commuted to time served, on Sept. 6, 1979, by President Jimmy Carter.

JUNE 9

Wealthy Evelyn Smith of Phoenix, Ariz., is kidnapped and held for $75,000 ransom by a lone abductor; the ransom is paid, the victim is released unharmed and the kidnapper is never caught.

1·9·5·5

MURDER

JAN. 26

Serge Rubinstein, international con man and swindler, is found strangled to death in his posh Manhattan apartment by his butler; Rubinstein's killer is never found.

APRIL 10

Nightclub hostess and bar shill Ruth Ellis shoots down her faithless lover, David Blakeley, on a London street in full view of passersby. The 28-year-old blonde states at her trial: "I intended to kill him." She would be found guilty within 14 minutes and, over a nationwide storm of protest, will be hanged on July 3 at Holloway Prison, the last woman in Great Britain to be executed.

APRIL 28

Burton W. Abbott of San Francisco strangles 14-year-old Stephanie Bryan in a sex killing; the girl's body is discovered by police on a lonely road some hours later; pieces of her clothing are found by Abbott's wife in her home, and she turns in her husband; Abbott will go to the gas chamber at San Quentin on March 15, 1957.

APRIL 29

Michael Queripel, a 17-year-old government employee in Potter's Bar, England, batters to death a Mrs. Currell on a golf course because, as he later tells police, he has a migraine headache; Queripel is caught after his bloody handprint, found on the golf club used to kill the victim, is matched to him, following the fingerprinting of more than 9,000 males in the community; Queripel is given a prison term of indefinite length because of his youth.

JUNE 14

Judge Charles E. Chillingworth and his wife, Marjorie, vanish from their West Palm Beach, Fla., estate; their disappearance will not be explained until 1960, when Floyd Albert Holzapfel, arrested for burglary, will tell police that he has taken the Chillingsworths out into the ocean and drowned them at the instigation of Judge Joseph A. Peel, Jr., whose rackets were interrupted by Judge Chillingsworth; Holzapfel will be sent to the electric chair; Peel will be given two concurrent life sentences.

JULY 22

Terence Armstrong, five-month-old infant of John and Janet Armstrong, dies ostensibly of eating poisoned berries in Gosport, England; but in 1956 Mrs. Armstrong, when separated from her husband, will infer that her husband poisoned their child; John Armstrong will deny his guilt but will be sent to prison; Mrs. Armstrong, acquitted, will later admit that she gave the child Seconal to help him sleep and therefore was responsible for his death. Her husband will be released.

AUG. 4

Arthur Ross Brown of San Francisco, a sex pervert, abducts Mrs. Wilma Frances Allen, 34, from a Kansas City, Mo., shopping center, robs her on a lonely road, strips her, then shoots her twice in the head, dumping her body in a field and stealing her car, which he later abandons; Brown, later turned in by his mother, who fears for her own life, will be sent to the gas chamber at the Missouri State Prison on Feb. 24, 1956.

SEPT. 1

Emmett Louis Till, a 15-year-old black, is mur-dered by a group of white men outside Greenwood, Miss., for allegedly whistling lewdly at a white woman; his body is thrown into the Tallahatchie River but floats to the surface; no one is prosecuted for this killing.

OCT. 6

Brothers John and Anton Schuessler, ages 13 and 11, respectively, and their friend Robert Peterson, 14, disappear from a northwestern Chicago bowling alley and are found 10 days later in the Robinson Woods Forest Preserve, all beaten, strangled to death and sexually molested; a citywide manhunt for the sex killer ensues with hundreds of deviates interrogated, but the murderer is never found.

NOV. 1

Jack Gilbert Graham heavily insures the life of his mother, Mrs. Daisie Walker King, then plants a bomb on board the plane she takes from Denver, United Air Lines Flight 629, which explodes 11 minutes after takeoff, killing all 44 persons on board; FBI agents find bomb apparatus in Graham's home, and he will be convicted and sent to the gas chamber at the Colorado Penitentiary on Jan. 11, 1957.

ROBBERY

AUG. 3

As a Brink's truck returns to the Buffalo branch office from the Fort Erie ractrack in Ontario, Canada, three bandits, who have broken into the garage, hold up the guards and, after a shoot-out, steal money boxes containing $489,500; Brink's guards, however, pursue the robbers and capture two of them and the money.

ORGANIZED CRIME

FEB. 27

Abner "Longy" Zwillman, syndicate boss of New Jersey, is found dangling from wires in the basement of his West Orange home; Vito Genovese later is named as Zwillman's killer by Meyer Lansky; many believe Lansky ordered the killing to eliminate a rival for his syndicate board seat.

MAY 31

IRS agents close their case of income-tax evasion against Meyer Lansky.

NOV. 4

Willie Bioff, who has informed on Chicago syndicate leaders, gets into his car in Phoenix, Ariz., where he has been living under the alias of Nelson, and is blown up as he steps on the accelerator.

NOV. 5

Authorities in Naples, Italy, hold hearings regarding resident Lucky Luciano and decide that he is "socially dangerous"; Luciano is barred from leaving his home between dusk and dawn.

WHITE-COLLAR CRIME

MARCH 14

In an odd decision, the U.S. Supreme Court rules that bookmaker Frank Lewis is subject to the $50 occupational tax on gambling, despite the law that prohibits gambling in Washington, D.C.

MISCELLANEOUS

MARCH 15

Frank Lew, a notorious international drug smuggler, opens operations in Hong Kong, using American sailors to smuggle hard drugs into the U.S.; T. A. Halverson, a U.S. sailor, takes one of Lew's opium packs aboard the M.S. *Fernhill,* where he turns informer and later collects $1,000 for smashing Lew's dope ring. Lew will be sent to prison.

JUNE 15

Notorious French criminal Roger Dekker escapes Fontevrault Prison near Paris while wearing a guard's uniform; Dekker is shot to death by gendarmes two days later.

DEC. 25

Customs officers in the U.S. Southwest conduct massive drug raids, chiefly in Houston, snaring dozens of dealers and pushers and collecting great drug caches and millions of dollars.

MURDER

FEB. 29

Social misfit Danny Metcalf is stopped by patrolman Gerald H. Mitchell near Paoli, Pa., as Metcalf drives through a stop sign; Metcalf shoots and kills the officer, drives through police barricades, crashing his car near Gladwyne, where he takes Mrs. Margaret Loweth and her 11-year-old son Billy hostage and attempts to drive through more police barricades in the Loweth car; the trio are cornered by police on March 1 in a rural area; Mrs. Loweth jams on the brakes, sending her car into a ditch; she flees as Metcalf grabs her son, using him as a shield, backing into some woods with a pistol to the boy's head as police close in; Metcalf stumbles, the boy escapes, and police open up a withering fusillade that kills Metcalf instantly.

AUG. 25

Freda Rumbold of Bristol, England, shoots her husband, Albert, as he sleeps, then puts up a sign on the bedroom door that reads: "Please do not enter." Police routinely investigating the disappearance of Albert Rumbold some days later smell the decomposing corpse and find the victim; Mrs. Rumbold will be sent to prison for life.

SEPT. 1

Ex-police officer William Lawrence Warren Nicholson of Fish Hook, South Africa, emerges from his house covered with blood and shouting, "My wife—I think she's been murdered!" Nicholson's wife, Sylvia, is found with her head crushed by a hammer; Nicholson states that a black intruder killed his wife, then struck him repeatedly with his own hammer, the murder weapon, one he has absentmindedly cleaned, wiping off his own fingerprints; he is arrested, and the prosecution will point out that it is unthinkable that an ex-police officer would destroy evidence unless he were guilty of the crime; Nicholson will be a miserable witness, will be convicted, and will be hanged on Aug. 12, 1957, maintaining his innocence until the end.

OCT. 2

Myrna Joy Aken, 18, vanishes from her Durban, South Africa, home; a medium tells the family that the girl's body will be found in a culvert some 60 miles distant; this proves to be true when the corpse is discovered near Umtwalumi; the girl has been raped, mutilated and shot several times with a .22-caliber weapon; Aken's next-door neighbor, Van Buuren, who has helped to search for her, is a prime suspect, admitting that he has been seeing her and that he took her for a drink on the night of the murder; Van Buuren, with a record of theft and forgery, claims that he left the girl alone in the car to buy some whiskey and when he returned he found her dead and panicked, driving the body to Umtwalumi, where he dumped it. Police find a large amount of .22-caliber ammunition in Van Buuren's home; he will be tried and convicted for the murder, hanged at Pretoria Prison on June 10, 1957.

DEC. 28

Patricia and Barbara Grimes, Chicago teenagers, vanish after seeing a movie and later are found naked, mutilated, sexually assaulted and strangled to death; an army of detectives follows hundreds of leads and arrests scores of suspects, but the case remains unsolved; it is thought that the killer is the same person who has slain the Schuessler brothers and Robert Peterson over a year earlier.

ROBBERY

JULY 18

William Liebscher, Jr. a California car salesman who takes up bank robbing when business drops off, robs the Bank of America in Daly City, Calif., of $1,750. (See "Robbery," May 10, 1957.)

ORGANIZED CRIME

JAN. 3

Joe Adonis (Joseph Doto), friend of film actor George Raft and one of the leaders of the U.S. crime syndicate, is deported to his native Italy, sailing on the *Conte Biancamano* from New York City en route to Naples, where he will meet with Lucky Luciano.

AUG. 18

Bill Bonanno, son of New York City boss Joe Bonanno, marries Rosalie Profaci, niece of Mafia don Joseph Profaci; attending the wedding are syndicate kingpins Frank Costello, Vito Genovese, Joseph Barbara, Albert Anastasia, Joseph Zerilli, Sam "Momo" Giancana, Tony Accardo and Stefano Magaddino.

OCT. 22

Dedan Kimathi, fierce Mau Mau leader in Kenya who is responsible for dozens of murders, last of the leaders of the secret criminal organization, is driven out of the Aberdares jungle, where he has been hiding for several years, and is captured. He will be tried, convicted and executed in 1957.

NOV. 9

Carmine Galante, New York City Mafia chief, receives a 30-day jail sentence and is fined $150 for trying to bribe a New Jersey traffic cop.

WHITE-COLLAR CRIME

APRIL 18–SEPT. 1

Bogus American Silver Mine stock is promoted by con man N. James Elliott, involving several motion-picture stars, but is exposed by the *New York Journal-American*.

MISCELLANEOUS

FEB. 28

Émile Buisson, one of France's most dangerous robbers, who has shot and killed several policemen, bank guards and messengers, is guillotined in Paris after calmly telling the executioner: "I am ready, Monsieur. You can go ahead. Society will be proud of you."

JULY 4

Peter Weinberger, a 32-day-old infant, is abducted from his Westbury, N.Y., home by Angelo John LeMarca and held for $2,000 ransom; LeMarca is tracked down by FBI agents after killing the child; he will be sent to the electric chair in Sing Sing on Aug. 8, 1958.

MURDER

MARCH 4

Edgar Herbert Smith is questioned when the body of 15-year-old Victoria Zielinski of Mahway, N.J., is found in a sandpit; though Smith, one of the girl's boyfriends, claims ignorance of her murder, he is convicted and sent to prison to await execution; he will spend 14 years on death row, writing appeal after appeal, authoring a successful book, *Brief Against Death,* and befriending through the mails columnist William F. Buckley, Jr., who will be instrumental in getting Smith released in 1971; in 1976, Smith will attack Lefteriya Ozbun while trying to steal her paycheck, repeatedly stabbing her in San Diego; he will then flee and call Buckley who, in turn, will inform FBI agents of the criminal's address in Las Vegas, where he will be arrested and returned to prison, where he remains at this writing.

MAY 3

Kenneth Barlow, a male nurse in London, calls police, telling them that his sick wife has drowned in their bathtub; he claims he has given her artificial respiration, but his pajamas are dry and there is no water on the bathroom floor from splashing, which would be evident in such a drowning; a careful inspection of the corpse reveals that Mrs. Barlow has been given two massive injections of insulin in the buttocks, enough to kill her; Barlow will be convicted and sent to prison for life.

JUNE 26

Melvin David Rees kills Margaret Harold as she sits in a car with an army sergeant near Annapolis, Md.; after subduing the sergeant, Rees will go on to murder Carroll Jackson, Carroll's wife and two children on a lonely road after raping Mrs. Jackson; the "Sex Beast," as Rees later is called, will be executed in 1961.

AUG. 1

Harvey Murray Glatman, who poses as a photographer for detective magazines, promises model Judy Ann Dull that her picture will appear in a national publication—"you know the typical bound-and-gagged stuff"—and when she is tied up, he rapes and strangles her in his Los Angeles home, burying her body in the desert; he will use the same *modus operandi* when killing Mrs. Shirley Bridgeford and Ruth Mercado in 1958; while later attempting to kill Lorraine Vigil he

will be apprehended and will confess his murders; Glatman will go to the gas chamber in San Quentin on Aug. 18, 1959.

AUG. 15–16

Judith Mae Anderson, 15-year-old Chicagoan, disappears from her West Side home; her chopped-up remains surface in 55-gallon drums floating in Montrose Harbor a week later; her killer is never found.

NOV. 1

One of the most beautiful and notorious call girls in Frankfurt, West Germany, Rosemarie Nitribitt, is found dead in her posh apartment, choked to death and her head bashed in; police interrogate hundreds of male clients in her phone book, many of whom panic and leave the country and a few of whom commit suicide rather than risk exposure of their sexual relationship with Rosemarie, but no one is convicted of the murder.

DEC. 1

Garbageman Charles Starkweather, a youth full of hate, kills gasoline station attendant Robert Colvert in Lincoln, Neb., then murders the mother, baby sister and stepfather of Caril Ann Fugate, his sweetheart, at her encouragement; within the month, Starkweather will kill six more persons, becoming one of the most dreaded mass murderers in America until he is cap-

Mass murderer Charles Starkweather, onetime Lincoln, Neb., garbage man. (Dec. 1, 1957)

tured near Douglas, Wyo.; Starkweather later will brag about his killings and go to Nebraska's gas chamber on June 25, 1959; Caril Fugate will go to prison for life but will be paroled in 1977, claiming that Starkweather compelled her to go along with him.

ROBBERY

MAY 10

William Liebscher, Jr., of Fairfax, Calif., robs a branch of the Bank of America in Napa City, Calif., of $2,555; on June 14 Liebscher, acting as a lone bandit, robs a single teller of $2,500 in the Western Bank in Fairfield, Calif.; on July 10 in San Francisco, Liebscher takes $700 from a teller in the American Trust Co. Liebscher's routine never varies: He makes his face up so that he looks older, goes into a bank to show the muzzle of a toy gun barely peeping from beneath a newspaper and hands the teller a note demanding only 20s, 10s and 5s; one teller finally notes part of the license plate identification on Liebscher's car, and Liebscher then is tracked down by FBI agents, to whom he meekly surrenders; he will be sentenced to 15 years in prison.

ORGANIZED CRIME

APRIL 16

Johnny Torrio, considered to be the grand architect of the national crime syndicate and who has been in retirement in New York City for a decade, dies of a heart attack in his bed.

MAY 2

Frank Costello is wounded by Frank "The Chin" Gigante as Costello returns home to his lavish apartment after dinner, in an abortive hit reportedly by Vito Genovese, who thinks to consolidate his power in New York City.

JUNE 10

Chicago Mafia chief Paul "The Waiter" Ricca has his U.S. citizenship revoked after a federal court rules he has entered the country illegally; Ricca wins a delay against deportation by facing charges of tax evasion.

AUG. 8

Johnny Dio (Dioguardi), high-ranking New York City gangster, takes the Fifth Amendment 140 times while testifying before the McClellan Senate committee investigating organized crime.

OCT. 25

Albert Anastasia, the most ruthless killer in the syndicate hierarchy, is shot to death while getting a shave in the barbershop of New York City's Park Sheraton Hotel; his two killers escape and are never identified.

NOV. 14

The notorious Mafia syndicate summit meeting at the Apalachin, N.Y., estate of Joseph Barbara is interrupted by invading state law-enforcement officers, who round up scores of mobsters from across the nation; dozens more flee on foot or by car through the surrounding hills.

WHITE-COLLAR CRIME

MAY 8

The U.S. Court of Appeals in a unanimous decision rules that wiretap evidence is admissible in federal courts if it is obtained by local police under a state court order.

DEC. 7

The U.S. Supreme Court overrules and reverses the conviction of the Court of Appeals in the Salvatore Bernanti case of tax-stamp violations, stating that the Court of Appeals had evidence that was inconsistent with ethical standards and destructive of personal liberty.

MISCELLANEOUS

SEPT. 22

George E. Collins abducts eight-year-old Lee Crary, demanding $10,000 ransom; the child, however, escapes three days later and leads police back to Collins's home, where he has been held; Collins will receive life imprisonment.

1·9·5·8

MURDER

APRIL 4

Cheryl Crane, 14-year-old daughter of film actress Lana Turner, stabs Turner's paramour, Johnny Stompanato, to death in her Beverly Hills mansion; she has killed the gangster, it is later said, to protect her mother from Stompanato, who has threatened to scar the actress for life for not advancing him money; the jury will conclude that the teenager has committed "justifiable homicide" in the defense of her mother.

MAY 13

While shopping after school, 16-year-old Gaetane Bouchard of Edmundston, N.B., Canada, disappears; later she is found in a gravel pit, stabbed to death; her boyfriend, John Vollman, an American, is arrested, though he denies any knowledge of the murder; yet his hair matches strands clutched in the hand of the dead girl, and his Pontiac has been seen near the gravel pit at the time of the murder; Vollman will be given a life sentence.

JULY 11

Peter Thomas Anthony Manuel is hanged at Barlinnie Prison in Glasgow, Scotland, for killing Doris and Peter Smart and their 11-year-old child in Glasgow during a robbery the previous January; before dying, Manuel, who has a long record of theft, rape and assault, admits to murdering two 17-year-old girls; leading police to their secret graves and stating coldly, while pointing to the hiding place of one of them: "I think I'm standing on her now."

JULY 17

King Faisal II of Iraq is assassinated with his entire family in the royal palace in Baghdad by General Qassim in a military takeover of the country; Qassim himself will be overthrown in 1963, being executed on Feb. 9, 1963.

SEPT. 8

Youngsters fishing on the banks of the Anacostia River in Washington, D.C., snag a body that proves to be that of Mrs. Ruth Reeves, who has been murdered; detectives match the wire used to tie weights to her body to a spool of wire in the home of her ex-boyfriend, Philmore Clark, who will be convicted of the killing and given a 25-year prison sentence.

NOV. 28

Lowell Lee Andrews, a 310-pound, 18-year-old honor student in Wolcott, Kan., shoots his sister, father and mother as they sit in the living room of their house; first he tells police burglars have done the murders, then admits to the killings, saying he wanted to gain the family inheritance to become a "hired gun" in Chicago; Andrews will devour two complete chicken dinners and go to the hangman in Leavenworth with indigestion.

DEC. 10

James D. French hitches a ride with Franklin Boone, whom he kills near Stroud, Okla.; later French will murder his cellmate, Eddie Shelton, and be electrocuted in the Oklahoma State Prison.

DEC. 14

Constable Raymond Summers is stabbed to death while attempting to break up a gang fight outside a London pub; his killer is not located, but the following year Ronald Henry Marwood, haunted by guilt, walks into a police station and admits the murder; he will be hanged at Pentonville Prison on May 8, 1959.

DEC. 20

Mary Olive Hattam, a nine-year-old in Ceduna, South Australia, disappears from a beach where she is playing with friends; her body is found in a beach cave some hours later; she has been raped, and her skull has been crushed by a rock, which, blood-coated, lies nearby; a man's footprints in the sand, local trackers conclude, have been made by an aborigine; Rupert Max Stuart, an aborigine traveling with a carnival and who has been arrested for drunkenness, admits the killing and, after a sensational trial and many appeals against a death sentence, is sent to prison for life.

ROBBERY

FEB. 27

A delivery truck of the Popular Bank of Milan is stopped on the Via Ospoppo by six bandits who loot the truck of 114 million lire ($182,000) and $750,000 in securities; all six bandits will be captured.

AUG. 10

Display windows at Tiffany's main store on Fifth

Avenue in New York City are smashed in the early-morning hours and, before alarms bring police, $163,000 in insured jewels are snatched up by thieves who are never caught.

ORGANIZED CRIME

JAN. 9

Elmer "Trigger" Burke, hit man for gangsters in New England who has attempted to kill Joseph "Specs" O'Keefe on orders of the Brink's robbery gang on whom O'Keefe has been informing, goes to the electric chair in Sing Sing for murdering Edward "Poochy" Walsh, a bartender who had insulted him.

FEB. 11

Meyer Lansky is arrested in New York City and interrogated about the 1957 murder of Albert Anastasia, then booked on a vagrancy charge and freed on $1,000 bond.

FEB. 24

Hearings in Naples, Italy, probe the activities of Lucky Luciano; he is labeled a "social danger."

MARCH 27

As part of well-designed government harassment, Meyer Lansky is arrested when arriving in Miami from Cuba for possessing painkilling pills; he explains that these are for his ulcer, posts a $50,000 bond and later provides a note from his doctor to that effect in court.

JUNE 2

Leroy Jefferson, reportedly one of the U.S.'s leading narcotics peddlers, is arrested in New York City for drug violations; he is released for lack of evidence.

JULY 8

Vito Genovese is released in New York City after posting a $50,000 bond on charges of conspiring to import and sell narcotics.

SEPT. 27

Igea Lissoni, Luciano's mistress in Italy, dies of breast cancer at age 37.

NOV. 12

Judge Marks in New York City sentences 12 leading policy racketeers of the syndicate to six months each in prison—these include Patsy Borelli, John Mangano and Pasquale Romano, all with long arrest records; then, stunning the prosecution, he suspends the sentences, saying that these hardened criminals are "victims of their environment."

DEC. 13

The Italian Court of Appeals decides that Lucky Luciano should be a free man, declaring that he "has nothing to do with murder, narcotics or illegal rackets."

WHITE-COLLAR CRIME

MARCH 16

The chief of New York City's Cornucopia Gold Mines, Earl Belle, who has allegedly gutted his firm through $2 million in bank loans, flees to Rio de Janeiro, where he is interviewed and admits that his books are "falsified and quite incomplete."

MISCELLANEOUS

SEPT. 5

Federal agents in New York City confiscate 2,454 gallons of illegal whiskey. No arrests are made.

MURDER

FEB. 1

Rosemarie Diane "Penny" Bjorkland, a pretty 18-year-old blonde, wakes up in her upper-middle-class San Francisco home and decides to murder someone, anyone—"just to see if I could and not worry about it afterwards." She shoots and kills gardener August Norry, father of two, in the hills surrounding San Francisco, where she has been driving, looking for a random victim; she will be tracked down through a gun shop where she has purchased bullets and will be sent to prison for life.

MARCH 3

Arms dealer George Puchert is blown up in Frankfurt, West Germany; Algerian terrorists are suspected of the murder, but no one is charged with the killing.

MARCH 7

At Southlands Beach, Bermuda, 72-year-old Gertrude Robinson is found raped and murdered; Dorothy Pearce, 59, will be found raped and horribly beaten to death, her body covered with bites and scratch marks, on May 9; like Mrs. Robinson, the second victim lived alone in a beach cottage; valuables in both killings were not taken by the killer; CID investigators from Scotland Yard are sent to Bermuda, a British Crown colony, to investigate, but their probes prove fruitless; secretary Dorothy Rawlinson, 29, will be found floating on the south-shore beach, her body half eaten away by sharks, on Sept. 28, but her remains still bearing the marks of a savage beating; some days later a beach shopkeeper will report to police that a black man, his clothes wet and using wet money to buy items, has been in his store; police will quickly pick up 19-year-old golf caddy Wendell Lightbourne, who will admit to the murders; he will be sentenced to death, then his sentence commuted to life imprisonment, which he will serve in England.

JULY 18

Dr. Bernard Finch, involved in a love triangle, murders his wife, Barbara, shooting her in front of their Los Angeles home while his lover, Mrs. Carole Tregoff, hides in bushes nearby; Finch will later be given a life term along with Mrs. Tregoff, who will be paroled in 1969.

NOV. 15

Thieves Perry Smith and Richard Eugene Hickock invade the Holcomb, Kan., home of Herbert Clutter; earlier, while in prison, Hickock has been informed by inmate Floyd Wells, who once worked for Clutter, that Clutter has large cash deposits in his home; when no valuables or cash are found, Smith and Hickock go berserk and kill Clutter, his wife and teenage son and daughter. They take about $40 and flee but later are caught in Las Vegas, where Hickock states: "Perry Smith killed the Clutters. I couldn't stop him. He killed them all!" Both men will be hanged in Lansing, Kan., on April 14, 1965.

DEC. 23

Police answering an alarm of a woman being attacked in a YWCA in Birmingham, England, find the headless body of 29-year-old Stephanie Baird; her severed head is perched on a nearby bed; more than 20,000 men in the city are interrogated; when 27-year-old Patrick Byrne is asked for his fingerprints, he becomes hostile; he is then grilled and eventually confesses the murder; Byrne will be given a life sentence.

ROBBERY

JAN. 30

Brian Donald Hume, British racketeer, robs a bank in Zurich, Switzerland, of $50,000, jumps into a cab and orders the driver to take him to safety; when the cabdriver refuses, Hume shoots him to death, a murder for which he will be given a life sentence; Hume will be returned to his native England and be imprisoned for life in Broadmoor, a prison for the criminally insane. (Hume figured in one of the more bizarre criminal incidents in Great Britain: On Oct 21, 1949, infamous fence Stanley Setty, who has received stolen cars from Hume, was found, his head severed; Hume later was charged with the murder but acquitted; knowing he could not be tried again for the same crime, Hume, in 1958, admitted murdering Setty in a confession purchased by and published in the *Sunday Pictorial*.)

JULY 16

Guenther Fritz Erwin Padola is taken into custody in his London flat after having robbed the home of Mrs. Verne Schiffman, taking more than £2,000 worth of furs and jewelry and then attempting to blackmail Mrs. Schiffman, who has called police; while pretending to negotiate with Padola, who pretended to be a

Roger "The Terrible" Touhy (right front, arm on table) with other defendants in a trumped-up kidnapping trial; he will be murdered by old gangland foes after serving more than 20 years. (Dec. 17, 1959)

detective having incriminating tapes in his possession, Mrs. Schiffman signals two Scotland Yard detectives who have run to her house; Padola shoots Detective Raymond Purdy to death and escapes; he will be hunted down and will be hanged at Wandsworth Prison on Nov. 5.

ORGANIZED CRIME

JUNE 22

It is revealed that the Department of Justice has been attempting to have Meyer Lansky's citizenship revoked since 1952, but the case has been stalled "for lack of prosecution" and subsequently dismissed; on Sept. 25, Lansky, now considered by many to be the chairman of the board of the national crime syndicate, after learning that Florida gambling boss Little Augie Carfano is attempting to oust him, allegedly orders Carfano's death; Little Augie, who is accompanied by former beauty queen Mrs. Janice Drake, picks up two men at New York City's LaGuardia Airport, emissar-

ies of Lansky's strong-arm man, Vincent "Jimmy Blue Eyes" Alo, whom he thinks is joining him; the two men get into Carfano's Cadillac, and when the car goes down a deserted street, they reportedly shoot Carfano and Mrs. Drake to death.

DEC. 17

Roger "The Terrible" Touhy, released from Stateville Penitentiary after serving more than 20 years for kidnapping Jake "The Barber" Factor, a kidnapping he did not do, is killed by goons wielding shotguns as he steps onto the front porch of his sister's Chicago home; the killers have reportedly been sent by onetime Capone henchman Murray "The Camel" Humphreys; no one is prosecuted in the case.

MISCELLANEOUS

MARCH 10

Anthony Marcello, a syndicate boss of Southern California, is arrested in Los Angeles for smuggling narcotics.

MURDER

FEB. 10

Adolph Coors III is abducted and held for ransom outside Denver, Colo.; the millionaire brewer later will be found dead, and his killer, Joseph Corbett, Jr., will be sent to prison for life.

MARCH 14

Three Chicago female socialites strolling through the woods in the Starved Rock, Ill., resort area are robbed and murdered by resort employee Chester Weger, who will be sent to prison for life.

JUNE 23

A tribal medicine man near Temuco, Chile, murders two young girls as sacrifices to ancient gods and throws their bodies into the ocean; when authorities are told of the killing they routinely investigate but fail to identify the medicine man.

JULY 3

Joseph Howk, Jr., alias Mohammed Abdullah, shoots student Sonja Lilliam Hoff on the library steps of the Berkeley campus of the University of California after she refuses to date him; for this senseless murder Howk will be given a life sentence.

AUG. 16

Graeme Thorne, who has just won a £100,000 lottery in Sydney, Australia, receives a phone call from Stephen Leslie Bradley, who states that he has kidnapped his eight-year-old son and demands £25,000 ransom; when authorities allow the press to publish details of the abduction, the kidnapper remains silent and the boy's body is found near Seaforth on Aug. 16; leaves from a rare species of cypress tree are found on the boy, and this type of tree is located about a mile from where the body is found, in the backyard of Stephen Bradley, who later confesses the kidnapping but claims that the boy has suffocated in his car trunk; he will be sent to prison for life.

OCT. 28

Brenda Nash, 12, is strangled to death in Heston, Middlesex, England, by a man chewing peppermints and driving a Vauxhall car, according to one of the victim's girlfriends; police quiz more than 5,000 owners of Vauxhall cars and stumble across Arthur Albert Jones, who is identified by the girlfriend as the man who picked up Brenda; Jones later will be sent to prison for life.

NOV. 13–14

Waitress Ann Gibson Tracy in Laguna Beach, Calif., has a candlelight dinner with her lover, Amos Stricker, a rich contractor, then shoots him to death because he is faithless and refuses to marry her; she will be given a life term.

ROBBERY

MAY 21–30

Scores of looters in a dozen towns in central Chile are shot to death by troopers following a violent earthquake that has devastated the country.

ORGANIZED CRIME

MARCH 30

Cataldo Tandoj, police commissioner in Palermo, Sicily, who has been cracking down on Mafia operations, is shot to death on the street.

JUNE 2

Mafia sachem Vincent Grafeo is shot to death near his home in Brooklyn, N.Y.

WHITE-COLLAR CRIME

JUNE 23

Chicagoan Angelo Inciso is convicted and sentenced to serve 10 years in a federal prison and is fined

$22,000 for illegally collecting $420,267 in fake life-insurance claims on people who were already dead.

DEC. 5

Charles T. Polhemus, Corky Vastola and others are arrested in New York City and accused of running a counterfeiting ring.

MISCELLANEOUS

FEB. 5

French master burglar Jean-Louis André and four

others tunnel out of Fresne Prison, to be recaptured weeks later.

APRIL 12

Eric Peugeot, four-year-old son of a millionaire manufacturer in Paris, is kidnapped but returned safe after a $300,000 ransom is paid; later two of the kidnappers will be apprehended and sent to prison for life.

SEPT. 3

Federal agents break into a huge New York City laboratory where morphine is being processed into heroin; millions of dollars in drugs are seized, and several dealers, including Frank Borelli, are arrested.

1·9·6·1

MURDER

JAN. 17

Patrice Lumumba, prime minister of the newly created Republic of the Congo (now the Republic of Zaire), is assassinated in Katanga Province while a prisoner of President Joseph Kasavubu.

MARCH 3

Mrs. Elsie May Batten, clerk in a London antique shop, is found dead, an ancient dagger plunged into her heart and another stuck in her neck; shopkeepers in the Cecil Court area later pick Edwin Bush, a black man, out of a police lineup as one who has been in the area recently attempting to sell an old sword; Bush tells police he has killed the clerk because "she made a remark about my color." The 21-year-old Eurasian will be executed at Pentonville Prison on July 6.

MARCH 25

Marthinus Rossouw, bodyguard and eccentric companion to 36-year-old Baron Dieter von Schauroth of Cape Town, South Africa, shoots his wealthy employer and later tells the police that he has been paid to do so by von Schauroth, who was unhappy in his home life and had taken out an enormous insurance policy on his life; police discover that von Schauroth has been illegally dealing in diamonds—many stones are found littering his body—and that Rossouw had murdered him during the course of a robbery; Rossouw will be hanged on June 20, 1962.

MAY 30

Rafael Leonidas Trujillo, strongman dictator of the Dominican Republic, is assassinated in his car en route

Dominican Republic strongman Rafael Trujillo, assassinated in 1961. (May 30, 1961)

to San Cristóbal from Ciudad Trujillo (the name of Santo Domingo during his regime). He is ambushed by army officers led by Pedro Cedeño.

AUG. 22

Michael Gregsten, a married man trysting with Valerie Storie in Slough, Buckinghamshire, England, is killed by a stranger invading his car and ordering him to drive down country roads, saying that the police are after him; after shooting Gregsten twice, the stranger rapes Miss Storie, then flees after firing two shots into her; James Hanratty, a professional criminal, is later identified by the paralyzed Valerie Storie, and he is picked out of lineups by witnesses who claim to have seen him driving Gregsten's car; Hanratty will be hanged at Bedford Prison on April 4, 1962, but controversy still surrounds the shaky identification made of him by a victim.

NOV. 5

Workmen near Swansea in Wales unearth the skeletal remains of Mamie Stuart, an ex-chorus girl who has disappeared in 1920; at the time, George Shotton, a married man who admitted to having an affair with Mamie Stuart, was charged with murdering her, but, for lack of a body, the case against him was dropped; from a detailed study of the remains, it will be determined that Mamie Stuart has been murdered; then a retired mailman will testify that, 40 years earlier, he had accidentally bumped into Shotton as he emerged from the cottage where he had stayed with Mamie Stuart in 1920; Shotton, who was laboring with a heavy sack, was at first shocked at seeing the mailman, saying: "Oh, God, for a minute I thought you were a policeman!" Shotton will be convicted post-mortem of murder, since he has died three years earlier at Bristol at age 78.

NOV. 21

In the Buriat ASSR of the Soviet Union in central Asia, a professional criminal called Nikolayev is convicted of murdering one Tabduyev and is sent to prison for life.

DEC. 15

Former Nazi official Adolf Eichmann is convicted in Israel of helping to murder millions of Jews during World War II as the man responsible for shipping tens of thousands of Jews in cattle cars to concentration camps. He will be executed.

ROBBERY

JULY 1

The Bank of Nova Scotia in Montréal is burglarized by a highly professional team allegedly organized and directed by master burglar Georges Lemay; the burglars make off with $633,605.

DEC. 26

Western bank and train robber Al Jennings of Oklahoma dies in near-poverty in Tulsa.

ORGANIZED CRIME

FEB. 18

Charles "Lucky" Luciano in Naples reads and approves a script for a movie to be based on his life; a week later the board of directors of the national crime cartel in New York City unanimously condemn such a movie, and Luciano scraps the idea.

AUG. 17

New York City syndicate killer Joey "Jelly" Gioelli, thought to have turned informer, reportedly is murdered and his body buried at sea.

AUG. 20

Larry Gallo is almost strangled by rival New York City gunmen.

SEPT. 13

The oldest living Mafia don, boss of bosses V. Ciccu, dies of old age in Palermo, Sicily.

OCT. 4

New York City gangster Joe Magnasco is shot to death on the street, a Gallo war victim.

OCT. 31

Mobster Bernard McLaughlin is killed during a local gang war over disputed rackets in Boston.

WHITE-COLLAR CRIME

MARCH 15

Agents raid policy houses in black districts of Washington, D.C., arresting 32 blacks on charges of collecting numbers without the $50 occupational tax stamp and 26 others on other policy charges.

APRIL 9

A report of the New York State Investigation Commission alleges that no single criminal activity has been more responsible for corruption of public officials than gambling.

AUG. 23

The Sportsman's Club, an enormous gambling operation in Newport, Ky., is raided by revenue agents and closed down.

NOV. 2

An elusive "bookiemobile," a truck moving constantly about New York City taking bets at street corners, finally is halted in Brooklyn by police, who have been searching for the bookmaking operation on wheels for many months. Several are arrested and given prison terms.

MISCELLANEOUS

FEB. 2

A hijacked Portuguese ocean liner, the *Santa Maria,* docks at Recife, Brazil, and lands 600 passengers; the errant crew, who intended to sell the cargo, is arrested, and the leaders are given long prison terms.

AUG. 3

Leon Bearden, having a long prison record, and his 16-year-old son Cody commit the first skyjacking, of a Continental Airlines Boeing 707, which Bearden takes over at the point of a gun in flight over New Mexico, ordering the pilot to fly to Cuba; the jet lands at El Paso for refueling, and Bearden explains that he is tired of life in the U.S. and wants to die abroad; FBI agents come aboard to "discuss" the matter, and Bearden tells them that he really can't afford to take an extended trip "because I've only got twenty-five bucks to my name." At that point both he and his son are overpowered by agents, and the passengers and crew are released. Bearden will be sent to prison for 20 years; his son will also be sent to prison but he will be released in 1963.

MURDER

JUNE 2

Dr. Harvey Lothringer, a wealthy physician living in posh Jamaica Estates in Queens, N.Y., takes $500 from 19-year-old Barbara Lofrumento to perform a secret abortion in his $85,000 ranch-style home, but he butchers her and she dies; Dr. Lothringer then chops up the patient-victim's body and grinds it through his kitchen disposal; he flees with a girlfriend to France, where he is arrested on Sept. 11 and extradited to the U.S., where he is found guilty of second-degree manslaughter.

JUNE 14

Anna Slesers, 55, is found strangled in her Boston apartment, the first of many victims whose death will be attributed to the Boston Strangler, later identified as Albert DeSalvo, who will be sent to the Walpole State Prison in Massachusetts, where another inmate will murder him, stabbing him through the heart on Nov. 26, 1973.

AUG. 28

Dr. Geza de Kaplany, a Hungarian anesthesiologist, insanely jealous of his former beauty queen wife, Hajna, turns up the music in his San Jose, Calif., home and, while his wife is tied to a bed, cuts her scores of times, pouring acid into her wounds, scarring her for life so that no man will ever again find her attractive; she dies in a hospital 36 hours later; de Kaplany will plead not guilty by reason of insanity but be sentenced to prison for life; he will be paroled in 1976 in one of the most controversial inmate releases in California history.

OCT. 11

Carol Ann White, 16, is murdered in London, her body found by Ted Donald Garlick; police become suspicious when they recall Garlick's acquittal on a murder charge when he and his wife had purportedly agreed to a suicide pact by turning on the gas and how she died and he survived; in the White slaying, Garlick becomes the prime suspect and, under heavy police grilling, confesses the killing, producing the knife with which he stabbed the teenager repeatedly; the killer will be sent to prison for life.

Dr. Geza de Kaplany, who tortured and murdered his beauty queen wife, here seen protesting evidence in court. (Aug. 28, 1962)

ROBBERY

AUG. 14

A gang of armed men stop a mail van on Route 3, near Cape Cod, Mass., taking $1,551,277 in many sacks, the bills being old and of small denomination, destined for destruction; the masked thieves wear white gloves during the robbery and later are dubbed "The White Glove Gang"; although suspects abound, no one will ever be indicted for this robbery.

NOV. 27

Five men subdue guards at London's Heathrow Airport, stealing £62,000; three of the alleged bandits are caught, Charles Wilson, Gordon Goody and Mickey Ball, with only Ball being convicted.

ORGANIZED CRIME

JAN. 24

Mario Caruso and Salvatore Mamesi, Mafia members, are arrested in the Palace Hotel in Madrid, Spain,

and later are convicted for narcotics violations and bail-jumping; each will recieve a 15-year sentence.

JAN. 26

While meeting a scriptwriter who is to write his life as a film, Charlie "Lucky" Luciano dies of a heart attack at Naples' Capodicino Airport. (The syndicate, at first opposed to the film, had reconsidered.)

APRIL 8

Mafia syndicate chieftain Tony Bender (Anthony Strollo) vanishes in New York City; he is presumed murdered.

JUNE 7

Joseph Profaci, a powerful Mafia don who controls one of New York City's five Mafia families and with whom the Gallo brothers have been warring, dies of cancer in South Side Hospital on Long Island, N.Y.

JUNE 22

Joseph Valachi murders John Joseph Saupp, a fellow inmate in the federal prison at Atlanta, thinking him to be Joseph DiPalermo, a Mafia henchman on orders from Vito Genovese to kill him; at this point

Joe Valachi, shown testifying on Cosa Nostra operations. (June 22, 1962)

Valachi begins to talk nonstop to federal agents, exposing the history of the New York City Cosa Nostra (Mafia).

AUG. 26

Edward J. "Spike" O'Donnell, onetime Prohibition bootlegger and fierce opponent of Al Capone and his allies, dies in bed of a heart attack in Chicago.

OCT. 15

Gallo gangsters Marco Marelli and Anthony DiCola disappear in New York City; they are presumed murdered.

WHITE-COLLAR CRIME

FEB. 2

Massive raids in the Bronx, N.Y., net 28,000 policy slips representing 920,000 players.

MARCH 29

Billie Sol Estes is charged with transporting fraudulent mortgages on anhydrous ammonia tanks across state lines; Estes' swindle has cost investors millions.

MISCELLANEOUS

FEB. 26

Frank "Buster" Wortman, a 1930s gangster, is convicted of tax evasion.

JUNE 12

Frank Lee Morris and Joseph and Clarence Anglin make plaster dummies of themselves that occupy their prison bunks while they escape Alcatraz through ventilating systems; though treacherous San Francisco Bay is thoroughly searched, their bodies are never found; many believe the trio successfully escaped, compelling federal authorities to conclude that "The Rock" no longer is escapeproof; Alcatraz will be closed down on May 15, 1963, its prisoners removed to other federal prisons; the last inmate to leave "The Rock" is Dillinger gangster James Henry "Blackie" Audett.

AUG. 5

Film star Marilyn Monroe is found dead in her Los Angeles home, her death first stated to be caused by an overdose of drugs; several persons at the scene later claim that Miss Monroe is given a lethal injection or is otherwise treated in such a way as to cause her death, claims that still are to be substantiated. Some claim the actress, who has been close to both President John F. Kennedy and U.S. Attorney General Robert F. Kennedy, has been murdered in a conspiratorial manner because of the important state secrets she had learned, claims that also are unsubstantiated.

1·9·6·3

MURDER

JAN. 3

Doris Saunders of Los Angeles is convicted of attempting to hire a man to rig an electric toothbrush to electrocute her husband, Larry; she receives a minimum sentence.

JAN. 22

Teofilo "Sparks" Rojas, a notorious bandit, is killed near Armenia, Colombia; Rojas is credited with murdering between 592 and 3,500 people, which makes him the greatest single mass murderer in recorded times.

JAN. 26

In a ruse to make police think a berserk sniper is loose in Bloomfield Township, Mich., 15-year-old Douglas Godfrey fires several random shots at passersby, then shoots his mother, Mary Godfrey, through the window of his home so that the sniper will be blamed; police note Douglas's indifference at the death of his 38-year-old mother; Douglas is interrogated and confesses the murder, saying that he killed Mary Godfrey because she was too strict.

FEB. 8

Arab leader Abdul Karim Kassem is executed by revolutionaries in Baghdad.

FEB. 14

Dr. Carlos Nigrisoli of Bologna, Italy, murders his wife, Anna, by injecting nerve tonic into her; he will receive a life sentence.

FEB. 28

Benjamin Lewis, Chicago alderman for the 24th Ward, is found murdered in his West Side office only two days after being reelected by an overwhelming majority; his killers have never been found.

MARCH 6

Carol Thompson of St. Paul, Minn., staggers to the home of a neighbor, her throat cut, managing to blurt: "Help—a man—his knife—my throat . . ." She dies within the hour. Her husband, Tilmer Eugene Thompson, a prominent criminal lawyer, draws police suspicion when he refuses to turn over a list of his clients as possible suspects, explaining that it's against professional ethics; detectives learn that Thompson has insured his wife's life with several companies for an aggregate amount exceeding $1 million; a Thompson neighbor reports having seen a strange car outside the Thompson home at the time of the murder, and this is traced to a hoodlum named Anderson, who confesses to police that he has been hired to kill Mrs. Thompson by Norman Mastrian, a college friend of Thompson's, at Thompson's request; Anderson gains immunity by becoming a state's witness; Mastrian and Thompson will be sent to prison for life.

MARCH 29

Klaus Gossman shoots down an elderly woman and her son who own a gunshop in Nuremberg, West Germany; Gossman, who has robbed a Deutsches Bank in Ochenbruch the previous year, killing the bank director, Erich Hallbauer, and later killing a porter, will be captured months later carrying a gun with the name of Elke Sommer scratched on it; he is obsessed with her and plans to kill her someday, he tells police; Gossman will be sent to prison for life.

APRIL 13

Mrs. Lorraine Clark, who murdered her husband in 1954 and dumped his body in a river, is released from the Women's Reformatory at Framingham, Mass., after serving nine years of a life sentence.

JUNE 12

Secretary for the NAACP Medgar Evers is shot in the back and killed as he steps from his car in Jackson, Miss., during the civil rights campaign in the Deep South. The killers are never identified.

JULY 30

Col. William Farber dies suddenly in Middletown, N.J., his death attributed to heart failure; two years later, in Sarasota, Fla., Farber's wife, Marjorie, will insist that her neighbor Dr. Carol Coppolino, with whom she was having an affair, gave her a muscle relaxant drug that she injected into her husband to kill him; the murder, she said, was planned by Dr. Coppolino so they could be together; the doctor's wife, Carmela, 32, mother of two, will die on Aug. 28, 1965, also of a sudden heart attack, another victim of Dr. Coppolino's, according to Marjorie Farber; two trials will be held, the first being a murder case against Dr. Coppolino for killing Col. Farber, for which he will be found innocent; in the second trial, Dr. Coppolino will be found guilty of second-degree murder in the death of his wife and be sent to prison for life.

AUG. 28

Niece of author Philip Wylie and daughter of journalist Max Wylie, 21-year-old Janice Wylie, is stabbed to death with her roommate, Emily Hoffert, 23, a teacher; police later charge a black man, George Whitmore, with the slayings, but he claims a confession has been beaten out of him; in 1964 Nathan and Marjorie Delaney will go to police to turn in a 22-year-old heroin addict and burglar who has been living with them, Richard Robles, who will be arrested on Jan. 26, 1965; Robles will break down and say that he had several sexual experiences with Janice Wylie, finally losing control and having an uncontrollable urge to murder her during intercourse, an obsession later exploited in the novel *Looking for Mr. Goodbar;* Robles will be given a life sentence.

NOV. 2

With their hands tied behind their backs as they ride in an armored personnel carrier, Ngo Dinh Diem, president of South Vietnam, and his brother and adviser, Ngo Dinh Nhu, are assassinated by unknown South Vietnamese officers in Saigon.

NOV. 22

Lee Harvey Oswald assassinates President John F. Kennedy in Dallas by shooting him in his car as it travels down a street overlooked by the Texas School Book Depository Building; Oswald fires from a sixth-floor window of a storage room in this building, striking Kennedy and wounding Texas Governor John Connally; Oswald does not live long enough to stand trial, being shot while in custody, on Nov. 24, by saloon owner Jack Ruby, who later will die of illness before his trial; though many claim there was a conspiracy to murder Kennedy, with unknown persons in high office involved, none of these theories has been proved.

Presidential assassin Lee Harvey Oswald moments before he was shot to death by Jack Ruby in Dallas, Tex. (Nov. 22, 1963)

ROBBERY

AUG. 8

Britain's Great Train Robbery occurs when the Royal Mail Train is stopped through a fixed stop signal a half hour from Euston Station by 30 of London's top heist men, led by mastermind Bruce Reynolds; once the train is stopped, bandits take over the engine, break into the mail car and, after striking the guard unconscious, take 120 mail bags, tossing them to other bandits, who pile the bags into Land-Rovers; the robbers, who must have obtained inside information that the train would be carrying this large shipment of unmarked, old bills, then drive off to Leatherslade Farm in Buckinghamshire, where they split up more than £2,600,000, about £150,000 apiece; all the bandits, after many chases and adventures, will be caught and imprisoned, with only one, Ronald Biggs, escaping later to Brazil where, at this writing, he is still enjoying his freedom.

SEPT. 21

French police, acting on a tip, break into the home of Yugoslav house painter Nikola Franusic to find more than $2 million in rare books and other *objets d'art* he has stolen over three decades.

ORGANIZED CRIME

MAY 6

Irving Vince, who has testified against gangster Murray "The Camel" Humphreys, is found dead—suffocated and stabbed—in Room 507 of Chicago's Del Prado Hotel; his killer has never been found.

JUNE 6

The bodies of Emile Colontuono and Alfred Mondello, Gallo gangsters killed by the Profaci gang in the Profaci-Gallo war, are found in New York City.

JUNE 30

A car explodes in the main square of Ciacelli, Sicily, injuring several passersby in a revived war between old and new Mafia factions.

JULY 24–AUG. 6

Ali Waffa and Hugh "Apples" McIntosh are killed in the Gallo-Profaci war in New York City.

DEC. 28

Joseph Magliocco, who has taken over the Profaci Mafia family in New York City, dies of a heart attack; he will be replaced by Joe Colombo.

WHITE-COLLAR CRIME

MARCH 28

Billie Sol Estes, friend to presidents and movie stars, is found guilty on five counts of mail fraud and one count of conspiracy.

MISCELLANEOUS

MARCH 29

In New York City, rock 'n' roll singer Jimmy "Baby Face" Lewis is arrested on a charge of possessing narcotics; police later state that his arrest led to the uncovering of a nationwide narcotics ring.

AUG. 2

Race riots break out in Chicago after three black families move into predominantly white neighborhoods; several persons are injured.

SEPT. 15

During race riots in Birmingham, Ala., a bomb explodes at the Sixth Avenue Baptist Church, killing four black girls and injuring many other people; the bomber has never been caught.

DEC. 8

Frank Sinatra, Jr., 19, is kidnapped and held for $240,000 ransom, which is paid by the victim's father; kidnappers Joseph C. Amsler, John W. Irwin and Barry Keenan will be sent to prison for long terms.

1·9·6·4

MURDER

JAN. 10

Anti-American riots break out in the Canal Zone of Panama, spurred on by radio broadcasts spewing a racial slogan of "a good Gringo is a dead Gringo." Dozens are injured.

JAN. 20

Store owner Max Feinberg is arrested in Philadelphia for allegedly selling Sterno to scores of skid-row bums, 31 of whom die after drinking it; Feinberg will be released for lack of evidence.

FEB. 2

Prostitute Hannah Tailford's body is found floating in the Thames; she is the first of six streetwalkers who will be horribly murdered in 1964–1965 in the London area by a night stalker the press dub "Jack the Stripper," since he strips his victims naked after killing them; this mass killer has never been found, although police believe that he was a retired security guard who drove trucks at night and later committed suicide.

MARCH 13

Early in the morning, Catherine "Kitty" Genovese is attacked in front of her Kew Gardens, N.Y., home by rapist Winston Moseley; for many minutes the girl cries for help as her assailant slashes her, runs away when someone shouts at him from a window, then returns to kill her while she cries in vain; dozens of neighbors have heard the cries but fail to respond, most saying later that they "didn't want to get involved." Moseley, a 29-year-old factory worker, will be arrested six days later and will confess the murder, along with two other killings; he will go to prison for life.

APRIL 7

Peter Anthony Allen and Gwynne "Ginger" Owen Evans murder John Alan West, a laundry driver, in London to steal his watch; the killers leave a raincoat, receipts and addresses of girlfriends at the scene of the murder, everything but printed calling cards; Allen and Evans will be the last two people to be hanged in Britain, on Aug. 13.

MAY 31

In Tucson, Ariz., Charles Schmid, a dim-witted 22-year-old, five-foot, three-inch braggart, tells friends John Saunders and Mary French that he wants "to kill a girl today" and, while all get drunk, Schmid entices Alleen Row, 15, into his car; his friends watch as he rapes her, then smashes the victim's head with a rock. Schmid buries the body in the desert; he will murder, on Aug. 16, 1965, the Fritz sisters—Gretchen, 17, and Wendy, 13—strangling them and throwing the bodies in a ditch; later he will show the rotting corpses to a friend, Richard Bruns, who will go to the police; Schmid will be arrested on Nov. 11, 1965; Mary French and John Saunders will attempt to avoid punishment by testifying against Schmid, who will receive the death penalty; French will get five years and Saunders will get life; Schmid, however, will manage to stay alive through appeals; he will escape the Arizona State Prison on Dec. 11, 1972, and terrify the countryside before being recaptured; Schmid later will die in prison.

JUNE 30

Jacques Mossler, millionaire financier, is bludgeoned to death in his Key Biscayne, Fla., home; his eccentric, attractive wife, Candace, and her nephew, Melvin Lane Powers, are tried for the killing but are acquitted.

AUG. 11

Odell Jones of Lake City, Fla., admits to drowning

"The Pied Piper" of Tucson, Ariz., thrill killer Charles Schmid. (May 31, 1964)

his wife in a pool, then putting her body into the trunk of her car, digging an enormous hole in nearby sand dunes and burying the entire car; police dig up the car and find the body; Odell will go to prison for life.

AUG. 27

Edmund Emil Kemper, who will grow to be a six-foot, nine-inch drooling sadist, shoots and kills his grandmother at age 15 and is sent to California's Atascadero State Hospital for psychiatric care; he will be released five years later by the California Youth Authority, going to live with his mother in Santa Cruz, where he will collect weapons and perform day labor to buy a car that he will use to pick up girls, making up a "hit" list; Kemper will begin killing coeds in 1972, calling the police a year later after hammering his mother to death and strangling her friend; he will admit to killing six female students, rattling off horrific details of necrophilia, cannibalism and decapitation; After being sent to prison for life, Kemper will

say of his victims: "They were dead, I was alive. That was the victory in my case."

OCT. 8

Lucille Miller drugs her husband, Dr. Gordon E. Miller, while he sits in his car near San Bernardino, Calif., then sets fire to the auto; police discover that Mrs. Miller has performed the murder to be with another man; and she will be sent to the women's prison at Fontana for life but will be paroled on May 10, 1972, serving less than eight years.

DEC. 26

Sadistic lovers Myra Hindley and Ian Brady of Manchester, England, abduct Lesley Ann Downey, murdering her and burying her body on the moors, where they have killed and buried another child in 1963, John Kilbride, 12; both thrill killers are turned in to police by David Smith and will be sent to prison for life with no possibility of parole.

ROBBERY

JULY 16

Hundreds of looters gut stores in Harlem, New York City, after a 15-year-old boy is shot to death as he attacks a policeman; one looter is killed and 140 more people are injured, including 48 policemen, in what develops into full-scale race riots.

ORGANIZED CRIME

JAN. 21

Anthony "Lover" Moschiano, a heroin addict and informant, is murdered by Thomas N. Durso, Chicago policeman and syndicate narcotics dealer, on orders of Michael Gargano, a syndicate terrorist.

JAN. 22

Meyer Lansky's new casino opens in the Lucayan Beach Hotel in the Bahamas.

MAY 15

Mafia leader Luciano Liggio is arrested in Palermo, Sicily, carried on a stretcher to jail (Liggio, 38, has been crippled by spinal tuberculosis); he has defied capture for 16 years but finally has been found helpless in bed, too ill to resist arrest.

JULY 31

Joseph ''Doc'' Stacher is convicted of income-tax evasion, fined $10,000 and given a five-year prison term.

WHITE-COLLAR CRIME

MARCH 27

George F. Knoop of Las Vegas pretends to drown, then drives to Los Angeles to live under an assumed identity so that his wife can collect insurance money on his life; later he will be identified, arrested, convicted and given a light sentence.

JULY 26

In his second conviction, Teamsters President James Hoffa is found guilty of fraud and conspiracy for mishandling union funds.

MISCELLANEOUS

JULY 1

Race riots in Philadelphia leave 150 injured and 165 arrested for attacking police officers.

OCT. 9

U.S. Air Force Lt. Col. Michael Smolen is kidnapped by Castroite terrorists in Caracas, Venezula, and held while terrorists demand the release in Saigon of Viet Cong terrorist Nguyen Van Troi, who has attempted to murder Defense Secretary Robert McNamara; Troi's execution is postponed, and Smoken is released; Troi will be executed on Oct. 19.

NOV. 29

Cleveland Williams, leading contender for the heavyweight boxing championship, is shot during a scuffle with a Houston, Tex., traffic cop who has arrested him for drunken driving; Williams will survive.

DEC. 10

Esther Carter, U.S. Commissioner, drops charges against 19 persons charged with conspiracy in slaying three civil rights workers on June 21; they are released.

1·9·6·5

MURDER

APRIL 1

Movie actor Tom Neal, who has been involved in several scandals—including beating actor Franchot Tone and hospitalizing him over the affections of Barbara Payton, later a streetwalker—is arrested for murdering his third wife, Gail, in their Palm Springs, Calif., home; Neal will be sent to prison for 15 years, serve seven and will die of a heart attack, penniless, in Hollywood on Aug. 7, 1972.

JULY 14

Marie Crimmins, four, and her brother Edward, five, are reported missing in New York City by their father who has been living apart from his wife, Alice; both children are found some days later, strangled; Mrs.

Crimmins can offer only feeble excuses why the children vanished in the middle of the night; in two trials, in 1968 and 1971, Mrs. Crimmins will be found guilty of murder and manslaughter, respectively, in the deaths of her children, whom she has killed, according to prosecution, because she feared her husband would obtain custody of them when her sexually promiscuous life-style was exposed; she will be sent to prison for life but is transferred in 1976 to a work-release program.

AUG. 11

In racial rioting at the outskirts of Cape Town, South Africa, 17 blacks are killed and 50 more injured.

OCT. 20

John Kilpatrick, president of the United Industrial Workers' Union, is found shot to death in a Chicago alley; his killer, Dana H. Nash, is sent to prison for a term of 150 years.

OCT. 26

In Indianapolis, sadist Gertrude Baniszewski encourages several neighbor boys and her own son to torture teenager Sylvia Likens to death in her basement; the young girl has been left in Mrs. Baniszewski's safekeeping by Sylvia's parents, who travel in their jobs; Mrs. Baniszewski will be sent to prison for life. Being juveniles, the boys will not be incarcerated.

ROBBERY

SEPT. 21

International bank robber Georges Lemay escapes from the Dade County Jail in Miami, Fla.

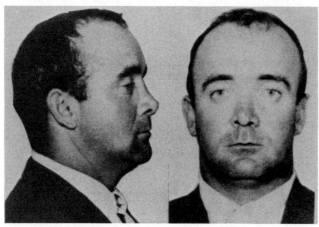

Canadian bank robber Georges Lemay, who stole millions. (Sept. 21, 1965)

ORGANIZED CRIME

MARCH 11

Gaspar DiGregoria, former aide to Joseph ''Joe Bananas'' Bonanno, takes over the Bonanno empire when his boss is kidnapped. (See ''Organized Crime,'' May 17, 1966.)

MAY 27

Sam ''Momo'' Giancana, syndicate boss of Chicago, appears before a federal grand jury and invokes the Fifth Amendment; it is pointed out that to receive immunity from prosecution for his testimony, Giancana must either answer all questions or go to jail for contempt; Giancana goes to jail after taking the Fifth.

SEPT. 11

Front man for syndicate gambling operations in Chicago Manny Skar, who is about to turn police informant, is murdered in the Gold Coast.

MISCELLANEOUS

AUG. 8

Blacks riot in suburban Watts, Calif., setting fires, then cutting fire hoses; half the area is gutted, and 34 persons die in the fires or are shot by police or rioters; more than 1,000 are injured, 4,000 are arrested, and damages exceed $34 million.

1·9·6·6

MURDER

JULY 13–14

Part-time seaman Richard Franklin Speck, who has a long history of burglary, breaks into the student quarters of nine nurses working at the Chicago Community Hospital, slaying eight; one, Corazon Amu-

rao, survives, hiding beneath a bed, and later she will identify the killer, who will be sentenced to more than 400 years with no hope of parole.

JULY 31

Ex-marine Charles Whitman, who has previously told a psychiatrist that he intends to go to the school tower at the University of Texas in Austin and begin

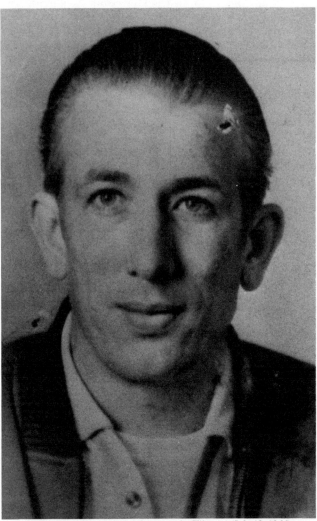

Richard Speck, killer of eight nurses in Chicago. (July 13, 1966)

shooting people, stabs his mother to death, then, on the following day, takes an arsenal to the tower and, from a 27th-floor perch, will shoot 46 persons, killing 16 before police rush him in a shoot-out that leaves him dead.

AUG. 12

Car thieves Harry Maurice Roberts, John Edward Witney and John Duddy shoot and kill three policemen when their car is stopped in Hammersmith, England; they all will be tracked down, and each will be given 30 years in prison.

SEPT. 16

Valerie Percy, 20, daughter of U.S. Senator-to-be Charles Percy, is slashed and stabbed to death in her bed inside the Percy mansion in Kenilworth, Ill.; though police conducted a widespread manhunt, the killer has never been found.

NOV. 12

Robert Benjamin Smith, a top high-school student in Mesa, Ariz., enters a beauty parlor and, after forcing five women and two children to lie on the floor, shoots them all to death before surrendering to police; Smith states that he has committed mass murder to become famous.

DEC. 17

Myron Lance and Walter Kelbach, homosexuals, kidnap and rape Salt Lake City gasoline station attendant Stephen Shea, then kill him; the rampaging pair will slay four more persons before being caught and sent to prison for life.

ROBBERY

AUG. 19

Bank robber Georges Lemay is captured in Las Vegas by FBI agents, carrying $10,000 in big bills and using the alias of Robert Palmer; Lemay will be sent back to Montréal to be convicted in 1968 of bank burglary, for which he will serve almost eight years, being released in 1975.

SEPT. 14

Larry Knohl is sentenced in Florida to five years in prison for illegal possession of $300,000 in stolen U.S. Treasury notes.

ORGANIZED CRIME

MARCH 11

Dominic Galiano, a Chicago syndicate gangster, is shot to death.

MAY 17

Almost 19 months after his disappearance—it is said that he has been kidnapped by syndicate chieftains and held until he informed on the operations of his own men—Joseph "Joe Bananas" Bonanno surrenders to federal authorities in New York City to face racketeering charges.

MAY 23

Ben Stein is convicted of labor racketeering in Chicago and sentenced to 18 months in a federal prison.

WHITE-COLLAR CRIME

JUNE 1–OCT. 1

Los Angeles is inundated with hundreds of door-to-door con artists belonging to the Williamsons clan; tens of thousands of dollars are lost in short cons.

JULY 15–OCT. 15

Willard Talbot, taking a leaf from the *The Music Man,* gleans $1.5 million after selling thousands of parents coast-to-coast cheap instruments and music lessons for their children, promising that all the students will play in a massive orchestra in the Rose Bowl at the end of the year.

MISCELLANEOUS

JAN. 29

Yugoslav dissidents bomb five Yugoslav consulates in the U.S.

MARCH 11

Dr. Timothy Leary is sentenced to 30 years in federal prison for transporting marijuana.

MARCH 25

Virginia Hill, onetime bagwoman for the syndicate who has been living in obscurity in Salzburg, Austria, after marrying a ski instructor, commits suicide by taking an overdose of sleeping pills.

SEPT. 29

A race riot in San Francisco is quelled by National Guardsmen; dozens have been injured.

SEPT. 30

Nazi war criminals Baldur von Schrach and Albert Speer are released from West Berlin's Spandau Prison, leaving Rudolf Hess as the lone occupant, guarded by dozens of troops.

OCT. 17

With the help of Soviet agents, spy George Blake saws his way through the bars of his cell and escapes Wormwood Schrubs Prison in England.

NOV. 9

Widespread riots in India leave hundreds injured after sacred cows are slaughtered by political dissidents; Prime Minister Indira Gandhi assumes control over police to put down outbreaks.

NOV. 13

A bomb blows up on the freighter *The Grand Inegrity* as it sails from Portland, Ore.; killed are the captain and a crew member; authorities have never determined the reason for the explosion.

DEC. 12

The U.S. Supreme Court upholds the conviction of Jimmy Hoffa on charges of jury tampering.

MURDER

FEB. 9

Mary Ellen Kaldenberg of Kenosha, Wis., a 17-year-old who has gone to a drugstore to buy a soda, is found in the back of an abandoned car, murdered; her killer IS never apprehended. She will be the first of seven ghastly murder victims in Kenosha from 1967 through 1981.

APRIL 5

In West Berlin 11 persons are taken into custody in an alleged plot to kill U.S. Vice President Hubert Humphrey during a visit to the city.

AUG. 19

Thomas Eugene Braun and Leonard Maine murder Samuel Ledgerwood in rural Oregon while he is fishing, stealing his car; the pair will go on to kill Mrs. Deanna Buse near Redmond, Wash., the same day and

Timothy Luce in northern California on Aug. 27, wounding Luce's companion, Susan Bartolomei, who later will identify them; they will receive life sentences.

Raymond Leslie Morris, who has bragged to his wife, "I've never made a mistake in my life," kidnaps 7-year-old Christine Ann Darby in Walsall, England, sexually assaults her, then suffocates the child; his car is spotted near the pickup site and the license traced to him; Morris will be sent to prison for life.

AUG. 23

August Jagusch, a New York City sex pervert who has strangled a prostitute, Mildred Fogarty, to death after she tells him she has gonorrhea in 1951, is released from Auburn State Prison.

AUG. 25

George Lincoln Rockwell, the leader of the American Nazi Party, is shot and killed in Arlington, Va.

ROBBERY

SEPT. 22

The Peoples Court in the Petrograd District (Leningrad) of the USSR sentences burglar V. I. Samarsky to three years in prison for stealing property and money under his control.

ORGANIZED CRIME

MARCH 7

Joseph Polito is shotgunned to death in his Chicago home after testifying against associates about their involvement in the $50,000 scam of Vogue Credit Jewelers.

MARCH 16

Alan Rosenberg, a Chicago businessman who re-

portedly owes Felix "Milwaukee Phil" Alderisio large sums of "juice," is beaten to death, becoming the city's 1,003rd gangland victim.

MISCELLANEOUS

JAN. 6

Mrs. Betty Hill of Boulder, Colo., is held captive in her home until $50,000 is paid for her release; the hostage-taker has not been apprehended.

JAN. 7

Deranged army deserter Richard James Paris hands his bride, Christine, a package containing 14 sticks of dynamite as they enter their honeymood suite in the Orbit Inn, Las Vegas, Nev.; he then fires a bullet into the dynamite, killing himself, his wife and five other honeymooners.

APRIL 3

Kenneth King, 11, is abducted from his Beverly Hills, Calif., home and, after a $250,000 ransom is paid, he is released on April 6. The kidnapper is never apprehended.

APRIL 8

Riots by blacks in Nashville, Tenn., result in 17 persons injured and dozens arrested.

APRIL 23

James Earl Ray escapes the Missouri State Penitentiary by hiding in the bread crate of a delivery truck. He will be recaptured a short time later.

JULY 12–17

Across the U.S. 127 race riots break out, leaving scores injured and millions of dollars in damage.

DEC. 26

Five convicted robbers slug a guard in Dartmoor Prison in England and escape over a wall; England suffers a total of 694 escapes in 1967, with 120 prisoners not caught.

1·9·6·8

MURDER

FEB. 24

Bank executive Albert Ricci of Lorrain, Ohio, allegedly sends a package containing a bomb to Samuel Hammons in Avon, Ohio; Ricci and Hammons are reportedly in love with the same woman; Hammons is killed while opening the package, and later Ricci is found dead in a car accident.

MARCH 19

Joan Robinson Hill, daughter of oil tycoon Ash Robinson of Houston, Tex., dies of a liver infection; her husband, a spendthrift and notorious philanderer who has married her purportedly to obtain the Robinson millions, will be convicted of "murder by omission"—in that he purposely withheld medicine that would have saved his wife's life; a mistrial will be declared when Hill's former wife claims he attempted to kill her; before Hill can be tried again, he will be murdered by a hired gunman, who will be shot to death by a police officer.

APRIL 4

James Earl Ray shoots civil rights leader Dr. Martin Luther King, Jr., to death as Dr. King stands on a balcony of a Memphis, Tenn. motel; Ray flees to Canada, then England and the Continent in a well-financed escape, which leads many to believe in a powerful conspiracy behind the assassination; Ray will be returned to the U.S., convicted of murder and sent to prison for life.

MAY 6

An irate, drunken customer, ejected from The Grave, a Forth Worth, Tex., nightclub, returns to throw a firebomb into the club; the fire bomb explodes, killing seven customers and injuring six more; the fire bomber has not been caught.

Dr. Martin Luther King, Jr. (April 4, 1968)

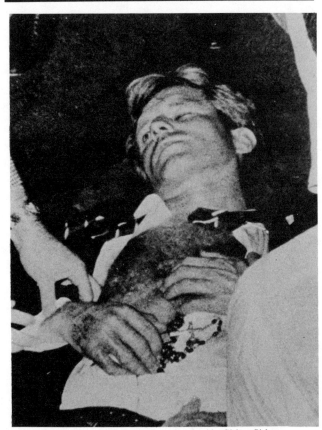

Senator Robert F. Kennedy dying of a bullet fired by Sirhan Sirhan.
(June 5, 1968)

MAY 14

Shelia Garvie and her lover, Brian Tevendale, murder Max Garvie, Shelia's husband, as he sleeps in bed in their West Cairnbeg Farm in western Scotland; after Garvie's body is found in an underground tunnel, his wife and her lover, who have been seen together, will be quickly convicted and given life sentences.

MAY 28

Martin Brown, age four, is found murdered in a deserted Newcastle, England, house; notes in childish handwriting are found next to his body; two months later Brian Howe, age three, is found strangled, with similar notes at the scene; the notes are traced to Mary Flora Bell, age 11, who will be found guilty of manslaughter and sentenced to life detention in a school for incorrigible children.

JUNE 5

Palestinian Sirhan Bishara Sirhan assassinates Robert F. Kennedy in Los Angeles as the senator is walking from the stage of the Ambassador Hotel after making a speech; the killer will receive a life sentence.

OCT. 30

Silent-screen idol Ramon Novarro is murdered in his posh Los Angeles home by Tom and Paul Ferguson, brothers from Chicago who have tortured Novarro to find out where he has hidden his fortune; the Fergusons are pinpointed after making a long-distance call to Chicago to talk to a girlfriend; both will be sent to prison for life.

ORGANIZED CRIME

MARCH 8

Raymond L. S. Patriarca, syndicate boss of New England, is convicted of conspiracy to kill Rocco Desiglio and is sentenced in Providence, R.I., to serve five years in prison.

WHITE-COLLAR CRIME

SEPT. 23

Italian wine inspectors learn that millions of quarts of Vina Ferrari have been doctored with tar, seaweed, banana paste and other strange ingredients in a giant importing swindle.

MISCELLANEOUS

FEB. 11

Pravda tells its reads that 3.7 million major crimes have been committed in the U.S. in 1967, adding that minor crimes add up to a total of 10 million offenses in the U.S., figures that even Soviet jurists find hard to believe.

APRIL 8

The U.S. Supreme Court removes the death penalty provision from the Lindbergh kidnapping law.

JUNE 30

After receiving a tip, Sheriff Roy Cunn in Meridian, Miss., orders deputies to surround the home of a local Jewish businessman, catching KKK supporters Thomas Tarrant and Kathy Ainsworth planting 22 sticks of dynamite; as police close in, Ainsworth fires a submachine gun at officers and is killed by return fire. Tarrant is sent to prison.

DEC. 17

Barbara Jane Mackle, daughter of rich contractor Robert F. Mackle of Miami, Fla., is kidnapped and buried alive by Gary Steven Krist, who collects a $500,000 ransom; an informant calls the FBI, and Barbara is found in her tomb outside Atlanta, Ga., just before her air supply gives out; Krist and an accomplice, Ruth Eisemann-Schier, are identified by the victim, and captured in Florida; Krist will go to prison for life, Eisemann-Schier will receive a seven-year sentence.

MURDER

FEB. 3

Dr. Eduardo Mondiane, president of the Mozambique National Liberation Front, is killed by a bomb in Tanzania. His assassin is never identified.

MARCH 28

Christiaan Buys is poisoned to death with arsenic by his wife, Maria, in rural South Africa; she confesses when confronted with autopsy findings, and will be hanged on Nov. 13, 1970.

MARCH 30

Following a meeting of the New Africa organization in Detroit, a policeman is killed, four black militants are wounded and 135 persons are arrested in a gun battle.

APRIL 10

Kenneth Ray Wright abducts and kills eight-year-old Camellia Jo Hand and her dog in Ocoee, Fla.; Wright will be traced through his car license plates, convicted, and sent to prison for life.

AUG. 4

San Francisco mass murderer "Zodiac" writes to newspapers gloating over the four murders he has already committed in lovers' lane slayings; witnesses to some of the murders describe a young white male wearing eyeglasses; he will kill two more persons before he is no longer heard from in 1971.

AUG. 8–9

Charles Manson unleashes his murder cultists in Los Angeles to murder and mutilate actress Sharon Tate, wife of film director Roman Polanski, and four others; the cultists will also murder Leno and Rosemary LaBianco, on Aug. 11; the demented Manson will go to prison for life, as will followers Susan Atkins, Leslie Van Houten and Patricia Krenwinkel.

OCT. 27

In Los Angeles, Indian student Prosenjit Poddar, after telling his psychiatrist that he intends to kill student Tatiana Tarasoff, who has rebuffed him several times, stabs the girl as she stands on her front porch; Poddar

will be deported to India after serving four years in prison.

DEC. 29

In London, England, Indian blackmailers Arthur and Nizamodeen Hosein kidnap and murder Mrs. Muriel McKay, demanding £500,000 ransom; later they increase their demand to 1 million, and are traced when attempting to pick up the money on the London–Cambridge Road outside London; both will be sent to prison for life, but the body of Mrs. McKay has not been found; it is presumed that the Indian brothers fed the

Charles Manson, hippie cult leader and director of mass murders in Los Angeles. (Aug. 8, 1969)

chopped-up remains to the pigs on their farm in Hertfordshire; ironically, the pair kidnapped the wrong woman, thinking Mrs. McKay was the wife of Rupert Murdoch, millionaire newspaper publisher.

ORGANIZED CRIME

FEB. 6

Thomas Zummo, a member of DiGregorio's New York City Mafia family, is shot to death as he walks into his girlfriend's house; it is the last killing in the Bonanno war, which has claimed 10 lives.

FEB. 11

Vito Genovese dies of a heart attack in the federal prison at Atlanta, Ga.; Tommy Eboli takes over his New York City Mafia family.

President Richard Nixon declares all-out war on organized crime, asking Congress for $61 million to combat worldwide drug trafficking; the governments of France, Turkey, Mexico, Iran and Italy are asked to cooperate.

DEC. 10

Mafia boss Michele Cavatajo and three others are killed when their car is raked with gunfire as they drive down a Palermo, Sicily, street during rush hour.

MISCELLANEOUS

JAN. 12

Hundreds are injured when smashing police lines in Rhodesia and South Africa during racial disturbances.

MARCH 1

In New Orleans, businessman Clay Shaw is acquitted on conspiring to assassinate President Kennedy.

MAY 13

More than 100 persons are killed in Kuala Lumpur, Malaysia, during race riots.

SEPT. 4

U.S. Ambassador to Brazil C. Burke Elbrick is kidnapped by terrorists who demand that their manifestos be published; they are, and Elbrick will be released on Sept. 7.

SEPT. 7

In Toronto, Ont., Canada, Mrs. Mary Nelles is kidnapped and is released a few days later after a $200,000 ransom is paid; the five kidnappers are caught, convicted and given long prison sentences.

SEPT. 21

Throughout western India massive riots take place between Moslems and Hindus over the alleged mistreatment of sacred Hindu cows and Hindu spiritual leaders, leaving more than 120 dead.

1·9·7·0

MURDER

MARCH 31

West German ambassador to Guatemala Count Karl von Spreti is kidnapped and a $700,000 ransom, along with the release of 22 political prisoners held in Germany, is demanded; Guatemala refuses to pay the ransom, and von Spreti will be found dead on April 6.

APRIL 5

Ronald John Vivian Cohen, son of a millionaire and himself a highly successful financier of home construction, wakes up the housekeeper in his lavish Cape Town, South Africa, home to tell her hysterically that an intruder has killed his wife; Susan, his second wife, lays in the library, her skull crushed; a bronze statue, the murder weapon, is nearby; investigating detectives note that Cohen has bruises and scratches on his arms and is covered with blood, but there is no sign of a struggle in the mansion; he is charged with murder and later will state he has had a blackout; Cohen will be found guilty, but having had what is termed "diminished responsibility" in committing the crime, he will be given 12 years in prison.

MAY 29

Former Argentine President Pedro Eugenio Arambaru is kidnapped and killed by terrorists when their demands for the release of political prisoners are refused in Argentina.

JUNE 22

Jeanette and Harvey Crewe, whose farm is near Pukekwa, New Zealand, are found shot and tied with weights in the nearby Waikato River; their neighbor, Arthur Alan Thomas, who once had courted Mrs. Crewe, is charged with the double murders because his rifle is the same caliber as that used on the victims and a spool of wire in his barn matches that used to tie the weights to the bodies; on this slim evidence, Thomas will be sent to prison for life.

JULY 31

U.S. diplomat Daniel A. Mitrone is kidnapped in Uruguay by terrorists who demand that that country free all its political prisoners; when the demand is rejected, Mitrone is killed, his body found in Montevideo on Aug. 10.

SEPT. 5

Dale Merle Nelson of West Creston, B.C., Canada, goes berserk and slays nine relatives; he is captured a short time later, blaming his actions on LSD; he will be sent to prison for life.

SEPT. 26

E. C. Mullendore III, alleged multimillionaire, is shot to death at his massive Cross Bell Ranch in Oklahoma; at first it is thought that Mullendore has been killed by intruders; then several ranch hands with criminal backgrounds are suspected, but no one is indicted, for lack of evidence; it is then discovered that Mullendore is almost penniless, living on enormous loans made against his failing ranch; his killing has never been solved.

OCT. 10

Canadian separatist terrorists kidnap Pierre Laporte, minister of labor; they have already kidnapped British Trade Commissioner John R. Cross; holding both men, they demand $4 million and that 20 members of their group be flown out of the country; when the Pierre Trudeau government refuses to negotiate, Laporte is killed, his body found in a trunk of a car parked at the airport outside Montréal; seven members of the kidnapping group are allowed to fly to Cuba, and Cross is released.

OCT. 28

Millionaire horse breeder George Jayne, of Iverness, Ill., an exclusive Chicago suburb, is shot through the window of his home while celebrating his son's 16th birthday. The murder is committed by Julius Barnes, working with Mel Adams, who has been hired for the killing by Edward Nefeld, onetime chief of detectives for the town of Markham, Ill., and Joseph LaPlaca, both of whom, in turn, were operating at the direction of Silas Jayne, the victim's brother. (The Jayne brothers have been notoriously feuding for years, with many attempts being made against each other's life.) Nefeld will receive three to 10 years in prison, Adams immunity for his testimony against the others. Silas Jayne and LaPlaca are given six to 20 years in prison, Barnes 25 to 35 years. Silas Jayne will be paroled on May 24, 1979, still insisting upon his innocence.

NOV. 26

A Bolivian disguised as a priest attempts to shoot Pope Paul VI in Manila, Philippines, during a visit, but the pontiff is unharmed.

ORGANIZED CRIME

MAY 5

High Judge Pietro Scaglione and his driver are shot dead in a Palermo, Sicily, street; Scaglione has been conducting trials of Mafia figures.

DEC. 30

Dixie Davis, onetime legal "mouthpiece" for beer baron Dutch Schultz, dies of a heart attack in New York City after his home is robbed and family threatened by burglars.

WHITE-COLLAR CRIME

SEPT. 22

Hugo J. Addonizio, former mayor of Newark, N.J., receives a 10-year prison term and a $25,000 fine after being convicted of conspiracy charges.

MISCELLANEOUS

MARCH 6

U.S. diplomat Sean M. Holly is seized by terrorists

in Guatemala and held until three terrorists are set free; he is released unharmed.

MARCH 24

USAF Lt. Col. Donald J. Crowley is kidnapped by Dominican Republic terrorists and held until 20 political prisoners are allowed to leave the country; he will be released unharmed.

APRIL 6

A four-story town house in Greenwich Village explodes; it has been used as a bomb factory by young New York City militants.

JUNE 11

The West German ambassador to Brazil is kidnapped but released unharmed a short time later when 40 Brazilian political prisoners are freed.

JULY 9

Colombian terrorists seize former Colombian Foreign Minister Fernando Londone y Londone, releasing him unharmed after his family pays a $200,000 ransom.

JULY 31

Aloysio Dias Gomide, Brazilian vice consul, is seized in Montevideo and released a short time later when his wife pays a ransom of $250,000.

AUG. 7

Terrorists in Montevideo, Uruguay, seize Claude L. Fly, a U.S. agronomist, but they release him before ransom is paid when he grows dangerously ill.

AUG. 18

Black activist Angela Davis is put on the FBI's 10 Most Wanted Fugitives list after a courtroom shooting in California.

OCT. 19

Conspiracy charges against Black Panther chief Bobby Seale are dropped following a declared mistrial of his case, in which he was charged with inciting to violence in Chicago during the 1968 Democratic National Convention.

DEC. 1

Basque separatists seize German businessman Eugene Beihl, demanding political sanctions; he will be released unharmed on Dec. 25.

DEC. 7

Swiss ambassador to Brazil Giovanni E. Bucher is kidnapped by revolutionaries in Rio de Janeiro but will be released on Dec. 16, 1971, after the Brazilian government releases 70 political prisoners.

1·9·7·1

MURDER

MARCH 29

Lt. William Calley is found guilty of mass murder in the My Lai, Vietnam, massacre. He is given a life term but later released.

JULY 12

Juan Vellejo Corona, 38-year-old Mexican immigrant and labor contractor, is indicted for murdering 25 itinerant workers. Carona has hired the migrants to work his farm, then killed them systematically over a long period of time in the bunkhouse of the Sullivan Ranch near Yuba City, Calif., to steal their belongings and meager pay; the bodies are found clubbed, stabbed and shot to death and buried in shallow graves; Corona's bloody machete and blood-crusted boots will horrify the jury hearing his case, and he will be found guilty, although shouting his innocence, and sentenced to serve 25 consecutive life terms in Soledad Prison; he will be stabbed 32 times by fellow prisoners in 1973, losing the sight in one eye and thereafter being isolated for his own protection.

MAY 17

Ephraim Elrom, Israeli consul, is abducted in Istanbul and held by Turkish terrorists, who demand that fellow terrorists be released; when the demand is ignored, Elrom will be murdered, his corpse discovered on May 23.

JUNE 21

At the instigation of Karen Glabe, former cop Preston Haig stabs Glabe's husband, Kenneth, to death in Arlington Heights, Ill.; Karen, a former airline stewardess, has paid Haig $5,000 to commit the murder so she can be with her young lover, Mitchell Link; Haig leaves for New Mexico, but his wife informs on him, and he in turn confesses, implicating Mrs. Glabe; Lake County Circuit Judge Robert K. McQueen will sentence both Mrs. Glabe and Haig in 1980 to 35 to 45 years in prison.

JULY 3

Francis Wyanan Vontsteen shoots and kills François Swanepoel, a policeman, in Pretoria, South Africa; Mrs. Sonjia Swanepoel, with whom Vontsteen has been having a decade-long love affair (she has had a child by him but has convinced her husband that it was his), tries to pass the blame for the killing onto a Bantu tribesman intruder, but a witness tells police that Vontsteen has approached him and asked him to help kill the officer; Vontsteen will be hanged in October 1971 and his mistress, Mrs. Swanepoel, will be given 15 years in prison.

AUG. 26

Jenny Janel Henderson, 11, is found naked and strangled in a gravel pit near her home in Odessa, Tex., the last victim, it is thought, of the so-called Texas Strangler, who has killed 11 females from 1968 to 1971.

SEPT. 3

John Gilbert Freeman, a demented upholsterer living in Phoenix, Ariz., murders seven neighbors as he enters the home of Norvella Bentley, blazing away with two .38 revolvers; Freeman will be confined to an asylum for four years, declared sane, then given seven consecutive life terms; as he is led away he will shout to the court that Communists have done the killings.

ROBBERY

AUG. 2–3

Frederick Joseph Sewell and other, unknown thieves rob a jewelry store in Blackpool, England, of £106,000 worth of jewelry, shooting several officers while making their escape, including Superintendent of Police Gerald Richardson; Sewell will be caught within a month and sent to prison for 30 years.

NOV. 24

A man buying a ticket on Northwest Orient Airlines for a Portland, Ore.,-to-Seattle flight gives his name as D. B. Cooper; in midflight he informs the pilots that he has a bomb in a briefcase on board and demands $200,000 and four parachutes, all of which are supplied when the plane lands; the plane, now with only Cooper as a passenger, then flies to Reno, but when it lands, the crew finds Cooper gone, the rear exit door open; it is thought that Cooper parachuted from the 727 jet somewhere over Washington; however, none of the marked money shows up until children playing along the bank of the Columbia River near Vancouver, Wash., find some of the bills; Cooper and the rest of the loot have never been found.

DEC. 31

The Hotel Pierre in New York City is robbed of jewelry kept in its safe, gems unofficially estimated to be worth $5 million; the thieves have not been caught.

ORGANIZED CRIME

MAY 18

The American Embassy in Tel Aviv writes to Meyer Lansky, then in Israel, to tell him that his passport has been canceled because of indictments against him in the U.S.

JUNE 28

Joe Colombo is crippled when he is shot three times by black gunman Jerome A. Johnson in New York City during the Italian-American Unity Day Parade at Columbus Circle, an event engineered by Colombo; the assailant is shot to death immediately by Colombo bodyguards.

WHITE-COLLAR CRIME

FEB. 15–AUG. 10

Con men establish a land-development scheme called Lake Havasu Estates in Arizona in a copycat offer similar to that of the legitimate McCulloch Corp., but they develop nothing except enormous payments from suckers.

MISCELLANEOUS

JAN. 8

British ambassador to Uruguay Geoffrey Jackson is

kidnapped in Montevideo by terrorists demanding that prisoners be released; the prisoners will set free and Jackson will be released unharmed on Sept. 9.

AUG. 18

A helicopter lands in the prison yard of the Mexico City Prison, guards thinking that important visitors are arriving; the 'copter, which is present only 15 seconds, takes aboard two inmates, counterfeiter Carlos Castro and American murderer Joel D. Kaplan; later it will be claimed that the break, which purportedly cost $1 million to engineer, has been masterminded by the CIA, for whom Kaplan works.

SEPT. 9

More than 1,000 prisoners at New York's Attica Prison riot, setting fire to buildings, taking 32 hostages and later killing three guards.

OCT. 18

Soviet Premier Alexei Kosygin is assaulted by a demonstrator on the grounds of the Canadian Parliament in Ottawa, but he is unharmed.

1·9·7·2

MURDER

APRIL 8

Sheik Abeid Amani Karume, ruler of Zanzibar, is assassinated.

APRIL 14

Uruguayan guerrillas murder four persons in terror attacks.

AUG. 4

Arthur Bremer of Milwaukee, Wis., is given a 63-year prison sentence for shooting Alabama Gov. George C. Wallace (who is paralyzed for life) and three others in a political meeting in Laurel, Md.

OCT. 5

Herbert Mullin of Santa Cruz, Calif., a neat, hippie-hating youth and the son of a retired Marine colonel, begins shooting and killing long-haired, eccentric people and will murder, until February 1973, 13 persons, later telling police he has done this to propitiate the gods and thwart earthquakes in California; he will be given a life sentence.

ROBBERY

NOV. 5

Two men force their way into the closed Barn Restaurant in Braintree, Essex, England, killing the owner, Bob Patience, his wife and child, and making off with £900; George Ince, who seems to match the description of one of the gunmen, is twice tried for the robbery-murder and found not guilty; a look-alike, John Brook, later is found, along with his partner, Nicholas de Clare Johnson; Brook will be sent to prison for life, Johnson for 10 years.

ORGANIZED CRIME

APRIL 7

Joey Gallo is shot to death in front of his wife and bodyguards (who are wounded) in Umberto's Clam Bar in New York City by unknown gangsters.

AUG. 8

A criminal fraternity is reported in the Georgian SSR of the Soviet Union; the group spends most of its efforts producing illegal brandy.

DEC. 22

Chicago Mafia syndicate chieftain Paul "The Waiter" Ricca dies of natural causes in that city.

White-Collar Crime

FEB. 14

Sharper Jerome Hoffman begins a bogus investment firm, REFA, and gleans $150 million from gullible investors; Hoffman becomes so rich that he tries to buy the New York Yankees baseball club, but his bid is turned down; later he will be sent to the federal correction institution at Marion, Ill., for two years, for his swindle.

Miscellaneous

JAN. 9

Detroit's ''dope war'' begins; it will claim 200 victims over nine months.

FEB. 3

Barry Glen Lipsky, a drug pusher in New York City, begins to talk to police, a confession that leads to one of the largest roundups of drug dealers in U.S. history.

MARCH 22

A bomb reportedly set by the IRA explodes in the biggest hotel and main railroad station in Belfast, Northern Ireland.

MAY 6

A skyjacker who has extorted $303,000 from Eastern Airlines parachutes into Central America, imitating the feat of D. B. Cooper five months earlier. He is never captured.

JUNE 3

An American terrorist hijacks a plane in San Francisco, obtains $500,000 ransom and takes another jet to sanctuary in Algeria.

JULY 15

Ulrike Meinhof of the German terrorist Baader-Meinhof gang is arrested by police; she will commit suicide in May 1976 inside her cell in Stammheim Prison.

JULY 27

Mrs. Virginia Piper is kidnapped and held for $1 million ransom; she is released upon payment.

OCT. 26

Frank Tummillo becomes the first federal agent to be killed in the four-year history of the Bureau of Narcotics and Dangerous Drugs, during a $160,000 cocaine ''buy'' in New York City.

1·9·7·3

Murder

JAN. 7

Mark James Robert Essex, a black man from Kansas, goes to the Howard Johnson Motel in downtown New Orleans, setting fires and shooting white guests; he kills a honeymooning couple, three policemen and two hotel employees and wounds 16 others before a helicopter loaded with police machine gunners cuts him in half with a spray of bullets as he shoots it out on the hotel roof.

APRIL 10

Calvin Jackson, a porter at the Park Plaza Hotel in New York City, suffocates Theresa Jordan, a 39-year-old hotel guest, stealing her TV and raping the body; he will murder and rape nine other women in the hotel through 1974 before confessing to police when under arrest for another offense; Jackson will go to prison for life.

MAY 14

Wayne Coleman, Carl and Billy Isaacs and George Dungee, escaped prisoners from a Maryland correction center, invade the Alday home in rural Seminole County, Ga., murdering the entire family of seven, including Mrs. Mary Alday, whom they have dragged along with them into the woods, where they all have repeatedly raped, sodomized, beat her and finally shot her to death; the four are sentenced to death and at this writing still await execution in Georgia's Reidsville Prison; says Coleman afterwards: "I'd like to kill about 1,000 more people."

JUNE 3

Driving on Highway I-57 outside Chicago, Henry Brisbon and three others run another car to the side of the road; Brisbon inexplicably shoots and kills its occupants, James Schmidt and his fiancée, Dorothy Cerny; Brisbon, tracked down through his license plate, will be sentenced to serve from 1,000 to 3,000 years in prison, making parole an impossibility.

AUG. 8

In Pasadena, Tex., 18-year-old Elmer Wayne Henley, Jr., calls police to tell them he has killed 33-year-old Dean Caroll, a raving homosexual who has killed over the past few years at least 27 youths, castrating them and burying their remains in a boathouse pit near his Pasadena, Tex., home. Henley tells Houston police that he has murdered Caroll because he thought he was about to be the next victim, although he admits helping the mass killer by enticing homosexual victims to Caroll's home; Henley will be sent to prison for life.

SEPT. 12

Marcus Wayne Chenault of Atlanta, Ga., is sentenced to death for murdering the mother of Dr. Martin Luther King, Jr., on June 30.

NOV. 6

Douglas Gretzler and William Stellman, stickup men, break into the Victor, Calif., home of Walter Parkin, forcing Parkin to give them $4,000; they then shoot to death Parkin, his wife, four children and three others present; the murderous pair are captured some days later and are sent to Death Row at San Quentin, where they remain as of this writing; in addition to the nine Parkin slayings, 11 other killings in Arizona and California are attributed by police to Steelman and Gretzler.

DEC. 31

Roseann Quinn takes John Wayne Wilson to her New York City apartment, but the homosexual prostitute, unable to perform, slashes the young woman to death; he will later become the protagonist of Judith Rossner's *Looking for Mr. Goodbar*.

ROBBERY

DEC. 2

Carl Dixon, Louis Mathis and Anthony B. Vaglica

break into the Fogg Museum at Harvard University and steal $5 million in antique coins; later they are caught while trying to fence the coins and will receive stiff prison terms.

ORGANIZED CRIME

APRIL 5

Mafia chief Angelo Mangano narrowly escapes assassination by unknown gunmen in Palermo, Sicily.

APRIL 14

Chicago Syndicate subchief Sam DeStefano is murdered in the garage of his home; DeStefano has been one of the outfit's most feared killers, considered crazy by many of his own kind.

WHITE-COLLAR CRIME

APRIL 15

Eighteen of France's most distinguished wine merchants are indicted for importing $800,000 worth of fake Bordeaux wines; the press dubs the scam "Winegate."

MISCELLANEOUS

MAY 2

Joanne Chesimard, a black terrorist, and Clark E. Squire, another radical, kill two policemen who stop their car on the New Jersey Turnpike; Chesimard will later be caught and sent to prison for life, only to escape on Nov. 2, 1979.

JUNE 10

Playboy J. Paul Getty III is kidnapped outside his Rome residence; when his kidnappers get no response from the 16-year-old's grandfather, J. Paul Getty I, who believes the kidnapping a stunt pulled by his grandson to obtain more spending money, they cut off one of the boy's ears and mail it to a Rome newspaper along with a photo showing the mutilated grandson;

Getty pays $2.9 million to the kidnappers, who release the grandson. They are never apprehended.

DEC. 6

An executive for the Exxon Corporation, Victor E.

Samuelson, is kidnapped in Buenos Aires, Argentina, by members of the Peoples' Revolutionary Army and held for a record $14.2 million ransom, which the oil company will pay. Samuelson will be released unharmed.

1·9·7·4

MURDER

FEB. 12

Eban Gossage, son of famous publicist Howard Gossage, stabs his sister Amy to death in her San Francisco apartment while he argues with her over their father's inheritance; Gossage will be sent to prison, convicted of voluntary manslaughter.

FEB. 14

Psychopathic Patrick Mackay, who thinks he is Hitler reincarnated, stabs 84-year-old Isabella Griffiths to death in her London apartment; his next victim is Adele Price, on March 10, 1975; March 21, 1975, he will ax to death Father Anthony Crean, a priest who has helped him in the past; police, knowing the priest's affiliation with Mackay, arrest the 23-year-old, and he confesses the murders and is sent to prison for life.

MARCH 23

An irate patron is ejected from an Allentown, Pa., bar; he returns within an hour to toss a Molotov cocktail into the bar, killing eight people and injuring a dozen more; the killer has never been found.

NOV. 4

Marthinus Choegoe breaks into the Cape Town, South Africa, home of wealthy Christopher van der Linde and stabs his wife, Susanna, to death while she sleeps, then flees; he is seen escaping and is identified to police; when captured, the killer says that he has been hired by Marlene Lehnberg, who wants Mrs. Van der Linde out of the way so she can marry her husband; both Marlene Lehnberg and Choegoe will be sent to prison for life.

DEC. 1

Charles Jackson, 46, a skid-row bum, is found slashed to pieces on the lawn of the Los Angeles Public Library; he is the first of eight skid-row men who will be murdered by a killer known as the Los Angeles Slasher, who will operate until early 1975 and who has never been caught.

DEC. 30

Anthony F. Barbaro, an honor student in Olean, N.Y., inexplicably sets fire to his school, kills three passersby with a rifle, then wounds 11 firemen attempting to put out the blaze; after his capture, Barbaro hangs himself in his cell.

ROBBERY

AUG. 24

A special commission to combat pilfering in Soviet industries is established in Moscow.

OCT. 20

Six men blow a hole in the wall of the main Chicago office of The Purolator Company and make off with $4.3 million; they will attempt to flee to Latin America with the untraceable old bills, but all will be captured and most of the money recovered.

ORGANIZED CRIME

JAN. 23

Carmine "The Cigar" Galante is paroled in New York after serving several years on a dope smuggling conviction.

JULY 6

The decomposing bodies of syndicate loan shark Sam Marcello and Mafia enforcer Joseph Grisafe are found in two oil drums behind a Western Avenue hot-dog stand in Chicago.

WHITE-COLLAR CRIME

SEPT. 2

Mark Colombo is found guilty in a Swiss tirla of defrauding Lloyd's Bank International Ltd. of £33 million.

MISCELLANEOUS

FEB. 2

Reg Murphy, editor of the *Atlanta Constitution* who has been kidnapped and held for $700,000 ransom, is released; his abductors, Mrs. Betty Ruth Williams and William H. Williams, soon will be captured and imprisoned.

FEB. 4

Patricia Hearst is allegedly kidnapped by Symbionese Liberation Army members in San Francisco.

APRIL 13

American businessman Alfred Albert Laun III, wounded in the stomach, escapes from his Marxist abductors in Córdoba, Argentina; he survives.

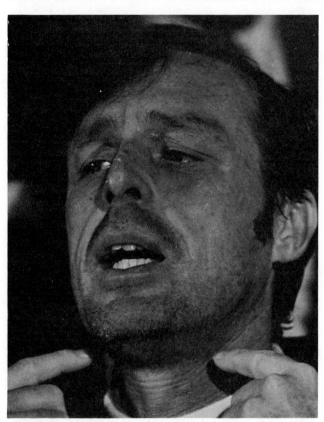

Reg Murphy, kidnapped editor of the *Atlanta Constitution*. (Feb. 2, 1974)

1·9·7·5

MURDER

JAN. 13

Donald Neilson kidnaps 17-year-old Lesley Whittle of Kidderminster, England, and demands £50,000 ransom from her wealthy family (not paid); on March 7 the girl's naked body is found hanging from a beam in a drainage shaft, a wire tied around her neck; Neilson, who has also murdered three postal officials and performed countless robberies and burglaries, will evade capture for nine months; when captured, he will be sent to prison for life.

MARCH 25

King Faisal of Saudi Arabia is assassinated in the Ri'Assa Palace by his playboy nephew Prince Faisal Bin Musaed Bin Abdulaziz, who is later decapitated and his head put on public display.

APRIL 3

James Ruppert of Hamilton, Ohio, kills 11 members of his family to obtain the family fortune of $300,000; he will be given 11 consecutive life terms.

MAY 15

Norma Jean Armistead, a middle-aged obstetrical

nurse, visits a pregnant unmarried mother in a Van Nuys, Calif., apartment, ostensibly to deliver her child; instead she cuts the woman's throat, killing her, then performs a Cesarean section, bundling up the live child and racing to a hospital where she checks in, telling doctors she has delivered *her own* child only hours earlier; a routine inspection proves her a liar, and she will be arrested and found guilty of first-degree murder; she will be given a life term.

MAY 16

Michael Abdul Malik, who called himself "Michael X" in London's black power movement of the 1960s, is hanged in Port-of-Spain, Trinidad, for slashing to death with a machete his cousin, Joseph Skerritt, and 27-year-old British divorcée Gale Ann Benson, a daughter of a former member of the British Parliament.

MAY 24

Russell Smith goes on a rampage through Dayton, Ohio, firing through windows and doors, then shooting people emerging from a movie theater; he will rape two girls, kill one, kill his girlfriend and three others and wound 11 before turning his gun on himself.

JULY 1

Patients in the VA hospital in Ann Arbor, Mich., begin to die at an alarming rate of respiratory failure, 11 in all; later two nurses will be charged with injecting Pavulon, a muscle relaxant, into the victims, but it will not be proved, and they will be released; the killings have never been solved.

JULY 30

James Riddle Hoffa vanishes from the parking lot of a Bloomfield Township, Mich., restaurant and is not seen again; the vitriolic Teamsters leader is believed to have been kidnapped and murdered on orders of the syndicate.

SEPT. 5

Lynette Alice "Squeaky" Fromme attempts to shoot President Gerald Ford at a political rally in Sacramento, Calif., but the .45 she aims misfires and she is quickly arrested; the onetime Charles Manson disciple will be sent to prison for life on Dec. 17.

SEPT. 22

Malcontent Sara Jane Moore attempts to shoot President Ford outside a San Francisco hotel, but her aim is spoiled by a marine in the crowd; she will go to prison for life.

DEC. 7

Playboy John S. Knight III, heir to the Knight-Ridder newspaper chain, is murdered for money in his Philadelphia penthouse by three hustlers—Steven Maleno, Felix Melendez and Salvatore Soli; Maleno and Soli murder Melendez and will be sent to prison for life.

DEC. 23

Richard S. Welsh, chief of the CIA in Athens, Greece, is shot to death as he returns home from a Christmas party given by Ambassador Jack Kubisch; Welsh is thought to be a victim of radicals attempting to oust the incumbent junta, but his killers have never been found.

ORGANIZED CRIME

OCT. 8

Mafia leader Candido Cuini is shot to death while lying wounded in a Palermo, Sicily, hospital.

MISCELLANEOUS

JAN. 20

A bloody riot begins in the Walpole, Mass., prison; the riot will last for five days and leave dozens injured.

MARCH 25

Youngsters Shelia and Kathy Lyon walk from their Wheaton, Ill., home to a nearby shopping plaza and vanish; neither has been seen since, and they are thought to be victims of foul play.

SEPT. 18

Patricia Hearst is captured by lawmen in San Francisco and later is charged with bank robbery as a member of the Symbionese Liberation Army, not its kidnap victim.

DEC. 14

After holding 23 people hostage for 12 days on a stalled train near Beilen, Netherlands, six Asian terrorists demanding political sanctions surrender to police.

DEC. 21

Palestinian terrorists raid a meeting of the Organization of Petroleum Exporting Countries, taking 11 OPEC members hostage in Vienna; two guards will be killed but later the hostages will be released.

DEC. 29

A bomb explodes in the main terminal of New York City's LaGuardia Airport, killing 11 persons and injuring 70 others; the bomber has not been caught.

1·9·7·6

MURDER

JAN. 15

Cynthia Cadieux, 16, disappears from her Roseville, Mich., home and later is found naked in a ditch, her skull crushed; hers is the first of seven child-murders in the bedroom communities surrounding Detroit that will plague police until late 1977, when the murders will cease; the killer has not been found.

FEB. 13

Actor Sal Mineo is found knifed to death in the carport of his West Hollywood, Calif., home; later robber Lionel Ray Williams will be identified as the killer by a tattoo on his arm and given a life sentence.

MARCH 21

Singer Claudine Longet accidentally shoots and kills her lover, ski instructor Vladimir "Spider" Sabich, in Aspen, Colo., she will be convicted of "criminally negligent homicide," be given a 30-day sentence and be placed on probation for two years.

APRIL 25

Moses Pearson, while high on cocaine, drives wildly through central Georgia, shooting persons at random, killing three and wounding 13 before police trap him, at which time he sends a bullet into his own brain.

MAY 4

Patricia Columbo and her boyfriend, Frank DeLuca, murder Patricia's mother, father and little brother in Elk Grove Village, Ill., so Patty can obtain the family fortune; DeLuca leaves telltale clues behind and both will be arrested shortly after the killings; several men will come forward to testify that Patricia had sex with them and offered them money to murder her parents; both DeLuca and Columbo will be sentenced to from 200 to 300 years in prison.

JULY 29

David Berkowitz, the infamous "Son of Sam" mass killer, pleads guilty to the murder of Stacy Moskowitz and to five other counts of second-degree murder in New York City; he is sentenced to 315 years in prison and is sent to Attica Correctional Facility in upstate New York.

AUG. 19

Michael Edward Drabing of Lincoln, Neb., stabs a farmer, Lloyd Schneider, his wife and 17-year-old daughter to death in that city in a "kill the rich" vendetta; he is captured before he can murder the governor of Illinois, who is next on his hit list; Drabing will go to prison for life.

Chicago killer Patricia Columbo, who traded sexual favors to have her family murdered. (May 4, 1976)

SEPT. 21

Former Chilean Foreign Minister Orlando Letelier is assassinated in Washington, D.C., when his car is blown up by explosives planted, police theorize, by political enemies.

OCT. 19

Michaiah Shobek is executed at Nassau in the Bahamas for murdering three U.S. tourists for their money.

OCT. 20

Tulio Oneto, an Argentine exchange broker, is killed in Buenos Aires by members of the Peoples' Revolutionary Army after Oneto's family fails to pay a $2 million ransom; the broker's son-in-law, Carlos Macri, also abducted, is released after the guerrilla group receives a $750,000 ransom for him.

DEC. 8

Mrs. Patty Bolin of Columbus, Ohio, pulls out a .22-caliber pistol and shoots to death her husband, her 12-year-old daughter and her 9-year-old son; she aims at her 15-year-old daughter, Alicia, but the weapon misfires; and the daughter runs for the police; by the time officers arrive, Mrs. Bolin has shot herself to death.

ROBBERY

JAN. 28

Guerrillas blow open the vaults of the British Bank of the Middle East in Bab Idriss, Lebanon, taking between $20 million and $50 million, which has never been recovered.

MARCH 30

A Brink's truck is stopped on a Montréal, Canada, street; aiming an antitank gun at the guards, five bandits take more than $2.8 million, the largest Brink's loss in history. The bandits are never apprehended.

APRIL 14

An estimated $6 million in gems are stolen from safe-deposit boxes in the Palm Towers Hotel in Palm Beach, Fla., the largest hotel burglary on record. The burglars are not apprehended.

JULY 16

Albert Spaggiari and nine others allegedly tunnel into the underground vault of the branch bank of the Société Générale in Nice, France, and for 48 hours loot the safe-deposit boxes of between $8 million and

$10 million in jewels, cash, bonds and securities; later, mastermind Spaggiari is captured but will make a spectacular escape from a French courtroom before his trial; as of this writing, he remains at large.

ORGANIZED CRIME

DEC. 15

Frederick "Rick" Manzie, husband of singer Barbara McNair, is shot several times in the head gangland style in his wife's 20-room Las Vegas home; Manzie has been strongly tied to syndicate members in Chicago.

WHITE-COLLAR CRIME

JULY 6

In Paris, French embezzler Herve de Vathaire; his girlfriend, Daniele Marquet; and associate Jean Kay vanish after de Vathaire embezzles more than $1.6 million from his employer, the Dassault airplane manufacturing firm; all three are tried *in absentia* and given long prison terms. At this writing they have yet to be apprehended.

OCT. 25

Former Argentine President Maria Estela Perón is found guilty of embezzling $500,000 by writing checks against a Perónist fund.

DEC. 1

French, Spanish and West German police break up an enormous counterfeiting ring, arresting Frederic Seuzan and three others and seizing $14 million in bogus American $20 bills. Seuzan will be sent to prison for several years.

MISCELLANEOUS

JAN. 5

Phonograph record executive Louis Hazan is released by kidnappers in Paris after a $3.5 million ransom is paid.

JAN. 9

Malaysian stevedore Teo Hock-song is sentenced to death in Singapore for smuggling morphine.

FEB. 19

Newspaper heiress Patricia Hearst invokes the Fifth Amendment 19 times during her trial for a 1974 bank robbery with the Symbionese Liberation Army.

MARCH 10

Donald Alexander Hay of Port Moody, B.C., Canada, kidnaps 12-year-old Abby Drover, keeping her in a dungeonlike room of his home; a curious police officer discovers Abby on Sept. 6, returning her safely to her family; Hay, 43, will be sent to prison for life.

APRIL 2

John Thomas Jova, 24, son of the U.S. ambassador to Mexico, is found guilty of drug smuggling and sent to prison in Maidstone, England, for 2½ years.

APRIL 14

In an apparent move to obtain judicial leniency, Patricia Hearst agrees to testify against SLA members.

MAY 1

Actress Louise Lasser is arrested in Beverly Hills, Calif., on charges of cocaine possession.

JUNE 2

Investigative reporter Don Bolles is blown up in his car in Phoenix, Ariz.; a national investigative team of reporters will descend on Phoenix, and later John Harvey Adamson and others will be indicted for the bombing murder; Adamson will then turn state's evidence, will admit to detonating the bomb, and will receive a 20-year sentence for second-degree murder.

JUNE 3

Five Americans who have been held hostage are released by members of the Eritrean Liberation Front in Asmara, Ethiopia.

JULY 15

Kidnappers James and Richard Schoenfeld and Fred Woods take over a school bus carrying 26 children near Chowchilla, Calif., and drive it to where they have dug a large hole, burying the entire bus and its riders; they demand a $5 million ransom but are captured before the money is paid; all 26 children and their driver, Ed Ray, buried for 30 hours, are found alive.

SEPT. 24

Patricia Hearst is sentenced to seven years in prison for a 1974 California bank robbery.

OCT. 28

Japanese police arrest 2,489 persons in Tokyo in massive drug raids, confiscating large amounts of illegal substances.

1·9·7·7

MURDER

JAN. 18

Murderer Gary Mark Gilmore is executed by a firing squad at the Utah State Prison after shouting to the riflemen: "Let's do it!"

FEB. 14

Self-styled Nazi Fred Cowan of New Rochelle, N.Y., goes on a murder rampage at a plant where he has been suspended, killing four employees and a police-

man; police and military personnel try to blast Cowan out of the plant, but he commits suicide.

MARCH 4

Student Taweeyos Sirikil meets with a prospective buyer for his car who has answered an ad; Sirikil goes off in a test drive with the buyer on Chicago streets and vanishes; Sirikil's body, stabbed several times, is found three weeks later; the killer has not been found.

MARCH 8

Three men convicted of murdering publisher Ab-

Fred Cowan, self-styled Nazi and murderer. (Feb. 14, 1977)

dulla al-Madani, who also is a National Assembly member, are executed by firing squad in Bahrain.

MARCH 27

Al Marjek, a 19-year-old child-killer who has raped and murdered three young boys—his crimes being the first of their kind in Syrian legal history—is hanged in a public square in Damascus.

MAY 27

Mrs. Gertrude Resnick Farber, daughter of a rich TV antenna manufacturer, is kidnapped and held for $1 million ransom; when the money is not paid, Mrs. Farber is killed, her body found near a Grahamsville, N.Y., reservoir. The murder is never solved.

NOV. 19

Mrs. Pam Pastorino of Chicago and her 15-year-old sister Debbie Saylor kill their stepfather, Leonard Warchol, when he tells them he does not want Debbie making pizza in the kitchen; Mrs. Pastorino, who hits Warchol over the head with a lead pipe while Debbie stabs him several times, will be sentenced to prison for 60 years; Debbie Saylor will go to a youth center.

ROBBERY

MAY 1

Richard Gantz, a convicted robber on a work-re-lease program, goes on a robbing spree in New York City, holding up a gasoline station and stealing three cars, taking a 19-year-old college student with him at gunpoint, raping and sodomizing the girl many times before he is arrested while attacking the student in a Brooklyn motel. He will be sent to prison for several years.

MAY 25

Two unknown burglars use a stolen blowtorch to break into a safe in a dynamite warehouse in Hunnerberg, Sweden; they blow themselves and the plant to pieces.

JUNE 6

More than $176,000 in jewelry is taken from West Virginia gemsmith Aubrey Hawkins who, with his wife, Alberta, is killed by the unidentified thieves in Jacksboro, Tenn.

OCT. 7–11

Exactly $1 million in cash is taken from the vault of the First National Bank of Chicago, obviously by someone working for the bank; the suspect will hold his job for several months before the bank dismisses him; knowing he is being watched around the clock by FBI agents, the suspect has made no move toward the money, nor fled, as of this writing.

ORGANIZED CRIME

APRIL 28

Hugh J. Addonizio, former mayor of Newark, N.J., is released from prison after serving part of a 10-year sentence for conspiring with syndicate members to extort $1.4 million from New Jersey contractors.

WHITE-COLLAR CRIME

FEB. 2

Lawmen raid the home of Virgil Hewell in Burke, Va., finding a large amount of counterfeit $20 bills and $200,000 worth of hard drugs. Hewell will receive a stiff sentence.

APRIL 8

Six men are arrested for unleashing a flood of counterfeit $20 bills in New York City, an estimated $1 million in bogus notes.

APRIL 26

Secret Service agents in Chicago raid a North Side apartment and confiscate a printing press, master negatives, plates and $700,000 in counterfeit $20 bills and $1.5 million in fake $10 bills.

MAY 3

Fernando Bonini, accused of being ringleader of a massive counterfeit ring operating internationally, is arrested in Rome after selling millions of dollars' worth of Citibank travelers' checks.

MISCELLANEOUS

FEB. 14

Edwin John Eastwood of Melbourne, Australia, who kidnapped a teacher and six students in 1972, goes on another kidnapping rampage, abducting 16 persons, including another teacher and nine students; Eastwood will be wounded in a gun battle with police and be sent to prison.

MARCH 11

Film director Roman Polanski is arrested at the Beverly Wilshire Hotel in Beverly Hills, Calif., and is charged with luring a 13-year-old girl to the home of actor Jack Nicholson (who is away in Europe) on the pretext of photographing her, then drugging and raping her; while police are searching the Nicholson home they find the actor's longtime friend Angelica Huston, 26, daughter of film director John Huston, whom they arrest on charges of possessing cocaine; Polanski will post a $2,500 bond and flee the country, remaining in Europe to avoid prosecution; he has not returned to the U.S. as of this writing.

MARCH 19

Kidnappers release industrialist Carlo Colombo in Bornago, Italy, after a ransom of $1.2 million is paid.

MARCH 23

Reno N. Fruzza, vice president of the First National Bank of Nevada in Las Vegas, and his wife, Polly, are injected with what extortionists claim is a lethal drug; they can have the antidote, which must be taken in eight hours, they are told, if Fruzza obtains $1.2 million from his bank, which he does; the extortionists escape, and the Fruzzas later learn that they have been injected with a harmless substance.

APRIL 3

Piero Scosta, 42, oldest son of one of Italy's wealthiest shipowners, is released by kidnappers after a $1.6 million ransom is paid in Genoa.

APRIL 18

Veronica Franovic, a model, and Zoltan Kakash of Torrance, Calif., kidnap Lou Adler, president of Ode Records, and hold him for a $25,000 ransom, which is paid; Adler will be released unharmed, and the kidnappers will be tracked down and given long prison terms.

JUNE 15

James Earl Ray, killer of Dr. Martin Luther King, Jr., escapes from the Brushy Mountain State Prison in Tennessee; he will be recaptured a short time later.

AUG. 29

Nazi war criminal Herbert Kappler, who is ailing and being held under arrest in a Rome, Italy, hospital, escapes guards by being carried out of the hospital between the legs of his wife. He is later recaptured.

OCT. 3

India's Prime Minister Indira Gandhi is arrested in New Delhi on two charges of corruption but is released the next day, these charges later dropped, say supporters, as fabrications of political foes.

DEC. 14

Achilleas Kyprianous, son of the president of Cyprus, is kidnapped and held by terrorists; he is released four days later after political sanctions are granted.

1·9·7·8

MURDER

JAN. 23–27

Richard Trenton Chase goes on a murder rampage, killing six persons in California; when captured he brags of drinking his victims' blood; he will be sent to prison for life.

MARCH 16

Former prime minister of Italy Aldo Moro is kidnapped by Red Guard terrorists; when their demands are not met, Moro will be killed 55 days later.

APRIL 10

Linda Goldstone, wife of a prominent Chicago physician, is abducted by Hernando Williams, who repeatedly rapes her before killing her and stuffing her body in the trunk of his car, where it will be found later; Williams will go to prison for life.

MAY 5

Mrs. Marilyn Dietl of Burlington, Vt., takes her 18-year-old daughter Judy for a drive and shoots and kills her in the car to prevent her, she later explains to the police, from becoming a prostitute; Mrs. Dietl will be sent to prison for five to 15 years.

JUNE 3

Loop secretary Bobbie Ryan goes to bed with Peter Hoban, a Democratic precinct captain, in his North Side Chicago apartment; while Hoban sleeps, Ms. Ryan robs the place and sets fires that cause Hoban's death; she will receive a 22-year prison sentence.

NOV. 18

Megalomaniac religious leader Jim Jones, whose cultist commune in Guyana is a front to collect millions for his People's Temple, is visited by U.S. Congressman Leo Ryan, who is investigating conditions at the jungle camp where reportedly members are held prisoner so their relatives will continue to send contributions; Jones, high on drugs, orders the congressman killed; a hit squad shoots Ryan, three journalists and two defectors to death on a small airport runway, then Jones orders all his followers to follow him into suicide; they drink a punch laced heavily with cyanide, most compelled to drink at the point of machine guns held by fanatics; children beg and women scream, but the mass suicide, which includes Jones, ensues, claiming the lives of 913 people, mostly illiterate blacks who have followed Jones into his jungle haven.

NOV. 27

Daniel James White, onetime San Francisco City Supervisor, kills San Francisco Supervisor Harvey Milk, an avowed homosexual, and Mayor George Moscone, shooting them in their City Hall offices; White, whose attorneys later argue that he has committed the killing while "high on junk food," is given an eight-year term for voluntary manslaughter; homosexuals react by staging mass riots on July 15, 1979.

DEC. 11

Robert Piest, a 15-year-old, disappears from a pharmacy in Des Plaines, Ill., after telling his mother to wait for him while he talks to a contractor about a job. Police investigate hours later and question John Wayne Gacy, owner of the PDM Contracting Company. Gacy admits knowing the Piest boy but denies knowledge of his whereabouts. Further interrogations prompt Gacy, a homosexual, to admit killing the Piest boy, along with thirty-one others. Twenty-seven bodies are unearthed beneath the narrow crawlspace of Gacy's Summerdale, Ill. home. The wealthy contractor's arrest causes neighbors to go into shock. He was well-liked and threw expensive summer picnics. He had the habit of appearing at fund-raisers in a clown costume, and was active in the Democratic party, once having his photo taken with Rosalynn Carter. Gacy will be convicted and sentenced to death for abducting and murdering his victims (whom he would chloroform, then sodomize and kill). He is the third worst mass killer in United States history, Johann Otto Hoch being second with about 50 murders to his credit and 19th-century archkiller for insurance money, H. H. Holmes (Herman Webster Mudgett) being first with more than 200 victims. At this writing Gacy awaits execution by lethal injection.

ROBBERY

MAY 17

The body of silent-film comedian Charlie Chaplin, earlier stolen from its grave for arcane reasons, is found in a Swiss cornfield.

San Francisco homosexuals rioting after learning of the lenient sentence given former Supervisor Dan White, killer of Mayor George Moscone and Supervisor Harvey Milk. (Nov. 27, 1978)

SEPT. 25

Dozens of looters pick the pockets of 135 persons killed in a Pacific Southwest Airlines jet that has crashed in San Diego.

OCT. 25

Stanley Mark Rifkin, a computer consultant, learns the code of the computer controlling funds of the Security Pacific National Bank and transfers $10.2 million to a New York account he draws from, using the money to buy up diamonds in Switzerland; Rifkin will be caught, and most of the money will be recovered; it is the largest bank theft in American history to date. Rifkin will get 10 years in prison.

DEC. 11

Six masked bandits rob more than $5 million in American currency and $1 million in gold, jewels and foreign currency from the Lufthansa Airlines cargo hold in New York City's Kennedy International Airport; they have not been apprehended.

DEC. 19

Three bandits dressed like workmen hold up a Wells Fargo armored car in Staten Island, N.Y., when guards stop for lunch at a delicatessen; the bandits take more than $3 million in cash, the largest such haul in history, escape in cars and have not been caught.

ORGANIZED CRIME

JULY 18

Chicago syndicate chief Louis "Blind Louie" Cavallaro is convicted of extortion and sent to prison for 18 months.

MISCELLANEOUS

AUG. 27

Extortionists in Stateline, Nev., threaten to blow up several casinos unless they are paid $3 million; when the money is not forthcoming, a large hole is blown into the side of Harvey's Hotel-Casino, causing widespread damage.

OCT. 4

In Nashville, Tenn., country singer Tammy Wynette is kidnapped by a masked stranger who terrorizes her for hours before she is released 90 miles away; the abductor has not been caught.

1·9·7·9

MURDER

APRIL 28

Steven Judy rapes and murders Mrs. G. Chasteen of Indianapolis, Ind., and drowns her three children after abducting them on an interstate highway near Mooresville, Ind., on March 8, 1981. He will be executed for these killings.

MAY 25

The seventh body in the worst murder chain in Australian history is found in Adelaide, all of the victims being young women murdered from 1976, presumably by the same killer.

MAY 29

Federal Judge John H. Wood, Jr., is shot to death near his chambers in San Antonio, Tex.; Charles V. Harrelson, who has been convicted of another for-hire murder in the late 1960s, is tried and convicted of the assassination, given two consecutive life terms; prosecutors insist that he was hired to murder Judge Wood by Jamiel Chagra, who feared the judge's future decision in a drug smuggling case involving Chagra; Chagra will be found not guilty of hiring Harrelson for the killing but will be convicted of tax evasion and sent to prison for 15 years.

JULY 4

Five members of a motorcycle gang—four men and a young woman—are slain in their rural clubhouse near Charlotte, N.C.; police find the shell casings from rapid-fire automatic weapons outside the clubhouse, but the killers have not been apprehended.

JULY 25

Theodore Bundy is convicted of killing five coeds in 1978 in Florida; he has been convicted of a 1974 kidnapping and is thought to have murdered two other coeds in Florida and Colorado; he is given the death penalty but remains alive on appeals at this writing.

AUG. 27

Lord Mountbatten, uncle of Britain's Prince Philip, is killed by an explosion on his yacht off the Irish coast; the IRA takes credit for the murder.

OCT. 26

South Korean CIA chief Kim Jae Kyu murders President Park Chung Hee and eight bodyguards in the Blue House complex next to the presidential palace in Seoul.

OCT. 29

It is reported that the fourth headless body of a young woman has been retrieved from the outskirts of Moscow, three other women within the year being murdered in a similar fashion. No suspect has ever been announced by the Soviet police.

NOV. 21

The U.S. Embassy in Pakistan is sacked by Communist mobs; two Americans are murdered.

ROBBERY

MAY 3

Chicago prostitute Cathy Nathaniel goes to the luxurious high-rise apartment of Steven Ticho in the Hancock Building to have sex with the lawyer; during the assignation, Nathaniel shoots her client in the back of the head, then, allegedly with the aid of accomplice Bernice Albright, loots the apartment; Ms. Nathaniel will receive a 35-year prison term; Albright will not stand trial.

JULY 24

Michael Brown of Chicago holds hostage five people in two home invasions, attempting to force captives to withdraw money from local banks, but he is foiled by lawmen and will be sentenced to 25 years.

MISCELLANEOUS

MARCH 28

Larry Flynt, publisher of *Hustler* magazine, is found guilty of distributing obscene material and is given a suspended prison term and fined $27,500 in Atlanta and ordered to keep his publications out of Georgia.

MAY 7

Mrs. Harry Chaddick, wife of a multimillionaire Chicago developer, is kidnapped in Palm Springs, Calif., and held for ransom; FBI agents, however, will track down the kidnapper and kill him, and Mrs. Chaddick will be released unharmed.

MAY 31

Corsican separatists set off 42 bombs all over Paris; scores are injured.

JUNE 20

Nikola Kaviaja, Serbian nationalist, is sentenced to 40 years' imprisonment in Yugoslavia; he had planned to crash-dive an airplane into the Belgrade headquarters of Marshall Tito.

AUG. 22

James R. Albee is sentenced in Oregon to 60 years for forcing a passenger jet en route to Los Angeles back to Portland, Ore., claiming that he had a bomb in his briefcase.

SEPT. 23

Inmates riot in Statesville Correctional Center outside Joliet, Ill., doing great damage in a three-hour rampage.

NOV. 4

Iranian militants seize the U.S. Embassy in Tehran, holding American personnel as hostages and demanding the return of the ousted Shah of Iran; the ransom is not met. On Nov. 16 eight Iranian militants will be arrested outside Washington, D.C., carrying high-powered rifles, ammunition and explosives along with a street map of the capital.

NOV. 20

The Grand Mosque in Mecca is seized by hundreds of fascist rebels, 63 of whom will be beheaded later.

DEC. 3

In a wild stampede by rock 'n' roll fans to obtain entry to a Cincinnati concert featuring The Who, 11 people are trampled to death.

1·9·8·0

MURDER

JAN. 7

William Comeans, a newsboy in New Rome, Ohio, is strangled to death after getting anonymous threats; his killer has not been found.

FEB. 27

John Young Bradford is bludgeoned to death by his wife, Priscilla, and her two friends Joyce Lisa Cummings and Janice Irene Gould while Mrs. Bradford compels her 14-year-old daughter to participate, in the lavish Bradford home in Melbourne, Fla.; all three women will be sent to prison for life, after explaining that they wanted to take over Bradford's business, making it an all-female operation.

MARCH 14

Demented Dennis Sweeney goes to the New York City law offices of Allard Lowenstein, shooting Lowenstein, his former political mentor, to death for mysterious reasons; Sweeney had become a political activ-

Dennis Sweeney (right), killer of political activist Allard Lowenstein. (March 14, 1980)

ist in the 1960s at Lowenstein's urgings. He will be sent to prison for life.

JUNE 6

Wealthy Bruce and Darlene Rouse are shotgunned to death in their suburban Libertyville, Ill., home while their three children are in and out of the house; nothing is stolen, so police rule out robbery or murder by strangers; the teenage children—Kurt, Robin and Billy—later claim they have heard nothing; Kurt, who has argued with his parents about drug use, lives in a shack behind the main house; he is present at the time of the killings but says he heard nothing from the main house; the murders remain unsolved at this writing.

JUNE 8

Oron Yarden, age eight, is kidnapped from a wealthy suburb in Tel Aviv (the third ransom kidnapping in Israeli history) but is not returned when his parents pay the demanded $40,000 ransom; his body will be found on June 30 near Netanya, a coastal city; his killers have not been found.

AUG. 14

Onetime pimp Paul Snider, from Vancouver, B.C., Canada, who has promoted statuesque blonde Dorothy Stratten to a *Playboy* centerfold (she is also from Vancouver) and has married her, blows her head off in a Los Angeles bungalow after learning she plans to wed film director Peter Bogdanovich; Snider then commits suicide.

AUG. 20

A Winona, Minn., girl, age 15, who has been arguing with her parents, after seeing the film *Tarantulas: The Deadly Cargo,* buys one of the hairy spiders from a local pet shop and plants it in the bed of her parents, who discover the spider before retiring; the girl will not be prosecuted.

SEPT. 9

Frustrated actor Paul DeWit stabs to death Everett Clarke, his acting coach, on the practice stage in Clarke's offices in Chicago's Fine Arts Building (Clarke had once been the voice of "The Whistler" in the 1940s radio series); DeWit will be given a life term.

NOV. 17

Six members of the KKK are found innocent of murder charges involving the deaths of five Communist Workers Party members in Greensboro, N.C., in November 1979.

DEC. 5

Master burglar Bernard C. Welch shoots and kills

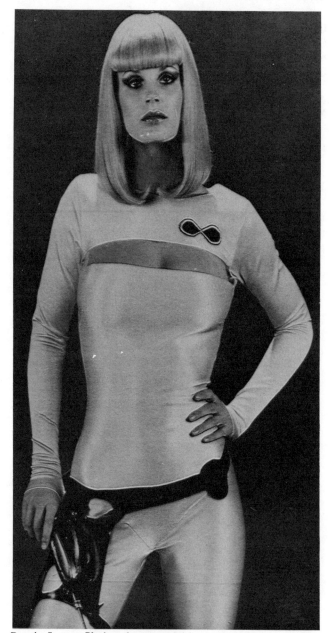

Dorothy Stratten, Playboy playmate and rising movie actress, murdered by her promoter-husband, Paul Snider. (Aug. 14, 1980)

writer-physician Michael J. Halberstam when the doctor interrupts a burglary at his Washington, D.C., town house; Halberstam, although mortally wounded, runs down Welch in his car before dying; Welch will be sent to prison for life.

DEC. 8

Mark David Chapman, thinking he is John Lennon, his obsessive idol, shoots and kills Lennon outside The Dakota apartment complex in New York City after asking for the singer's autograph; he will be sent to prison for life.

Mark David Chapman, killer of John Lennon. (Dec. 8, 1980)

ORGANIZED CRIME

JULY 2

William E. "Billy" Dauber, Chicago hit man and mob terrorist, leaves the Will County (Ill.) courthouse with his wife, Charlotte, where both are on trial for drug smuggling. Dauber has bragged to reporters that he has been marked by the mob for death because syndicate chieftains think he might turn informer to have the drug charges dropped and that he has been sleeping in a bed with a self-designed bulletproof blanket. As he drives with his wife away from the courthouse, a car forces his own auto to the side of a country road and mob men spray the Dauber vehicle with gunfire, killing Dauber and his wife. Reporters later remember Dauber as having once quipped: "The only thing we have to sell is fear."

WHITE-COLLAR CRIME

JULY 24

Former U.S. Representative Charles C. Diggs, Jr., of Michigan begins serving a three-year sentence for mail fraud and payroll kickbacks.

MISCELLANEOUS

JAN. 27

In Tokyo, former Beatle Paul McCartney is released from jail after being held for 10 days for possession of marijuana, and ordered never to return to Japan; he flies to Amsterdam but is ordered to leave the country before leaving Schiphol Airport; he then flies to England, where he expresses amazement at Japanese regulations: "I did not realize drug laws were so severe over there. I thought it was more like America."

FEB. 3

At least 32 persons die and scores are injured following a bloody riot in the New Mexico State Prison.

MAY 19

More than 3,500 National Guard troops enter Miami to stem race riots in which 15 have been killed.

JUNE 1

Hundreds of Cuban refugees, many of them criminals who have been "dumped" on the U.S. in massive deportation by Fidel Castro, riot at a Ft. Chaffee, Ark., relocation center, wounding 15 lawmen trying to quell the disturbance.

JULY 6

The bodies of 10 Salvadorans being smuggled into the U.S. are found in the Arizona desert, making a total of 13 corpses of aliens abandoned by smugglers.

OCT. 7

Film producer Robert Evans is given a year's probation for possession of cocaine in New York City.

NOV. 3

Iranian thugs release 52 Americans held hostage in Tehran since 1979, ending the crisis.

NOV. 8

In Piacenza, Italy, Countess Giovanna Portapulia, who has been born with physical deformities, is released from a broom-closetlike room where the 65-year-old woman has been chained for 50 years by members of her blueblood family; family members, who later are charged in court with unlawful restraint and maltreatment, indifferently state that ''we had to do it to save the family's honor.''

William and Tracy Melton, who are about to be sentenced for possession of cocaine and marijuana, swallow cyanide poison and die in a Rockville, Md., court, shocking witnesses; the couple faced a minimum sentence.

1·9·8·1

MURDER

MARCH 7

American Chester Bitterman, who has been abducted by terrorists in Bogotá, Colombia, is found shot to pieces in an abandoned bus parked on a city street; his killers have not been found.

MARCH 20

Jean Struven Harris, director of an exclusive girls' school, who has been convicted of shooting to death her lover, wealthy Dr. Herman Tarnower, coauthor of the best-selling book *The Complete Scarsdale Medical Diet,* in his lavish Purchase, N.Y., home on March 10, 1980, is sentenced to from 15 years to life in prison for second-degree murder.

MARCH 24

Burbank machinist Lawrence Sigmond Bittaker, 40, is found guilty of the torture-murders of five teenage girls in Torrance, Calif.; Bittaker has lured the girls to his van, where he has raped them, then using a sled-

Jean Struven Harris, given 15 years to life for shooting Dr. Herman Tarnower. (March 20, 1981)

Millionaire doctor-author Herman Tarnower of Scarsdale, N.Y. (March 20, 1981)

gehammer, pliers and ice pick, mutilated and tortured them before strangling them to death; he will be given the death sentence but is alive at this writing.

MAY 13

Pope John Paul II, while riding through Vatican Square during a religious celebration that thousands attend, is shot and wounded by Mehmet Ali Agca, a Turkish terrorist later credited with being a Communist envoy whose special mission was to assassinate the politically involved pontiff. Agca will be given a long prison term. (The Pope has told U.S. Secretary of State George P. Shultz that he believes the KGB has been behind his attempted assassination.) In July 1983 15-year-old Emanuela Orlandi, whose father is a minor official at the Vatican, will be kidnapped and held by terrorists who demand that Agca be released.

MAY 19–JULY 30

Three teenage children are abducted and murdered in and about Vancouver, B.C., Canada; Canadian lawmen have been unable to find the killer.

JUNE 10

Town bully Kenneth Rex McElroy is shot to death in Skidmore, Mo., as more than 70 persons watch; the killer is not turned in by townspeople, who have had a meeting shortly before the shooting to decide what to do about the burly menace.

SEPT. 26

Insurance claims adjuster Michael Mekler receives a call on his beeper to investigate an accident on Chicago's South Side; arriving at the scene, he is shot and killed from ambush; his killer has not been found.

ROBBERY

OCT. 20

Militant black and white fanatics bent on establish-ing a separate nation for blacks (arbitrarily selecting six southern U.S. states) stop a Brink's truck in Nanuet, N.Y., killing three guards and taking $1.6 million in cash. Caught later, the defendants are Kuwasi Balagoon, a black and a member of the so-called Black Liberation Army, and Weather Underground members David Gilbert and Judith Clark, both white; after hearing their sentences over loudspeakers hooked up to their cells—they have boycotted the trial—the defendants applaud. Three hours later Gilbert marries another Weatherman prisoner, Kathy Boudin, daughter of civil rights lawyer-activist Leonard Boudin; Balagoon, Gilbert and Clark each are given a sentence of 25 years to life.

ORGANIZED CRIME

JULY 25

Alfred Pilotto, chief of Chicago's south suburban rackets, is playing golf on a Crete, Ill., course when a gunman steps from behind a bush and shoots him several times. Pilotto will survive, but the 70-year-old gangster will go to prison for 20 years for labor racketeering in 1982. His assailant is never found.

MISCELLANEOUS

JULY 5

Rioting against the Thatcher government injures more than 200 policemen in Liverpool, England.

DEC. 17

U.S. General James Dozier is kidnapped in Milan, Italy, by members of the Red Brigade but later will be released unharmed when Italian police burst into the kidnappers' quarters.

1·9·8·2

MURDER

APRIL 3

A mailman discovers the body of Wanda Faye Reddick, 16, of Richland, Ga., who has been dragged screaming from her bed days earlier, (her family had rushed to her side but the kidnapper had removed all the light bulbs in the house and they had to grope blindly about while the abductor dragged Wanda through the front doorway); the Reddick girl is the third victim of abductor-killers in Richland who have kidnapped and slain Tanya Nix, 14, and Valerie Marie Sellers, 17, in 1981; at this writing the killers have not been found.

APRIL 12

Margaret Barbera, controller for the Candor Diamond Co. of New York City, is shot and killed in the parking lot atop Pier 92 at 52nd Street in Manhattan. When three CBS employees attempt to intervene, a gunman shoots them to death also. Barbera was to be a witness in the $5.5 million fraud case against Candor's owner, Irwin M. Margolies, who has previously been convicted of fraud and tax evasion and has been sentenced to 28 years in prison, being held in a detention center in Manhattan. Later Donald Nash is arrested and charged with the four murders as well as disposing of another Candor employee, Jenny Soo Chin, who has disappeared on Jan. 15 and who was to have testified against Margolies; Nash will be convicted on May 24, 1983, and will be sentenced to four consecutive life terms.

JUNE 9

Werner Hartmann, a 38-year-old German immigrant who has become a millionaire by installing stereos in cars, is found shotgunned to death in his palatial Northbrook, Ill., home. Though much of the investigation still revolves around Hartmann's attractive 29-year-old wife, Debra, the case remains unsolved at this writing.

AUG. 9

Former McLean (Ill.) County prosecutor Jeffrey Joseph Gurga allegedly blackens his face and climbs into the second-story apartment of Kathleen Pearson in Chicago, then he stabs to death Mrs. Pearson and wounds her 19-year-old daughter Jeannine, women he has never met. The struggle put up by Mrs. Pearson rouses a male neighbor, who confronts Gurga as he attempts to escape. Cries Gurga: "My God, I've gone

bananas. . . . When are the paramedics coming? I don't know these women." He is charged with murder, his defense being insanity.

SEPT. 29–30

An unknown killer or killers doctor with cyanide poison several containers of Tylenol capsules, which are sold through five Chicago-area outlets, capsules that kill seven residents—Mary Kellerman; Theresa, Stanley and Adam Janus; Mary Reiner; Mary McFarland; and Paula Prince. When poison is found in Tylenol capsules elsewhere, the over-the-counter product is withdrawn nationally. A nationwide manhunt ensues but the random, seemingly motiveless killer or killers are still at large at this writing.

OCT. 20

Claude Dallas of Caldwell, Idaho, is found guilty of manslaughter and sent to prison for the shooting deaths of game wardens Bill Pogue and Conley Elms, whom Dallas has shot at his remote southwestern Idaho camp on June 1, 1981, after they have accused him of trapping and hunting without a license.

DEC. 2

Christine Falling, a 19-year-old baby-sitter, pleads guilty to murdering three children in Blountstown and Perry, Fla., suffocating 2-year-old Cassidy "Muffin" Johnson and two-month-old Travis Coleman in 1980 and killing eight-month-old Jennifer Daniels in 1981. She will get life.

ROBBERY

FEB. 14

Surprising a lone guard at a Bronx armored car firm in New York City, two robbers wearing ski masks, one robber wielding a shotgun, after cutting a hole in the roof of the Sentry Armored Car Courier Company, take 10 to 12 canvas bags containing $50 and $100 bills that were neatly stacked in the "money room" on carts, a total estimated to exceed $5.3 million. The thieves have yet to be caught as of this writing.

OCT. 5

Four bank robbers holding nine persons hostage in

a Koblenz, West Germany, bank are allowed to flee with an undetermined sum after they threaten to kill the hostages.

ORGANIZED CRIME

FEB. 20

Onetime basketball star James Bradley is killed on a downtown Portland, Ore., street by members of the syndicate, according to police, who feel that Bradley, earlier arrested for narcotics violations, will begin to talk, giving information on the Northwest drug trafficking ring controlled by the syndicate.

WHITE-COLLAR CRIME

OCT. 19

Joel Johnson, 52, is arrested in New York City after allegedly scamming city banks of more than $10 million in seven years, forging checks that female accomplices then cash; Johnson has reportedly been leading a double life, operating out of a Harlem fleabag hotel but retreating to a 14-room country estate to enjoy his ill-gotten riches.

John DeLorean, onetime General Motors marketing wizard and car manufacturer whose firm in Northern Ireland is failing, is arrested in Room 501 of the Sheraton Plaza in Los Angeles for attempting to buy and sell millions of dollars' worth of cocaine in a huge ''buy'' in order, authorities later claim, to shore up his collapsing financial empire.

DEC. 16

Carl Henry Johnson, who has allegedly embezzled $614,000 from the National Bank of Albany Park, Ill., where he has worked as an assistant comptroller, agrees to lead FBI agents to $50,000 of the loot, which is hidden ''in the woods'' outside Cincinnati; Johnson, four FBI agents and Patrick Daly, a retired Chicago Police detective, take a small twin-engined plane from Chicago to Ohio, but the plane crashes near Montgomery, Ohio, killing the pilot and the other six men on board.

MISCELLANEOUS

MARCH 15

Film actress Theresa Gilda Saldana is wounded in a knife attack in Los Angeles.

AUG. 4

James B. Moran is given a 15-year prison term for a kidnapping spree, leaving an Akron, Ohio, hospital on April 26 and forcing four persons to accompany him on his escape route to Pittsburgh, where he commandeered a car driven by a woman he forced to accompany him to Baltimore and from there to Aurora, Colo.

SEPT. 30

White Sox star Ron Le Flore is arrested in Chicago and accused of possession of illegal drugs and weapons. (LeFlore has served a prison term in Michigan for armed robbery as a youth.)

OCT. 3

Gaby Kiss Maerth, 18-year-old daughter of retired

Teamsters boss Jimmy Hoffa, declared officially dead in 1982 after vanishing from a Detroit-area restaurant seven years earlier. (Dec. 10, 1982)

British businessman Oscar Maerth and who has been held in Como, Italy, by kidnappers demanding $3.5 million ransom, is released after her father pays $119,000, according to police officials.

OCT. 4

U.S. Representative Ike F. Andrews of North Carolina is arrested for drunk driving in Washington, D.C., and for speeding, driving 67 miles per hour in a residential zone.

OCT. 5

Michael Fagin, a dim-witted housebreaker who has broken into Queen Elizabeth's bedroom in Buckingham Palace in London (the Queen quietly talked with him until able to summon guards, who dragged Fagin away), is sent to a maximum-security asylum for life.

OCT. 10

Actor Richard Dreyfuss is arrested for driving under the influence of drugs when he crashes his car in Beverly Hills, Calif. He will admit his guilt and receive a minimal sentence.

OCT. 24

Marta Corsetti, who has been held by kidnappers in Rome for more than three months, is released even though ransom is not paid.

NOV. 27

Heather Michelle Ross, 22, Bermuda's entry in the Miss World contest, is arrested in London and charged with smuggling $250,000 worth of cocaine into Britain.

DEC. 10

Detroit Judge Norman R. Barnard declares Teamsters President James R. Hoffa officially dead as of July 30, exactly seven years after his disappearance from a Detroit-area restaurant. His $1.2 million estate is turned over to his son and daughter. Most police officials assume Hoffa has been killed, his body hidden.

DEC. 14

Dr. Xiomara Suazo, daughter of Roberto Suazo Cordova, president of Honduras, is kidnapped en route to a Guatemala City hospital by terrorists and held until their propaganda statement is widely published by the Guatemalan government.

1·9·8·3

MURDER

JAN. 24

An Italian jury sentences 32 members of the notorious Red Brigade to life terms for the 1979 assassination of former Prime Minister Aldo Moro; other sentences, ranging from four months to 30 years, are given to 27 more defendants; four are found innocent; the entire mob of defendants has been held in an enormous cage in the courtroom in Rome, Italy, screaming and interrupting proceedings over nine nerve-wracking months (the life sentences are the most severe that can be handed down in that Italy has no death penalty).

MAY 20

The ANC (African National Congress) takes responsibility for a bomb set off in downtown Pretoria, South Africa, that kills 19 persons and wounds another 200; the ANC has been branded an outlaw organization by the South African government, which will hang three ANC members the following month.

JUNE 4

Gordon W. Kahl, who belongs to a paramilitary tax protestation group called Posse Comitatus and who on Feb. 13 has killed two U.S. marshals who have followed him from a meeting in Medina, N.D., shoots it out with officers in a farmhouse outside Walnut Ridge, Ark., killing Sheriff Gene Matthews before he himself is killed and then burned when the farmhouse catches fire.

JUNE 5

Douglas R. Ryen; his wife, Peg; his daughter, Jessica; and Christopher Hughes, a neighbor's boy, are brutally stabbed to death in the Ryens' hilltop home in the ranching area of Chino, Calif. Ryen's eight-year-old son Joshua, though wounded severely by the attacker, escapes. Later police will arrest Kevin Cooper, 25, an escaped mental patient who has been convicted of burglary, and charge him with the murders.

JUNE 9

Convicted of murdering four white policemen between 1979 and 1981, three men—Simon Mogerane, 23; Jerry Mosololi, 25, and Marcus Motaung, 27—are hanged at the Pretoria Prison in South Africa.

JUNE 25

Two sisters, Zita Blum and Honora Lahmann, are found in their Joliet, Ill., home shot and stabbed to death, their house ransacked and set afire. These are the first of 15 murder-robberies that will occur in Joliet through August. The home-invading killers still are being sought at this writing.

JULY 7

Ex-model and onetime mistress to the late millionaire Alfred Bloomingdale, Vicki Morgan, is beaten to death with a baseball bat. Her lover, Marvin Pancoast, with whom she has been living, reportedly calls Los Angeles police, saying: ''I just killed someone.'' He is held for the murder of the 31-year-old Morgan who, a year earlier, has filed a $10 million palimony suit against Bloomingdale. (The couple met in 1970 when Morgan was 17 and Bloomingdale was in his 50s.) Only days later Beverly Hills lawyer Robert K. Steinberg announces that he has video tapes showing Vicki Morgan in a sex orgy with Bloomingdale, two high-level ''appointed officials'' and a congressman. The tapes, however, will disappear, Steinberg later stating that someone in the Los Angeles press corps has stolen the ''sex tapes,'' but the newsperson remains anonymous.

AUG. 1

Sidney Wells, a senior at the University of Colorado in Boulder and the boyfriend of Shauna Redford, daughter of actor Robert Redford, is found shotgunned to death in his luxurious Spanish Towers condominium. His killer still is being sought at this writing.

AUG. 4

Peter Sutcliffe, the confessed Yorkshire Ripper who has murdered 13 women in England in 1981, is ordered to pay a compensation claim to the mother of one of his victims; the legal order is the first of its kind in British history. Sutcliffe's $45,000 home will be sold to pay the claim. The onetime truck driver is serving a life sentence at Parkhurst Prison on the Isle of Wight off England's southern coast.

AUG. 10

Self-avowed Nazi Frank G. Spisak, who has mur-

dered three men at Cleveland State University within the year, is sentenced to death in Cleveland, Ohio.

AUG. 16

Maria Velten, a 67-year-old woman in Kempten, West Germany, admits poisoning her father in 1963 and her 78-year-old aunt in 1970 because they were sick and she could not care for them. To this list she adds two husbands and a boyfriend, poisoned in 1976, 1978 and 1980, respectively. The last three, Frau Velten confesses, have been killed for their money. She will receive a life term.

AUG. 21

Benigno Aquino, opposition leader to Philippines dictator Ferdinand Marcos, is shot to death on the runway of Manila's international airport while returning to his native country from a U.S. exile to establish democratic elections. Marcos denies any connection with the killing, but it is said that one of the guards on the plane, ostensibly there to protect Aquino, has shot the politician. Government officials, however, insist that Aquino's assassin is the unidentified killer shot to death by guards immediately after the 50-year-old Aquino has been shot in the back of the head while disembarking the plane. Later the dead assassin is reported to be Rolando Vizcarra, onetime bodyguard of Ferdinand Marcos. Hundreds of thousands of Aquino's supporters will riot, with scores wounded, in the ensuing weeks.

SEPT. 2

Jimmy Lee Gray, 34, is sent to the gas chamber in the Mississippi State Prison for raping and smothering a three-year-old girl. He is the first person to be executed in the state since 1964, eighth in the nation since a 1976 U.S. Supreme Court ruling that allowed capital punishment.

Peter Arne, British character actor, is found beaten to death in his London apartment. Arne, who has appeared in such films as *The Return of the Pink Panther* and *Straw Dogs* and who was a close friend of late playwright Sir Noel Coward, was killed, according to police, by an ''intimate friend'' and that they believe the murder to be the result of a ''homosexual relationship.''

SEPT. 3

Anthony Joyner, 24, a former kitchen worker in a Philadelphia home for the elderly, is charged with raping and murdering six women who ranged in age from 83 to 92 in recent months. As of this writing, the case is still before the courts.

SEPT. 13

According to the National Coalition to Ban Handguns, Odessa, Tex., becomes the nation's murder capital with 29.8 homicides per 100,000 residents, compared with the former murder capital, Miami, which had 29.7 homicides per 100,000 residents in 1982.

SEPT. 17–18

Unknown killers slaughter the Osborne family of Fort Wayne, Ind., sexually assaulting a two-year-old girl and locking her in a closet (from which she is later rescued by police) before bludgeoning to death her father, Dan Osborne, an editorial-page writer for the *Fort Wayne News-Sentinel;* his wife, Jane; and their 11-year-old son, Ben.

SEPT. 26

Mystery writer Muriel Davidson, who has complained of receiving many crank calls in recent weeks, is found murdered in her Santa Monica mountain home. Later police will attribute the murder to Robert Thom, an unemployed aerospace worker who had received counseling from the writer in an alcoholic rehabilitation center. As of this writing, the case is still before the courts.

SEPT. 29

Rudy Blythe, president of the Buffalo Ridge State Bank of Ruthton, Minn., and Deems Thulin, a bank loan officer, are lured to a farm once owned by James Lee Jenkins, a farm the bank has reclaimed, and are allegedly shot to death by Jenkins, who then flees with his 18-year-old son Steve to another family-owned farm near Paducah, Tex., where Jenkins, down to his last pennies, shoots himself.

OCT. 5

Willie Mak, a Hong Kong immigrant, is convicted of 13 counts of aggravated first-degree murder, having shot to death 13 middle-aged men and women in a Chinatown gambling club in Seattle, Wash., on Feb. 19. One accomplice, Benjamin Ng, has already been given life for the robbery-murders. Tony Ng, the other alleged accomplice, remains at large at this writing.

OCT. 15

Dr. John M. Brannion, Jr., who has served as a personal physician to Ugandan dictator Idi Amin, is returned to Chicago to begin serving a jail sentence for having murdered his socialite wife, Donna, in 1971.

OCT. 20

Oscar Gerber and Bruno Spiewak, officers in a suburban Chicago firm, visit employee James Stavrolakis to fire him. Both men are shot to death as they enter Stavrolakis' Lincolnwood hotel room. Stavrolakis then turns his pistol on himself, committing suicide.

OCT. 21

Otis Elwood Toole, a vagrant picked up by Hollywood, Fla., police, admits that he has murdered six-year-old Adam Walsh, decapitating the boy in 1981, the brutal slaying that has led to the passing of the Missing Children's Act by Congress in 1982. Toole, who has served time for killing his mother, also confesses to murdering at least 50 other persons, working in tandem with multiple killer Henry Lee Lucas, who has confessed to having murdered 200 women. Both will receive a life term.

Hutchie T. Moore, a former Chicago policeman, shoots and kills Judge Henry A. Gentile in a Daley Center courtroom in downtown Chicago, then shoots James A. Piszcor, the attorney representing his wife in a settlement of Moore's divorce. Moore, who allegedly is paralyzed (it is later claimed that he fakes his injury from a gunshot wound received when he and his son struggled for Moore's weapon years earlier), has fired a pistol hidden on his person from his wheelchair in court. Terrorized courtroom officials and spectators flee the court, then return minutes later when Moore calmly tells them: "You can come out now. . . . I'm through."

ROBBERY

FEB. 26

Several thieves attempt to hold up a large bank in Tegucigalpa, Honduras, but are surrounded by police; Capt. Louis Moran Morel is killed in an exchange of gunfire before the robbers surrender.

AUG. 5

Two robbers enter the swanky Sofitel Hotel in Avignon, France, a resort town on the banks of the Rhône River and attempt to break into safe-deposit boxes. Failing to do so, they kill four guests and three hotel employees before jumping from a three-story window to a waiting car and then speeding off. The thieves remain unknown as of this writing.

ORGANIZED CRIME

FEB. 10

Ken Eto, syndicate gambling boss in Chicago, is shot three times in the head but survives the assassination attempt allegedly by hit men John Gattuso and

Jasper Campise, who are both later arrested, named by Eto as his assailants. Gattuso and Campise, free on high bond, are found dead five months later, their bodies stuffed into a car trunk.

MARCH 12

Reputed head of organized crime in Kansas City Nick Civella dies of lung cancer at age 70.

AUG. 3

Reported syndicate gangster Lawrence Neumann is convicted of murdering mob-connected Chicago jeweler Robert Brown in 1979. It is the first time in Cook County history that a mob figure faces the death sentence.

AUG. 14

Italian police officials in Rome release murder figures dealing with organized crime in Sicily, Campania and Calabria, stating that more than 850 murders are attributable to organized crime, particularly the Mafia in Sicily, the Camorra in Campania and the Ndrangheta in Calabria. Though most of these murders are the result of internecine wars between the criminal factions, victims also include magistrates, police chiefs even military generals who have vowed to eradicate organized crime in Italy. Police estimate that the Sicilian Mafia alone is netting $1 billion from international drug traffic and other rackets, money that is being plowed into legitimate business interests.

WHITE-COLLAR CRIME

MARCH 10

Gus Econopoulos, a 51-year-old warehouse worker from San Francisco, and confederates allegedly rig the largest slot-machine jackpot at Harrah's Casino in Lake Tahoe, replacing a computer chip in seconds after a minor diversion, which compels the machine to pay Econopoulos $1.7 million. The winner, however, begins hyperventilating and is taken to the manager's office to lie down, where the scheme begins to unravel. Econopoulos and others are charged with theft. At the time of this writing, the case is still in the courts.

MARCH 13

Hugo B. Magain, former Mexican ambassador to the U.S., charges that widespread corruption is taking place between Mexican officials and American businessmen bribing with millions of dollars for Mexican business concessions.

JUNE 18

Roberto Calvi, who has reportedly misappropriated funds from Vatican accounts, transferring millions of dollars into his own name in Swiss accounts, is found hanging by the neck beneath Blackfriars Bridge in London. Calvi, who has been the president of Italy's largest private bank, Banco Ambrosiano of Milan, is found with bricks in his pockets, as if he had also intended to drown himself, then opted for hanging. Though his death is ruled a suicide, many believe Calvi has been murdered. Michele Sindona, Calvi's closest friend, has gutted the Franklin National Bank of New York, faked a kidnapping when free on bond, fled to Europe, and then returned to the U.S., where he has been given a 25-year prison sentence. Linked to both Sindona and Calvi through a Masonic lodge is financial wizard Licio Gelli, who vanished in August from a Swiss jail where he was being held on charges of bank fraud. Gelli remains at large at this writing.

SEPT. 12

Government officials claim that Robert Vesco, who has fled the U.S. for South America in 1972 with a reported $60 million in stolen funds, has set up a deal wherein he buys heroin and cocaine that has been confiscated by Cuban coast guard authorities and has the drug shipments funneled through cooperating leftists in Nicaragua and then into other Latin American countries en route to the U.S., gleaning untold millions of dollars.

SEPT. 28

Alan D. Saxon, the mysterious founder and chairman of the burgeoning-with-wealth Bullion Reserve of North America, which maintains plush offices on Sunset Boulevard in Los Angeles, slips into the sauna of his posh Marina del Rey oceanfront condominium and inhales the fumes he has piped from a running moped. Saxon's suicide occurs only hours after New York State Attorney General Robert Abrams opens an investigation into the firm's operations in that state. Thousands of investors soon are in shock when they learn that Bullion Reserve's mountaintop storehouse for precious metals does not contain $1 billion in gold and silver but less than $1 million. An estimated $60 million is owed to investors who have been convinced of the firm's legitimacy because the company has promptly issued monthly statements and appeared healthy.

OCT. 9

Bernard Whitney is arrested in Los Angeles and charged by federal authorities with committing one of the largest land frauds in U.S. history, a swindle that might amount to upward of $2 billion. Whitney, a Manhattan Beach, Calif., lawyer, real-estate developer and C.P.A., along with Rienk Kamer, a Dutch journalist who is in hiding, have allegedly sold thousands of investors in the Netherlands, Belgium and the U.S. shares in a 10,000-home development project north of Los Angeles, one that did not exist except on Whitney's promise to build it. According to authorities, Whitney, through his firms, also bought up about $5 million of land in Utah, claiming the land to be a prime resort area and selling it to Dutch investors for more than $15 million. As of this writing, the case is still in the courts.

OCT. 16

Former Japanese Prime Minister Kakuei Tanaka is found guilty of accepting in the years 1973–74 bribes amounting to $1.8 million from the Lockheed Corp. for persuading Nippon Airways to purchase 21 Lockheed L-1011 TriStar airliners. Tanaka is fined $2 million and given a four-year prison sentence but remains free on appeal and retains his seat in the Diet (Parliament).

MISCELLANEOUS

JAN. 5

Giavanni Vigliotto, who admits to having married 82 women around the world for their money, is tried in Phoenix, Ariz., for bigamy. The convicted bigamist will be sent to prison to serve a long term.

JAN. 10

More than 550 prisoners at Sing Sing riot, taking 17

guards hostage and demanding reforms in the ancient prison. Within 24 hours the guards are released after officials promise to put reforms into effect.

FEB. 21

TV actor Raymond Anthony Vitte, costar of *The Quest,* who is turned in by neighbors for chanting and shouting late at night, lunges at investigating officers coming to his Studio City, Calif., apartment. Vitte, according to later reports, places "a curse on them," then charges the officers. He is sprayed three times with tear gas and struck once with a baton with no apparent effect. Vitte is dragged to a patrol car but inexplicably stops breathing as the car heads for the police station. He is pronounced dead a short time later.

MARCH 10

Hilda Hoffman of Chicago, who has brought suit against that city's police department for being "strip-searched" as an invasion of her civil rights, is awarded $60,000 in damages by a Chicago jury. Hoffman, who has been stopped for an illegal left turn and was taken to a Chicago police station, was forced to disrobe in a hallway there while male officers watched matrons search for drugs.

MAY 29

Joseph M. Majczek, wrongfully convicted of murdering Chicago policeman William Lundy in 1933 and given a 99-year term, dies in Chicago. Majczek was famous for the movie based on his case, *Call Northside 777.*

INDEX